Deploying SharePoint 2016

Best Practices for Installing, Configuring, and Maintaining SharePoint Server 2016

Vlad Catrinescu

Trevor Seward

Apress®

Deploying SharePoint 2016: Best Practices for Installing, Configuring, and Maintaining SharePoint Server 2016

Vlad Catrinescu
Greenfield Park, Québec, Canada

Trevor Seward
Sultan, Washington, USA

ISBN-13 (pbk): 978-1-4842-1998-0
DOI 10.1007/978-1-4842-1999-7

ISBN-13 (electronic): 978-1-4842-1999-7

Library of Congress Control Number: 2016958033

Managing Director: Welmoed Spahr
Acquisitions Editor: Gwenan Spearing
Technical Reviewer: Thomas Vochten
Editorial Board: Steve Anglin, Pramila Balan, Laura Berendson, Aaron Black, Louise Corrigan, Jonathan Gennick, Todd Green, Robert Hutchinson, Celestin Suresh John, Nikhil Karkal, James Markham, Susan McDermott, Matthew Moodie, Natalie Pao, Gwenan Spearing
Coordinating Editor: Nancy Chen
Copy Editor: Brendan Frost
Compositor: SPi Global
Indexer: SPi Global
Cover Image: Courtesy of Freepik

Distributed to the book trade worldwide by Springer Science+Business Media New York, 233 Spring Street, 6th Floor, New York, NY 10013. Phone 1-800-SPRINGER, fax (201) 348-4505, e-mail orders-ny@springer-sbm.com, or visit www.springer.com. Apress Media, LLC is a California LLC and the sole member (owner) is Springer Science + Business Media Finance Inc (SSBM Finance Inc). SSBM Finance Inc is a Delaware corporation.

For information on translations, please e-mail rights@apress.com, or visit www.apress.com.

Apress and friends of ED books may be purchased in bulk for academic, corporate, or promotional use. eBook versions and licenses are also available for most titles. For more information, reference our Special Bulk Sales–eBook Licensing web page at www.apress.com/bulk-sales.

Any source code or other supplementary materials referenced by the author in this text are available to readers at www.apress.com. For detailed information about how to locate your book's source code, go to www.apress.com/source-code/. Readers can also access source code at SpringerLink in the Supplementary Material section for each chapter.

To my lovely wife Leana, and my kids, Victoria and Jameson. Thank you for all of your love, guidance, and support over the years as I followed my passions!
—Trevor

This book is dedicated to my parents, Mircea and Iuliana, who have been an inspiration to me and believed in me, even when I didn't. Thank you for your support, without which none of my success would be possible!
–Vlad

Contents at a Glance

Contents

About the Authors

Vlad Catrinescu is an Office Servers and Services MVP who lives in Montréal, Canada. Vlad works as an independent consultant specializing in SharePoint and SharePoint Online deployments as well as hybrid scenarios. As a Pluralsight Author, Microsoft Certified Trainer, and recognized international speaker, Vlad has helped thousands of users and IT Professionals across the globe to better understand and to get the most out of SharePoint.

Trevor Seward is an Office Servers and Services MVP who resides in Washington State. He lives with his wife Leana, daughter Victoria, and son Jameson. Trevor has over a decade of experience with SharePoint administration and architecture, along with experience in Azure, Active Directory, virtualization, SQL Server, and other services that support SharePoint.

About the Technical Reviewer

Thomas Vochten is a Microsoft MVP and SharePoint architect. He focuses on platform architecture, planning, deployment, availability, and operations—whether on-premises or in the cloud. Thomas is a very active public speaker who travels the world to talk about implementing SharePoint and Office 365 and to prevent people from making the same expensive mistakes he did. He has a deep affection for SQL Server, teaches the occasional classroom full of IT professionals, and is getting around deploying hybrid SharePoint environments. Thomas works for Xylos, a consultancy company based in Belgium.

Acknowledgments

We would like to thank the SharePoint Product Group for producing this great platform, with a special thanks to the Program Group members in the SharePoint 2016 beta program for all of their help.

Introduction

This book is written to be a reference for SharePoint Administrators and IT Professionals willing to learn how to deploy SharePoint Server 2016 in their organizations. This book is geared towards the intermediate to advanced crowd, and most of the configurations are done through PowerShell instead of the user interface.

This book will start with an introduction to what is new—and gone—from SharePoint Server 2016 and cover the planning and installation of SharePoint Server 2016, as well as all the features such as SharePoint Add-ins, Business Intelligence, and connected systems such as Workflow Manager and Office Online Server. Other topics that you will learn about in this book are

- Hybrid SharePoint Deployments
- User Synchronization using Microsoft Identity Manager
- Integration between SharePoint and Exchange Server
- Migrating to SharePoint Server 2016
- Implementing High Availability and Disaster Recovery
- Patching SharePoint Server 2016 and the Zero Downtime Patching concept

CHAPTER 1

■ ■ ■

Introduction to SharePoint 2016

In this chapter, we will introduce SharePoint 2016, a bit of history about where is SharePoint coming from, and Microsoft's goals for the 2016 version. We will also have a high-level overview of the new features in SharePoint 2016.

SharePoint 2016 is the sixth version of SharePoint Server that Microsoft shipped to the public. First introduced in 2001, SharePoint Portal Server (the name back then) was nowhere as popular as it is now. It took a few versions, but starting with Office SharePoint Server 2007 (MOSS), SharePoint went from a CD Microsoft gave away, including 25 user licenses, to one of Microsoft's most lucrative products. After two huge successes with SharePoint 2010 and SharePoint 2013, more than 75,000 enterprises accounting for 160 million users now use SharePoint.

A fact that is less known about Microsoft is that Microsoft has been offering cloud SharePoint solutions since around 2003, back when it was known as Microsoft Managed Solutions. Back then, Microsoft was taking the On-Premises version of the product, and simply hosted it for the client. Microsoft's cloud offering was then renamed to BPOS, which is now known as Office 365.

Office 365 changed the way that Microsoft worked with their cloud offering. Instead of creating software for On-Premises, and then hosting it for clients in the cloud, Microsoft kept updating Office 365 in intervals going as low as two weeks.

After adding features and improving both stability and productivity features in SharePoint Online for three years since SharePoint 2013 came out, Microsoft has packed a lot of the new features into the SharePoint 2016 On-Premises product. It was the first time ever that Microsoft took the code branch of SharePoint online, to build an On-Premises SharePoint Server.

To take a trip back in time, and to realize how new some features are in SharePoint, Figure 1-1 shows a bit of SharePoint history and the important features for SharePoint Administrators that each version introduced.

Electronic supplementary material The online version of this chapter (doi:10.1007/978-1-4842-1999-7_1) contains supplementary material, which is available to authorized users.

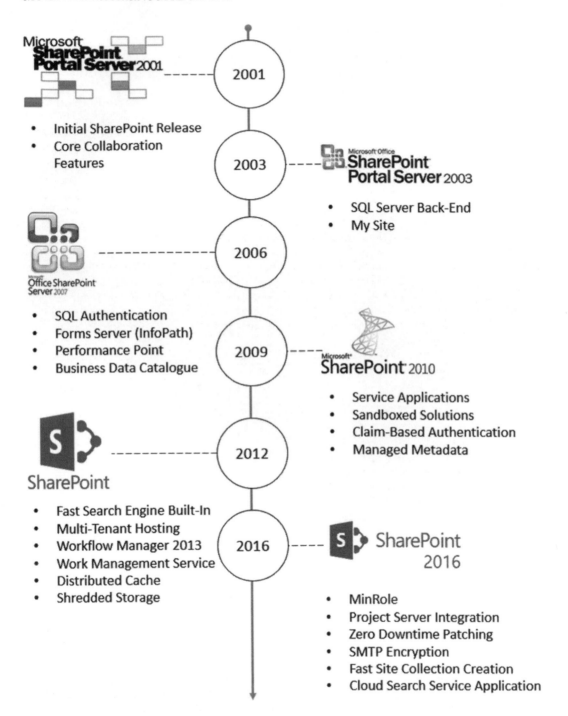

Figure 1-1. A small history of new features in every SharePoint version

However, Microsoft also made it clear that some of the new features in the cloud will never make it to On-Premises. For example, Delve, Microsoft's new tool that runs on the Office Graph to show documents before you even search for them, will never make it as a stand-alone On-Premises product. This is not only due to Microsoft marketing and keeping everything "cloud-first" but also because of the complexity and infrastructure needed would not be possible On-Premises.

Microsoft understands that for plenty of reasons, some enterprises will never go fully to the cloud. Some of them are due to legal or compliance reasons, while some of them are blocked by the customizations limits on SharePoint Online. This is where Hybrid deployments come in. By implementing a Hybrid deployment between SharePoint Server 2016 and Office 365, you offer users the newest features available in the cloud, while documents that need to stay On-Premises can stay On-Premises! While the integration is not 100% seamless between SharePoint Server 2016 and Office 365, there are some amazing improvements compared to SharePoint Server 2013.

What's New in SharePoint Server 2016

In this section, we will take a high-level look at the new features included in SharePoint Server 2016, as well as reference the chapters in which those features will be covered in detail.

MinRole

After running SharePoint for millions of users every day in the cloud and needing to provide an SLA of 99.9%, Microsoft implemented some changes directly in the SharePoint topologies in order to bring speed and stability and to simplify SharePoint deployments. This new topology is called MinRole. In MinRole, instead of starting services manually on servers, as we did before, Microsoft hard-coded which services run on which server. Every server in the MinRole farm has a role out of the six available roles:

- Front-End
- Application
- Distributed Cache
- Search
- Custom
- Single-Server Farm

Once the SharePoint Server 2016 farm is setup in MinRole mode, SharePoint will automatically start the services on the right server when they are needed, and stop those services if the Service Application no longer exists in the farm. The new MinRole concept will be explained in more detail in **Chapter 2.**

Data Loss Prevention

Data Loss Prevention (DLP) is one of the features that Microsoft first introduced in SharePoint Online, and made its way to SharePoint Server 2016. DLP is a system which gives the capability for the administrators and the enterprise compliance managers to find sensitive information in documents, and make sure their use respects the company's policies. Since DLP is an industry-wide term, there are three ways in which a DLP system functions: in-use, in-motion, and at-rest. When talking about SharePoint, we are talking about a DLP system that looks for sensitive data while it's at rest.

The DLP system in SharePoint Server 2016 allows us to find over 51 information types, including credit cards, Social Security Numbers, bank account numbers, passports, and so on. The DLP system in SharePoint 2016 doesn't only find and report the sensitive information in the whole SharePoint farm; it can also block it so other users can't access it. Figure 1-2 shows you an example of a document library, with two documents that have been blocked because they contain sensitive information. Only the Site Owner, User who created the document, and the last person who modified it are even able to see the documents.

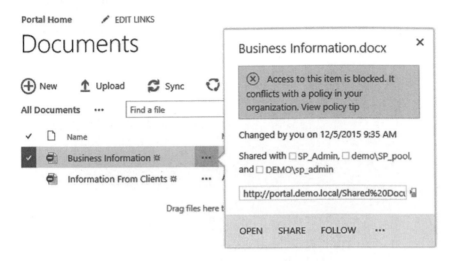

Figure 1-2. *Both Documents are blocked because they conflict with a DLP Policy*

Durable Links

Durable Links is another feature that originated in the cloud, and made its way back to the server room in SharePoint 2016. Before looking at the solution, let's look at the problem. When using SharePoint 2010, SharePoint 2013, and even File Shares, the URL of each document is a path-based URL. In a file share, the path to a document would be as follows:

\\Share\folder\document.docx

In a SharePoint 2013 document library the link to that same document would be as follows:

`https://webapplication.domain.com/Document%20Library/Document.docx`

In both cases, if I rename the document or move it to a different folder or document library my links will break, and all the users who bookmarked that document, or users who linked to that document in other lists or documents, would get a *"Document not Found"* exception.

The Durable links feature allows users to rename a document, and even move it throughout the same site collection, and the links will still work. This feature works with Office documents (Word, Excel, OneNote, and PowerPoint) as well as PDF files. Furthermore, in order to have access to this feature, you need to install and configure Office Online Server 2016 (new name for Office Web Apps Server). We will learn how to configure Office Online Server in **Chapter 9**.

Large File Support

In past versions of SharePoint, the maximum file size for any file was 2047MB, or 2GB. While most companies didn't store documents that big in SharePoint, a lot of enterprises were forced to use third-party file share connectors to display those big files in SharePoint, and take advantage of all the rich features SharePoint has to offer. With SharePoint Server 2016, Microsoft has updated the recommended maximum file size to 10GB as a *supported* limit. If needed, you can go above the recommended 10GB maximum file size; however, Microsoft recommends that you do your own load and performance testing if you choose to do so. If you plan to store large files in SharePoint, make sure to properly plan for space end performance.

As with previous versions of SharePoint, the SharePoint Administrator can control the max file size from the SharePoint Central Administration, for each Web Application individually.

SMTP Encryption

In past versions of SharePoint, the outgoing e-mail was always sent unencrypted and on port 25. This could have led to a security hole since sometimes e-mail alerts contain full information about a list item, or the properties of a document. As you can see in Figure 1-3, the new Outgoing E-Mail settings page allows us to use TLS connection encryption as well as change the SMTP Server port, to a non-default port.

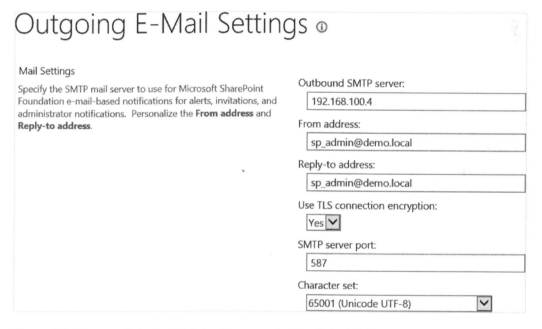

Figure 1-3. *The new Outgoing E-Mail settings page in SharePoint 2016*

Zero Downtime Patching

In SharePoint 2013 patching an environment could have taken hours if you didn't stop the right services before applying patches. For international companies with offices all over the world, taking hours to patch a SharePoint farm, and bringing the business-critical services down during office hours, was not acceptable.

In SharePoint Server 2016 Microsoft redesigned the way that Cumulative Updates are delivered, in a way that you could patch your SharePoint Server 2016 farm without any visible downtime for your users. However, there are certain restrictions and requirements that you must meet in order to get the Zero Downtime Patching to work. This feature will be covered in detail in **Chapter 17.**

Project Server Integration

In past versions of SharePoint Server, Project Server was an add-on that needed to be installed and patched separately from SharePoint. This often led to enterprises having a dedicated farm for Project Server, instead of hosting Project Server on the same farm as the enterprise SharePoint farm.

In SharePoint Server 2016, Project Server is fully baked inside. SharePoint 2016 binaries, patches, and language packs include all the fixes needed for Project Server. Project Server is now simply a Service Application you have to configure. However, the licensing for Project Server is still an add-on on the price of the SharePoint license.

List View Threshold

Let me start by saying the 5000-item list view threshold was never a SharePoint limit. The 5000-item threshold was a *recommendation* by the SharePoint team in order to make sure that lists load fast. Since SharePoint stores its data in SQL, it is also subject to SQL limitations. In SQL server, if you do a query that returns more than 5000 results, SQL will lock that table until the query finishes executing. The table lock would delay other operations, thereby having an impact on your SharePoint performance. The two ways to go around this recommendation would be to create views that would contain fewer than 5000 items, or to ask the SharePoint Administrator to put that limit higher.

SharePoint 2016 includes several new improvements in order to improve performance in large lists. First, SharePoint 2016 databases are no longer subject to lock escalation. Furthermore, SharePoint 2016 now has a timer job that runs by default on all the lists with views over 2,500 items. This timer job evaluates every view and would calculate if a view would benefit from an indexed column. If it would, then SharePoint will automatically create that index.

An important item to remember is that by default, the list threshold in SharePoint 2016 is still at 5000, so if you need views larger than 5000 items, the SharePoint Administrator must still change the list throttling settings in the Central Administration.

Fast Site Collection Creation

Different Site Collections in SharePoint all start from the base blank template model, and then SharePoint activates the required features to get the template that you want. This process can take a few minutes. In SharePoint 2016, Microsoft introduced a new concept of Fast Site Collection Creation. Instead of starting by a blank site, and then activating features, SharePoint will create a master copy of the template at the Content Database level, and when asked to create a new site collection, it will copy the master directly from the database. This reduced the time needed to create certain site collections from minutes to seconds. This feature will be covered in detail in **Chapter 13.**

Recently Shared Items

SharePoint 2016 introduced a new feature called the Recently Shared Items (RSI) cache. The RSI Cache serves to immediately populate the "Shared with Me" view in a user's OneDrive for Business when using it On-Premises. By default in past versions of SharePoint, the "Shared with Me" view was only populated after items were crawled, therefore introducing a delay between the time when someone shared a document, and it appeared in the view.

This feature is not enabled by default in SharePoint Server 2016 because it can also introduce some small security concerns. We will learn the benefits and implications of this feature in more detail in **Chapter 6**.

TLS 1.2 Encryption

Past versions of SharePoint only supported TLS 1.0. SharePoint Server 2016 allows enterprises to use TLS 1.2 for a better security.

Hybrid Features in SharePoint 2016

In SharePoint Server 2016, Microsoft invested heavily in hybrid experiences, in order to allow enterprises that want to keep content On-Premises, to benefit from the latest features in the cloud. In this section, we will have a brief overview of the newest features and benefits, and in **Chapter 14** we will learn how to configure them.

Some of those features have been made backwards compatible with SharePoint 2013 by Microsoft, so even if your organization doesn't have SharePoint 2016 yet and you are planning a migration in the future, you could already start offering some of those hybrid features to your users.

Hybrid OneDrive for Business

When you connect SharePoint 2016 to SharePoint Online you have the option of setting the OneDrive for Business of your users to be in the cloud, instead of keeping it in your On-Premises environment. On-Premises, OneDrive for Business is a part of each user's MySite and you need to store and back up the data from your user's OneDrive for Business, as well as open the MySite web application to the outside network if you want your users to be able to work from home.

When you put OneDrive for Business in Office 365, depending on the plan, users will receive between 1TB and unlimited storage in OneDrive for Business. Microsoft backs up this data in their datacenters instead of your datacenter. OneDrive for Business in Office 365 is available from all over the world via the Internet. You don't need to open up your On-Premises SharePoint farm to the Internet or require the user to be connected to VPN.

Hybrid Sites

In SharePoint 2013 Hybrid mode, when users followed a site On-Premises, they had their shortcut in their On-Premises MySite. When they followed a site in SharePoint Online, it showed up in the Sites section of Office 365. As you see in Figure 1-4, with the new Hybrid Team Sites functionality in SharePoint 2016, when a user follows a site whether it's in SharePoint Server 2016 or SharePoint Online, it will show up in the Office 365 SharePoint section.

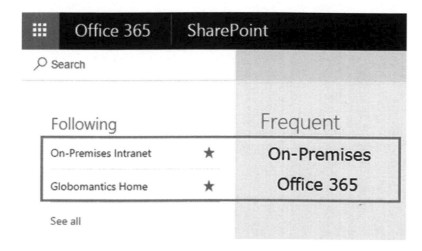

Figure 1-4. The Sites section in Office 365 shows us followed sites, both in SharePoint Online and in SharePoint Server 2016 On-Premises

Hybrid Profiles

In a SharePoint 2016 Hybrid implementation, we can tell SharePoint to always redirect a user's profile to its Office 365 profile, which is now Delve. In the past, users had to maintain two profiles, one for the MySite On-Premises, and the Office 365 profile in Delve. After setting up Profile Redirection, whenever someone clicks on a user, that person will be redirected to the user's profile in the cloud. Figure 1-5 shows a preview of what a user's profile looks like in Delve.

Figure 1-5. *The Profile of Vlad Catrinescu in Delve*

Extensible App Launcher

The App Launcher is one of the few UI changes in SharePoint 2016 compared to previous versions, and it makes it look a lot more integrated with Office 365. When enabled, the Extensible App Launcher will display the Office 365 Delve and Video Apps, along with your custom Office 365 tiles in the SharePoint Server 2016 App Launcher. In Figure 1-6, we can see the Delve and Video apps have been added to the default app launcher.

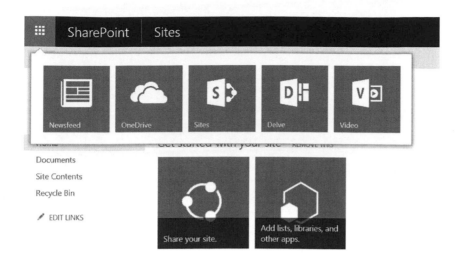

Figure 1-6. *Extensible App Launcher in action*

Hybrid Search

SharePoint 2016 allows us to configure Hybrid Search in two different ways. The first is called Hybrid Federated Search. With Hybrid Federated Search, the index is not replicated between Office 365 and SharePoint. With each user query, the SharePoint Query Engine will query the other system to get results, which allows us to get result from both SharePoint On-Premises and SharePoint Online, on both systems. However, the user experience is not as good as you may hope. In order to show SharePoint Online results from SharePoint On-Premises, we need to use result blocks. The downside of result blocks is that items from both systems are separate from one another, and not shown in order of relevance. In addition, result blocks are limited to 10 results. An example of a Federated Search with result blocks can be seen in Figure 1-7.

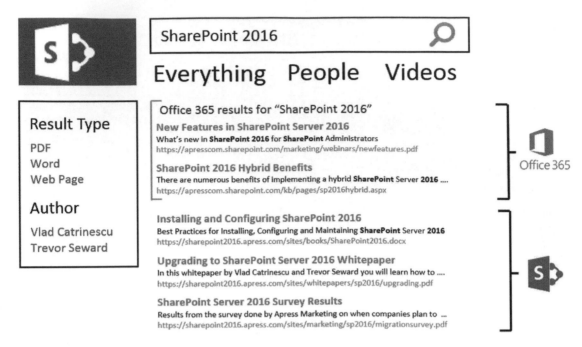

Figure 1-7. *SharePoint Federated Search with Result Blocks to show Office 365 and SharePoint On-Premises results on the same page*

Another way to sort Federated Search results was to include them in different pages, also known as Search Verticals. Adding a different search vertical will be like adding another choice along the built in Everything, People, and Videos in your Search Center, and users could change vertical by selecting it from the top menu. If we look at Figure 1-8, we see that users can only search in SharePoint On-Premises or SharePoint Online, but not the two at the same time.

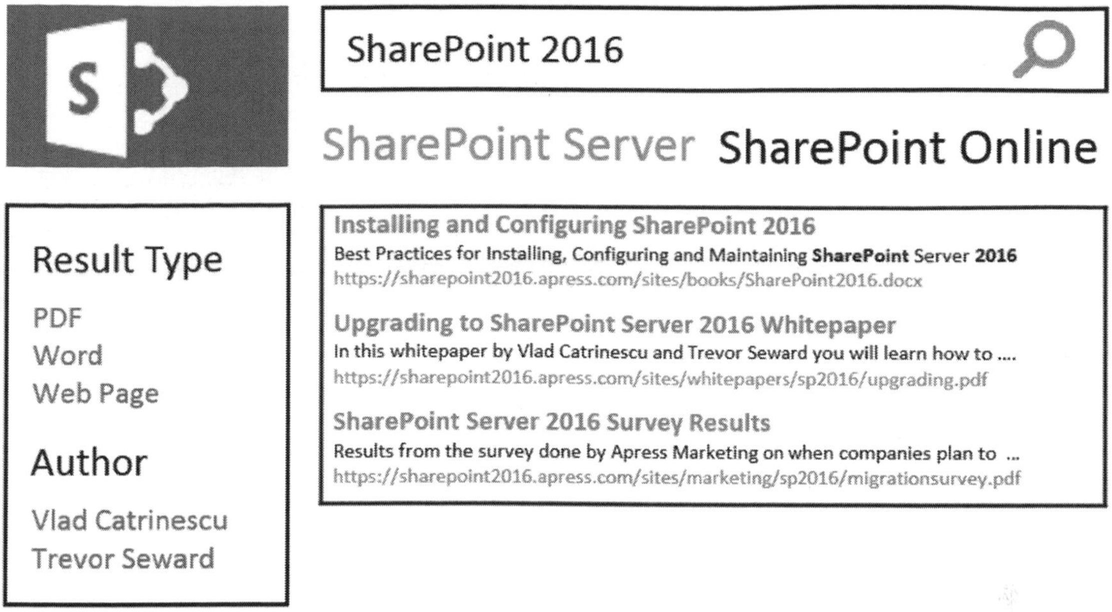

SharePoint 2016

SharePoint Server **SharePoint Online**

Result Type

PDF
Word
Web Page

Author

Vlad Catrinescu
Trevor Seward

Installing and Configuring SharePoint 2016
Best Practices for Installing, Configuring and Maintaining **SharePoint** Server **2016**
https://sharepoint2016.apress.com/sites/books/SharePoint2016.docx

Upgrading to SharePoint Server 2016 Whitepaper
In this whitepaper by Vlad Catrinescu and Trevor Seward you will learn how to ….
https://sharepoint2016.apress.com/sites/whitepapers/sp2016/upgrading.pdf

SharePoint Server 2016 Survey Results
Results from the survey done by Apress Marketing on when companies plan to …
https://sharepoint2016.apress.com/sites/marketing/sp2016/migrationsurvey.pdf

Figure 1-8. *The Federated Search Experience when displaying results from SharePoint Server and SharePoint Online on different pages*

The problem with displaying the search results in different pages, or different result blocks, is that the user has to look at two places to find the best result for his query. Furthermore, result blocks have limits that can get annoying, for example a maximum of 10 results per result block. That is why Microsoft introduced the Cloud Search Service Application, which introduces a new Hybrid Search experience. Instead of having two separate indexes between On-Premises and the cloud, the Cloud Search Service pushes all the On-Premises index to Office 365. Therefore, after the entire configuration is done, users will query a single index from On-Premises or from the cloud. This brings a much better experience for the user, as you see in Figure 1-9, since the best result is shown, whatever system that result is in.

Figure 1-9. Mockup of results in the new Hybrid Search Experience between SharePoint and Office 365

Since the index is now in the cloud, your users will be able to use a majority of Delve features for their On-Premises documents, as well as control the DLP feature for both On-Premises and SharePoint Online in a single place! The Cloud Search Service Application can also crawl File Shares and remote SharePoint sites.

SharePoint 2016 Insights

SharePoint 2016 Insights is a new hybrid feature to help SharePoint Administrators and Compliance Officers to more easily view SharePoint audit logs for enterprises using SharePoint Hybrid. By enabling SharePoint 2016 Insights, SharePoint 2016 and SharePoint Online audit logs will be easily viewable and filterable in the Office 365 Protection Center.

Removed Features

While SharePoint Server 2016 brings us some amazing new features, we also lost a few. Some of those losses we could see coming, and some are more of a surprise. In this section, we will only overview the list of features, and specify the chapter in which their implications will be explained in more detail.

SharePoint Foundation

Microsoft will not be offering SharePoint Foundation. Enterprises currently using SharePoint Foundation 2013 will have to either stay on 2013, upgrade to SharePoint Server, or go to SharePoint Online.

User Profile Service Synchronization

Previous versions of SharePoint had a built-in synchronization service based on Forefront Identity Manager in order to synchronize User Profiles between Active Directory and SharePoint. Forefront Identity Manager came from a different team at Microsoft and introduced a lot of complexity and issues.

By default, SharePoint 2016 will have the option to use Active Directory Import to bring in user profiles from the Active Directory, and we can setup SharePoint 2016 to use an external identity provider such as

Microsoft Identity Manager to have the same rich set of features we had before. We will cover best practices and limitations of AD Import and Microsoft Identity Manager in **Chapter 7**.

Excel Services in SharePoint

The Excel Services Service Application doesn't exist in SharePoint Server 2016 anymore. This may be a big shock, especially to enterprises which use SharePoint for Business Intelligence. While we did lose some features, most of the Business Intelligence features will still work in SharePoint Server 2016; however, you will need to install and configure Office Online Server 2016. We will talk about Office Online Server in **Chapter 9** and about Business Intelligence Features in **Chapter 12**.

Tags and Notes

The Tags and Notes feature is gone from SharePoint Server 2016. Users will not be able to create new tags or notes, and they will not be able to view existing ones either. However, Microsoft provided a new PowerShell cmdlet that allows the SharePoint Administrator to export them so they are not lost. The loss of this feature was to be expected, as Microsoft discontinued it from SharePoint Online in September 2014.

Work Management Service

The Work Management Service was a feature that got introduced in SharePoint Server 2013 and allowed users to show their tasks from all of the SharePoint and Project Server sites and even from Outlook. Those tasks were then shown in the "Tasks" view in a user's MySite as seen in Figure 1-10.

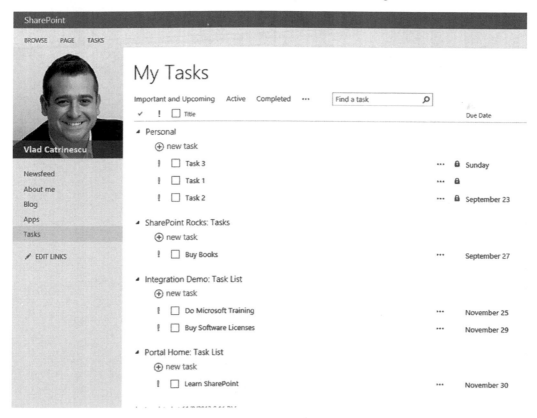

Figure 1-10. *Aggregated view of a user's task in an On-Premises MySite*

Standalone Install Mode

Previous versions of SharePoint included a "Standalone Install" mode, in which the SharePoint installer not only installed SharePoint, but SQL Express as well. In SharePoint 2016, it is still possible to install both SharePoint and SQL on a single machine; however, the installer does not install SQL Express anymore. This is partly because SharePoint 2016 does not support SQL Express as a back end anymore. We will cover possible architecture options in **Chapter 2**.

Next Steps

Now that we are familiar with what improvements SharePoint Server 2016 has to offer, in the next chapter we will learn how to design our SharePoint 2016 farm topology in order to achieve maximum performance and stability with a variety of potential options.

CHAPTER 2

■ ■ ■

Designing a Physical Architecture

In this chapter, we will be reviewing physical architectures for SharePoint Server 2016, as well as networking, virtualization, and other farm considerations.

Decisions on architectures are dependent on content size, concurrent user support, overall user count, and of course monetary considerations. While this book will cover a highly available architecture with disaster recovery systems, many architectures remain valid for a variety of use cases and should be designed with your use case and requirements in mind.

SharePoint Server 2016 Farm Architecture

Choosing a farm architecture is a difficult decision, more so when a SharePoint has never been previously deployed to the environment.

Deciding on a farm architecture largely relies on these factors:

- Monetary investments available for hardware and software licensing

- High Availability and Disaster Recovery Requirements (RTO/RPO)

- Anticipated Content Size

- Overall User Count

- Anticipated Concurrent User Count

- Provisioned Services

All of these play a factor in determining hardware and software requirements. For Enterprises implementing a SharePoint farm for the first time, the anticipated content size and concurrent user count may not be easily determined, but there are load generation tools which this chapter will touch on to assist in determining what may be appropriate.

SharePoint Server can represent a significant monetary cost. Hardware requirements are on the upper end of many Document Management Systems. Each SharePoint Server must be licensed, along with each SharePoint User. Another licensing point to consider is SQL Server, and as SharePoint Server 2016 does not support SQL Express, the only option is the licensed editions of SQL Server.

Creating a highly available SharePoint farm will also raise costs not only in initial investment, but also in operational costs. The more servers and services there are to manage, the more expensive the farm becomes over time.

What services are provisioned on the farm will also impact performance. In a farm where you have over 500 million items to crawl, it is necessary to provision a new Search Service Application. If you have additional Search Service Applications, you may also want to provision additional SharePoint Servers to handle that load.

© Vlad Catrinescu and Trevor Seward 2016
V. Catrinescu and T. Seward, *Deploying SharePoint 2016*, DOI 10.1007/978-1-4842-1999-7_2

Microsoft introduced the concept of MinRole and Zero Downtime patching. MinRole specifies a specific server runs specific services. MinRole provides the best service placement based on Microsoft's experience with SharePoint Online. Per Table 2-1, MinRole service placement cannot be changed as it is defined in code. This may be an important consideration if you want to run any custom services within the farm. Zero Downtime patching allows for patching of a SharePoint farm without taking the farm offline, but Zero Downtime patching does not prevent any one particular server in the farm from going offline; for example, a SharePoint patch may require a reboot. This means that for effective high availability, all services within the farm must be allocated to at least two servers.

Table 2-1. *MinRole Matrix*

Service	Custom	Single Server	Front-end	Distributed Cache	Search	Application
Access Services	Y	Y	Y			
Access Services 2010	Y	Y	Y			
App Management Service	Y	Y	Y			Y
Application Discovery and Load Balancer Service		Y			Y	
Business Data Connectivity Service	Y	Y	Y			Y
Claims to Windows Token Service	Y	Y	Y	Y	Y	Y
Distributed Cache	Y	Y		Y		
Document Conversions Launcher Service	Y	Y				
Document Conversions Load Balancer Service	Y	Y				
Information Management Policy Configuration Service		Y	Y			Y
Lotus Notes Connector	Y	Y				

(*continued*)

Table 2-1. (*continued*)

Service	Custom	Single Server	Front-end	Distributed Cache	Search	Application
Machine Translation Service	Y	Y	Y			Y
Managed Metadata Web Service	Y	Y	Y			Y
Microsoft Project Server Calculation Service	Y	Y	Y			Y
Microsoft Project Server Events Service		Y	Y			Y
Microsoft Project Server Queuing Service		Y	Y			Y
Microsoft SharePoint Foundation Administration		Y	Y	Y	Y	Y
Microsoft SharePoint Foundation Database		Y	Y	Y	Y	Y
Microsoft SharePoint Foundation Incoming E-Mail		Y				Y
Microsoft SharePoint Foundation Sandbox Code Service	Y	Y	Y			Y
Microsoft SharePoint Foundation Subscription Settings Service	Y	Y	Y			Y
Microsoft SharePoint Foundation Timer Service		Y	Y	Y	Y	Y

(*continued*)

Table 2-1. (*continued*)

Service	Custom	Single Server	Front-end	Distributed Cache	Search	Application
Microsoft SharePoint Foundation Tracing Service		Y	Y	Y	Y	Y
Microsoft SharePoint Usage Service		Y	Y	Y	Y	Y
Microsoft SharePoint Foundation Web Application Service		Y	Y	Y		Y
Microsoft SharePoint Foundation Workflow Timer Service	Y	Y				Y
Microsoft SharePoint Insights	Y	Y	Y	Y	Y	Y
PerformancePoint Service	Y	Y	Y			
Portal Service		Y	Y	Y		Y
PowerPoint Conversion Service	Y	Y				
Project Server Application Service	Y	Y	Y			Y
Request Management	Y	Y	Y	Y		Y
Search Administration Web Service		Y			Y	
Search Host Controller Service		Y			Y	
Search Query and Site Settings Service		Y			Y	
Secure Store Service	Y	Y	Y		Y	Y

(*continued*)

Table 2-1. (*continued*)

Service	Custom	Single Server	Front-end	Distributed Cache	Search	Application
Security Token Service		Y	Y	Y		Y
SharePoint Server Search		Y	Y		Y	
SSP Job Control Service		Y	Y	Y	Y	Y
User Profile Service	Y	Y	Y			Y
Visio Graphics Service	Y	Y	Y			
Word Automation Services	Y	Y				Y

With this data in hand, a better determination can be made as to what your farm should look like.

When a server is out of compliance with a specific MinRole, it will be notated in Central Administration under Manage Servers in Farm, as shown in Figure 2-1, as well as for the specific service in Manage Services in this Farm.

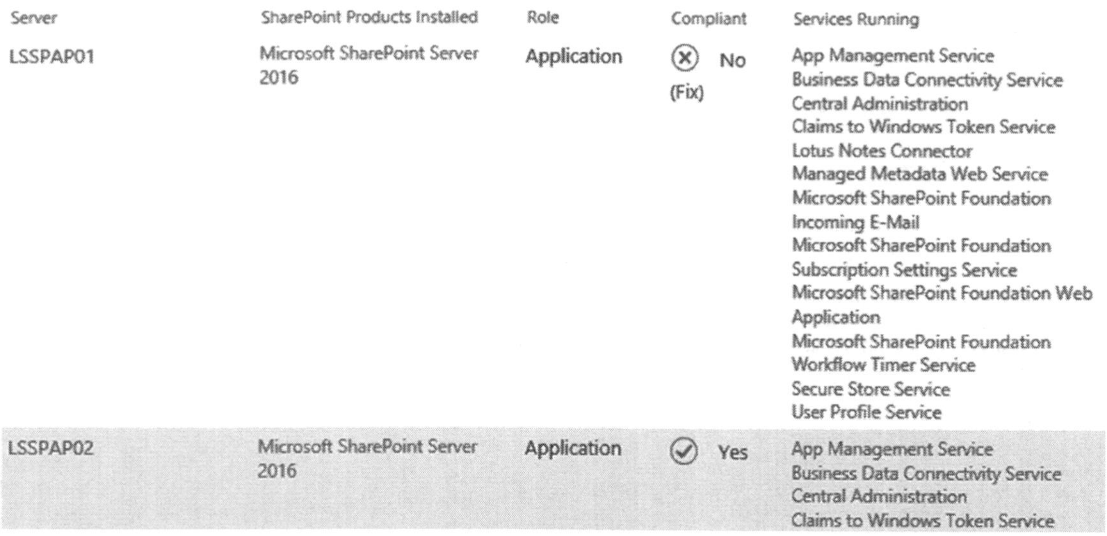

Server	SharePoint Products Installed	Role	Compliant	Services Running
LSSPAP01	Microsoft SharePoint Server 2016	Application	(✗) No (Fix)	App Management Service Business Data Connectivity Service Central Administration Claims to Windows Token Service Lotus Notes Connector Managed Metadata Web Service Microsoft SharePoint Foundation Incoming E-Mail Microsoft SharePoint Foundation Subscription Settings Service Microsoft SharePoint Foundation Web Application Microsoft SharePoint Foundation Workflow Timer Service Secure Store Service User Profile Service
LSSPAP02	Microsoft SharePoint Server 2016	Application	(✓) Yes	App Management Service Business Data Connectivity Service Central Administration Claims to Windows Token Service

Figure 2-1. *Compliant role information in Central Administration*

Dedicated MinRole requires a minimum of eight servers within the SharePoint farm to keep all services highly available, while shared MinRole requires four servers. High Availability will be covered further in Chapter 17.

With the basic concepts of farm architecture, the next step in the architecture process is reviewing the hardware and software requirements for SharePoint Server 2016.

Hardware and Software Requirements

SharePoint Server 2016 hardware requirements remain largely unchanged from SharePoint Server 2013, and any production hardware provisioned for SharePoint Server 2013 can be used with SharePoint Server 2016, as noted in Table 2-2. These are *minimum* requirements. Production deployments often require significantly higher specifications.

Table 2-2. *Hardware Requirements*

Server	Processor	Memory	Primary Disk	Secondary Disk
SharePoint Server	4 Cores, 64-bit	12 – 24GB	80GB	80GB
SQL Server	4 Cores, 64-bit	12 - 16GB	80GB	N/A
SharePoint Single Server Farm	4 Cores, 64-bit	12 - 24GB	80GB	100GB

SharePoint Server 2016 can be installed on Windows Server 2012 R2 Standard or Datacenter, as well as Windows Server 2016 Standard or Datacenter.

Each SharePoint Server requires the following prerequisites.

- Active Directory Rights Management Services Client 2.1

- Cumulative Update 7 for AppFabric 1.1 for Windows Server

- Microsoft CCR and DDS Runtime 2008 R3

- Microsoft .NET Framework 4.6

- Microsoft Identity Extensions

- Microsoft Information Protection and Control Client

- Microsoft ODBC Driver 11 for SQL Server

- Microsoft SQL Server 2005 Analysis Services ADOMD.NET

- Microsoft Silverlight 3 (optional)

- Microsoft Sync Framework Runtime v1.0 SP1 (x64)

- SQL Server 2012 Native Client

- Visual C++ Runtime Package for Visual Studio 2012

- Visual C++ Runtime Package for Visual Studio 2015

- WCF Data Services 5.6

- Windows Server AppFabric 1.1

Additional software may be required when installing other services on top of SharePoint, such as Microsoft's Business Intelligence functionality.

Supported versions of SQL Server are SQL Server 2014 Service Pack 1 and SQL Server 2016, Standard and Enterprise editions. SQL Express is no longer supported for a SharePoint Server farm.

When deploying Business Intelligence services, such as SQL Server Reporting Services, PowerPivot, and Power View, SQL Server 2016 is required with SharePoint Server 2016.

The choice for using SQL Server Standard or Enterprise will largely come down to what method of SQL Server High Availability and Business Intelligence services are deployed to and for the farm.

Virtualization plays an important role in today's data center as well as the cloud; next we will take a look at virtualization options, as well as restrictions with regards to SharePoint Server 2016.

Virtualization

Microsoft fully supports virtualizing SharePoint Server and SQL Server on Hyper-V and other hypervisors, such as VMware ESXi, via the Server Virtualization Validation Program at https://www.windowsservercatalog.com/svvp.aspx. For SharePoint Server, there are restrictions on supported virtualization technologies.

Virtualization is an important technology in today's world, providing greater density in the enterprise environment. It is important to thoroughly test performance of the underlying host hardware in order to properly plan the layout and configuration of virtual machines. For example, placing SQL Server virtual disks on the same LUN as a SharePoint Server may not be appropriate, or allocating a large number of vCPUs when a SharePoint Server may only require four vCPUs, thereby causing CPU oversubscription and reducing overall performance.

Virtualization Limitations and Restrictions

Dynamic memory techniques, which adjust the amount of virtual RAM allocated based on the load of the virtual machine, such as Hyper-V Dynamic Memory or VMware Memory Ballooning, are not supported by SharePoint Server. The Distributed Cache service and Search Server Service create memory allocations based on the memory available when those respective services start. If memory is removed from the system below the amount of memory allocated when the SharePoint Server has started, these two services would be unaware of that change in allocation and cannot adjust their memory quotas appropriately.

Differencing disks are virtual disks that multiple virtual machines may use as a "base." For example, a virtual disk with Windows Server 2012 R2 and the appropriate SharePoint Server 2016 prerequisite installed could serve as that base, and each SharePoint Server virtual machine would have its own, separate virtual disk where changes would take place. This can cause performance penalties for SharePoint Server, thus Microsoft does not support them.

"Online" virtual machine backups are backups of an entire virtual machine, including virtual machine configuration as well as any virtual disks. The operating system in the virtual machine, as well as any applications, is unaware of the online backup. Microsoft does not support these operations with SharePoint Server as online backups do not happen at exactly the same time throughout the farm. This could lead to inconsistencies between farm members if the backups were to be restored, including inconsistencies between the SharePoint Servers and SQL Server databases.

Like online virtual machine backups, online checkpoints, also called snapshots, are also not supported by Microsoft for the same reason. Not only do checkpoints present the same issue of farm consistency during a checkpoint rollback, but they may lead to performance issues, as checkpoints generate a new differencing virtual disk for any changes after the checkpoint was taken.

Replication of SharePoint Server virtual machines is not supported. This includes any form of replication, such as Hyper-V Replica, VMware vSphere Replication, or even Storage Area Network (SAN) block level or file level replication.

Time synchronization services at the virtual machine level should be disabled. The Windows virtual machine will then leverage an authoritative time source within the domain, either the Active Directory Domain Controller with the PDC Emulator FSMO role, or another Domain Controller member server. This ensures time is consistent between SharePoint servers within the farm.

Networking plays a very important role with SharePoint, and next we will examine the required ports for SharePoint as well as networking bandwidth and latency limitations.

Network Requirements

Microsoft recommends the use of the Windows Firewall when possible. With this in mind, and with the potential of other firewalls between SharePoint farm members, SQL Servers, and/or Domain Controllers, it is important to make sure the appropriate ports are open for SharePoint to operate properly. SharePoint will automatically create the Windows Firewall rules when SharePoint is installed. Review Table 2-3 for the ports required by SharePoint and related services.

Table 2-3. *Ports Required for SharePoint*

Service	TCP Port	UDP Port	Protocols
Distributed Cache	22233, 22236	N/A	ICMP Type 0 (ping)
People Picker	53, 88, 135, 137 - 139, 389, 445, 636, 749, 750, 3268, 3269	53, 88, 137 - 139, 389, 445, 749	N/A
Sandbox Service	32846	N/A	N/A
Search Crawler	Web Application Ports Used (e.g. 80, 443)	N/A	N/A
Search Index	16500 - 16519	N/A	N/A
Service Applications	32843, 32844	N/A	N/A
SQL Server	1433 (default)	1434 (default)	N/A
WCF Services	808	N/A	N/A
User Profile Service	53, 88, 389, 5725, 1025 - 5000, 49152 - 65536	53, 88, 389, 464	N/A
SMTP	25 (default)	N/A	N/A

SharePoint Server requires that all servers in the farm are connected with at least 1Gbps network connectivity and 1ms response time over an average of ten minutes. Latency can be measured using any preferred tool, including ping, Psping, Hrping, and others. Microsoft does expect some latency above 1 ms due to various factors, including the use of virtualization or switch fabrics adding latency. The latency limits a SharePoint member server placement to 186 miles (299 km) from each other in a vacuum; however, given that we do not live in a vacuum, the distance may be significantly reduced.

Like SharePoint Servers in the farm, the SQL Servers must also have 1 ms or less latency to each SQL Server running in a synchronous form of replication, as well as the SharePoint servers that the SQL Servers are supporting. This means a SQL Server using AlwaysOn Availability Groups in Synchronous mode will likely need to be within a very short distance of one another.

SharePoint is heavily dependent on a healthy Active Directory forest. Domain Controllers for all domains from which SharePoint users and services reside in should be close to the SharePoint farm, preferably within 1ms RTT and connected with at least 1Gbps connectivity. Each Active Directory Domain should have two or more Domain Controllers for high availability.

Chapter 3 will discuss in further depth how Active Directory is secured for the SharePoint Server 2016 farm.

■ **Note**   Psping is a Microsoft Sysinternals Utility available from https://technet.microsoft.com/en-us/sysinternals/jj729731.aspx. Hrping is available from CFOS Software at https://www.cfos.de.

Network Load Balancers

Network Load balancers are key to providing high availability to SharePoint for your end users. While many load balancers offer SSL Offloading, this should be avoided where possible. Using SSL Offloading removes the encryption on the load balancer and sends the resulting request in clear text to the target services, such as SharePoint. SharePoint uses OAuth tokens for a variety of purposes, such as communicating with Office Online Server, Workflow Manager, and SharePoint Add-ins. OAuth tokens are plain text and rely on transport security, such as SSL, in order to remain secure. While SSL Offloading no longer provides a performance advantage in terms of CPU utilization on a server with a modern AMD or Intel processor, it can reduce the impact of the SSL handshake, which can add up to a few hundred milliseconds. Browsers will reuse the HTTP session, which may reduce the likelihood of another SSL handshake from being required. SSL Offloading may also be used for traffic inspection, looking for exploits, data validation, and so on.

In either case, explore using SSL Bridging instead of SSL Offloading. SSL Bridging decrypts the end user's SSL session at the load balancer, and re-encrypts the SSL session from the load balancer to the SharePoint server. This allows the load balancer to reuse the SSL sessions and reduce the impact of any SSL handshake.

With networking requirements restrictions, and load balancer options covered, we will take a look at the Active Directory service accounts that SharePoint requires.

Service Accounts

Guidance for Service Accounts varies. In this book, we will be taking the minimalist approach, which has proven performance benefits and no known security risks. There are four recommended Managed Accounts for SharePoint; the Farm Account, Service Application, Web Application Pool Account, and Claims to Windows Token Service account. In addition, non-Managed Accounts include a Crawl Account (for Search), User Profile Synchronization (for the AD Import synchronization connection), Portal Super User (for Publishing), and Portal Super Reader (for Publishing). SQL Server should also be run as a Domain User account.

Each account has a specific purpose and supports various services of the SharePoint environment as outlined in Table 2-4.

Table 2-4. *Service Account Rights*

Service Account	System/Service	Permission/Role	Notes
Farm Account	SQL Server	dbcreator securityadmin	Roles are optional but recommended; database creation/security may be managed by DBA
Farm Account	SharePoint Server	Farm Administrator Shell Administrator WSS_ADMIN_WPG Local Group WSS_RESTRICTED_WPG_V4 Local Group WSS_WPG Local Group	On Farm creation, these permissions are assigned automatically

(continued)

Table 2-4. (*continued*)

Service Account	System/Service	Permission/Role	Notes
SQL Server Account	SQL Server	sysadmin Perform Volume Maintenance Tasks Lock Pages in Memory	Fixed role is added automatically when the SQL Server service is configured to run as the Domain User. Perform Volume Maintenance Tasks and Lock Pages in Memory are Local Security Policy User Rights. These will allow instant initialization of database files and prevent Windows from paging out memory in use by SQL Server, respectively.
Web Application Pool Account	SharePoint Server	WSS_WPG Local Group	Other permissions may vary
Service Application Pool Account	SharePoint Server	WSS_WPG Local Group	Other permissions may vary
Claims to Windows Token Service Account (C2WTS)	SharePoint Server	Local Administrator User Rights Assignment: Act as part of the Operating System Impersonate a client after authentication Log on as a service	These rights must be assigned on any SharePoint Server running the C2WTS service, in addition to configuring Kerberos Constrained Delegation for external services where required
Search Crawl Account	SharePoint Web Applications	Full Read User Policy	
User Profile Synchronization Account	Active Directory	Delegated Rights: Replicate Directory Changes Replicate Directory Changes All	Can be configured via Active Directory Users and Computers or ADSI Edit
Portal Super User Account	SharePoint Web Applications	Full Control User Policy	
Portal Super Reader Account	SharePoint Web Applications	Full Read User Policy	

It should be noted that the Farm Account account no longer requires Local Administrator rights on any SharePoint server. This is due to the User Profile Synchronization Service (Forefront Identity Manager) no longer being part of the SharePoint Server 2016 product. The Claims to Windows Token Service account is now the only account that continues to require Local Administrator rights, but depending on the features deployed to the farm, does not necessarily need to be provisioned.

With all of the basic requirements for SharePoint Server 2016 covered, let's take a look at the various topology options available to us.

SharePoint Farm Topology Options

SharePoint topology strategies are numerous. Here we will go over the most common topologies, as well as the minimum required topology for the new "Zero Downtime" patching functionality.

Single Server Farm

A single server farm, as depicted in Figure 2-2, consists of a single SharePoint Server with SQL Server installed on the same server. It is possible that SQL Server may also be running on its own server. This farm architecture has a specific installation role named "Single Server Farm." With this role, it is not possible to add additional SharePoint Servers to the farm, although it is possible to change the role postinstallation to accommodate a farm expansion.

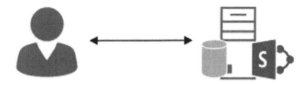

Figure 2-2. *Single Server Farm*

Single server farms have the disadvantage of high memory requirements in order to operate effectively, especially when SQL Server is installed on the same server. Careful memory management with SQL Server is key to acceptable performance. Continuously monitoring the SQL Server memory requirements via Performance Counters is required in order to properly set the Maximum Memory value.

Single Server farms are suited to specialized roles, such as the Microsoft Identity Manager Portal, or Team Foundation Server integration, but are otherwise not recommended for production purposes due to potential significant load and lack of high availability.

One advantage of Single Server farms with SQL Server on the SharePoint Server over all other farm types is that these farms may be checkpointed/snapshotted, replicated (via a hypervisor or SAN block or file level replication), and online virtual machine backups may be taken for this farm type.

If a Single Server farm is under consideration, it may be worth looking into leveraging SharePoint Online for the lower cost of ownership.

Three-Tier Farm

The three-tier farm is one of the most common farm types. These farms consist of a single Web Front End, single Application Server, and single SQL Server. Web Front End is simply defined as the SharePoint Server that is handling end-user traffic, while the Application Server is defined as a SharePoint Server that is not handling end-user facing traffic while typically handling most SharePoint services, such as Business Data Connectivity Services, Managed Metadata Service, and so on.

When installing SharePoint Server with the three-tier farm architecture, shown in Figure 2-3, the Custom role option must be selected for each SharePoint Server. This will allow you to set which services run on each server. The Custom option is the same approach to deploying a SharePoint farm as one would have taken with SharePoint Server 2010 and 2013.

For the three-tier farm architecture, it is recommended to run Distributed Cache, Microsoft SharePoint Foundation Web Application, Search Query Processing role, and Search Index Partition role on the Web Front End. This provides the best end-user experience for these services, although you may want to consider running additional services on the Web Front End for improved performance. See the Streamlined Architecture section later in this chapter.

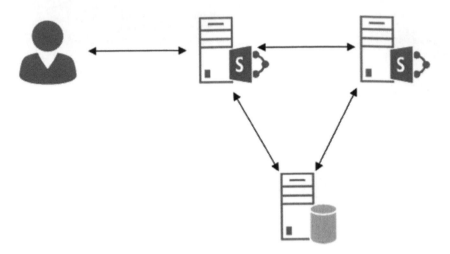

Figure 2-3. *Three-Tier Farm*

The Web Front End Server is where all other services will run, such as Business Data Connectivity Services, Managed Metadata Service, User Profile Service, and any other service which will not run on the Web Front End but is required within the farm. This may lower the memory requirements for the Application Server compared to the Web Front End.

Traditional Highly Available Farms

Other topologies provide basic high availability, as Figure 2-4 shows. These topologies can suffer the loss of one or more SharePoint Servers and SQL Servers while still serving users.

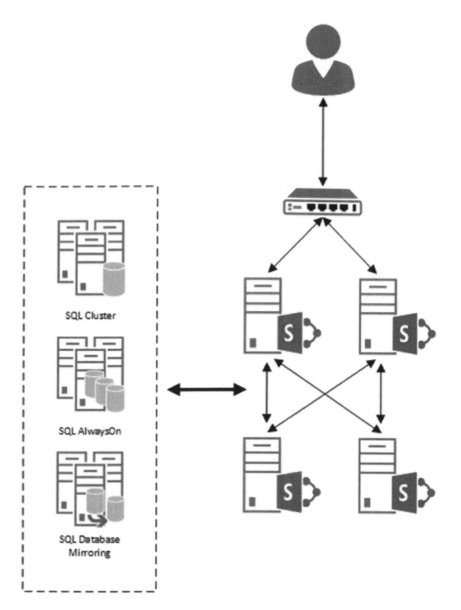

Figure 2-4. *Highly Available Traditional Topology Farm*

An example of this would be two Web Front Ends, two Application Servers, and two SQL Servers using a form of high availability, such as SQL Clustering, Database Mirroring, or AlwaysOn Availability Groups with Failover Clustering.

The Web Front Ends would be behind a load balancer, such as an F5 Big-IP or KEMP LoadMaster. The load balancers would detect a server failure and automatically route traffic to the available Web Front End. For Service Applications, SharePoint operates in a round-robin load balancing when two or more SharePoint Servers in the farm are running any one particular Service Instance. For example, if two SharePoint Servers are running the Managed Metadata Service and one SharePoint Server fails, the SharePoint Topology Service will automatically remove the failed SharePoint Server from the round-robin load balancing and the Managed Metadata Service would continue to be available within the farm. More information on the Topology Service and round-robin load balancing can be found later in this chapter.

MinRole Farms

Microsoft introduced the new concept of "MinRole" to SharePoint Server 2016. Dedicated MinRole is a set of SharePoint Server roles that are defined by the services required for that role. Roles are enforced through SharePoint code. For example, if a SharePoint Server is deployed with the "Distributed Cache" MinRole, SharePoint will automatically provision the Distributed Cache service. If other services are started that do not comply with the MinRole selected, such as the Managed Metadata Service, the SharePoint Server with the Distributed Cache MinRole will be considered out of compliance and notated as such in Central Administration.

MinRole consists of the following new installation roles.

- Distributed Cache. This role runs Distributed Cache, but does not handle end-user traffic directly.

- Front-end. This role not only handles end-user traffic, but runs many services that require low latency for end users, such as the Managed Metadata Service, or User Profile Service.

- Application. The Application role runs what are considered non-latency-sensitive services, such as workflow or PowerPoint Conversion Service.

- Search. Search runs the specific Search roles such as the Admin or Content Processing roles.

Dedicated MinRole farms can be deployed with a minimum of four SharePoint Servers in the farm, although this provides no high availability for SharePoint. Dedicated MinRole farms comply with the Streamlined Topology, discussed later in this chapter.

Zero Downtime MinRole Farms

Downtime patching requires the SharePoint farm be highly available for all services, as shown in Figure 2-5. This means there must be a minimum of eight SharePoint Servers within the farm when using dedicated MinRole and four servers when using shared MinRole.

There are two servers deployed with the Distributed Cache MinRole. The next two SharePoint Servers run the Front-end MinRole, and these two SharePoint Servers are behind a load balancer that can detect server failure and route end-user traffic to the available server. Next, there are two Application MinRole servers, and finally, two Search MinRole servers for a highly available Search Service. In this configuration, any one particular role can suffer a single SharePoint Server failure, or multiple server failures across roles. For example, a single Front-end and single Application server can be down at the same time.

A Zero Downtime MinRole farm, of course, would be supported by one or more highly available SQL Server configurations, such as one or more SQL Clusters or AlwaysOn Availability Groups with Failover Clustering.

The November 2016 Public Update brings Feature Pack 1 where Microsoft has introduced the concept of shared MinRoles. These consist of the following new installation roles.

- Distributed Cache and Front-end

- Application and Search

The enhanced MinRole options allow for smaller farms than the original MinRole options, but the roles are otherwise identical to the dedicated MinRoles described above.

This book will be using dedicated MinRoles, although shared MinRoles are a viable option for the smaller installations where prior to the November 2016 Public Update, the custom MinRole option had to be used.

As with previous MinRoles, it is possible to convert a server from the dedicated to shared MinRoles, or visa versa.

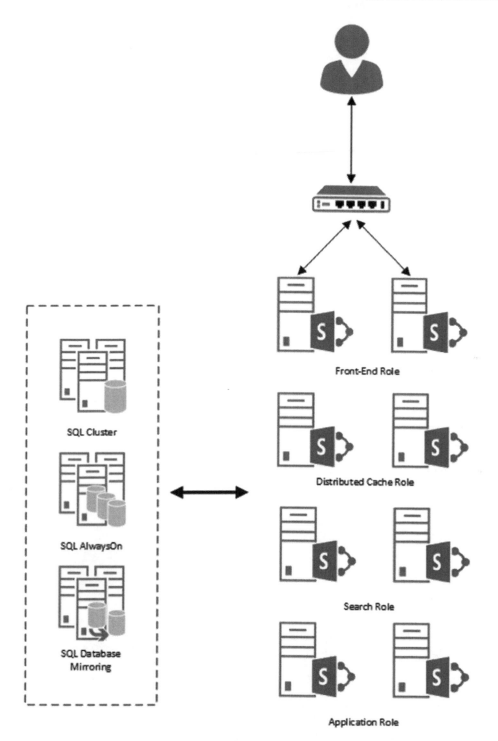

Figure 2-5. *Highly Available MinRole with Zero Downtime Patching Support*

Zero Downtime Traditional Farms

Zero Downtime patching can also be used with more traditional farms, such as a three-tier highly available farm configuration. Each server would use the Custom role with all services remaining highly available within the farm.

Traditional Service Application Topology

The Traditional Topology is a topology that has been used for many years, and is often deployed today with SharePoint Server 2013.

This model follows installation of the Microsoft SharePoint Foundation Web Service on the Web Front End server. The topology may also add Distributed Cache to the Web Front End, as well.

The Application server runs all other services in this topology. This places a higher load on the Application server in comparison to other topologies, while potentially reducing the load of the Web Front End. Increased network traffic may result from this topology due to services communicating from the Application server to the Web Front End; for example, a call to a Managed Metadata field would travel from the Web Front End to the Application server, then back through the Web Front End before reaching the user's browser.

Streamlined Service Application Topology

The Streamlined Topology was born out of Microsoft's experience with SharePoint Online and is the preferred topology. This topology was introduced about a year into the SharePoint Server 2013 lifecycle.

Microsoft tiered services in the Streamlined Topology based on latency for end users. Services that required lower latency, that is, faster access for end-user requests, were placed on the Web Front Ends. Services that were not end user interactive, such as the workflow service, were placed on back-end Application servers (also called "batch" servers).

In certain conditions, this farm topology provided better performance and responsiveness for end users over the Traditional farm topology. Farms using MinRole leverage this topology.

Topology Service

The Round Robin Service Load Balancer, the core function of the Topology Service, is responsible for adding and removing available Service Application endpoints, along with endpoint availability.

The Round Robin Service Load Balancer will enumerate all Service Application Proxies in the farm and determine what endpoints are available. Each Service Instance on a SharePoint server is exposed via an endpoint.

In SharePoint Server 2013 with the Streamlined Topology configuration (and in certain scenarios, the Traditional Topology), because the Round Robin Service Load Balancer would add endpoints to the internal round-robin load balancer, it was possible that even if a particular endpoint was available on the SharePoint Server the end user was connected to, their request may be routed to another SharePoint Server in the farm. This is less than ideal, as the idea behind the Streamlined Topology was to keep end-user requests on the local SharePoint Server.

With SharePoint Server 2016, Microsoft introduced the ability for the Round Robin Service Load Balancer to keep the end-user requests on the same server when MinRole is enabled. This provides the best latency and performance for end-user requests and reduces network load between SharePoint farm member servers.

Hybrid Considerations

SharePoint Server 2016 offers Hybrid Search, where the Search Index is unified with a SharePoint Online Tenant Search Index. If Hybrid Search is used, the On-Premises farm does not utilize a local Search Index. This may factor into plans to reduce the number of Search Servers within the farm.

Utilizing OneDrive for Business in hybrid configuration (redirection) can also help reduce the necessary On-Premises hardware required for SharePoint and SQL Server by offloading all MySite-related activity and storage to SharePoint Online. Chapter 14 will go into further detail on Hybrid.

SQL Server architecture is also an important consideration for a performant SharePoint farm. We will take a look how measure performance and a brief look at high availability architecture.

SQL Server Architecture

SQL Server plays a very important role for SharePoint Server 2016 performance, availability, and Disaster Recovery. Performance measurements of SQL Server prior to deployment are crucial in to gauge limitations of the system and determine when a scale up or scale out of SQL Server is required.

Performance

The first step is to measure the potential performance of SQL Server is the disk I/O subsystem. Microsoft has created a tool, Diskspd, to measure disk performance. This tool will provide valuable data in terms of the number of IOPS the disk subsystem is capable of supporting. Note that testing *write* performance (the DiskSpd -w switch) will cause data loss. Only test write performance on a disk with no data.

■ **Note**   Diskspd is available from Microsoft on the TechNet Gallery. `https://gallery.technet.microsoft.com/DiskSpd-a-robust-storage-6cd2f223`

In addition to disk, the amount of memory available to SQL Server plays a critical role in SharePoint Server performance. The more memory is available to SQL Server, the larger datasets the memory can hold and the longer SQL Server can keep those datasets in memory.

Lastly, CPU performance is crucial. Modern physical SQL Servers will typically have two sockets with four or more cores per CPU. However, in a virtual environment, be sure to allocate two or more vCPUs, depending on performance requirements. A single vCPU may lead to very poor performance in all but the very smallest of environments.

Setting an appropriate Maximum Memory value for SQL Server is important to reserve memory for the operating system and any ancillary programs running on the SQL Server. This will help prevent paging of either SQL Server memory or other process memory to disk, which may reduce overall SQL Server performance.

High Availability and Disaster Recovery

SharePoint Server supports SQL Server High Availability including SQL Server Clustering, Database Mirroring, and SQL Server AlwaysOn Availability Groups. As SQL Server Database Mirroring is deprecated, this book will focus on leveraging AlwaysOn with SharePoint Server databases. We will be reviewing AlwaysOn Availability Groups in Synchronous mode with automatic failover for a local site. SQL Server Clustering is also a valid option; however, SQL Server Clustering does not provide high availability for storage. Conversely, AlwaysOn doubles the storage requirements.

As with disk performance testing for SQL Server, we need to perform load testing for SharePoint, covered in the next section.

Load Generation/Load Testing

While having an architecture outlined is important, so is testing it! Microsoft has two primary tools for testing, Visual Studio 2013 Ultimate or Visual Studio 2015 Enterprise, and the SharePoint Load Generation Tool. These Visual Studio editions include recording specific actions taken in a browser, with the ability to run multiple controllers concurrently to test many users accessing a farm at once.

The SharePoint Load Generation Tool is an add-in for Visual Studio 2013 Ultimate and Visual Studio 2015 Enterprise that performs the following tests:

- CSOM List Read and Write load test

- MySite Read and Write load test

- MySiteHost Read and Write load test

The SharePoint Load Generation Tool also has additional options for authentication and number of servers to test, and automatically records pertinent performance counters for review post-test.

■ **Note** `The SharePoint Load Generation Tool is available on the Visual Studio Gallery.
`https://visualstudiogallery.msdn.microsoft.com/04d66805-034f-4f6b-9915-403009033263`

Now we will examine the SharePoint Server, SQL Server, Workflow Manager, and Office Online Server architecture used in this book. This farm architecture demonstrates the High Availability MinRole architecture.

Architecture in Action

The farm architecture chosen for this book, depicted in Figure 2-6, we will be using the minimum viable farm for a highly available MinRole configuration and "Zero Downtime" patching.

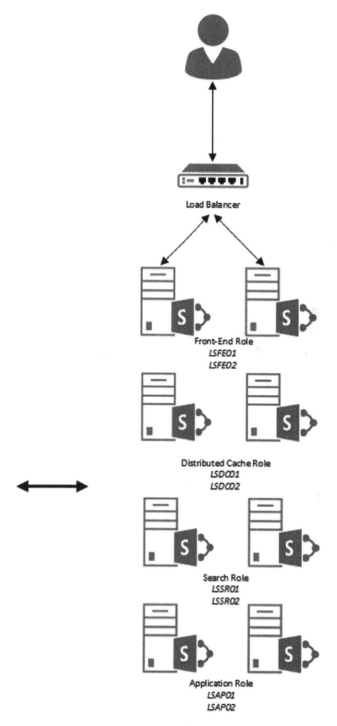

Figure 2-6. *Farm Architecture chosen for this book*

The SQL Servers will be part of an Availability Group using Failover Clustering to provide an AlwaysOn Availability Group for the SharePoint Server databases. In addition, the Failover Cluster quorum will reside on a file server, LSQUORUM01, in order to provide automatic failover. The SharePoint servers fulfilling the Front-end role will reside behind a load balancer. This load balancer offers detection of failed hosts to provide the highest availability possible to clients. In addition to the SharePoint farm, a Workflow Manager farm will also be provisioned with the following architecture, shown in Figure 2-7.

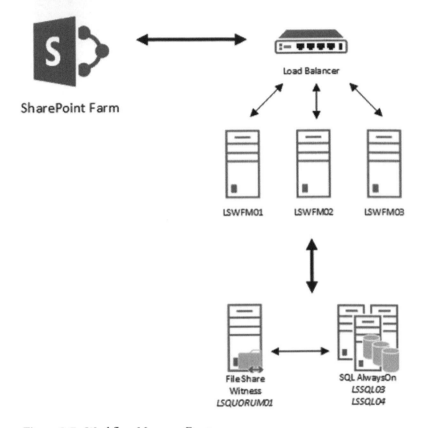

Figure 2-7. *Workflow Manager Farm*

Workflow Manager will be covered in further detail in Chapter 10; however, Workflow Manager can be set up with either a single server or three servers. No other valid configuration is available. In addition, Workflow Manager only supports up to SQL Server 2012, hence the addition of two SQL Servers configured with an AlwaysOn Availability Group.

Lastly, the environment shown in Figure 2-8 consists of an Active Directory Rights Management Services server, Exchange Server 2016, Microsoft Identity Manager 2016, and Office Online Server in a three server highly available environment.

Active Directory
Domain Controller
LSDC01

Exchange Server 2016
LSEXCH01

Office Online Server
LSOOS01
LSOOS02
LSOOS03

SharePoint Farm

Active Directory Rights
Management Services
LSRMS01

Microsoft Identity
Manager 2016
LSMIM01

Figure 2-8. *The Learn-SP2016.com environment*

Business Intelligence

SQL Server will continue providing Business Intelligence features for SharePoint Server 2016. Features such as SQL Server Reporting Services, PowerPivot, and Power View will require SQL Server 2016 for Business Intelligence services, although the SQL Server Database Engine may continue to run on SQL Server 2014 with Service Pack 1. Previous versions of SQL Server for Business Intelligence services are not compatible with SharePoint Server 2016. Business Intelligence will be discussed further in Chapter 12.

Next Steps

We covered some of the basic decisions required to determine what farm topology is right for your configuration and touched on a variety of viable farm topologies, along with reviewing the MinRole and Zero Downtime patching features.

In the next chapter, we will go through an end-to-end installation of SQL Server 2014 with Service Pack 1 on Windows Server 2012 R2 with a Core installation, as well as SharePoint Server 2016 in a highly available MinRole farm. The chapter will also cover security fundamentals for Active Directory, SQL Server, and SharePoint Server.

CHAPTER 3

■ ■ ■

Installing SharePoint Server 2016

In this chapter, we will learn the necessary steps for installation and configuration, from Active Directory, SQL Server, and finally to SharePoint Server 2016. We will also review basic Service Application, Web Application, and Site Collection deployment and configuration. This chapter will provide you with the knowledge to walk through each component using PowerShell as the primary deployment and configuration scripting language. Once you are finished with this chapter, you will have a fully functional, highly available SharePoint Server 2016 MinRole farm. In this chapter, some of the configurations outlined are Microsoft requirements while others are recommendations from Microsoft and the author.

Active Directory Configuration

Your Active Directory domain should consist of two or more Domain Controllers in the physical location where the SharePoint farm and SQL Servers will reside. This will provide the fastest authentication and DNS lookup performance to SharePoint. The Domain Controllers should also have a Server Authentication certificate (e.g., SSL) in order to encrypt LDAP traffic between SharePoint and the Domain Controller. These certificates are typically deployed via Active Directory Certificate Services, but you can also use a public Certificate Authority as well.

Securing Active Directory will primarily be done via Group Policy. SharePoint is provisioned in the domain CORP, which has an fully qualified domain name (FQDN) of CORP.Learn-SP2016.COM. All domain computers, with the exception of Domain Controllers, fall under the Default Domain Policy.

Review Table 3-1 and Table 3-2 for the applied Group Policy Security options.

Table 3-1. *Default Domain Policy Security Options*

Security Policy Name	Policy Setting
Network security: Configure encryption types allowed for Kerberos	AES128_HMAC_SHA1, AES256_HMAC_SHA1, Future encryption types
Microsoft network client: Send unencrypted password to third-party SMB servers	Disabled
Network access: Allow anonymous SID/Name translation	Disabled
Network access: Let Everyone permissions apply to anonymous users	Disabled
Domain member: Digitally encrypt or sign secure channel data (always)	Enabled

(continued)

© Vlad Catrinescu and Trevor Seward 2016
V. Catrinescu and T. Seward, *Deploying SharePoint 2016*, DOI 10.1007/978-1-4842-1999-7_3

Table 3-1. (*continued*)

Security Policy Name	Policy Setting
Domain member: Require strong (Windows 2000 or later) session key	Enabled
Microsoft network client: Digitally sign communications (always)	Enabled
Microsoft network server: Digitally sign communications (always)	Enabled
Network access: Do not allow anonymous enumeration of SAM accounts	Enabled
Network access: Do not allow anonymous enumeration of SAM accounts and shares	Enabled
Network security: Do not store LAN Manager hash value on next password change	Enabled
Network security: Minimum session security for NTLM SSP based (include secure RPC) clients	Require NTLMv2 session security; Require 128-bit encryption
Network security: Minimum session security for NTLM SSP based (include secure RPC) servers	Require NTLMv2 session security; Require 128-bit encryption
Domain controller: LDAP server signing requirements	Require signing
Network security: LDAP client signing requirements	Require signing
Network security: LAN Manager authentication level	Send NTLMv2 response only; Refuse LM & NTLM

Table 3-2. *Default Domain Controller Policy Security Options*

Security Policy Name	Policy Setting
Network security: Configure encryption types allowed for Kerberos	AES128_HMAC_SHA1, AES256_HMAC_SHA1, Future encryption types
Microsoft network client: Send unencrypted password to third-party SMB servers	Disabled
Network access: Allow anonymous SID/Name translation	Disabled
Network access: Let Everyone permissions apply to anonymous users	Disabled
Domain member: Digitally encrypt or sign secure channel data (always)	Enabled
Domain member: Require strong (Windows 200 or later) session key	Enabled
Microsoft network client: Digitally sign communications (always)	Enabled
Microsoft network server: Digitally sign communications (always)	Enabled

(*continued*)

Table 3-2. (*continued*)

Security Policy Name	Policy Setting
Network access: Do not allow anonymous enumeration of SAM accounts	Enabled
Network access: Do not allow anonymous enumeration of SAM accounts and shares	Enabled
Network security: Do not store LAN Manager hash value on next password change	Enabled
Network security: Minimum session security for NTLM SSP based (include secure RPC) clients	Require NTLMv2 session security; Require 128-bit encryption
Network security: Minimum session security for NTLM SSP based (include secure RPC) servers	Require NTLMv2 session security; Require 128-bit encryption
Domain controller: LDAP server signing requirements	Require signing
Network security: LDAP client signing requirements	Require signing
Network security: LAN Manager authentication level	Send NTLMv2 response only; Refuse LM & NTLM

And finally, SharePoint Server is assigned a Group Policy to disable Windows Updates. Alternatively, you may choose to deploy an enterprise patch management solution, such as Windows Software Update Services and disable SharePoint-related updates from being deployed to SharePoint servers, but allow all other forms of updates.

All computers in the domain have the Windows Firewall with Advanced Security enabled. SharePoint and SQL Server will make exceptions in the firewall automatically during installation, but manual exceptions can be made. Note for SQL Server, an exception for TCP/5022 must be made for the AlwaysOn Availability Group.

At this point we have set up basic security for Active Directory and key policies for SharePoint. In the next section, we will cover service accounts leveraged by SQL Server and SharePoint.

Service Accounts

SharePoint and SQL Server require a few service accounts in order to function. There are a variety of strategies available for the number of service accounts to use and for what functions. This book will use a minimal number of service accounts to maintain the best possible performance by creating the least number of Application Pools in SharePoint. By using a single service account for Web Applications, as an example, we can deploy a single Application Pool for all Web Applications. This provides lower startup time for secondary Web Applications after the first Web Application has started up, and also allows each Web Application to "share" memory. With .NET, there is very little sharable memory between processes, even if they contain the same code. As SharePoint processes can consume a significant amount of memory, this provides a very large memory savings.

The Service Accounts in Table 3-3 have been provisioned in Active Directory to run SQL Server and SharePoint and will be used throughout this guide.

Table 3-3. *SQL Server and SharePoint Service Accounts*

Account Name	Account Purpose
CORP\s-sql	SQL Server Service Account
CORP\s-farm	SharePoint Farm Account
CORP\s-svc	SharePoint Service Application Pool Account
CORP\s-web	SharePoint Web Application Pool Account
CORP\s-c2wts	Claims to Windows Token Service Account
CORP\s-sync	User Profile Import Account
CORP\s-su	Portal Super User Account
CORP\s-sr	Portal Super Reader Account
CORP\s-crawl	Search Crawl Account

With the service accounts provisioned in Active Directory, we will look at the Power Management options that can improve performance for both SQL Server and SharePoint Server 2016.

BIOS and Windows Power Management

There are a few changes that can be performed on any server prior to installing SQL Server and SharePoint to increase the performance.

Taking a look at the BIOS/UEFI options for the hardware running SharePoint (whether SharePoint is installed on the physical hardware or if deploying a virtualization host that will run a SharePoint virtual machine), disabling Intel C-States (SpeedStep)/AMD Cool'n'Quiet will prevent the CPU from scaling back when not under load. In addition, disable C1E support ("enhanced halt state"), which is available on both Intel and AMD CPUs. Because SharePoint can spike in CPU load, this may cause a seesaw effect when this CPU technology is enabled. An OEM specific option, such as the HP Power Regulator Mode, may also help improve performance. For HP, setting the Power Regulator Mode to Static High Performance, and for Dell, the Power Management Mode to Maximum Performance. Lastly, disabling QPI power management will prevent throttling of lanes between multiple CPUs and physical memory.

BIOS/UEFI generally does not include an option to disable what is known as "Core Parking." Core Parking is when a specific core within a CPU is halted as it has no work. Core Parking is managed by the Operating System, and on supported Operating Systems for SharePoint Server 2016 and SQL Server, can be disabled by setting the "Minimum Processor State" to 100%, or setting the Power Profile to "High Performance." Power Management profiles can be set via Group Policy.

With the BIOS/UEFI adjusted for best performance, we will take a brief look at antivirus configuration for SQL Server and SharePoint Server 2016. Don't forget to adjust the Power Management settings for SQL Server and SharePoint once Windows is installed!

Host-Based Antivirus

Many companies use or require host-based antivirus. SharePoint Server requires numerous antivirus exclusions in order to prevent file locking and performance problems. For example, host-based antivirus scanning the Timer Service Configuration Cache may cause the Timer Service to pause running jobs due to unexpected high activity within the folder. Microsoft outlines the required exclusions at `https://support.microsoft.com/en-us/kb/952167`.

For SQL Server, exclude the SQL Server processes, MDF, LDF, and NDF file types, along with the locations where SQL Server writes logs or holds data.

Many enterprise antivirus vendors offer centralized management and configuration. If available, make generalized rules for both SQL Server and SharePoint Server 2016 to prevent the need to configure these options locally.

Next, let's start the installation and configuration process for our highly available MinRole farm, starting with the Windows configuration for SQL Server!

Windows Server Configuration for SQL Server

While SQL Server is often configured by a Database Administrator, at times the SharePoint Administrator may be responsible for provisioning the complete environment. Here we will cover the steps necessary to provision the SQL Server environment.

This farm will be utilizing SQL Server 2014 Service Pack 1 running on Windows Server 2012 R2 Standard using a Core installation (no GUI). Windows Core installations offer increased security through a reduced attack surface, lower management overhead, and a significantly smaller footprint with up to a 75% disk space savings. While Windows Core installations are supported for SQL Server, it is not possible to use Windows Core installations with SharePoint Server.

SQL Server will be configured to use AlwaysOn Availability Groups and automatic failover via a file share witness.

Each SQL Server has the following volumes:

- C: Operating System and SQL shared components

- M: Database data files (MDB)

- L: Database log files (LDF)

- T: TempDb data and log files

- Z: Backup volume

Volumes M:, L:, and T: have been formatted using an allocation (cluster) size of 64Kb. SQL Server extent reads are often eight pages in size, each page being 8Kb, thus a single extent read is 64Kb in size. Matching the cluster size to the extent data read size offers the best performance.

Each SQL Server has two network adapters. The primary is for client access and data synchronization over the Availability Group. The second is for a heartbeat between the SQL Servers.

As the SQL Servers are using a Core installation, PowerShell will be the primary configuration method for each SQL Server.

Network Adapter Configuration

The steps involve getting the appropriate network adapter in PowerShell, assigning an IP address, subnet, and gateway; disable DHCP, and finally setting the DNS client addresses. The client-facing adapter will be renamed to "Intranet" while the heartbeat adapter between SQL Servers will be named "Heartbeat." The Heartbeat network adapter will be allocated a private subnet not used by other general devices on the network.

Primary "Intranet" adapter:

- LSSQL01 IP Address: 172.16.0.20

- LSSQL02 IP Address: 172.16.0.21

Use Get-NetAdapter to display all available network adapters on the system. These steps should be repeated for the secondary SQL Server.

```
$adapter = Get-NetAdapter "Ethernet 2"
$adapter | Set-NetIPInterface -Dhcp Disabled
$adapter | New-NetIPAddress -AddressFamily IPv4 -IPAddress 172.16.0.20 -PrefixLength 16
-Type Unicast -DefaultGateway 172.16.0.1
Set-DnsClientServerAddress -InterfaceAlias $adapter.Name -ServerAddresses 172.16.0.10
Rename-NetAdapter -Name "Ethernet 2" -NewName "Intranet"
```

Secondary "Heartbeat" adapter:

- LSSQL01 IP Address: 192.168.5.1

- LSSQL02 IP Address: 192.168.5.2

```
$adapter = Get-NetAdapter "Ethernet"
$adapter | Set-NetIPAddress -Dhcp Disabled
$adapter | New-NetIPAddress -AddressFamily IPv4 -IPAddress 192.168.5.1 -PrefixLength 24
-Type Unicast
Rename-NetAdapter -Name "Ethernet" -NewName "Heartbeat"
```

Disable the DNS registration on the Heartbeat adapter for both servers using the following:

```
Set-DnsClient -RegisterThisConnectionAddresss $false -InterfaceAlias "Heartbeat"
```

This prevents the Heartbeat network from performing dynamic DNS registration, which may cause a connectivity loss as AlwaysOn relies on DNS A records.

Storage Configuration

The next step will be to provision the storage for each SQL Server. For the disks "M:," "L:," and "T:," the disks will be using an allocation size of 64Kb, while the disk "Z:" will use an allocation size of 4Kb.

Use Get-Disk to display all of the disks on the system.

```
Initialize-Disk 1 -PartitionStyle GPT
New-Partition 1 -UseMaximumSize -DriveLetter M
Format-Volume -DriveLetter M -FileSystem NTFS -AllocationUnitSize 65536
```

Repeat this process for each disk, replacing the disk number ("1" in the preceding) with the next uninitialized disk, and the drive letter parameters. For the "Z:" drive, or backup volume, remove the -AllocationUnitSize parameter in Format-Volume, which will set a default allocation unit size of 4096 (4Kb).

Identity Configuration

The next step in the process is to rename the server, restart for the name change to take effect, finally join the server to active directory, and then of course reboot again.

```
Rename-Computer -NewName <value> -Restart
$cred = Get-Credential #User credentials to join the computer to the domain
Add-Computer -Credential $cred -DomainName CORP
Restart-Computer
```

Failover Cluster Configuration

The final step is to install the Failover Cluster service and management tools. Using PowerShell, on each server, run the following:

```
Install-WindowsFeature Failover-Clustering,NET-Framework-Core -IncludeManagementTools
```

In order to create the Failover Cluster via PowerShell, the "-IncludeManagementTools" parameter is required.

Prior to creating the cluster, first test the cluster from one of the SQL Servers by running the Test-Cluster cmdlet and resolving any issues that may appear. As this cluster is not sharing storage, like a traditional failover cluster would, any storage-related warnings do not apply.

```
Test-Cluster -Node LSSQL01,LSSQL02
```

Create the cluster. The cluster name in this example is "LSSPSQLClus" with an IP address of 172.16.0.22, ignoring the heartbeat network and ignoring the local storage.

```
New-Cluster -Name "LSSPSQLClus" -Node LSSQL01,LSSQL02 -StaticAddress 172.16.0.22
-IgnoreNetwork 192.168.5.0/24 -NoStorage
```

Once the cluster has been created, it is a good idea to rename the cluster network adapters for clarity when administering the cluster. First get a list of the cluster networks as well as what subnet each cluster network is on. Based on the Address value of each cluster network adapter, rename the adapter appropriately.

```
Get-ClusterNetwork | fl *
$clusadapt = Get-ClusterNetwork -Cluster LSSPSQLClus -Name "Cluster Network 1"
$clusadap.Name = "Intranet"
$clusadapt = Get-ClusterNetwork -Cluster LSSPSQLClus -Name "Cluster Network 2"
$clusadap.Name = "Heartbeat"
```

The last step is to configure the Failover Cluster Quorum witness. For this cluster, we've chosen to use a file share witness to lower costs and administration complexity, although a SQL Server may be used as a cluster witness as well.

On the cluster witness, LSQUORUM01, create a new directory and share. The physical path is C:\SharePointCluster and the CIFS path is \\lsquorum01\sharepointcluster.

```
Mkdir C:\SharePointCluster
New-SmbShare -EncryptData $true -CachingMode None -Name SharePointCluster -Path C:\
SharePointCluster
```

When the share has been created, disable NTFS inheritance, copying the existing permissions, and then remove the permissions assigned to local Users. Assign "Everyone" with Change rights on the Share Permissions.

Set the Cluster Quorum settings to the file share witness from one of the cluster nodes.

```
Set-ClusterQuorum -FileShareWitness \\lsquorum01\sharepointcluster
```

The cluster configuration is completed and ready for the installation of SQL Server 2014 with Service Pack 1.

SQL Server 2014 Installation

SQL Server 2014 Service Pack 1 is the minimum version compatible with SharePoint. We will go over the installation of SQL Server 2014 with Service Pack 1 on a Windows Server 2012 R2 Standard Core install, first installing SQL Server via the Command Prompt and completing the configuration via PowerShell.

For SQL Server, we will use the Enterprise Core edition. The SQL Server service account will be CORP\s-sql. In order to run the SQL Server setup on Windows Core, it must be executed from cmd.exe (Command Prompt) rather than PowerShell. This is due to a .NET 3.5 Framework dependency that cannot be loaded under future versions of the .NET Framework.

SQL Server Installation

The SQL Server installation itself is configured via an .ini file, while the installation is processed through a batch file. The .ini file parameters must be adjusted accordingly for the specific environment.

```
[OPTIONS]
ACTION="Install"
FEATURES=SQLENGINE,REPLICATION,IS
INSTANCENAME="MSSQLSERVER"
SQLSVCACCOUNT=CORP\s-sql
SQLSVCPASSWORD="<Password>"
SQLSYSADMINACCOUNTS="CORP\Domain Admins"
IAcceptSQLServerLicenseTerms="True"
QUIET="True"
UpdateEnabled="False"
ERRORREPORTING="False"
INSTANCEDIR="M:\\Program Files\\Microsoft SQL Server\\"
AGTSVCACCOUNT=CORP\s-sql
AGTSVCPASSWORD="<Password>"
AGTSVCSTARTUPTYPE=Automatic
SQLSVCSTARTUPTYPE=Automatic
SQLTEMPDBDIR=T:\Data\
SQLTEMPDBLOGDIR=T:\Data\
SQLUSERDBDIR=M:\Data\
SQLUSERDBLOGDIR=L:\Logs\
ISSVCACCOUNT=CORP\s-sql
ISSVCPASSWORD="<Password>"
ISSVCStartupType=Automatic
TCPENABLED=1
BROWSERSVCSTARTUPTYPE=Automatic
```

Once the Configuration.ini file is created, create a SQLInstall.bat file in the same directory, specifying the environment specific installation parameters.

```
@ECHO OFF
set CDRoot=D:
@ECHO ON
%CDRoot%\Setup.exe /ConfigurationFile=sqlconfig.ini /Q
```

Execute SQLInstall.bat on both SQL Servers to install SQL in an unattended mode.

The last step for the installation process is to install the PowerShell module, SQLPS. This module allows administration of SQL Server from PowerShell. For SQL Server installations on Windows Server Core, download the following components from the SQL Server 2014 with Service Pack 1 Feature Pack:

- PowerShellTools.msi
- SharedManagementObjects.msi
- SQLSysClrTypes.msi

Use the following script to install them on both SQL Servers.

```
msiexec /i SharedManagementObjects.msi /passive /norestart
msiexec /i SQLSysClrTypes.msi /passive /norestart
msiexec /i PowerShellTools.msi /passive /norestart
```

Log off of Windows and log back in again in order to use the new module. This is required as the PATH variable has been updated.

■ **Note**   The SQL Server 2014 Service Pack 1 Feature Pack is available on the Microsoft Download Center. Verify you install the 64bit versions of the required software.

https://www.microsoft.com/en-us/download/details.aspx?id=46696

SQL Server AlwaysOn Availability Group Configuration

The SQL Server AlwaysOn Availability Group configuration takes place on the primary SQL Server. A blank user database must be created prior to creating the AlwaysOn Availability Group. Availability Groups have a boundary of 100 databases for performance purposes. While this can be exceeded, if creating databases on a per–Site Collection basis where there are a significant number of databases, it is recommended to create multiple Availability Groups.

Windows Core logs in a user with cmd.exe as the Command Prompt. Switch to PowerShell by typing in PowerShell at the command prompt. Next, import the SQLPS module.

```
Import-Module SQLPS -DisableNameChecking
Enable-SqlAlwaysOn -Path SQLSERVER:\SQL\LSSQL01\DEFAULT -Force
Enable-SqlAlwaysOn -Path SQLSERVER:\SQL\LSSQL02\DEFAULT -Force
```

■ **Tip**   If you do not want the Enable-SqlAlwaysOn cmdlet to automatically restart the SQL Server instance, use the -NoServiceRestart switch. You must then manually restart the SQL Server instance in order to enable AlwaysOn.

Create the Backup share to store the temporary user database. This PowerShell creates a new folder named "Backup" on the Z: drive, create a new Share named "Backup" (\\LSSQL01\Backup\) with Everyone Full Control on the Share permissions, then finally set the NTFS permissions. The NTFS permissions remove inherited permissions as well as the existing permissions (with the exception of BUILTIN\Administrators, who retain Full Control) and then create a new NTFS permission with NTFS Modify rights for the Domain User "CORP\s-sql," which runs the SQL Server service, and finally applies the permissions to Z:\Backup.

```
New-Item Z:\Backup -ItemType Directory
New-SmbShare -Name Backup -Path Z:\Backup -FullAccess "Everyone"
$acl = Get-Acl Z:\Backup
$acl.SetAccessRuleProtection($true,$false)
$rule = New-Object System.Security.AccessControl.FileSystemAccessRule("CORP\s-sql",
"Modify", "ContainerInherit,ObjectInherit", "None", "Allow")
$acl.AddAccessRule($rule)
Set-Acl Z:\Backup $acl
```

To create the blank database, on the primary SQL Server from the PowerShell prompt, run the following:

```
Invoke-SqlCmd "CREATE DATABASE AOTemp;" -ServerInstance LSSQL01
```

This will create the blank database we need in order to perform the backup and restore and create the AlwaysOn Availability Group. Create the Backup share on the primary SQL Server.

■ **Tip**   Make sure you're on the correct SQL Server! You can change the SQL Server from the PowerShell Command Prompt by going to the path SQLSERVER:\SQL\ServerName\InstanceName. If no Instance Name was specified during SQL Server installation, it is "DEFAULT."

Create the AlwaysOn endpoint and take a backup of the temporary database, AOTemp. If you have not created a Firewall exception yet, you will need to implement an exception for TCP/5022.

```
New-SqlHADREndpoint -Path SQLSERVER:SQL\LSSQL01\DEFAULT -Name SPHADR -Port 5022 -Encryption
Required
New-SqlHADREndpoint -Path SQLSERVER:\SQL\LSSQL02\DEFAULT -Name SPHADR -Port 5022 -Encryption
Required
Set-SqlHADREndpoint -Path SQLSERVER:\SQL\LSSQL01\DEFAULT\Endpoints\SPHADR -State Started
Set-SqlHADREndpoint -Path SQLSERVER:\SQL\LSSQL02\DEFAULT\Endpoints\SPHADR -State Online
Backup-SqlDatabase -Database AOTemp -BackupFile Z:\Backup\AOTemp.bak -ServerInstance LSSQL01
-NoRecovery
Backup-SqlDatabase -Database AOTemp -BackupFile Z:\Backup\AOTemp_Log.bak -ServerInstance
LSSQL01 -BackupAction Log -NoRecovery
```

Create the replicas and the Availability Group named SPHADR. We only have two replicas in Synchronous Commit mode to provide local high availability. Finally, join the Secondary Replica to the Availability Group.

```
$replicaA = New-SqlAvailabilityReplica -Name LSSQL01 -EndpointUrl TCP://LSSQL01.corp.learn-
sp2016.com:5022 -FailoverMode Automatic -AvailabilityMode SynchronousCommit -Version 12
-AsTemplate
$replicaB = New-SqlAvailabilityReplica -Name LSSQL02 -EndpointUrl TCP://LSSQL02.corp.learn-
sp2016.com:5022 -FailoverMode Automatic -AvailabilityMode SynchronousCommit -Version 12
-AsTemplate
Cd SQL\LSSQL01\DEFAULT
New-SqlAvailabilityGroup -Name SPHADR AvailabilityReplicas ($replicaA, $replicaB) -Database
AOTemp
Cd SQLSERVER:\SQL\LSSQL02\DEFAULT
Join-SqlAvailabilityGroup -Name SPHADR
```

Create the Availability Group Listener, "SPAG," with a static IP address. This IP address must be unused. This will be the endpoint SharePoint connects to, with a Full Qualified Domain Name of spag.corp.learn-sharepoint2016.com:1433.

```
New-SqlAvailabilityGroupListener -Name SPAG -StaticIp "172.16.0.23/255.255.0.0" -Path
SQLSERVER:\SQL\LSSQL01\DEFAULT\AvailabilityGroups\SPHADR
```

Restore the temporary database to the secondary node and then add the temporary database to the Secondary Replica.

```
Cd SQLSERVER:\SQL\LSSQL02\DEFAULT
Restore-SqlDatabase AOTemp -ServiceInstance LSSQL02 -BackupFile \\LSSQL01\Backup\AOTemp.bak
-NoRecovery
Restore-SqlDatabase AOTemp -ServiceInstance LSSQL02 -BackupFile \\LSSQL01\Backup\AOTemp_Log.
bak -RestoreAction Log
$ag = Get-Item SQLSERVER:\SQL\LSSQL02\DEFAULT\AvailabilityGroups\SPHADR
Add-SqlAvailabilityDatabase -InputObject $ag -Database AOTemp
```

The Availability Group setup is now completed. The Availability Group can continue to be managed with PowerShell, but may also be managed through SQL Server Management Studio for ease of use or those unfamiliar with SQLPS.

Kerberos Configuration

Kerberos is a significantly more secure protocol when communicating between services. Kerberos can be leveraged, as it will be here, between SQL Server and SharePoint. This not only increases security, but also improves authentication performance. To configure Kerberos for an AlwaysOn Availability Group, three SPNs are required: one for each SQL Server, and an additional SPN for the Availability Group Listener. The SPN is registered against the Service Account running the SQL Server service, or in this case, CORP\s-sql. Setspn.exe can be executed from any domain-joined machine by a Domain Administrator.

```
setspn -S MSSQLSvc/LSSQL01.corp.learn-sp2016.com:1433 CORP\s-sql
setspn -S MSSQLSvc/LSSQL01:1433 CORP\s-sql
setspn -S MSSQLSvc/LSSQL02.corp.learn-sp2016.com:1433 CORP\s-sql
setspn -S MSSQLSvc/LSSQL02:1433 CORP\s-sql
setspn -S MSSQLSvc/SPAG.corp.learn-sp2016.com:1433 CORP\s-sql
```

Once the SPNs have been created, the SQL Server service must be restarted on both SQL Servers.

■ **Tip**   For more information on Kerberos, see the article "What is Kerberos?" on TechNet.

https://technet.microsoft.com/en-us/library/cc780469(v=ws.10).aspx

---

Model Database

The model database in SQL Server is the template for all future databases created on the SQL Server. The model database initial values are not always optimal, and can be adjusted with T-SQL. The initial file size will vary depending on how heavily used the environment is, and for this environment it will be set at a conservative 100MB for modeldev (data file) and modellog (log file). To complete this, on the Primary and Secondary Replica, run the following T-SQL command.

```
ALTER DATABASE [model] MODIFY FILE (NAME = modeldev, SIZE = 100MB, MAXSIZE = UNLIMITED)
ALTER DATABASE [model] MODIFY FILE (NAME = modellog, SIZE = 100MB, MAXSIZE = UNLIMITED)
```

Note that we are not specifying the FILEGROWTH property as SharePoint ignores this value when creating databases.

MAXDOP

Provided the account installing SharePoint has the sysadmin Fixed Role in the SQL Server instance, MAXDOP will automatically be set. SharePoint Server 2016 will refuse to deploy if MAXDOP is not set to 1. If the user installing SharePoint does not have the appropriate rights on the SQL Server, the SQL Server administrator may set this value via T-SQL or through SQL Server Management Studio. It may also be necessary to manually set this value on any secondary servers in the Availability Group.

```
sp_configure 'show advanced options', 1;
GO
RECONFIGURE WITH OVERRIDE;
GO
sp_configure 'max degree of parallelism', 1;
GO
RECONFIGURE WITH OVERRIDE;
GO
```

Instant File Initialization

Instant file initialization is a feature that creates the MDF instantly. It bypasses the need to write zeros to the disk where the file is being created. As our service account is not a Local Administrator, we must grant the "Perform Volume Maintenance Tasks" to the service account. Because Windows Server Core does not offer the MMC, in order to perform this task we must use a Windows Server with a full GUI installation. The steps to complete this are as follows:

Use secpol.msc to make changes on the Windows Server with the full installation. Within the Local Security Policy management console, export the policy under Actions to an INF. Copy this INF to the Windows Server Core system. From there, run the following:

```
secedit.exe /configure /db secedit.sdb /cfg C:\export.INF
```

This completes the SQL Server installation. With a fully functional SQL Server AlwaysOn setup, we're ready to finally install SharePoint Server 2016!

SharePoint Server 2016 Installation

SharePoint will be set up on nine servers. The setup process will consist of running the prerequisite installer in a silent mode. Once the prerequisite installer has been completed, the SharePoint binaries will be installed. A wildcard certificate for *.learn-sp2016.com has been deployed to all SharePoint servers to be used for Web Applications.

Disable Insecure Transport Security Protocols

SharePoint Server 2016 introduces support for TLS 1.2. Because of this, it is highly recommended to disable previous protocols, including SSL 3.0, TLS 1.0, and TLS 1.1. By default, SSL 2.0 is disabled in Windows Server 2012 R2.

To disable the previous protocols, run the following PowerShell script on each SharePoint Server. This configuration change requires a reboot to take effect.

```
#Disable PCT 1.0
ni "HKLM:\SYSTEM\CurrentControlSet\Control\SecurityProviders\SCHANNEL\Protocols\" -Name "PCT
1.0" -Value "DefaultValue" -Force
ni "HKLM:\SYSTEM\CurrentControlSet\Control\SecurityProviders\SCHANNEL\Protocols\PCT 1.0\"
-Name "Server" -Value "DefaultValue" -Force
New-ItemProperty "HKLM:\SYSTEM\CurrentControlSet\Control\SecurityProviders\SCHANNEL\
Protocols\PCT 1.0\Server\" -Name Enabled -Value 0 -PropertyType "DWord" -Force
#Disable SSL 2.0
ni "HKLM:\SYSTEM\CurrentControlSet\Control\SecurityProviders\SCHANNEL\Protocols\" -Name "SSL
2.0" -Value "DefaultValue" -Force
ni "HKLM:\SYSTEM\CurrentControlSet\Control\SecurityProviders\SCHANNEL\Protocols\SSL 2.0\"
-Name "Server" -Value "DefaultValue" -Force
New-ItemProperty "HKLM:\SYSTEM\CurrentControlSet\Control\SecurityProviders\SCHANNEL\
Protocols\SSL 2.0\Server\" -Name Enabled -Value 0 -PropertyType "DWord" -Force
#Disable SSL 3.0
ni "HKLM:\SYSTEM\CurrentControlSet\Control\SecurityProviders\SCHANNEL\Protocols\" -Name "SSL
3.0" -Value "DefaultValue" -Force
ni "HKLM:\SYSTEM\CurrentControlSet\Control\SecurityProviders\SCHANNEL\Protocols\SSL 3.0\"
-Name "Server" -Value "DefaultValue" -Force
New-ItemProperty "HKLM:\SYSTEM\CurrentControlSet\Control\SecurityProviders\SCHANNEL\
Protocols\SSL 3.0\Server\" -Name Enabled -Value 0 -PropertyType "DWord" -Force
#Disable TLS 1.0
ni "HKLM:\SYSTEM\CurrentControlSet\Control\SecurityProviders\SCHANNEL\Protocols\" -Name "TLS
1.0" -Value "DefaultValue" -Force
ni "HKLM:\SYSTEM\CurrentControlSet\Control\SecurityProviders\SCHANNEL\Protocols\TLS 1.0\"
-Name "Server" -Value "DefaultValue" -Force
New-ItemProperty "HKLM:\SYSTEM\CurrentControlSet\Control\SecurityProviders\SCHANNEL\
Protocols\TLS 1.0\Server\" -Name Enabled -Value 0 -PropertyType "DWord" -Force
#Disable TLS 1.1
ni "HKLM:\SYSTEM\CurrentControlSet\Control\SecurityProviders\SCHANNEL\Protocols\" -Name "TLS
1.1" -Value "DefaultValue"  -Force
ni "HKLM:\SYSTEM\CurrentControlSet\Control\SecurityProviders\SCHANNEL\Protocols\TLS 1.1\"
-Name "Server" -Value "DefaultValue"  -Force
New-ItemProperty "HKLM:\SYSTEM\CurrentControlSet\Control\SecurityProviders\SCHANNEL\
Protocols\TLS 1.1\Server\" -Name Enabled -Value 0 -PropertyType "DWord" -Force
```

Prerequisite Silent Installation

To install all of the prerequisites in a silent mode, they must be downloaded from Microsoft and placed into a directory on the SharePoint server. In this example, the SharePoint binaries have been copied to C:\SharePoint2016, where PrerequisiteInstaller.exe resides.

```
Start-Process "C:\SharePoint2016\PrerequisiteInstaller.exe" -ArgumentList "/SQLNCli:`"C:\
SharePoint2016\PrerequisiteInstallerFiles\sqlncli.msi`" `
/Sync:`"C:\SharePoint2016\PrerequisiteInstallerFiles\Synchronization.msi`" `
/AppFabric:`"C:\SharePoint2016\PrerequisiteInstallerFiles\WindowsServerAppFabricSetup_x64.
exe`" `
/IDFX11:`"C:\SharePoint2016\PrerequisiteInstallerFiles\MicrosoftIdentityExtensions-64.msi`" `
```

```
/MSIPCClient:`"C:\SharePoint2016\PrerequisiteInstallerFiles\setup_msipc_x64.exe`" `
/KB3092423:`"C:\SharePoint2016\PrerequisiteInstallerFiles\AppFabric-KB3092423-x64-ENU.exe`" `
/WCFDataServices56:`"C:\SharePoint2016\PrerequisiteInstallerFiles\WcfDataServices.exe`" `
/ODBC:`"C:\SharePoint2016\PrerequisiteInstallerFiles\msodbcsql.msi`" `
/DotNet452:`"C:\SharePoint2016\PrerequisiteInstallerFiles\NDP452-KB2901907-x86-x64-AllOS-
ENU.exe`" `
/MSVCRT11:`"C:\SharePoint2016\PrerequisiteInstallerFiles\vcredist_x64.exe`" `
/MSVCRT14:`"C:\SharePoint2016\PrerequisiteInstallerFiles\vc_redist.x64.exe`""
```

The prerequisite installer will only require a single reboot, unlike previous versions of SharePoint. When logging back into the SharePoint Server after a reboot, the prerequisite installer will start automatically to validate the installation.

■ **Note** The Links for each prerequisite is available from the following links.

Windows Management Framework 3.0 for Windows Server 2008 R2 SP1 (Windows6.1-KB2506143-x64.msu): `http://go.microsoft.com/fwlink/?LinkID=233187`

Microsoft Sync Framework Runtime v1.0 SP1 (x64) (Synchronization.msi): `http://go.microsoft.com/fwlink/?LinkID=224449`

Microsoft SQL Server 2012 Native Client (sqlncli.msi): `http://go.microsoft.com/fwlink/?LinkId=622997`

Microsoft ODBC Driver 11 for SQL Server (msodbcsql.msi): `http://go.microsoft.com/fwlink/?LinkId=517835`

Windows Server AppFabric (WindowsServerAppFabricSetup_x64.exe): `http://go.microsoft.com/fwlink/?LinkId=235496`

Microsoft Identity Extensions (MicrosoftIdentityExtensions-64.msi): `http://go.microsoft.com/fwlink/?LinkID=252368`

WCF Data Services 5.6 Tools (WcfDataServices.exe): `http://go.microsoft.com/fwlink/?LinkId=320724`

Cumulative Update 7 for Microsoft AppFabric 1.1 for Windows Server (AppFabric-KB3092423-x64-ENU.exe): `http://go.microsoft.com/fwlink/?LinkId=627257`

Active Directory Rights Management Services Client 2.1

(setup_msipc_x64.exe): `http://go.microsoft.com/fwlink/?LinkID=544913`

Microsoft .NET Framework 4.6 (NDP46-KB3045560-Web.exe): `http://go.microsoft.com/fwlink/?LinkID=691472`

Microsoft Visual C++ 2012 Redistributable (x64) (vcredist_x64.exe): `http://go.microsoft.com/fwlink/?LinkId=627156`

Microsoft Visual C++ 2015 Redistributable (x64) (vc_redist.x64.exe): `http://go.microsoft.com/fwlink/?LinkId=623013`

The SharePoint binaries are installed via setup.exe. Per Figure 3-1, during the installation of SharePoint Server, you will be prompted for location of where to install SharePoint as well as where to locate the Search Index. If deploying a Search Server, you may wish to locate the Index on an alternate volume dedicated to the Search Index. Also consider changing the path to an alternate volume as the analysis and temporary file creation for content processing will be used for this location, regardless of the location of the Search Index. At the end of the installation, uncheck the Run the SharePoint Products Configuration Wizard now." checkbox, as this will guide you through using the SharePoint Management Shell to deploy SharePoint.

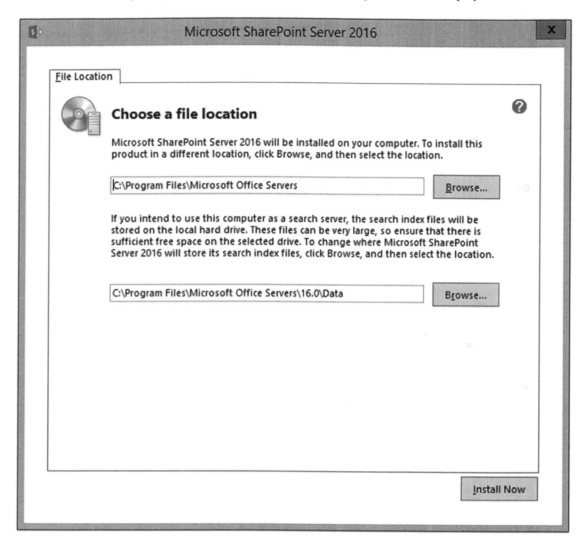

Figure 3-1. *Specifying the installation and Search Index location for SharePoint*

SharePoint Server 2016 has now been installed on all of the nine farm members. We are now ready to start the SharePoint Server 2016 configuration.

SharePoint Server 2016 Configuration

Instead of running the SharePoint Configuration Wizard, this book will display how SharePoint is installed via PowerShell. The goal of this section is to create all nine servers with the assigned MinRole, set transport encryption on Central Administration, and finally configure Central Administration authentication with Kerberos.

Run the SharePoint Management Shell as an Administrator on the server that will host Central Administration. In this example, it is LSSAP01. The -FarmCredential parameter will be the Domain User service account, CORP\s-farm.

```
New-SPConfigurationDatabase -DatabaseName Configuration -AdministrationContentDatabaseName
Administration -DatabaseServer spag.corp.learn-sp2016.com -Passphrase (ConvertTo-
SecureString "FarmPassphrase1" -AsPlainText -Force) -FarmCredentials (Get-Credential)
-LocalServerRole Application
```

Note the use of the Availability Group Listener for the -DatabaseServer parameter. Instead of using a SQL Alias configured through cliconfg.exe on the SharePoint server, the Availability Group Listener is used. As we can add and remove SQL Servers from the Availability Group, or even move the Availability Group Listener name to another Availability Group completely, it is no longer necessary to specify a SQL Alias.

■ **Tip**   If using cliconfg.exe to create a SQL Alias, make sure to run cliconfig.exe on all SharePoint Servers in the farm. Each SharePoint server must have the SQL Alias configured.

Additionally, note the new parameter, -LocalServerRole, which takes a value of Application, DistributedCache, WebFrontEnd, Search, Custom, or SingleServerFarm. This specifies the MinRole used for the particular server. As this will be hosting Central Administration, the Application role is the appropriate choice.

Central Administration

To configure Central Administration to use Kerberos as the authentication mechanism, a new SPN must be set on the Farm Account. The SPN will take the format of HTTP/CentralAdminFQDN.

```
Setspn -S HTTP/ca.corp.learn-sp2016.com CORP\s-farm
```

■ **Tip**   The SPN for a web site will always start with "HTTP," even if the site is using the SSL protocol, as HTTP is a Kerberos service, not a protocol description.

Create Central Administration using Kerberos and SSL.

```
New-SPCentralAdministration -Port 443 -WindowsAuthProvider Kerberos
-SecureSocketsLayer:$true
```

The next step is to change the default Alternate Access Mapping to align with the SPN and SSL certificate. Use Get-SPWebApplication -IncludeCentralAdministration to see what the current URL of Central Administration is, then modify it.

```
Set-SPAlternateUrl -Identity https://lsspap01 -Url https://ca.corp.learn-sp2016.com
Remove-SPAlternateUrl -Identity https://lsspap01
```

The next series of cmdlet secure permissions on the files and registry entries in use by SharePoint, provision SharePoint Features, Services, and Help.

```
Initialize-SPResourceSecurity
Install-SPFeature -AllExistingFeatures
Install-SPService
Install-SPHelpCollection -All
```

■ **Tip**   You can find the definition for the ACLs Initialize-SPResourceSecurity is applying by looking at the registry! Navigate to HKEY_LOCAL_MACHINE\SOFTWARE\Microsoft\Shared Tools\Web Server Extensions\16.0\ WSS\ResourcesToSecure\. Each resource is defined by a GUID, but under the key in the format of a GUID is a ResourceName which is the path to the item to be secured, along with the Permissions (Read (R), Write (W), Execute (E), Full Control (FC), and Change Permission (D)).

If a custom URL was set for Central Administration that does not include the machine name, make sure to create an A record in DNS to resolve the new hostname. In addition, validate that the IIS Site Bindings for the SharePoint Central Administration site are set correctly as shown in Figure 3-2. Because this server will only have a single IP address but will need to support multiple SSL certificates, Server Name Indication will be used. SNI is compatible with all browsers that SharePoint Server 2016 supports.

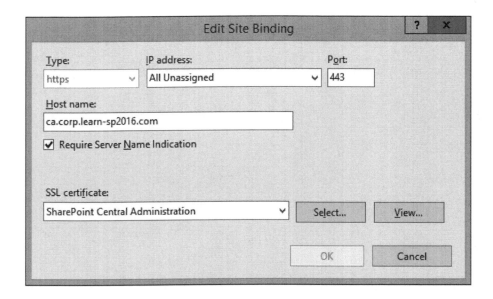

Figure 3-2. *Validating the Central Administration IIS Site Binding*

The next step is to make the Administration and Configuration databases highly available.

In order to achieve high availability for the databases, when a SharePoint database is created, you must add it to the Availability Group. This can be achieved through SQL Server Management Studio from a client computer. The first step is to take a Full Backup of the database. In this example, we will use the Configuration database, although it must be done with all databases created for the farm.

On the Primary Replica, using T-SQL, backing up the database as well as the transaction log as an Availability Group requires the use of the Full Recovery Model for each database that is part of the Availability Group. Specify the file path. Each file should have a unique name. Add the database to the Availability Group, named SPHADR in this scenario.

```
BACKUP DATABASE Configuration TO DISK = N'Z:\Backup\Configuration.bak';
BACKUP LOG Configuration TO DISK = N'Z:\Backup\Configuration_Log.bak';
ALTER AVAILABILITY GROUP SPHADR ADD DATABASE Configuration;
```

Finally, restore the database and log file on the Secondary Replica from the file share on the Primary Replica, and begin data movement for the database.

```
RESTORE DATABASE Configuration FROM DISK = N'\\LSSQL02\Backup\Configuration.bak' WITH
NORECOVERY;
RESTORE LOG Configuration FROM DISK = N'\\LSSQL02\Backup\Configuration_Log.bak' WITH
NORECOVERY;
ALTER DATABASE Configuration SET HADR Availability GROUP = SPHADR;
```

To add a database through the Availability Group wizard, first take a Full Backup through the wizard, shown in Figure 3-3. Right-click the database and go to the Tasks node, and then Backup. Specify the backup location that is shared (Z:\Backup) and a file name, in this example, Administration.bak.

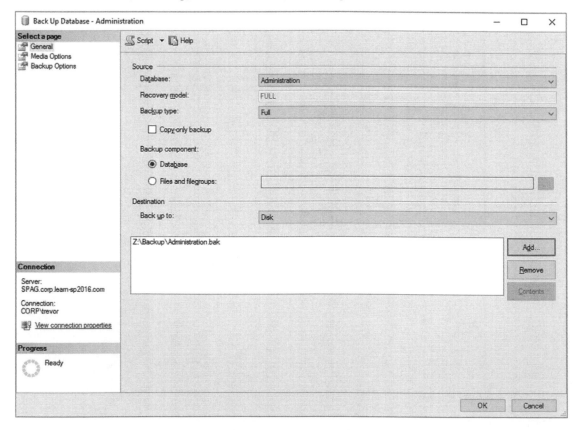

Figure 3-3. Taking a backup of the Central Administration Content Database from SQL Server Management Studio

To complete the addition of the database to the Availability Group, right-click the Availability Group in SQL Server Management Studio under the AlwaysOn High Availability\Availability Groups node, and then click Add Database…. The status on the Select Database screen should read "Meets prerequisites" for the database to be added, shown in Figure 3-4. The next steps will be to add the database to the Availability Group through the UI, specifying the UNC path to the location of the database backup, shown in Figure 3-5.

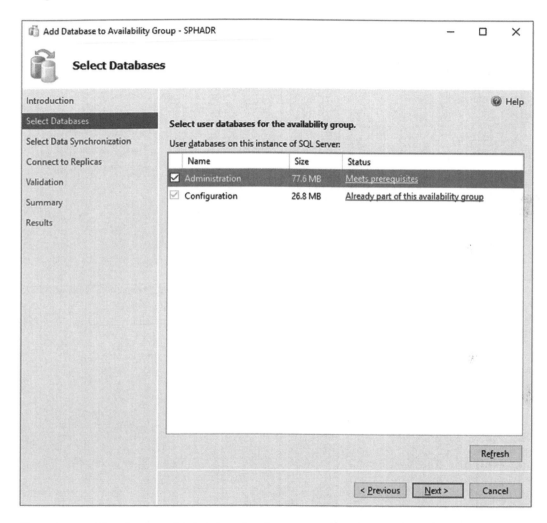

Figure 3-4. *Adding the Central Administration Content Database through the Add Database to Availability Group Wizard*

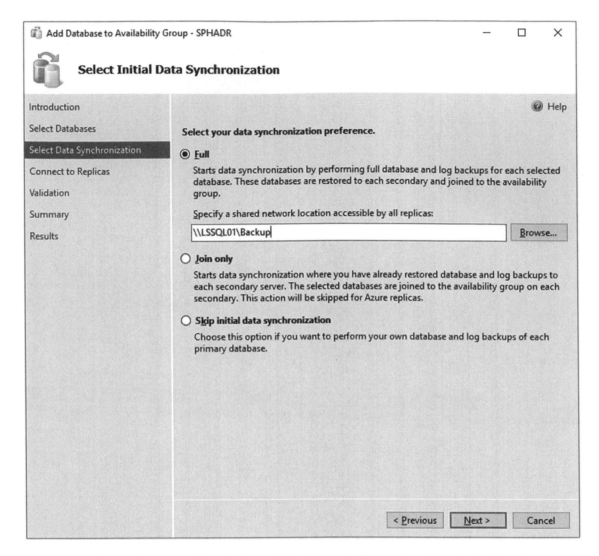

Figure 3-5. *Selecting the UNC path to the Central Administration Content Database backup location*

Connect to the Secondary Replica. The Validation step will notify you of any errors that will prevent the database from being added to the Availability Group. A summary of the steps will be provided, and the last step will add the database to the Availability Group. As the databases are initially small, this process should be quick.

At this time, it is safe to remove the temporary user database (AOTemp) from the Availability Group and delete the database from the Primary and Secondary Replicas. This completes the Availability Group configuration for the Configuration and Administration databases, but remember that all newly created databases for SharePoint, with notable exceptions you will find in this chapter, must be added to the Availability Group as they're created.

SQL Kerberos Validation

In order to validate that SharePoint is connecting to SQL Server using Kerberos, run the following script in SQL Server Management Studio while connected to the Availability Group. Note the WHERE clause specifying the first part of the name of all SharePoint servers in this farm. This WHERE clause may be dropped, if necessary.

```
SELECT
    s.session_id,
    c.connect_time,
    s.login_time,
    s.login_name,
    c.protocol_type,
    c.auth_scheme,
    s.HOST_NAME,
    s.program_name
FROM sys.dm_exec_sessions s
JOIN sys.dm_exec_connections c
ON s.session_id = c.session_id
WHERE HOST_NAME like 'LSSP%'
```

If the servers are connecting via Kerberos, the auth_scheme value will show KERBEROS, as shown in Figure 3-6.

session_id	connect_time	login_time	login_name	protocol_type	auth_scheme	HOST_NAME	program_name
54	00:00.3	56:44.3	CORP\s-farm	TSQL	KERBEROS	LSSPAP01	SharePoint[OWSTIMER][1][Administration]
55	25:00.6	57:30.4	CORP\s-farm	TSQL	KERBEROS	LSSPAP01	SharePoint[OWSTIMER][1][Configuration]
56	15:00.1	57:00.3	CORP\s-farm	TSQL	KERBEROS	LSSPAP01	SharePoint[OWSTIMER][1][Configuration]
59	06:26.6	56:53.4	CORP\s-farm	TSQL	KERBEROS	LSSPDC01	SharePoint[DistributedCacheService][1][Configuration]
63	55:00.2	57:00.4	CORP\s-farm	TSQL	KERBEROS	LSSPAP01	SharePoint[OWSTIMER][1][Configuration]
70	07:26.1	56:57.4	CORP\s-farm	TSQL	KERBEROS	LSSPDC02	SharePoint[DistributedCacheService][1][Configuration]
71	40:00.4	55:00.2	CORP\s-farm	TSQL	KERBEROS	LSSPAP01	SharePoint[OWSTIMER][1][Configuration]

Figure 3-6. *The SharePoint Timer and Distributed Cache Service connecting to the SQL Server via Kerberos*

If Kerberos has not been configured correctly on the SQL Server, the auth_scheme will display NTLM. Note that it is normal for certain connections to display as NTLM, such as if you are connected to SQL Server locally.

Adding SharePoint Servers

Adding the remaining SharePoint Servers to the farm is simple. Based on their role, only a single parameter will change, -LocalServerRole.

For the next server, LSSPAP02, an Application server, we need to run the following cmdlet from the SharePoint Management Shell.

```
Connect-SPConfigurationDatabase -DatabaseName Configuration -DatabaseServer spag.corp.
learn-sp2016.com -Passphrase (ConvertTo-SecureString "FarmPassphrase1" -AsPlainText -Force)
-LocalServerRole Application
```

As LSSPAP02 will also run Central Administration, make sure to install the Central Administration SSL certificate on LSSPAP02.

Once connected, move onto the two Search servers, LSSPSR01 and LSSPSR02, running the same cmdlet with -LocalServerRole Search.

```
Connect-SPConfigurationDatabase -DatabaseName Configuration -DatabaseServer spag.corp.
learn-sp2016.com -Passphrase (ConvertTo-SecureString "FarmPassphrase1" -AsPlainText -Force)
-LocalServerRole Search
```

Then the Web front end servers, LSSPFE01 and LSSPFE02 with the -LocalServerRole parameter Web.

```
Connect-SPConfigurationDatabase -DatabaseName Configuration -DatabaseServer spag.corp.
learn-sp2016.com -Passphrase (ConvertTo-SecureString "FarmPassphrase1" -AsPlainText -Force)
-LocalServerRole WebFrontEnd
```

And finally, the two Distributed Cache servers, LSSPDC01 and LSSPDC02 with the -LocalServerRole parameter DistributedCache.

```
Connect-SPConfigurationDatabase -DatabaseName Configuration -DatabaseServer spag.corp.
learn-sp2016.com -Passphrase (ConvertTo-SecureString "FarmPassphrase1" -AsPlainText -Force)
-LocalServerRole DistributedCache
```

For each server, we will also need to run cmdlets to provision services, features, help content, and set security on file system and registry objects. The notable exception is that the Search servers do not need to run Install-SPApplicationContent.

```
Initialize-SPResourceSecurity
Install-SPHelpCollection -All
Install-SPService
Install-SPFeature -AllExistingFeatures
Install-SPApplicationContent
```

Once the cmdlets have completed, if the SharePoint Timer Service is not started, start it via Services. msc or use the following PowerShell cmdlet.

```
Start-Service SPTimerV4
```

When all servers have been joined to the farm, validate that they have the correct services provisioned. This can be done in Central Administration by going to "Manage servers in farm," per Figure 3-7.

Server	SharePoint Products Installed	Role	Compliant	Services Running	Status	Remove Server
LSSPAP01	Microsoft SharePoint Server 2016	Application	✓ Yes	App Management Service Business Data Connectivity Service Central Administration Claims to Windows Token Service Managed Metadata Web Service Microsoft SharePoint Foundation Incoming E-Mail Microsoft SharePoint Foundation Subscription Settings Service Microsoft SharePoint Foundation Web Application Microsoft SharePoint Foundation Workflow Timer Service Secure Store Service User Profile Service	No Action Required	Remove Server
LSSPAP02	Microsoft SharePoint Server 2016	Application	✓ Yes	App Management Service Business Data Connectivity Service Central Administration Claims to Windows Token Service Managed Metadata Web Service Microsoft SharePoint Foundation Incoming E-Mail Microsoft SharePoint Foundation Subscription Settings Service Microsoft SharePoint Foundation Web Application Microsoft SharePoint Foundation Workflow Timer Service Secure Store Service User Profile Service	No Action Required	Remove Server
LSSPDC01	Microsoft SharePoint Server 2016	Distributed Cache	✓ Yes	Claims to Windows Token Service Distributed Cache Microsoft SharePoint Foundation Web Application	No Action Required	Remove Server
LSSPDC02	Microsoft SharePoint Server 2016	Distributed Cache	✓ Yes	Claims to Windows Token Service Distributed Cache Microsoft SharePoint Foundation Web Application	No Action Required	Remove Server
LSSPFE01	Microsoft SharePoint Server 2016	Front-end	✓ Yes	App Management Service Business Data Connectivity Service Claims to Windows Token Service	No Action Required	Remove Server

Figure 3-7. *Central Administration Manage servers in farm, showing all servers and roles*

Central Administration High Availability

To make Central Administration highly available, we need to start it on the second Application server, LSSPAP02. To do this, in Central Administration, navigate to Manage services on server. Select the second Application server from the Server drop-down, and then Start the Central Administration service. Once the service is started, modify the IIS binding and select the SharePoint Central Administration SSL certificate installed earlier, along with specifying the hostname of ca.corp.learn-sp2016.com and ticking the SNI checkbox.

At this point, Central Administration is ready to be placed behind a Load Balancer. Any A record for the Central Administration FQDN may now be pointed at the Load Balancer when configured.

Service Auto Provision

Services can be automatically provisioned in the farm, but each service must be set to do so. In Central Administration under Manage services in farm, note that a select few, by default, are set to Auto Provision as Figure 3-8 displays. This can be changed by clicking the Enable Auto Provision link. Other services are auto provisioned when the Service Application is created.

Services in Farm

	View: Configurable ▾		
Service	Auto Provision	Action	Compliant
Access Services	No	Manage Service Application	✓ Yes
Access Services 2010	No	Manage Service Application	✓ Yes
App Management Service	No	Manage Service Application	✓ Yes
Business Data Connectivity Service	No	Manage Service Application	✓ Yes
Claims to Windows Token Service	Yes	Disable Auto Provision	✓ Yes
Distributed Cache	Yes	Disable Auto Provision	✓ Yes
Document Conversions Launcher Service	No	Enable Auto Provision	✓ Yes
Document Conversions Load Balancer Service	No	Enable Auto Provision	✓ Yes
Machine Translation Service	No	Manage Service Application	✓ Yes
Managed Metadata Web Service	No	Manage Service Application	✓ Yes
Microsoft SharePoint Foundation Sandboxed Code Service	No	Enable Auto Provision	✓ Yes

Figure 3-8. Services in Farm showing which services are set to Auto Provision

In this scenario, we will be auto provisioning the following additional services.

- Microsoft SharePoint Foundation Subscription Settings Service

- Request Management

The service will initially show as Processing, prior to display the outcome in the Action column, such as "Disable Auto Provision" if the Service was set to Auto Provision.

Only set Auto Provision for services that will be used within the farm.

Outgoing E-Mail

Outgoing e-mail can now be configured using TLS. Outgoing e-mail can be configured from Central Administration under System Settings, Configure outgoing e-mail settings, per Figure 3-9. SharePoint 2016 is unable to authenticate with an SMTP host and must leverage an anonymous receive connector.

Outgoing E-Mail Settings ⓘ

Mail Settings

Specify the SMTP mail server to use for Microsoft SharePoint Foundation e-mail-based notifications for alerts, invitations, and administrator notifications. Personalize the **From address** and **Reply-to address**.

Outbound SMTP server:

```
lsexchg01.corp.learn-sp2016.com
```

From address:

```
sharepoint@learn-sp2016.com
```

Reply-to address:

```
sharepoint@learn-sp2016.com
```

Use TLS connection encryption:

```
Yes ∨
```

SMTP server port:

```
587
```

Character set:

```
65001 (Unicode UTF-8)            ∨
```

Figure 3-9. Outgoing e-mail settings in Central Administration

It may also be set via the SharePoint Management Shell.

```
$ca = Get-SPWebApplication -IncludeCentralAdministration | ?{$_.IsAdministrationWebApplication
-eq $true}
$senderAddr = "sharepoint@learn-sp2016.com"
$replyAddr = "sharepoint@learn-sp2016.com"
$smtpServer = "mail.learn-sp2016.com"
$ca.UpdateMailsettings($smtpServer, $senderAddr, $replyAddr, 65001, $true, 587)
```

65001 is the default code page. The $true value is to enable SSL, and the port specified is 587.

To validate the mail settings are working successfully, mail can be sent through the SharePoint Object Model in the SharePoint Management Shell. Simply fill in the blanks, using the URL of Central Administration as the specified site.

```
$email = "recipient@learn-sp2016.com"
$subject = "Email through SharePoint OM"
$body = "Message body."

$site = Get-SPSite http://centralAdministrationUrl
$web = $site.OpenWeb()
[Microsoft.SharePoint.Utilities.SPUtility]::SendEmail($web,0,0,$email,$subject,$body)
```

If the result returns True, the mail has been sent successfully. If not, investigate the mail receive connector logs for any potential errors. In addition, you can also use the Send-MailMessage cmdlet.

```
Send-MailMessage -To "recipient@learn-sp2016.com" -From "sharepoint@learn-sp2016.com"
-Subject "Testing Smtp Mail" -Body "Message Body" -SmtpServer "mail.learn-sp2016.com"
-UseSsl -Port 587
```

This cmdlet bypasses the SharePoint Object Model and may provide additional diagnostic information.

Information Rights Management

Information Rights Management settings may be found in Central Administration under Security, Configure information rights management. If a Service Connection Point has been created in Active Directory for Rights Management Services (a default setting), then specify "Use the default RMS server specified in Active Directory"; otherwise, select "Use this RMS server" and enter the fully qualified domain name of the RMS cluster. If an error is encountered, validate that the RMS cluster domain name can be resolved from the SharePoint server, and that ServerCertification.asmx on the RMS server (by default at "C:\inetpub\ wwwroot_wmcs\certification\ServerCertification.asmx") has NTFS permissions for the Farm Account and any Web Application Pool accounts.

IRM settings may also be enabled via the SharePoint Management Shell.

To set the setting "Use the default RMS server specified in Active Directory," run the following:

```
$webSvc = [Microsoft.SharePoint.Administration.SPWebService]::ContentService
$webSvc.IrmSettings.IrmRMSEnabled = $true
$webSvc.IrmSettings.IrmRMSUseAD = $true
$webSvc.Update()
```

To specify a specific server, run the following:

```
$webSvc = [Microsoft.SharePoint.Administration.SPWebService]::ContentService
$webSvc.IrmSettings.IrmRMSEnabled = $true
$webSvc.IrmSettings.IrmRMSUseAD = $false
$webSvc.IrmSettings.IrmRMSCertServer = "https://rms.learn-sp2016.com"
$webSvc.Update()
```

When using the SharePoint Management Shell, it may take a few seconds for the results to be displayed in Central Administration.

Managed Accounts

Managed accounts are the service accounts that run SharePoint services. The Farm Account account is added by default when the SharePoint farm is created. In this farm, we have three additional managed accounts that must be registered, s-svc to run the Service Applications, s-web to run the Web Applications, and s-c2wts for the Claims to Windows Token Service. To register Managed Accounts, run the following:

```
$cred = Get-Credential -UserName "CORP\s-svc" -Message "Managed Account"
New-SPManagedAccount -Credential $cred
```

Repeat the process for CORP\s-web and CORP\s-c2wts.

Service Application Pool

Because we will be using the minimal number of Application Pools possible in the farm, we will only create a single Application Pool for all Service Applications. This is done via PowerShell, and may also be done while creating the first Service Application in the farm. Using a single Application Pool reduces overhead as .NET processes cannot share memory even though the same binaries have been loaded into the process (for example, Microsoft.SharePoint.dll cannot be shared between two w3wp.exe processes).

```
New-SPServiceApplicationPool -Name "SharePoint Web Services Default" -Account (Get-
SPManagedAccount "CORP\s-svc")
```

When creating Service Applications, we will now select the "SharePoint Web Services Default" Application Pool.

Diagnostic Logging

Out of the box, SharePoint logs to the Unified Logging Service (Diagnostic Logging) to "C:\Program Files\ Common Files\microsoft shared\Web Server Extensions\16\LOGS\." Logging to the C: drive may not be ideal, not only for space reasons, but also for performance due to being on the same volume as all other SharePoint web-based resources that users access. The ULS location can be moved via Central Administration under Monitoring, Configure diagnostic logging. Set the Path to a specific location, such as "E:\ULS." Note that this path must be on all SharePoint servers in the farm. In addition, you may specify the maximum number of days to retain log files as well as the maximum disk space log files can consume. It is advisable to set the maximum disk space log files can use below the volume size they reside on.

From the SharePoint Management Shell, this can be set by running the following using any or all of the parameters. Note to restrict the maximum disk space log files can use, you must specify both the -LogDiskSpaceUsageGB and -LogMaxDiskSpaceUsageEnabled:$true parameters.

```
Set-SPDiagnosticConfig -DaysToKeepLogs 7 -LogDiskSpaceUsageGB 150 -LogMaxDiskSpaceUsageEnabl
ed:$true -LogLocation E:\ULS
```

If moving the ULS logs to an alternate location, it is also recommended to move the Usage logs, as well. In Central Administration, under Monitoring, Configure usage and health data collection, specify the Log path to the same root directory as the ULS logs, for example, E:\ULS.

Setting this through the SharePoint Management Shell is accomplished via the following:

```
Set-SPUsageService -UsageLogLocation E:\ULS
```

Claims to Windows Token Service

The Claims to Windows Token Service should always run under a dedicated account. This account is the only account that requires Local Administrator rights on the SharePoint servers where it runs. For a MinRole configuration, the Claims to Windows Token Service runs on all MinRoles (Application, DistributedCache, Search, WebFrontEnd).

Manually add the Claims to Windows Token Service to the Local Administrators group on each SharePoint server. In addition, using the Local Security Policy MMC (secpol.msc), add the Claims to Windows Token Service to the following User Rights Assignments, under Local Policies.

- Act as part of the operating system

- Impersonate a client after authentication

- Log on as a service

Claims to Windows Token Service must connect to data sources with Kerberos Constrained Delegation with Protocol Transition enabled. In order for the Delegation tab to appear in Active Directory Users and Computers for the Claims to Windows Token Service account, create a "dummy" SPN using setspn.exe.

```
Setspn.exe -S C2WTS/Dummy CORP\s-c2wts
```

To set the Claims to Windows Token Service account, use the SharePoint Management Shell.

```
$account = Get-SPManagedAccount "CORP\s-c2wts"
$farm = Get-SPFarm
$svc = $farm.Services | ?{$_.TypeName -eq "Claims to Windows Token Service"}
$svcIdentity = $svc.ProcessIdentity
$svcIdentity.CurrentIdentityType = [Microsoft.SharePoint.Administration.
IdentityType]::SpecificUser
$svcIdentity.UserName = $account.Username
$svcIdentity.Update()
$svcIdentity.Deploy()
```

Once completed, the Claims to Token Service will be running under the new identity on all SharePoint servers in the farm running the Claims to Windows Token Service.

Distributed Cache Service

The Distributed Cache service requires two modifications. The first is to set the backgroundGc application configuration value. The second is to set the amount of memory for Distributed Cache.

In order to set the backgroundGc parameter, from an elevated PowerShell window, run the following on each server in the farm running the Distributed Cache role.

```
$xmlDoc = [xml](Get-Content "C:\Program Files\AppFabric 1.1 for Windows Server\
DistributedCacheService.exe.config")
$createAppElement = $xmlDoc.CreateElement("appSettings")
$appElement = $xmlDoc.configuration.AppendChild($createAppElement)
$createAddElement = $xmldoc.CreateElement("add")
$addElement = $appElement.AppendChild($createAddElement)
$addElement.SetAttribute("key", "backgroundGC")
$addElement.SetAttribute("value", "true")
$xmlDoc.Save("C:\Program Files\AppFabric 1.1 for Windows Server\DistributedCacheService.exe.
config")
```

This creates the XML changes to the file and saves it. A restart of the Distributed Cache service is required; however, the next cmdlet will restart the service on our behalf.

An alternative to using the preceding script is to run Notepad.exe as an Administrator, open the file at C:\Program Files\AppFabric 1.1 for Windows Server\DistributedCacheService.exe.config. Directly above the closing </configuration> element, add the following text.

```
<appSettings>
<add key="backgroundGC" value="true" />
</appSettings>
```

As there are already multiple Distributed Cache hosts in this farm, we need to stop the service on the other hosts prior to updating this value, and then start Distributed Cache on those hosts.

```
Update-SPDistributedCacheSize -CacheSizeInMB 3096
```

On a single Distributed Cache host, run this cmdlet with a maximum value of 16384 for a server with 34GB or more RAM. In many instances, the 10% default allocation is sufficient. Microsoft recommends a value of 1GB for farms with fewer than 10,000 users; 2.5GB for farms with more than 10,000 users and fewer than 10,000 users; and finally, for farms with more than 10,000 users, 16GB per server allocation (this requires 34GB RAM for Distributed Cache plus 2GB overhead).

To run the Distributed Cache service as the Service Application Pool account, or CORP\s-svc, execute the following commands. Distributed Cache will otherwise run as the Farm Account (CORP\s-farm) account.

```
$acct = Get-SPManagedAccount "CORP\s-svc"
$farm = Get-SPFarm
$svc = $farm.Services | ?{$_.TypeName -eq "Distributed Cache"}
$svc.ProcessIdentity.CurrentIdentityType = "SpecificUser"
$svc.ProcessIdentity.ManagedAccount = $acct
$svc.ProcessIdentity.Update()
$svc.ProcessIdentity.Deploy()
```

In order to complete the identity change, stop the Distributed Cache service, remove the Distributed Cache instance, and finally add the Distributed Cache instance.

```
Stop-SPDistributedCacheServiceInstance
Remove-SPDistributedCacheServiceInstance
Add-SPDistributedCacheServiceInstance
```

This will complete the base changes required for the Distributed Cache service. The Distributed Cache service will be discussed further in Chapter 17 as it relates to service restarts.

With the basic services configured, we're ready to move onto Service Application setup and basic configuration.

Service Applications

Service Application creation will primarily be done via the SharePoint Management Shell, but with a few exceptions, Service Applications may also be created via Central Administration. Not all Service Applications must be provisioned on every farm. The best strategy is determining, via business requirements, to only provision Service Applications as they're required. Service Applications will typically add or activate timer jobs, which increases the load within the farm.

In this section, we will be provisioning the following Service Applications. Certain Service Applications will be covered in depth in later chapters.

- State Service

- Usage and Health Data Collection Service Application

- App Management Service

- Secure Store Service

- Business Data Connectivity Service

- Managed Metadata Service

- SharePoint Enterprise Search Service

- User Profile Service

As Service Applications are provisioned, those that require databases must have those databases added to the AlwaysOn Availability Group. The steps are the same as noted previously in this chapter and will not be covered here.

State Service

The State Service is used for the Session State management for filling out InfoPath Forms Service. If InfoPath Forms Services is not required, this Service Application is not required. This Service Application can only be configured via PowerShell.

```
$db = New-SPStateServiceDatabase -Name "StateService"
$sa = New-SPStateServiceApplication -Name "State Service" -Database $db
New-SPStateServiceApplicationProxy -Name "State Service" -ServiceApplication $sa
-DefaultProxyGroup
```

Usage and Health Data Collection Service Application

The Usage and Health Data Collection Service Application provides data collection that can be used for farm health and performance analysis via the Usage database. Note that this is a database that should not be part of the Availability Group. The data is transient. If the database becomes unavailable due to a failover, there is no end-user impact. Other Service Applications will also continue running correctly. If an Availability Group is required, a new Availability Group running in Asynchronous mode should be used as the Usage database may overwhelm the Availability Group with the large number of writes to this database. If this database is a member of an Availability Group, it will prevent the Configuration Wizard form executing and the database must be removed from the Availability Group until the Configuration Wizard has completed successfully on all SharePoint servers in the farm.

The Usage database will be created automatically when the Search Service Application is created; however, the name of the database will be set to "WSS_UsageApplication_<GUID>," which may not be desired.

This database will be created targeting the Primary Replica.

```
New-SPUsageApplication -Name "Usage and Health Data Collection Service Application"
-DatabaseServer LSSQL01 -DatabaseName Usage
```

App Management Service

The App Management Service is required for SharePoint Add-ins and Hybrid scenarios. This is the first Service Application where we will be specifying the new Service Application IIS Application Pool.

```
$sa = New-SPAppManagementServiceApplication -Name "App Management Service Application"
-DatabaseName "AppManagement" -ApplicationPool "SharePoint Web Services Default"
New-SPAppManagementServiceApplicationProxy -Name "App Management Service Application"
-ServiceApplication $sa -UseDefaultProxyGroup
```

Secure Store Service

The Secure Store Service provides credential delegation and access to other services inside and outside of SharePoint. The -AuditlogMaxSize value is in days.

```
$sa = New-SPSecureStoreServiceApplication -Name "Secure Store Service Application"
-ApplicationPool "SharePoint Web Services Default" -AuditingEnabled:$true -AuditlogMaxSize 7
-DatabaseName "SecureStore"
New-SPSecureStoreServiceApplicationProxy -Name "Secure Store Service Application"
-ServiceApplication $sa
```

Once the proxy has been created, set the Master Key and keep it in a safe place for Disaster Recovery purposes.

```
$proxy = Get-SPServiceApplicationProxy | ?{$_.TypeName -eq "Secure Store Service Application
Proxy"}
Update-SPSecureStoreMasterKey -ServiceApplicationProxy $proxy -Passphrase
"SecureStorePassphrase1!"
Start-Sleep 15
Update-SPSecureStoreApplicationServerKey -ServiceApplicationProxy $proxy -Passphrase
"SecurestorePassphrase1!"
```

Business Data Connectivity Service

Business Data Connectivity Service provides connectivity to external data sources, such as SQL databases for exposing them as External Lists.

```
New-SPBusinessDataCatalogServiceApplication -Name "Business Data Connectivity Service
Application" -DatabaseName "BCS" -ApplicationPool "SharePoint Web Services Default"
```

Managed Metadata Service

The Managed Metadata Service provides taxonomies for end-user consumption and SharePoint services, such as Search, User Profile Service, and more. The Managed Metadata Service should be created prior to the User Profile or Search Service.

```
$sa = New-SPMetadataServiceApplication -Name "Managed Metadata Service" -DatabaseName "MMS"
-ApplicationPool "SharePoint Web Services Default" -SyndicationErrorReportEnabled
New-SPMetadataServiceApplicationProxy -Name "Managed Metadata Service" -ServiceApplication
$sa -DefaultProxyGroup -ContentTypePushdownEnabled -DefaultKeywordTaxonomy
-DefaultSiteCollectionTaxonomy
```

An optional parameter for New-SPMetadataServiceApplication is -HubUri, which is a Site Collection for the Content Type hub. If a Site Collection has been previously created, this option may be specified. When this option is specified, an additional parameter on New-SPMetadataServiceApplicationProxy is available, -ContentTypeSyndicationEnabled. Setting the HubUri will be covered later in this chapter.

SharePoint Enterprise Search Service

The Enterprise Search Configuration is a complex script, and is often easier to complete via Central Administration. However, when created via Central Administration, the Search Server databases will have GUIDs appended to them.

This PowerShell must be run from a SharePoint server running the Search MinRole. In this case, the topology will be created on LSSPSR01.

```
$sa = New-SPEnterpriseSearchServiceApplication -Name "Search Service Application"
-DatabaseName "Search" -ApplicationPool "SharePoint Web Services Default"
-AdminApplicationPool "SharePoint Web Services Default"
New-SPEnterpriseSearchServiceApplicationProxy -Name "Search Service Application"
-SearchApplication $sa
$si = Get-SPEnterpriseSearchServiceInstance -Local
$clone = $sa.ActiveTopology.Clone()
```

Create the initial topology.

```
New-SPEnterpriseSearchAdminComponent -SearchTopology $clone -SearchServiceInstance $si
New-SPEnterpriseSearchContentProcessingComponent -SearchTopology $clone
-SearchServiceInstance $si
New-SPEnterpriseSearchAnalyticsProcessingComponent -SearchTopology $clone
-SearchServiceInstance $si
New-SPEnterpriseSearchCrawlComponent -SearchTopology $clone -SearchServiceInstance $si
```

```
New-SPEnterpriseSearchIndexComponent -SearchTopology $clone -SearchServiceInstance $si
-IndexPartition 0 -RootDirectory F:\SearchIndex\0
New-SPEnterpriseSearchQueryProcessingComponent -SearchTopology $clone
-SearchServiceInstance $si
```

Create the topology for the second Search Server, LSSPSR02.

```
$si2 = Get-SPEnterpriseSearchServiceInstance | ?{$_.Server -match "LSSPSR02"}
New-SPEnterpriseSearchAdminComponent -SearchTopology $clone -SearchServiceInstance $si2
New-SPEnterpriseSearchAnalyticsProcessingComponent -SearchTopology $clone
-SearchServiceInstance $si2
New-SPEnterpriseSearchContentProcessingComponent -SearchTopology $clone
-SearchServiceInstance $si2
New-SPEnterpriseSearchCrawlComponent -SearchTopology $clone -SearchServiceInstance $si2
New-SPEnterpriseSearchIndexComponent -SearchTopology $clone -SearchServiceInstance $si2
-IndexPartition 0 -RootDirectory F:\SearchIndex\0
New-SPEnterpriseSearchQueryProcessingComponent -SearchTopology $clone -SearchServiceInstance
$si2
$clone.Activate()
```

From LSSPSR02, clone the topology again in order to create the Index Partition 1 as the primary replica.

```
$si = Get-SPEnterpriseSearchServiceInstance -Local
$sa = Get-SPEnterpriseSearchServiceApplication
$active = Get-SPEnterpriseSearchTopology -SearchApplication $sa -Active
$clone = New-SPEnterpriseSearchTopology -SearchApplication $sa -Clone -SearchTopology
$active
New-SPEnterpriseSearchIndexComponent -SearchTopology $clone -SearchServiceInstance $si
-IndexPartition 1 -RootDirectory F:\SearchIndex\1
$si2 = Get-SPEnterpriseSearchServiceInstance | ?{$_.Server -match "LSSPSR01"}
New-SPEnterpriseSearchIndexComponent -SearchTopology $clone -SearchServiceInstance $si2
-IndexPartition 1 -RootDirectory F:\SearchIndex\1
$clone.Activate()
```

Finally, remove the inactive topologies.

```
$sa = Get-SPEnterpriseSearchServiceApplication
foreach($topo in (Get-SPEnterpriseSearchTopology -SearchApplication $sa | ?{$_.State -eq
"Inactive"})){Remove-SPEnterpriseSearchTopology -Identity $topo -Confirm:$false}
```

Set the Crawl Account for the Search Service Application.

```
$sa = Get-SPEnterpriseSearchServiceApplication
$content = New-Object Microsoft.Office.Server.Search.Administration.Content($sa)
$content.SetDefaultGatheringAccount("CORP\s-crawl", (ConvertTo-SecureString "<Password>"
-AsPlainText -Force))
```

Set the Full Crawl schedule of the Local SharePoint sites Content Source.

```
$source = Get-SPEnterpriseSearchCrawlContentSource -SearchApplication $sa -Identity "Local
SharePoint sites"
```

```
Set-SPEnterpriseSearchCrawlContentSource -Identity $source -ScheduleType Full
-WeeklyCrawlSchedule -CrawlScheduleRunEveryInterval 1 -CrawlScheduleDaysOfWeek "Sunday"
-CrawlScheduleStartDateTime "03:00 AM"
```

Configure the same Content Source to use Continuous Crawls.

```
$source.EnableContinuousCrawls = $true
$source.Update()
```

Initiate a Full Crawl of the content source. This will prep the farm to perform the Continuous Crawls.

```
$source = Get-SPEnterpriseSearchCrawlContentSource -SearchApplication $sa -Identity "Local
SharePoint sites"
$source.StartFullCrawl()
```

User Profile Service

The User Profile Service synchronizes User and Group objects from Active Directory into the SharePoint Profile Service. This service is also responsible for managing Audiences and configuration of MySites. Creating the service Application may be done via PowerShell.

```
$sa = New-SPProfileServiceApplication -Name "User Profile Service Application"
-ApplicationPool "SharePoint Web Services Default" -ProfileDBName "Profile" -SocialDBName
"Social" -ProfileSyncDBName "Sync"
New-SPProfileServiceApplicationProxy -Name "User Profile Service Application"
-ServiceApplication $sa -DefaultProxyGroup
```

One thing you'll notice is that we are specifying a name for the Sync database even though the database isn't used as User Profile Synchronization Service is no longer part of SharePoint. This is because SharePoint will create it regardless, although the database will be empty with no tables.

Add the Default Content Access Account, CORP\s-crawl, to the Administrator permissions of the newly created User Profile Service Application in order to enumerate People Data for Search.

```
$user = New-SPClaimsPrincipal "CORP\s-crawl" -IdentityType WindowsSamAccountName
$security = Get-SPServiceApplicationSecurity $sa -Admin
Grant-SPObjectSecurity $security $user "Retrieve People Data for Search Crawlers"
Set-SPServiceApplicationSecurity $sa $security -Admin
```

You may also want to consider adding additional accounts, such as SharePoint Administrators, who will need to manage the User Profile Service Application from PowerShell. In this example, we are providing a user with Full Control rights on the User Profile Service Application. The "-Admin" switch denotes the "Administrators" button in the ribbon, while the lack of the "-Admin" switch denotes the "Permissions" button in the ribbon.

```
$user = New-SPClaimsPrincipal "CORP\user" -IdentityType WindowsSamAccountName
$security = Get-SPServiceApplicationSecurity $sa -Admin
Grant-SPObjectSecurity $security $user "Full Control"
Set-SPServiceApplicationSecurity $sa $security -Admin
$security = Get-SPServiceApplicationSecurity $sa
Grant-SPObjectSecurity $security $user "Full Control"
Set-SPServiceApplicationSecurity $sa $security
```

Update the Search Server Service Content Source to use the SPS3S:// protocol (People Crawl over SSL, if using HTTP, use the SPS3:// protocol).

```
$sa = Get-SPEnterpriseSearchServiceApplication
$source = Get-SPEnterpriseSearchCrawlContentSource -SearchApplication $sa -Identity "Local
SharePoint sites"
$source.StartAddresses.Add("sps3s://sharepoint-my.learn-sp2016.com")
$source.Update()
```

Completing Service Application Setup

When all Service Applications are created, do not forget to add the Service Application databases, with the exception of the Usage database, to the Availability Group.

In addition, manually add the SharePoint Managed Accounts, CORP\s-farm, CORP\s-svc, CORP\s-c2wts, and CORP\s-web to the SQL Logins on the Secondary Replica or script the logins using the sp_help_revlogin stored procedure. Logins are not replicated automatically; however, during a database failover, the SQL Logins will have the appropriate rights to the databases.

■ **Tip**   Information on how to script the logins for transfer to the secondary replica is available at the Microsoft KB918992 - `https://support.microsoft.com/en-us/kb/918992`.

Web Application Setup

Web Application configuration is straight forward with PowerShell. We will walk through creating two Web Applications, `https://sharepoint.learn-sp2016.com`, which will hold Team Sites, Portals, and so on, and `https://sharepoint-my.learn-sp2016.com`, which will contain the MySite host and user's MySites, also known as OneDrive for Business sites.

With the first Web Application, we will be creating the IIS Application Pool named "SharePoint" that both Web Applications will leverage. Both Web Applications will also be configured to use Kerberos. This requires registering two SPNs.

```
Setspn -S HTTP/sharepoint.learn-sp2016.com CORP\s-web
Setspn -S HTTP/sharepoint-my.learn-sp2016.com CORP\s-web
```

Create the Authentication Provider, enabling Kerberos, and then create the Web Application.

```
$ap = New-SPAuthenticationProvider -DisableKerberos:$false
New-SPWebApplication -Name "SharePoint" -HostHeader sharepoint.learn-sp2016.com -Port 443
-ApplicationPool "SharePoint" -ApplicationPoolAccount (Get-SPManagedAccount "CORP\s-web")
-SecureSocketsLayer:$true -AuthenticationProvider $ap -DatabaseName SharePoint_CDB1
```

This will take a few minutes to complete; then, we can create the MySite Web Application.

```
New-SPWebApplication -Name "SharePoint MySites" -HostHeader sharepoint-my.learn-sp2016.com
-Port 443 -ApplicationPool "SharePoint" -SecureSocketsLayer:$true -AuthenticationProvider
$ap -DatabaseName SharePoint-My_CDB1
```

Validate the IIS Bindings are correct and that the SSL certificate has been correctly selected. SharePoint may not set the SSL certificate for you. This must be done on all servers running Microsoft SharePoint Foundation Web Application. For MinRole, this includes DistributedCache, WebFrontEnd, and Application roles.

To support Publishing sites, add the Portal Super User and Portal Super Reader to the SharePoint Web Application. These accounts are used for permission comparison purposes only and the password for these accounts is not required. If there is the possibility that a Publishing site may be created on the SharePoint MySite Web Application, add the accounts there as well. We must set the initial properties on the SharePoint Web Application via the SharePoint Management Shell.

```
$wa = Get-SPWebApplication https://sharepoint.learn-sp2016.com
$wa.Properties["portalsuperuseraccount"] = "i:0#.w|CORP\s-su"
$wa.Properties["portalsuperreaderaccount"] = "i:0#.w|CORP\s-sr"
$wa.Update()
```

Adding the users to the Web Application Policy may be done through Manage Web Applications under Central Administration, or through the SharePoint Management Shell.

```
$wa = Get-SPWebApplication https://sharepoint.learn-sp2016.com
$zp = $wa.ZonePolicies("Default")
$policy = $zp.Add("i:0#.w|CORP\s-su", "Portal Super User")
$policyRole = $wa.PolicyRoles.GetSpecialRole("FullControl")
$policy.PolicyRoleBindings.Add($policyRole)
$policy = $zp.Add("i:0#.w|CORP\s-sr", "Portal Super Reader")
$policyRole = $wa.PolicyRoles.GetSpecialRole("FullRead")
$policy.PolicyRoleBindings.Add($policyRole)
$wa.Update()
```

The Farm Account account will be on the Policy for each Web Application as it was previously set as the Default Content Access Account in the Search Service. This can be removed.

When the Zone Policy has been changed, it will require an IISReset to take effect. To perform this, from the SharePoint Management Shell, run the following:

```
foreach($server in (Get-SPServer | ?{$_.Role -ne "Invalid" -and $_.Role -ne "Search"}))
{
    Write-Host "Resetting IIS on $($server.Address)..."
        iisreset $server.Address /noforce
}
```

Add the required Managed Path, "personal," to the SharePoint MySite Web Application.

```
New-SPManagedPath -RelativeUrl "personal" -WebApplication https://sharepoint-my.learn-
sp2016.com
```

Then, enable Self-Service Site Creation.

```
$wa = Get-SPWebApplication https://sharepoint-my.learn-sp2016.com
$wa.SelfServiceSiteCreationEnabled = $true
$wa.Update()
```

These two steps are required in order to enable MySite creation by users.

Root Site Collections

Web Applications are required to have a root Site Collection. This is the Site Collection that resides at the path "/". For the SharePoint Web Application, we will deploy a standard Team Site Template, and for the SharePoint MySite Web Application, we will deploy the MySite Host Template.

```
New-SPSite -Url https://sharepoint.learn-sp2016.com -Template STS#0 -Name "Team Site"
-OwnerAlias "CORP\trevor"
New-SPSite -Url https://sharepoint-my.learn-sp2016.com -Template SPSMSITEHOST#0 -Name "Team
Site" -OwnerAlias "CORP\trevor"
```

Content Type Hub and Enterprise Search Center Configuration

In addition to these Site Collections, we will also create a Content Type Hub and an Enterprise Search Center. The Content Type Hub will be created and then configured in the Managed Metadata Service, and the Enterprise Search Center will be created and set as the Search Center URL.

The Content Type Hub can be a standard Team Site Template.

```
New-SPSite -Url https://sharepoint.learn-sp2016.com/sites/CTHub -Template STS#0 -Name
"Content Type Hub " -OwnerAlias "CORP\trevor"
```

Set the Managed Metadata Service Content Type Hub URL.

```
Set-SPMetadataServiceApplication -Identity "Managed Metadata Service" -HubUri
https://sharepoint.learn-sp2016.com/sites/cthub
```

Next, create the Enterprise Search Center using the SRCHCEN#0 template.

```
New-SPSite -Url https://sharepoint.learn-sp2016.com/sites/search -Template SRCHCEN#0 -Name
"Search Center" -OwnerAlias "CORP\trevor"
```

Finally, set the Enterprise Search Center in the SharePoint Search Service.

```
$sa = Get-SPEnterpriseSearchServiceApplication
$sa.SearchCenterUrl = "https://sharepoint.learn-sp2016.com/sites/search/Pages"
$sa.Update()
```

Additional information on the Search Service Application is in Chapter 6.

MySite Configuration

To configure MySites for the User Profile Service, the only option we must set is the MySite Host. All other settings are optional, but can be found in Central Administration under Manage Service Applications in the User Profile Service Application. In the Setup MySites link are a variety of options to control the MySite configuration.

```
$sa = Get-SPServiceApplication | ?{$_.TypeName -eq "User Profile Service Application"}
Set-SPProfileServiceApplication -Identity $sa -MySiteHostLocation https://sharepoint-my.
learn-sp2016.com
```

User Profile User Import

The User Profile User Import supports "Active Directory Import" mode from SharePoint. While this method of import is very fast, it does not support exporting properties from SharePoint to other systems. The User Profile Service Application also supports "External Synchronization," this method requires Microsoft Identity Manager 2016.

More information about the User Profile User Import and Microsoft Identity Manager 2016 configuration are covered in Chapter 7.

With all of the basic Service Applications provisioned, we will take a brief look at Virtual Machine Templates, which will allow for faster deployment of SharePoint Server 2016.

Virtual Machine Templates

Many of the initial steps of installing SharePoint Server may be templated with virtualization technologies. When planning on using templates, a virtual machine template for SharePoint Server may have the SharePoint prerequisites installed, as well as the SharePoint binaries (setup.exe). You cannot run the SharePoint Configuration Wizard, psconfig.exe, or PowerShell (New-SPConfigurationDatabase or Connect-SPConfigurationDatabase) prior to templating the virtual machine. Templating processes, such as Sysprep, should be run against the virtual machine prior to creating the template.

Next Steps

In this chapter, we walked through an advanced step-by-step process to install SQL Server 2014 with Service Pack 1 to SharePoint Server 2016 in a highly available configuration through the Command Prompt and PowerShell. This should provide you with the tools required to develop your own scripts and processes to provision a highly available farm.

Next, we will discuss Authentication and Security, covering NTLM, Kerberos, and SAML authentication. In addition, we will cover transport security and firewall access rules.

CHAPTER 4

■ ■ ■

Configuring Authentication and Security

In this chapter, we will cover the various mechanisms for authentication, authorization, and security for your SharePoint farm. NTLM, Kerberos, and SAML will be covered, along with their advantages and disadvantages throughout the farm. We'll also take a look at transport security via TLS (SSL) and IPsec. Lastly, we'll take a look at the Windows Firewall and what the best practices are for the SharePoint environment.

Authentication Methods

SharePoint Server supports a variety of authentication methods. We will cover each authentication method and their advantages and disadvantages. Authentication, also known as AuthN, is performed by IIS or services; SharePoint itself does not perform AuthN.

Basic

Basic authentication is where the user's username and password are sent in clear text to the SharePoint server. IIS performs authentication to Active Directory based on the supplied username and password. This is form of authentication is one of the least used and generally is unnecessary with the other options we have available to us. It is also not recommended to use Basic authentication without using SSL to encrypt the transport of the credentials.

NTLM

Authentication via NTLM is one of the most common forms of authentication used in SharePoint environments. It requires no additional configuration on the part of SharePoint Administrators or Domain Administrators. "It just works," however, is not the most secure or performant form of authentication available to us. As the web, including SharePoint, is stateless, authentication must be performed for each request. This authentication method must perform multiple trips between the user, SharePoint (IIS) and Active Directory, increasing the amount of time it takes to authenticate. This flow is shown in Figure 4-1.

© Vlad Catrinescu and Trevor Seward 2016
V. Catrinescu and T. Seward, *Deploying SharePoint 2016*, DOI 10.1007/978-1-4842-1999-7_4

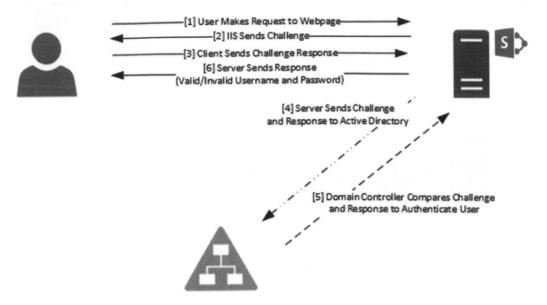

Figure 4-1. NTLM Challenge and Response Flow

NTLMv1 and NTLMv2 are considered insecure authentication protocols. NTLMv1 can take a matter of minutes to hours to crack an NTLM hash, while NTLMv2 may take up to 4 to 5 times longer. For highly complex NTLMv2 passwords, Rainbow Tables exist which are files that are precomputed cryptographic hash functions, reducing the amount of time it takes to reverse an NTLM hashed password into its plaintext variant. Microsoft now includes Group Policies to disable NTLM on computers that are members of Active Directory.

Kerberos

Kerberos is a modern authentication protocol in use in every Active Directory implementation. Instead of passing password hashes to and from services, Kerberos passes what are known as tickets. Certain tickets are created upon user login to the client machine and are retrieved from the Kerberos Distribution Center (KDC), which is an Active Directory Domain Controller. As shown in Figure 4-2, these tickets are steps one and two. When a user makes a request to an external service, such as SharePoint, steps three and four are executed to retrieve a Ticket Granting Service ticket (TGS). The user then sends the TGS to the target service. That service sees the ticket is valid, and in a mutual authentication scenario, the service sends information back to the client confirming the identity of the service. Each ticket has a specific lifetime, but these are generally long enough for users to not have to reauthenticate to the KDC to retrieve a new ticket. In a scenario with Active Directory domain-joined clients, this reauthentication, or retrieval of a new, valid ticket, would happen automatically.

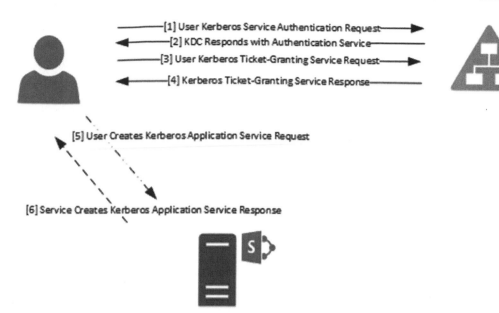

[1] User Kerberos Service Authentication Request

[2] KDC Responds with Authentication Service

[3] User Kerberos Ticket-Granting Service Request

[4] Kerberos Ticket-Granting Service Response

[5] User Creates Kerberos Application Service Request

[6] Service Creates Kerberos Application Service Response

Figure 4-2. *Kerberos Ticket Flow*

There is generally a perception among administrators that Kerberos is difficult to configure and setup. Luckily, it is quite easy for IIS (and SharePoint). It simply involves creating a Service Principal Name (SPN) for the HTTP service for the Domain User account running the IIS Application Pool. To put it simply, create an SPN for HTTP/<FQDN> for the Web Application Pool account and set the SharePoint Web Application to use Kerberos. By default, this requires Domain Administrator privileges. To use the example in this book, sharepoint.learn-sp2016.com is the FQDN of our Web Application and the Service Account assigned to it is CORP\s-web. ·

Using a console from any domain-joined machine, run the following command to assign the service (HTTP) to the principal (CORP\s-web).

```
setspn.exe -X -U HTTP/sharepoint.learn-sp2016.com CORP\s-web
```

The -X switch searches for duplicate SPNs. Duplicate SPNs will prevent the service from functioning properly. The -U switch tells setspn.exe that the account we're assigning the HTTP service to is a user account. Lastly, while we're using SSL, the name of the service is simply "HTTP." If using a port number other than 80 or 443, specify the port number after the FQDN, in the format of FQDN:nnnn.

In addition, we created SPNs for SQL Server. The service for SQL Server is "MSSQLSvc." Again, using SPN we are going to assign the MSSQLSvc service to CORP\s-sql. As our SQL implementation is represented by two SQL Servers and a SQL AlwaysOn Availability Group, we need to set three SPNs. We are also indicating the port number that SQL Server is listening on. Note in this example, instead of explicitly specifying to search for duplicates and that we are using a Domain User account, we are simply telling it to add an arbitrary SPN after validating that no duplicate SPNs exist.

```
Setspn.exe -S MSSQLSvc/LSSQL01.corp.learn-sp2016.com:1433 CORP\s-sql
Setspn.exe -S MSSQLSvc/LSSQL01:1433 CORP\s-sql
Setspn.exe -S MSSQLSvc/LSSQL02.corp.learn-sp2016.com:1433 CORP\s-sql
Setspn.exe -S MSSQLSvc/LSSQL02:1433 CORP\s-sql
Setspn.exe -S MSSQLSvc/SPAG.corp.learn-sp2016.com:1433 CORP\s-sql
```

The benefit of Kerberos is the authentication request does not need to make the round trip between the User, Active Directory, back to the User, and then to the target service. The tickets are considered valid until they expire by the service the user is accessing. This also limits the potential for intercepting and decrypting tickets. Active Directory also offers, through Group Policy, encryption algorithms that currently have no known practical attacks. This includes AES256 encrypted tickets. Unlike NTLM, which may be brute-forced within a matter of hours, AES128 or AES256 encrypted tickets would take billions of years to brute-force to retrieve the plaintext password.

Kerberos does have a significant downside as it requires the client to be able to access the KDC. If the KDC is inaccessible, the client cannot retrieve a Kerberos ticket. This is best represented in an external authentication scenario, such as the user authenticating to a SharePoint site over the Internet. Without further implementation of preauthenticating reverse proxies, SharePoint, or IIS more accurately, will fall back to allow the client to authenticate over NTLM, which is undesirable.

Lastly, certain clients may be unable to connect to a Web Application using Kerberos if nonstandard ports (TCP/80 or TCP/443) are used for the Web Application. Examples include the Search Crawler as well certain browsers. This is primarily an issue when the Web Application is configured using TCP/88, the same port as Kerberos, although it is strongly recommended to only use the standard TCP/80 or TCP/443 ports.

Security Assertion Markup Language

Security Assertion Markup Language, or SAML, is a modern form of authentication which presents *claims* about a user to a service. Based on the *identity claim* contained in the SAML assertion, the service will authorize the user to the service.

SAML is a favorite with modern services due to the ability to federate with disparate services that do not have a dependency on the authentication service the user authenticates with. For example, a user may authenticate against a local Active Directory Federation Services server using NTLM or Kerberos, and due to federation, may assert their identity to a SharePoint farm running within a separate organization. Based on rules within the federation trust, SharePoint will authorize the user to access SharePoint resources. This configuration is significantly easier to manage than an Active Directory forest trust over the Internet (which would generally take place within a VPN tunnel).

One of the SAML drawbacks, as it directly relates to SharePoint, is no validation of the information entered into the People Picker. The authentication source (for example, Active Directory), is abstracted away from SharePoint, thus SharePoint does not know where to "look" for accounts when using SAML. This is leads to a poor user experience, as it is not possible for SharePoint to validate what is a valid or invalid value.

■ **Tip**   LDAPCP, a free open source project on CodePlex, implements methods for SharePoint to validate the information inputted into the People Picker is valid. The validation only works when SharePoint has LDAP or LDAPS access to the target authentication service (such as Active Directory.

```
http://ldapcp.codeplex.com/
```

SharePoint is only compatible with SAML 1.1, unlike many other services which are compatible with SAML 2.0.

Forms-Based Authentication

Forms-based authentication (FBA) is often used when using non–Active Directory identity providers, such as a SQL database data store or Active Directory Lightweight Directory Services. FBA relies on *providers* which implement the logic to authenticate the user against the data store where the username and password is held. These are often custom developed, although Microsoft does include a provider out of the box to authenticate against LDAP services. FBA is often chosen in scenarios where IT does not or cannot use Active Directory for external partners.

When a user browses to a SharePoint site with FBA enabled, they are presented with a username and password dialog box to enter their credentials. The configured authentication provider will then validate those credentials against the authentication store.

When using FBA, the username and password are transmitted over the wire in clear text. Like with Basic authentication, it is strongly recommended to use SSL to encrypt the transport of credentials. FBA also requires manual implementation in SharePoint, modifying the Membership and Role providers within the Web Application, Security Token Service, and Central Administration web.config files. These files must also contain the same configuration values across all members of the SharePoint farm.

Authorization

SharePoint performs what is known as *authorization*, or AuthZ. Authorization is where a user has already performed *authentication* (AuthN), which is performed by IIS when using Basic, NTLM, or Kerberos authentication, and in the case of SAML, the Identity Provider (e.g., ADFS). AuthN takes place when a user attempts to access a resource. SharePoint evaluates the permissions of the resource against the permissions held by the user. If they have proper permissions, then they're authorized to access that content.

Now that we've looked at the various forms of authentication that SharePoint supports, along with the difference between authentication and authorization, let's take a look at the available transport security options we have to use with SharePoint.

Transport Security

Transport security is the act of securing, or encrypting, the information passed over the network. One of the most used forms of transport security is SSL, now known as TLS. This section will walk through TLS, IPsec, and available modern encryption protocols.

TLS

TLS, or Transport Layer Security, the replacement of SSL, or Secure Socket Layer, encrypts data as it is sent between services or between the end user and services. TLS is a very important in today's modern implementation of network services in order to protect data in transit over the network.

IPsec

IPsec is a form of encrypting all data across the network without specifically implementing an encryption protocol such as TLS. IPsec, for example, would encrypt data over the network even if the user sent data to a service where the service was requesting the information in clear text. IPsec has a high barrier to entry with a significant investment into planning and security. IPsec is also only useful within an internal network, while TLS would still be required to encrypt data over the Internet.

Encryption Protocols

TLS, or SSL, have different revisions, some of which are now considered insecure. SSL has the following versions.

- SSL 2.0
- SSL 3.0

Both SSL 2.0 and SSL 3.0 are considered insecure and should be disabled server-side. TLS has the following versions.

- TLS 1.0

- TLS 1.1

- TLS 1.2

TLS 1.1 and TLS 1.2 are considered modern, and for now, secure. TLS 1.0 should be disabled if possible. SharePoint Server 2016 and Office Online Server both support disabling all protocols except for TLS 1.2. Workflow Manager 1.0 only supports SSL 3.0 and TLS 1.0, but can communicate with SharePoint Server via TLS 1.2. For Workflow Manager 1.0, it is best to disable SSL 3.0 while leaving TLS 1.0 enabled.

Protocols can be disabled server-side through the registry. When these registry settings are changed, the server must be restarted in order for the change to take effect. For each protocol to disable, under the \ Protocols\<Protocol Version>\Server folder, create a DWORD of "Enabled" equal to 0.

```
Windows Registry Editor Version 5.00

[HKEY_LOCAL_MACHINE\SYSTEM\CurrentControlSet\Control\SecurityProviders\SCHANNEL\Protocols]

[HKEY_LOCAL_MACHINE\SYSTEM\CurrentControlSet\Control\SecurityProviders\SCHANNEL\Protocols\
PCT 1.0]
@="DefaultValue"

[HKEY_LOCAL_MACHINE\SYSTEM\CurrentControlSet\Control\SecurityProviders\SCHANNEL\Protocols\
PCT 1.0\Server]
@="DefaultValue"
"Enabled"=dword:00000000

[HKEY_LOCAL_MACHINE\SYSTEM\CurrentControlSet\Control\SecurityProviders\SCHANNEL\Protocols\
SSL 2.0]
@="DefaultValue"

[HKEY_LOCAL_MACHINE\SYSTEM\CurrentControlSet\Control\SecurityProviders\SCHANNEL\Protocols\
SSL 2.0\Server]
@="DefaultValue"
"Enabled"=dword:00000000

[HKEY_LOCAL_MACHINE\SYSTEM\CurrentControlSet\Control\SecurityProviders\SCHANNEL\Protocols\
SSL 3.0]
@="DefaultValue"

[HKEY_LOCAL_MACHINE\SYSTEM\CurrentControlSet\Control\SecurityProviders\SCHANNEL\Protocols\
SSL 3.0\Server]
@="DefaultValue"
"Enabled"=dword:00000000

[HKEY_LOCAL_MACHINE\SYSTEM\CurrentControlSet\Control\SecurityProviders\SCHANNEL\Protocols\
TLS 1.0]
@="DefaultValue"
```

```
[HKEY_LOCAL_MACHINE\SYSTEM\CurrentControlSet\Control\SecurityProviders\SCHANNEL\Protocols\
TLS 1.0\Server]
@="DefaultValue"
"Enabled"=dword:00000000

[HKEY_LOCAL_MACHINE\SYSTEM\CurrentControlSet\Control\SecurityProviders\SCHANNEL\Protocols\
TLS 1.1]
@="DefaultValue"

[HKEY_LOCAL_MACHINE\SYSTEM\CurrentControlSet\Control\SecurityProviders\SCHANNEL\Protocols\
TLS 1.1\Server]
@="DefaultValue"
"Enabled"=dword:00000000
```

As an alternative to implementing the registry changes on individual servers, consider using Group Policy to implement the settings.

■ **Tip** A Group Policy ADMX file to implement these changes is freely available from `https://github.com/Nauplius/SchannelConfiguration`.

In order for Office Online Server and Workflow Manager 1.0 to be able to communicate with SharePoint Server 2016 where TLS 1.2 is enforced, use the following registry entry on the Office Online Server or Workflow Manager 1.0 server. Reboot the server once implemented.

```
Windows Registry Editor Version 5.00

[HKEY_LOCAL_MACHINE\SOFTWARE\Microsoft\.NETFramework\v4.0.30319]
"SchUseStrongCrypto"=dword:00000001
```

HTTP Strict Transport Security

HTTP Strict Transport Security (HSTS) is another form of enforcing TLS. HSTS has two primary functions.

- Redirecting clients from HTTP to SSL.
- Telling clients that the site should only be accessed over SSL for all future requests.

This helps prevent man-in-the-middle attacks, where, after the client has connected to the valid site, the client is "tricked" into connecting to an insecure site of the same name (e.g., via DNS poisoning). Because HSTS was enabled on the valid site, the client will refuse to connect to the invalid site, regardless if the invalid site uses SSL or HTTP. This is because HSTS also tells the client to validate the SSL certificate on the site.

HSTS has a max-age value. This value is what tells the client that for future sessions, only connect over SSL. The max-age value should be 18 weeks or greater, and should be for at least as long as the site is expected to support SSL. If the site removes SSL support within the max-age timeframe, the client will refuse to connect to the site. HSTS can be set on a per–Web Application basis in SharePoint Server 2016 using the SharePoint Management Shell.

```
$wa = Get-SPWebApplication https://sharepoint.learn-sp2016.com
$wa.HttpStrictTransportSecuritySettings.IsEnabled = $true
$wa.HttpStrictTransportSecuritySettings.MaxAge = 31536000
$wa.Update()
```

The MaxAge property is a value in seconds. The default value, 31536000, is 365 days.

SSL Bridging and SSL Offloading

SSL Bridging is when a load balancer terminates the client's SSL session at the load balancer. The load balancer, in turn, decrypts the session, but resecures the session prior to connecting to the target resource, such as a SharePoint site, using SSL. This is illustrated in Figure 4-3.

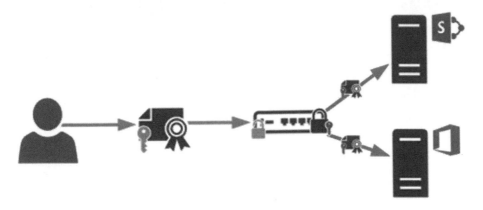

Figure 4-3. *SSL Bridging*

SSL Bridging may be used when administrators want to intercept and inspect the SSL traffic on the load balancer, want to speed up SSL session negotiation for clients (the load balancer maintains the SSL session for a longer period of time than the client would), or wants to translate the SSL or TLS protocol used by the client to a more or less strict version of the protocol.

SSL Offloading is when the load balancer decrypts a client session and then sends the information to the service over HTTP, as shown in Figure 4-4.

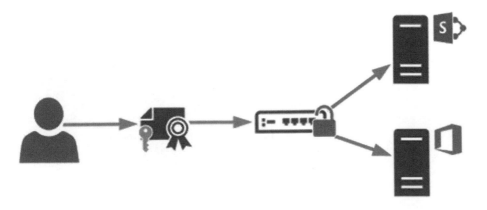

Figure 4-4. *SSL Offloading*

SSL Offloading is considered insecure as it transmits sensitive information in the clear. This may include OAuth2 tokens, which contain information that may be intercepted on the network and replayed to gain the same privileges to the requested resource (or user). As OAuth2 tokens are used between SharePoint, Office Online Server, Workflow Manager, and SharePoint Add-ins, it is critical that OAuth2 remain encrypted by transport security.

Firewalls

Firewalls are an important aspect in network security. Firewalls provide ingress and egress rules to allow or deny traffic based on patterns, source and destination IP addresses, and so on. We will cover two types of firewalls: host-based firewalls and stand-alone firewall appliances.

Windows Firewall

The Windows Firewall is built into all modern versions of Windows. It provides a fairly extensive ruleset to allow and deny traffic based on Network Location Awareness (where the server detects if it is on a public, private, or domain network), source and destination IP address, authentication, and so on.

While it may be uncommon to use in many environments, IT departments should consider implementing it on SharePoint servers. SharePoint does create specific Windows Firewall rules during installation to make management easier. Windows Firewall rules can also be easily deployed via Group Policy to sets of servers. The Windows Firewall can present the last line of defense from an attacker who has already gained internal network access.

Firewall Appliances

Many manufactures create hardware appliances, as well as software firewalls which run on commodity hardware. These firewalls are often used as an edge firewall (the firewall between the corporate network and the DMZ as well as back channel firewalls, or firewalls used between the DMZ and internal corporate network. These firewalls are the primary line of defense for a corporate network.

DMZ

Placing web servers in a DMZ while SQL Servers and other non-web services reside in the internal network is common place in many environments, and generally accepted as a secure option. However, as it pertains to SharePoint, this may in fact be the less secure option, as shown in Figure 4-5.

External User   **Edge Firewall**   **SharePoint DMZ** **Back Channel Firewall**   **SharePoint**

Figure 4-5. SharePoint in the DMZ with multiple ports open in the Back Channel Firewall

SharePoint must have not only a port open to SQL Server, but also ports open between SharePoint Servers *and* Active Directory Domain Controllers for authentication, authorization, People Picker, as well as the User Profile Service when using AD Import. Any other integrated services, such as Workflow Manager 1.0, Office Online Server, or hosted High Trust Add-ins must also be taken into consideration. This leads to a significant number of ports that must be opened in the back channel firewall between the DMZ and internal corporate network.

Reverse Proxies

Reverse Proxies are either preauthentication reverse proxies, such as Microsoft's Web Application Proxy, or do not provide any authentication mechanisms, such as Apache's mod_proxy or mod_ssl. Reverse proxies are typically deployed in a DMZ. Their function is to terminate the user's session, while the proxy passes the session to the services behind it. This is illustrated in Figure 4-6.

External User   **Edge Firewall**   **Reverse Proxy Back Channel Firewall   SharePoint**

Figure 4-6. *Reverse proxies to handle external user sessions*

This allows SharePoint and related services to reside in the internal corporate network and have a single port, tcp/443 (HTTPS), as an example, open in the back channel firewall. In general, this is considered more secure versus placing SharePoint servers within the DMZ when they need access to resources within the internal corporate network.

Access Rules

Strict Access Rules should be created, where possible: for example, blocking client networks from directly communicating with SharePoint servers not running end-user facing roles, such as those servers which are not the WebFrontEnd role.

Likewise, rules for SQL Server should also be put in place. Only SharePoint servers, backup systems, monitoring systems, and certain administrator systems should be allowed to communicate with the SQL Server over various ports (CIFS, standard SQL ports, as two examples). Table 4-1 provides the essential inbound ports for each type of server.

Table 4-1. *Inbound Ports for Servers*

Server Type	Port Number	Notes
SQL Server	TCP/1433	Database Engine
SQL Server	TCP/1434	Optional (SQL Browser)
SQL Server	TCP/5022	Optional (Availability Group Listener)
SharePoint Server	TCP/80	Optional (if using HTTP)
SharePoint Server	TCP/443	Optional (if using SSL)
Office Online Server	TCP/80	Optional (if using HTTP)
Office Online Server	TCP/443	Optional (if using SSL)
Workflow Manager	TCP/12291	Optional (if using HTTP)
Workflow Manager	TCP/12290	Optional (if using SSL)
SharePoint Server	TCP/32843	Service Application (HTTP)
SharePoint Server	TCP/32844	Service Application (SSL)
SharePoint Server	TCP/32845	Service Application (net.tcp)
SharePoint Server	TCP/22233	Distributed Cache
SharePoint Server	TCP/22234	Distributed Cache
SharePoint Server	ICMP (0)	Distributed Cache (Ping)
Microsoft Identity Manager	RPC Dynamic Ports	Synchronization Service
Microsoft Identity Manager	RPC Endpoint Mapper	Synchronization Service

Next Steps

We have taken a look at the available authentication and security options for SharePoint Server 2016. Next, we will learn how to set up and configure SharePoint Add-ins.

CHAPTER 5

■ ■ ■

Configuring Add-ins

According to Microsoft Best Practices, you should use Add-ins (previously known as apps) when customizing your SharePoint 2016 deployment. Furthermore, plenty of third-party vendors offer Add-ins in the SharePoint Store, which is similar to Apple iTunes or Google Play, but for SharePoint.

However, compared to your smartphone, you need more than an Internet connection to install Add-ins in SharePoint. Being able to consume Add-ins in SharePoint requires some configuration not only in SharePoint, but in DNS as well.

In this chapter, you will learn how to configure a SharePoint 2016 Environment to support Add-ins as well as how to manage them by using the App Catalog.

SharePoint Add-in Architecture Overview

Before we get started configuring Add-ins for SharePoint 2016, it's important to understand the Add-in architecture, to have a preview of all the different elements we will configure in this chapter.

First, technically speaking, every Add-in you add to your SharePoint Farm becomes a subsite under the SharePoint site you added it under. In Figure 5-1 we can see a SharePoint Site with two Add-ins deployed.

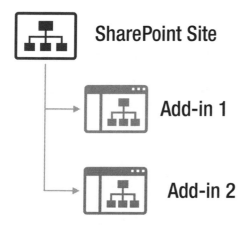

Figure 5-1. *Basic Add-in Architecture in SharePoint*

Furthermore, SharePoint Add-ins run under a different lookup zone in DNS for security reasons. If your main domain is **learn-sp2016.com,** your *Add-in Domain* could be **learn-sp2016addins.com**. If you plan to open your site to the internet and allow users to connect to it without a VPN, you will need to make sure your Add-in Domain is a real public domain, and since your site will probably be using SSL (Secure Sockets Layer), you will also need a wildcard certificate on your Add-in Domain provided by a public certification authority such as Digicert.

■ **Note**   Microsoft recommends using a completely new forward lookup zone, and not a subdomain such as addins.learn-sp2016.com. This recommendation is made to prevent Cross-Site Scripting (XSS) attacks.

The URL of each Add-in deployment is also given a unique ID. Therefore, even if we deploy the same Add-in on two different Site collections, each deployment has a different URL. The URL is composed of a prefix that you can choose, the Add-in ID, and the Add-in Domain. In Figure 5-2, we can see the same SharePoint site, with the URLs of both the site and Add-ins. For this book we will use the "app" prefix for our Add-ins.

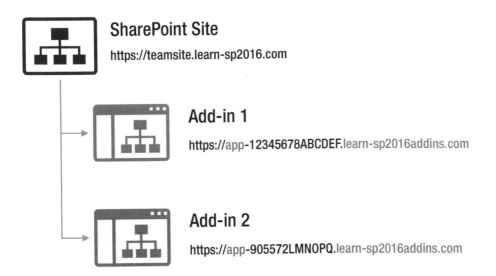

Figure 5-2. *Add-in URLs in SharePoint 2016*

We can choose the Add-in Prefix ourselves, as well as the Add-in domain; however, we cannot choose the ID that is assigned to the Add-in deployment. Therefore, that is why we need a dedicated forward lookup zone in our DNS that has a wildcard entry, so everything in our Add-in domain will point directly either to our SharePoint Server, or to the network load balancer that will forward the request to one of our SharePoint Web Front Ends. In Figure 5-3, you can see a sample of the Learn-SP2016 DNS, which will contain the *Learn-SP2016.com* forward lookup zone containing all your SharePoint Sites, as well as all the servers and everything in your domain. We can also find the *Learn-SP2016Addins.com* forward lookup zone that simply has a wildcard entry, so everything in that forward lookup zone will go to our SharePoint Web Front End.

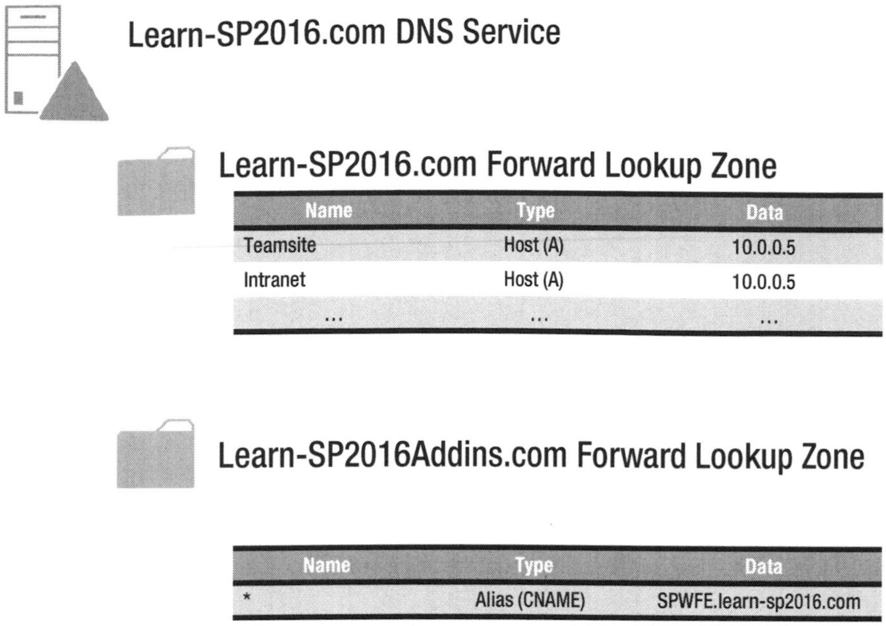

Learn-SP2016.com DNS Service

Learn-SP2016.com Forward Lookup Zone

Name	Type	Data
Teamsite	Host (A)	10.0.0.5
Intranet	Host (A)	10.0.0.5
...	...	...

Learn-SP2016Addins.com Forward Lookup Zone

Name	Type	Data
*	Alias (CNAME)	SPWFE.learn-sp2016.com

Figure 5-3. *DNS Architecture for SharePoint Add-ins*

Now that we know how we get our users to the SharePoint Server from DNS, let's take a look at how SharePoint handles those requests. In Figure 5-4, we see a user requesting an Add-in; the request goes to the DNS that directs the request to the SharePoint Server called SPWFE. However, since we do not have any Web Applications with that name, the Internet Information Services (IIS) Server running under SharePoint will not know to which site to send the request.

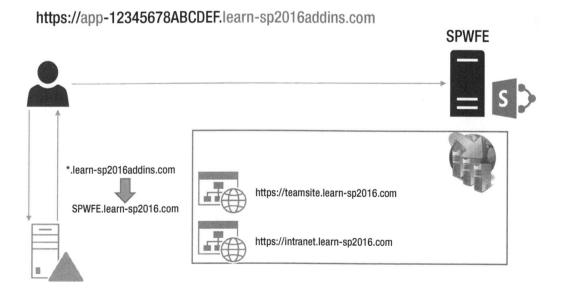

Figure 5-4. *What happens in the network when a user tried to access an Add-in*

One of the requirements we have on the SharePoint side is to create a Web Application that has no host header at all. The requests to our server will automatically go to that Web Application, which will forward the request to a Service Application called the *App Management Service Application.* That application knows what Add-in belongs to what Site, and will be able to direct the user to the right Add-in, in the right site. The process will then look as in Figure 5-5.

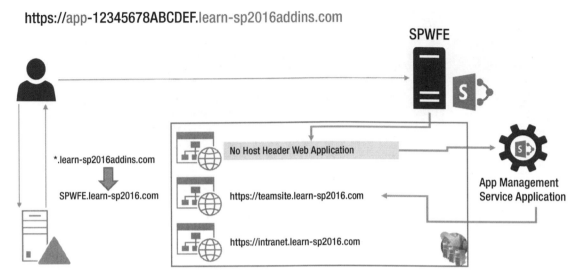

Figure 5-5. *What happens in the network when a user tried to access an Add-in*

Another Service Application that we will need to get the Add-ins working is the Subscription Settings Service Application. Now that we know what the architecture looks like, let's start to configure Add-ins for SharePoint 2016.

Configuring DNS

To configure DNS, you will need to be a Domain Administrator and have access to the DNS Manager console. First, open up the DNS Console, right-click "forward lookup zones," and select "New Zone" as seen in Figure 5-6.

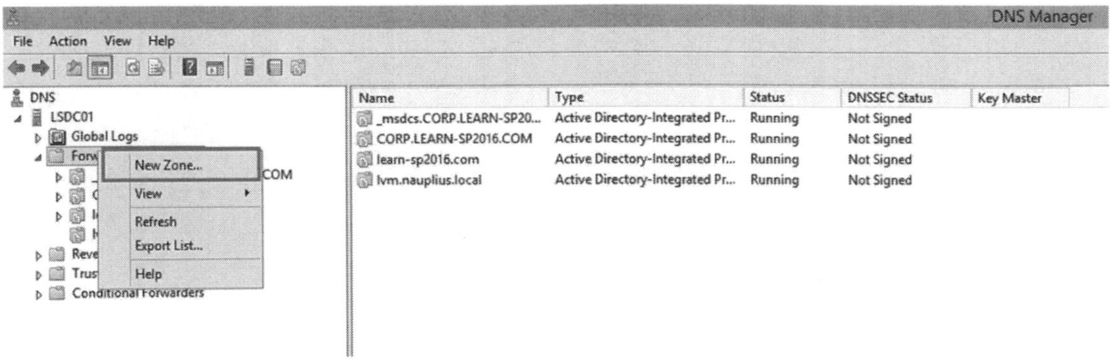

Figure 5-6. *Adding a New Zone to our DNS*

On the first screen, click "Next" as seen in Figure 5-7.

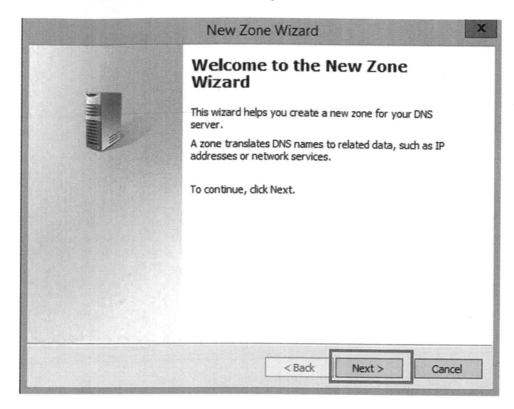

Figure 5-7. *New Zone Wizard*

The Zone must be of type "Primary Zone" and also check the "Store the zone in AD" box as seen in Figure 5-8.

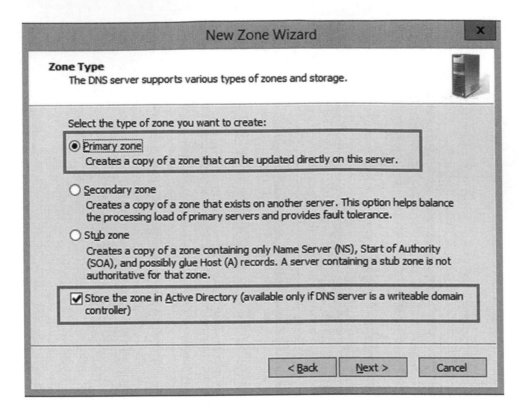

Figure 5-8. *Selecting the Zone Type*

Select if you want the data replicated to all the Domain Controllers in your domain, or in your forest. Since we only have one domain in our farm for this book, we choose the second option as seen in Figure 5-9.

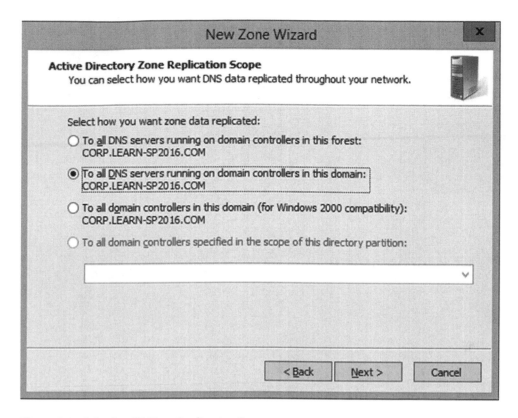

Figure 5-9. *Selecting AD Zone Replication Scope*

On the next screen you need to enter your new Add-in domain as seen in Figure 5-10.

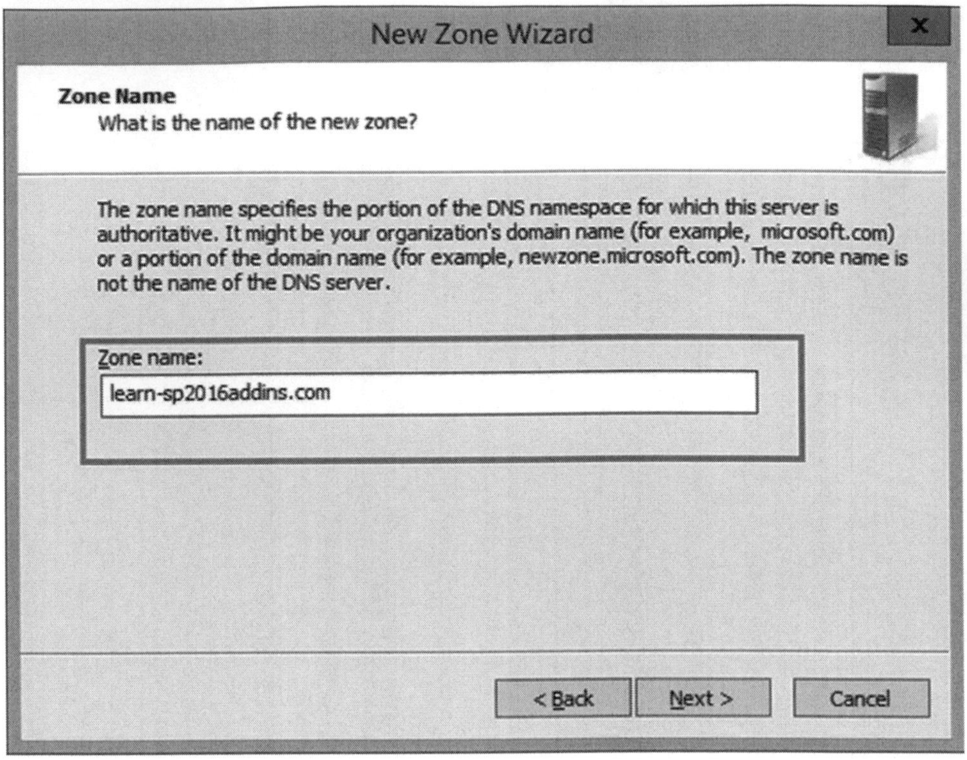

Figure 5-10. *Entering the Add-in Domain as our new Zone Name*

Lastly, select the type of Dynamic Updates for your Domain. Since there won't be any new records except the initial one, we should select "Do not allow dynamic updates" as seen in Figure 5-11.

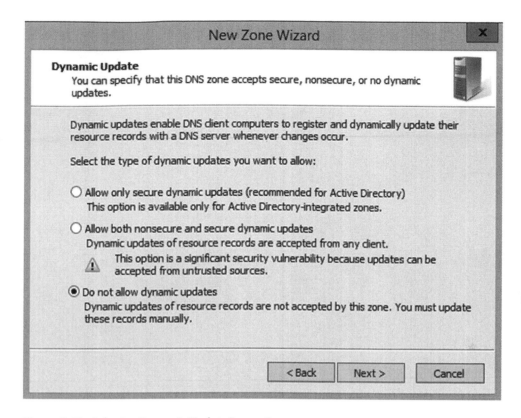

Figure 5-11. *Selecting Dynamic Update Properties*

After the zone is created, we need to create either an Alias (CNAME) or a Host (A) toward our SharePoint Servers. If you only have one SharePoint Web Front End, you can use a CNAME; however, if you use a network load balancer, you will want to use a HOST since you will probably forward your users to a Virtual IP Address. In our case, we will forward all requests for our Add-in domain to 172.16.0.105, a Virtual IP Address that goes to the load balancer, which then forwards the requests to one of our two Web Front Ends.

While still in the DNS Management Window, right-click our new forward lookup zone and select a "New Host (A or AAAA)" as seen in Figure 5-12.

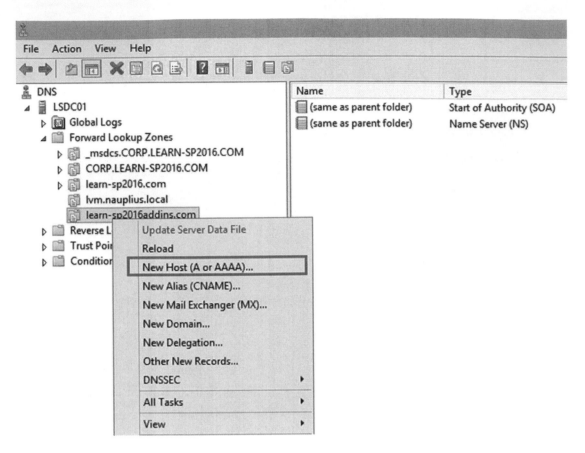

Figure 5-12. *Creating a new Host entry in DNS*

Afterward, enter a Wildcard (*) in the name, as well as the IP address you want to point it to as seen in Figure 5-13.

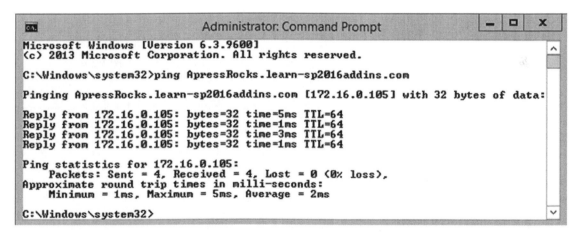

Figure 5-13. *Entering New Host Record Properties*

To test, simply do a PING request to <random word>.Add-inDomain.TLD. In my example in Figure 5-14 I used ApressRocks.learn-sp2016addins.com and the result was successful as it forwarded me to 172.16.0.105.

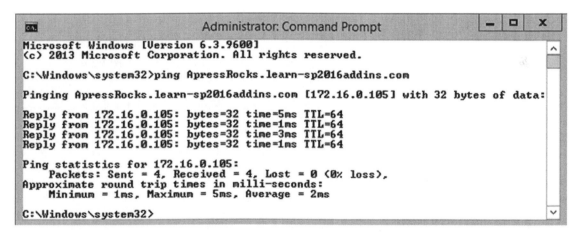

Figure 5-14. *Testing the configuration with Command Prompt*

If the ping test is successful, it means that the DNS has been configured successfully. We can now move to configuring our SharePoint Server 2016 to accept Add-ins.

Configuring SharePoint

The first step we need to do to get our SharePoint Server ready for Add-ins is to create the two required Service Applications:

- App Management Service Application
- Subscription Settings Service Application

If you are doing this procedure in a full MinRole farm, the services will start automatically when creating the Service Applications. If you are running on a Custom mode farm, you will need to manually turn on the *App Management Service* as well as the *Microsoft SharePoint Foundation Subscription Settings Service* on at least one SharePoint Server.

■ **Note**   In a Streamlined topology it is recommended to turn on those services on all the Web Front Ends in your SharePoint Server Farm.

While the App Management Service Application can be created by both the Central Administration and PowerShell, the Subscription Settings Service Application can only be created by using PowerShell. In this book we will create both Service Applications by using PowerShell, and run them both under our only Service Application Pool called *SharePoint Web Services Default*.

We first need to get our Service Application Pool and save it into a variable.

```
$apppool = Get-SPServiceApplicationPool "SharePoint Web Services Default"
```

Afterward, we create the Subscription Settings Service Application, as well as its proxy.

```
$SubscriptionSA = New-SPSubscriptionSettingsServiceApplication -ApplicationPool $apppool -
Name "Subscription Settings" -DatabaseName SubscriptionSettings

$proxySub = New-SPSubscriptionSettingsServiceApplicationProxy -ServiceApplication
$SubscriptionSA
```

Lastly, we create the App Management Service Application as well as its proxy:

```
$AppManagementSA = New-SPAppManagementServiceApplication -ApplicationPool $apppool -Name
"App Management" -DatabaseName AppManagement

$proxyApp = New-SPAppManagementServiceApplicationProxy -ServiceApplication $AppManagementSA
```

After the Service Applications are created and working, we need to set the Add-in Domain as well as the Add-in Prefix. This can be done in Central Administration > Apps > Configure App URLs as seen in Figure 5-15 or via PowerShell.

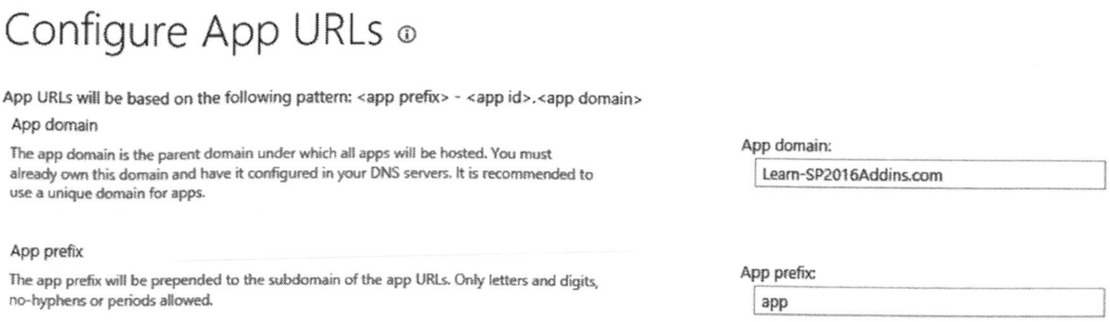

Configure App URLs ⓘ

App URLs will be based on the following pattern: <app prefix> - <app id>.<app domain>

App domain

The app domain is the parent domain under which all apps will be hosted. You must already own this domain and have it configured in your DNS servers. It is recommended to use a unique domain for apps.

App domain:

Learn-SP2016Addins.com

App prefix

The app prefix will be prepended to the subdomain of the app URLs. Only letters and digits, no-hyphens or periods allowed.

App prefix:

app

Figure 5-15. *The Configure App URL Screen in SharePoint 2016*

First, configure the Add-in domain using the following cmdlet:

```
Set-SPAppDomain Learn-SP2016Addins.com
```

And afterward the Add-in Prefix.

```
Set-SPAppSiteSubscriptionName -Name "app" -Confirm:$false
```

The only thing that we need now is a Web Application with no host header. Without that Web Application, users will see a HTTP 404 error when trying to access an Add-in. A Web Application with no host header simply means that when you create the Web Application, you leave the "Host Header" field blank as seen in Figure 5-16.

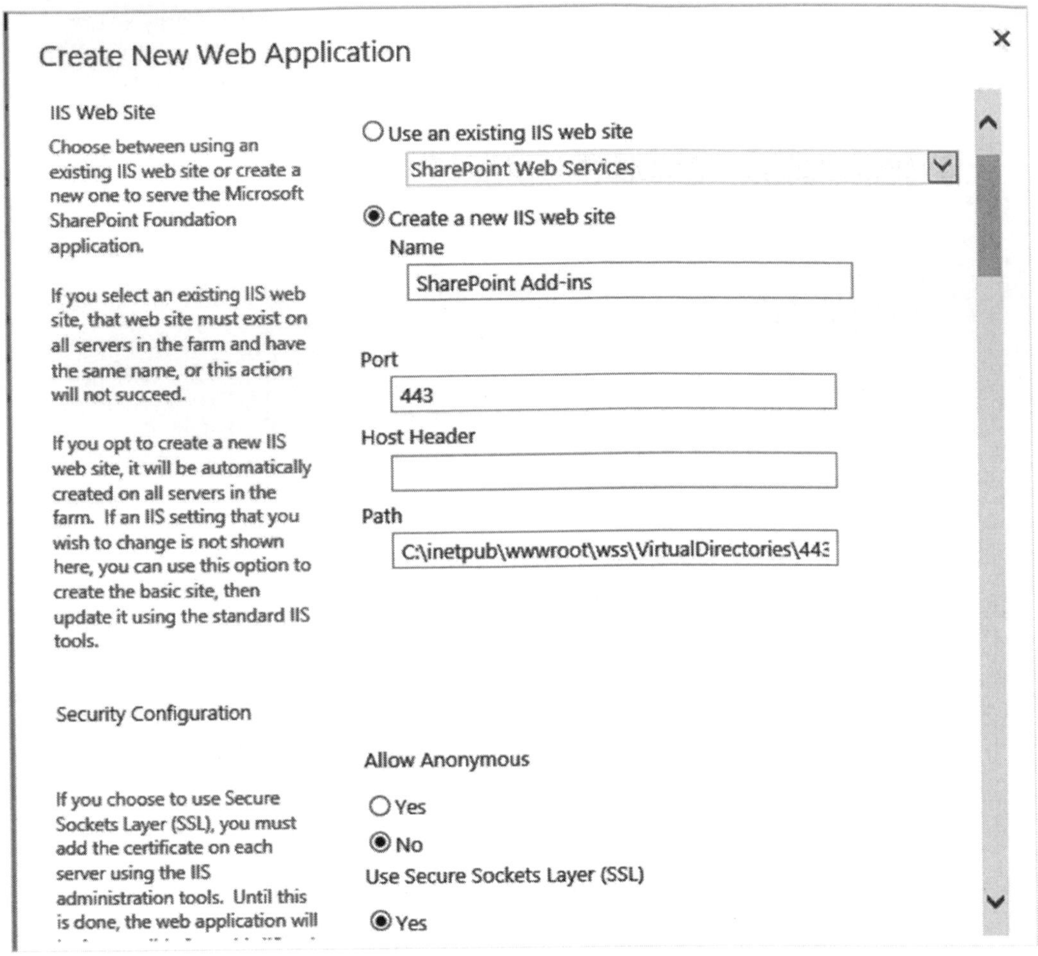

Create New Web Application   ✕

IIS Web Site

Choose between using an existing IIS web site or create a new one to serve the Microsoft SharePoint Foundation application.

If you select an existing IIS web site, that web site must exist on all servers in the farm and have the same name, or this action will not succeed.

If you opt to create a new IIS web site, it will be automatically created on all servers in the farm. If an IIS setting that you wish to change is not shown here, you can use this option to create the basic site, then update it using the standard IIS tools.

○ Use an existing IIS web site

SharePoint Web Services ▾

● Create a new IIS web site
Name

SharePoint Add-ins

Port

443

Host Header

Path

C:\inetpub\wwwroot\wss\VirtualDirectories\443

Security Configuration

If you choose to use Secure Sockets Layer (SSL), you must add the certificate on each server using the IIS administration tools. Until this is done, the web application will

Allow Anonymous

○ Yes
● No

Use Secure Sockets Layer (SSL)

● Yes

Figure 5-16. *Creating a new Web Application in SharePoint 2016*

If you already have a Web Application using the Alternate Access Mapping of https://servername or an IIS site with that binding, SharePoint will not allow you to create the new Web Application on port 443. If you have setup the Central Administration on SSL as we did in this book, make sure you have deleted the default Alternate Access Mapping on it, since we created a new URL for it.

You will also need to create a root site collection on that Web Application. There is no specific template or permissions needed; however, it needs to exist for SharePoint to work properly.

Since we are using SSL, we will also need to add the certificate into IIS. To do so, you first need to import the wildcard certificate for your Add-in domain into IIS as shown in Figure 5-17.

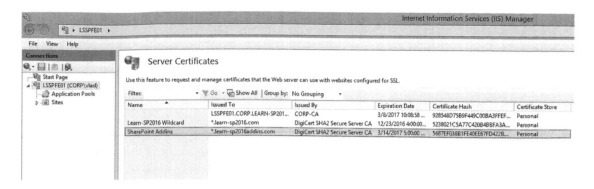

Figure 5-17. *Certificates in IIS Manager*

Afterward, you need to add a binding on the IIS Site we just created, on post 443 (SSL) and select the certificate that we just imported as shown in Figure 5-18.

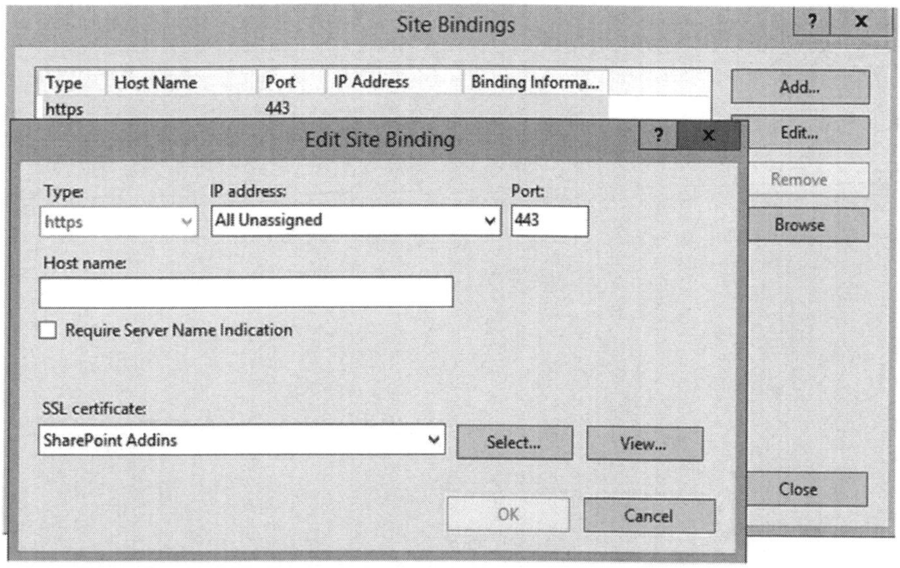

Figure 5-18. *Adding a Binding in IIS*

Due to limitations in the TLS/SSL architecture, you usually couldn't run more than one SSL site on the same Web Server because there wasn't a way in TLS to specify a "hostname" for the traffic. With Windows Server 2012 R2 and IIS8 we have Server Name Identification (SNI) on the other Web Applications, allowing this to work.

If you do not use SNI, you will have to add another IP to the SharePoint Server and redirect all Add-in requests to that IP.

■ **Note**   You need to repeat this step on every server that has the Foundation Web Application Service running. If you are running in a MinRole configuration those servers are the Front End, Distributed Cache, and Application roles. The Search Role doesn't have Foundation Web Application activated; therefore, you cannot do any changes on the Search Servers.

Securing all your SharePoint sites with SSL is extremely important in SharePoint, since the OAuth token is passed in a packet on the request, and you could be subject to a man-in-the-middle attack if that token is not secured.

After this is done, you can go to the store and add an Add-in from the SharePoint Store, and everything should work!

We have now successfully configured Add-ins, but there are a few settings we can change to make the experience more enjoyable for our end users.

Post Configuration Settings

After Add-ins are configured on our SharePoint environment, there are some configurations we might need do in some cases to improve user experience, or enable extra functionality. The first one is mainly for user experience. Usually, we add our main domain, for example *.learn-sp2016.com to the Intranet zone in Internet Explorer for all our users so they don't have to enter their username and password every time they go on a SharePoint site. However, since our Add-ins run in a different domain, users will get prompted to enter their username and password each time they access an Add-in, or have an Add-in Part on a SharePoint Page as seen in Figure 5-19.

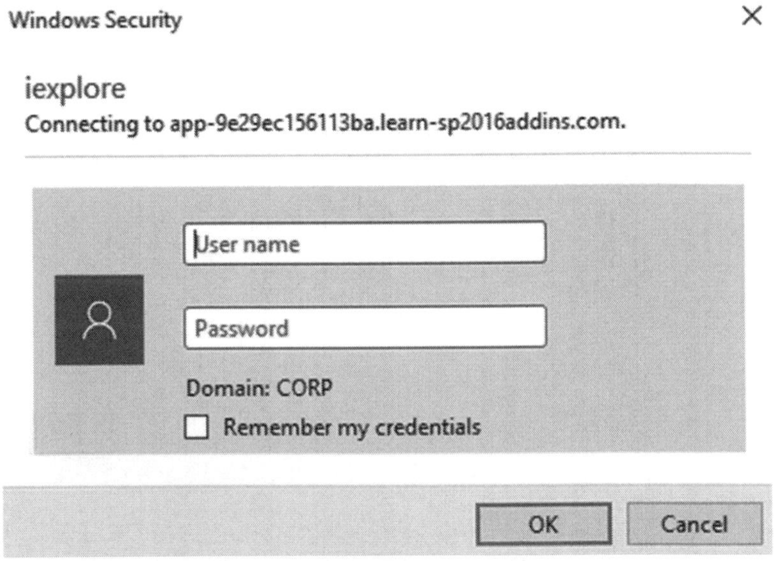

Figure 5-19. *Authentication Prompt on Add-in Domain*

Microsoft recommends not adding the Add-in Domain to our Intranet or Trusted sites zone since those zones do not provide a sufficient level of isolation of Add-ins from user data in SharePoint Sites. The consequences, as described before, are having a Windows Authentication prompt every time a user accesses an Add-in, or navigates to a page with an Add-in Part embedded.

In order to avoid this behavior and provide a seamless experience for your users, make sure you add the Add-in domain to the Intranet Zone of all your users, by Group Policy or any other tools you have in your organization. As a SharePoint Administrator you must decide whether to follow Microsoft's security best practices, or opt for the best end-user behavior and UX best practices.

The second setting which is a bit more SharePoint Specific is enabling users to deploy apps that require sites with Internet-facing endpoints. Those apps are greyed out by default and users cannot deploy them. If your farm is configured to allow Internet-facing end points, you can activate the *Apps that require accessible internet facing endpoints* feature on each Web Application on which you want to enable this functionality. The feature is disabled by default as shown in Figure 5-20.

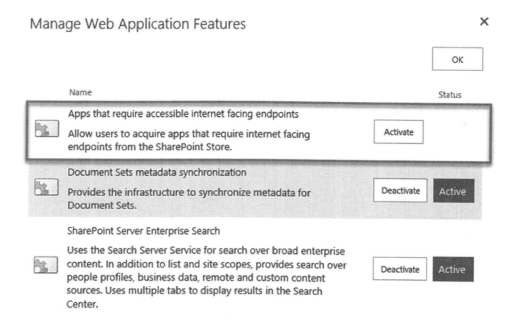

Figure 5-20. *Activating Web Application Features*

We have now successfully finished configuring Add-ins in our environment, and users can add, and consume Add-ins from the SharePoint Store. In the next section we will learn how to control what Add-ins are bought and how to distributed custom Add-ins to your users.

The App Catalog

The App Catalog is a special site collection on each Web Application that allows SharePoint Administrators to manage and control the Add-ins that are installed on the farm. By configuring an App Catalog, we can force users to get an administrator to approve all Add-in purchases, as well as upload in-house-built Add-ins and make them available to all our users.

Creating an App Catalog Site Collection

The App Catalog can be created either from the Central Administration in *Apps > Manage App Catalog* or through PowerShell by using the *"APPCATALOG#0"* template. When creating the App Catalog through Central Administration, we choose to create a new App Catalog Site as seen in Figure 5-21.

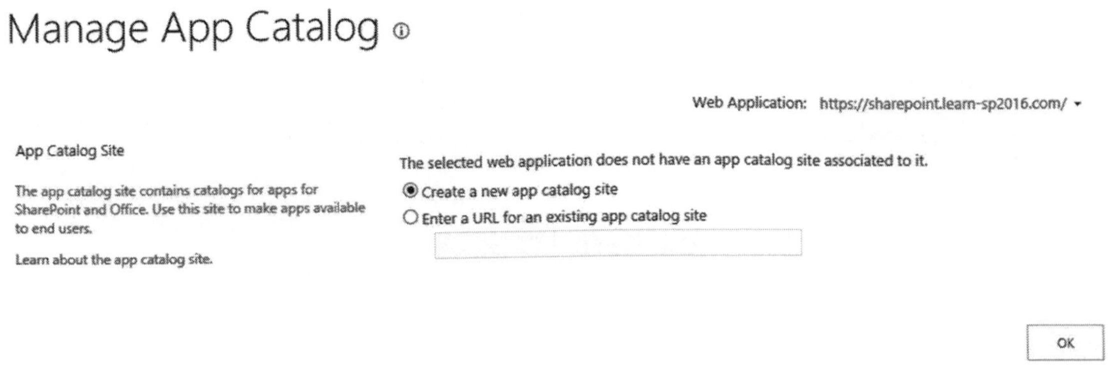

Manage App Catalog ⓘ

Web Application: https://sharepoint.learn-sp2016.com/ ▾

App Catalog Site

The app catalog site contains catalogs for apps for SharePoint and Office. Use this site to make apps available to end users.

Learn about the app catalog site.

The selected web application does not have an app catalog site associated to it.

◉ Create a new app catalog site
○ Enter a URL for an existing app catalog site

[   ]

[OK]

Figure 5-21. The Manage App Catalog Page in SharePoint 2016

The App Catalog Site creation page is very similar to a normal Site Collection creation page; the only difference is that we have a new box called "End Users" in which we enter the users that are allowed to see Add-ins from this App Catalog Site. In our scenario, we want the App Catalog to be open to all SharePoint Users, so we simply entered the Domain Users group as shown in Figure 5-22.

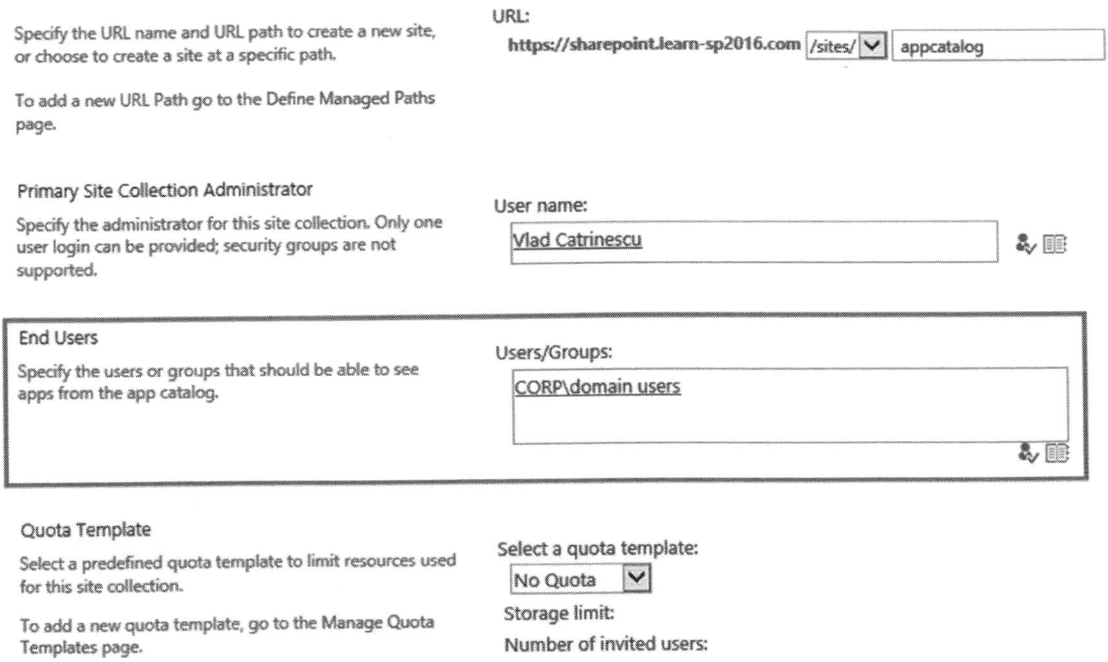

Specify the URL name and URL path to create a new site, or choose to create a site at a specific path.

To add a new URL Path go to the Define Managed Paths page.

URL:

https://sharepoint.learn-sp2016.com /sites/ ▾ appcatalog

Primary Site Collection Administrator

Specify the administrator for this site collection. Only one user login can be provided; security groups are not supported.

User name:

Vlad Catrinescu   👤 📇

End Users

Specify the users or groups that should be able to see apps from the app catalog.

Users/Groups:

CORP\domain users

👤 📇

Quota Template

Select a predefined quota template to limit resources used for this site collection.

To add a new quota template, go to the Manage Quota Templates page.

Select a quota template:

No Quota ▾

Storage limit:

Number of invited users:

Figure 5-22. Creating a new App Catalog Site Collection

Configure Requests

To block users from buying Add-ins from the SharePoint Store themselves and forcing them to place a request, we need to do some changes in the *Central Administration > Apps > Configure Store Settings* page. If we set it to No as seen in Figure 5-23, users will need to request an Add-in before being able to buy it.

SharePoint Store Settings

App Purchases
Specify whether end users can get apps from the SharePoint Store.

Should end users be able to get apps from the SharePoint Store?
○ Yes
◉ No

App Requests
View the list used to capture app requests. Users will request apps if they aren't allowed to get apps directly from the SharePoint Store or if they prefer to request an app rather than getting it directly.

Click here to view app requests

Figure 5-23. *The SharePoint Store Settings Page in SharePoint 2016*

This change can also be done with PowerShell with the following cmdlet by replacing `https://sharepoint.learn-sp2016.com` with the Web Application you wish to apply the change on.

```
Set-SPAppAcquisitionConfiguration -WebApplication https://sharepoint.learn-sp2016.com
-Enable:$false
```

When you force your users to request Add-ins instead of them being able to install them themselves, the button to add an Add-in will change from "Add it" as seen in Figure 5-24 to "Request it" as seen in Figure 5-25.

Team Site ▶ Add Apps ▶   USA $ ▾   English (United States) ▾   ?

Anniversary Timeline
from MAQ LLC

Find an app 🔍

Free
ADD IT

By acquiring this app you agree to its permissions.

Figure 5-24. *Button when users are allowed to add Add-ins themselves*

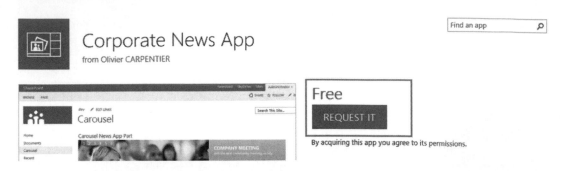

Figure 5-25. *Button when users must request an Add-in to be approved before being able to add it*

When a user requests an Add-in, they must specify how many licenses they need, or if it's for the whole organization as seen in Figure 5-26. Users also need to provide a business justification for the Add-in.

App Request: Corporate News App   ✕

User licenses

○ Request this app for a specific number of users.

     1

◉ Request this app for everyone in my organization.

Request justification

                                                          Request   Cancel

Figure 5-26. *The App Request for end users*

When an Add-in Request is done, SharePoint Server 2016 will place the request in the "App Requests" list in the App Catalog of that Web Application as seen in Figure 5-27.

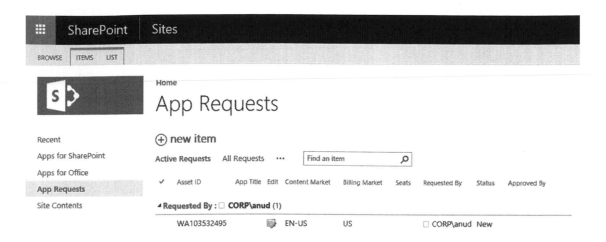

Figure 5-27. *The App Requests list in the App Catalog*

Once we click the list entry, we can see the title of the app, how many seats are required, the Justification as well as a Status field and Approver comments. Changing the Status to "Approved" will not allow the user to install the Add-in; the App Catalog admin will need to get the Add-in from the Store by clicking the "Click here to view app details and purchase or manage licenses" link as seen in Figure 5-28.

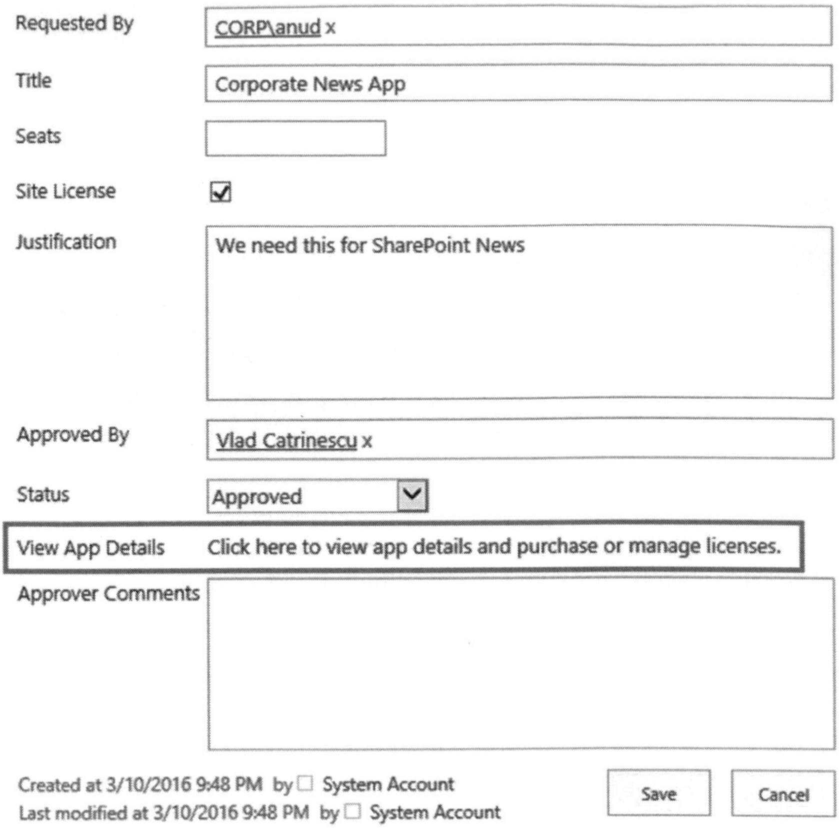

Requested By	CORP\anud x
Title	Corporate News App
Seats	
Site License	☑
Justification	We need this for SharePoint News
Approved By	Vlad Catrinescu x
Status	Approved ▾

View App Details   Click here to view app details and purchase or manage licenses.

Approver Comments

Created at 3/10/2016 9:48 PM by ☐ System Account
Last modified at 3/10/2016 9:48 PM by ☐ System Account

Save   Cancel

Figure 5-28. *The details of an Add-in Request*

Once the admin acquired the Add-in, users will be able to see the Add-in in the "Apps you can add" section in the Site Collection as seen in Figure 5-29.

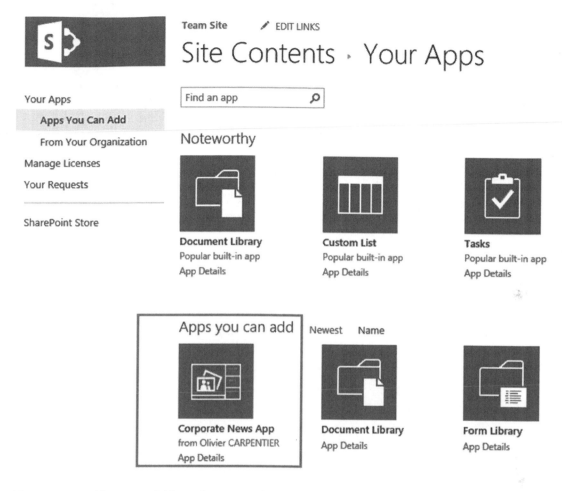

Figure 5-29. Add-in is available on the requested Site Collection

We have now successfully configured the App Catalog in our SharePoint 2016 Farm.

Next Steps

In this chapter, we learned how to configure our SharePoint 2016 Server Farm to allow users to consume Add-ins either from the SharePoint Store or built in-house. We also learned what the App Catalog is, and how we can request an admin approval before Add-ins are added to SharePoint Sites in our organization.

In the next chapter, we will learn how to create and configure the Search Service Application!

CHAPTER 6

■ ■ ■

Configuring the Search Service Application

Search is a very important part of SharePoint and many companies rely on the strong SharePoint Search Engine to find documents and information for their day-to-day jobs.

In this chapter, you will learn the architecture of the SharePoint Search Service Application, as well as how to configure it from both Central Administration and PowerShell.

SharePoint Search Service Application Architecture

Before starting to configure the Search Service Application, we will need to better understand the architecture and how it works internally. The SharePoint 2016 Search Engine is built on the FAST Search Engine that Microsoft acquired in 2008 from a Norwegian company then called Fast Search & Transfer ASA, and has fully integrated in SharePoint since SharePoint 2013. The SharePoint Search Service Engine is broken up into six different components:

1. **Crawl Component**

   The Crawl Component is responsible for crawling different types of content such as Local SharePoint Sites, Remote SharePoint Sites File Shares, and more. We call those Content Sources.

2. **Content Processing Component**

   The Content processing components receives data from the Crawl component, and breaks it down into artifacts that can be included in the Index. Some Search customizations such as Custom Entity Extractions are done by the Content Processing Component.

3. **Index Component**

   The Index Component is a logical representation of an index file. The Index component receives items from the Content Processing Component and writes them into an index file. For systems where there are a lot of crawled items, the Index can be split into different Index Partitions, a logical portion of the entire search index.

© Vlad Catrinescu and Trevor Seward 2016
V. Catrinescu and T. Seward, *Deploying SharePoint 2016*, DOI 10.1007/978-1-4842-1999-7_6

4. **Query Component**

   The Query Processing Component is the component that interacts with the SharePoint Front End. The Query Processing Component gets the queries done by users, analyzes it and submits it to the Index Components. The Index component will then return the relevant results to the Query component, which will then return the results to the end user. The Query Component is also responsible for the Security Trimming on the search results.

5. **Analytics Processing Component**

   The Analytics Processing Component creates search analytics as well as usage analytics. Those analytics are used for search relevance, generate recommendations as well as create search reports.

6. **Search Administration Component**

   The Search Administration Component runs the administration tasks as well as provisioning the other Search Components.

All those components work together to offer the end-to-end search experience for your users. Unlike most Service Applications, which only have one database, the Search Service application has four different types of databases, and you can have more than one of each type in your Search Service Application, depending on your requirements. We will cover those cases and when and how to scale out your Search Service Application a bit later into this chapter. The different types of databases that you will find in the Search Service Application are as follows:

1. **Crawl Database**

   The Crawl Database contains tracking and historical information about crawled items as well as information about the last crawl times, types of crawls and durations.

2. **Search Admin Database**

   The Search Admin Database stores configuration data such as the topology, managed properties, query and crawl rules.

3. **The Link Database**

   The Link database stores information extracted by the Content Processing component as well as information about search clicks and popularity.

4. **The Analytics Reporting Database**

   The analytics report database stores statistics information and analytics results.

There is another data storage location, which is not a database, but log files on the server that hosts the analytics processing component. This is called the **Event Store**. The Event store holds usage events such as the number of items an item is viewed. Now that we know the components of a Search Service Application, let's see how we can create it.

It's important to remember that the Index Component is also stored on the file system, and not in the database. Therefore, it's important to plan extra disk space for the servers running the Index Component.

All those search components must be hosted on a SharePoint Server that is configured as a "Search" MinRole server, or "Custom" MinRole server with the Search Services started.

Search Service Application Limitations

When planning our Search Service Application topology, we need to respect both the business requirements as well as the software boundaries of SharePoint Server 2016. Business requirements might be around index freshness as well as separation between the indexes of two different clients hosted on the same SharePoint farm. The number of items that you plan to crawl using the SharePoint Search Service application might require you to add multiple servers to your Search Topology in order to get around the software boundaries in SharePoint.

■ **Tip**   You can view all the SharePoint Server Software boundaries on TechNet at the following link:
`https://technet.microsoft.com/en-ca/library/cc262787(v=office.16).aspx#Search`.

Creating a Search Service Application

The Search Service Application can be created both from the SharePoint User Interface and from the SharePoint Management Shell. When creating the Search Service Application via Central Administration, the Search databases will have a GUID appended to them, unlike when creating the Search Service Application via the SharePoint Management Shell, where you have control over the database naming convention. It's also important to know that while it's possible to create the Search Service Application with Central Administration, the Search Service Application Topology can only be modified via PowerShell. Search Service Applications created with the Central Administration will host all components on a single server. For those reasons, we strongly recommend using PowerShell in this book to create your Search Service Application. We will still cover both options of creating the Search Service Application in this chapter.

Creating a Search Service Application from Central Administration

To create a Search Service Application from the User Interface, from the Manage Service Applications page in the Central Administration, click New, and select Search Service Application as seen in Figure 6-1.

Figure 6-1. *New Search Service Application from the User Interface*

In the new Create New Search Service Application window seen in Figure 6-2, we will first have to give it a name, select if it's a normal Search Service Application or a Cloud Search Service Application, and also give it the Service account that will run the Windows Search Service. In this chapter, we will not cover the Cloud Search Service Application, as this will be covered in Chapter 14. While it's possible to set a dedicated Search Service account for an extra layer of security, we recommend using the same account that runs the other services, which in our case is Corp\s-svc.

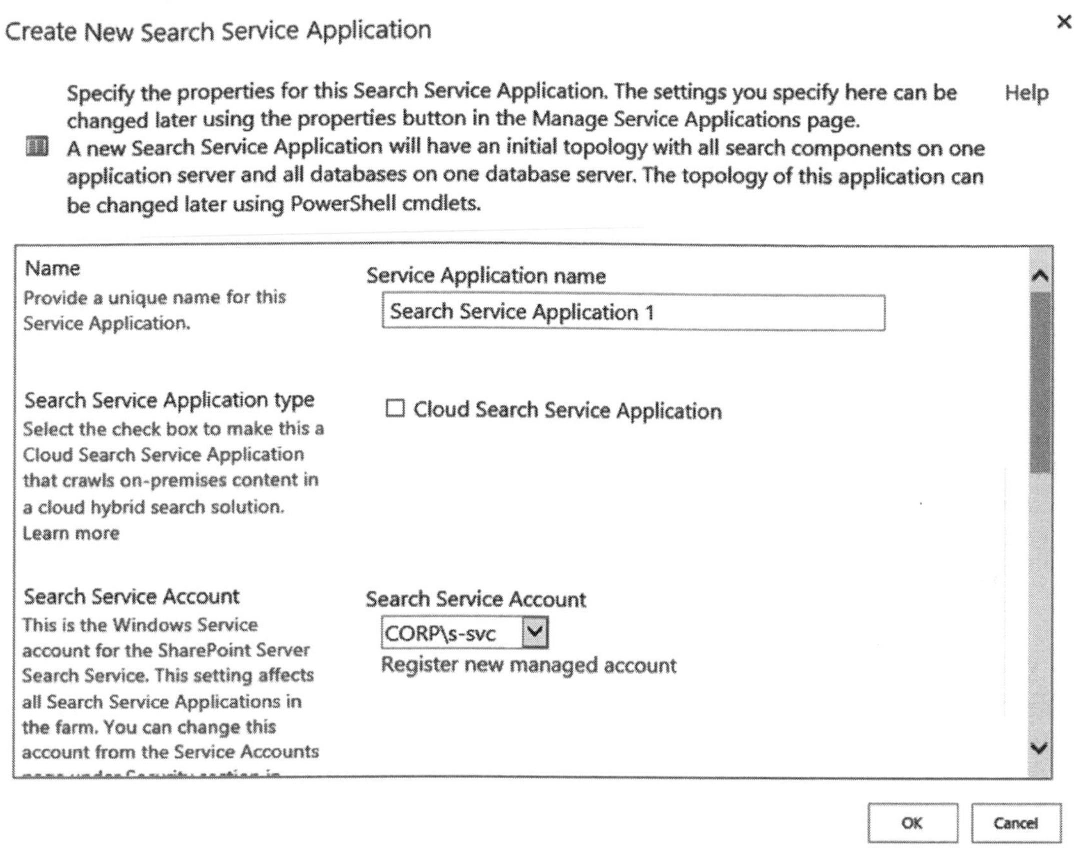

Figure 6-2. *New Search Service Application Window*

On the second part of the Create New Search Service Application Window seen in Figure 6-3, we need to select if we want to create new Service Application Pools for the Search Admin Web Service and Query and Site Settings Web Service, or use an existing one. While creating new ones could increase the isolation of the Search Service Applications, it will result in additional resources being used on your servers. In this book we recommend using the same Application Pool as the rest of your service applications, in this case "SharePoint Web Services Default," unless you have specific business or security requirements to isolate this Service Application from the other Service Applications.

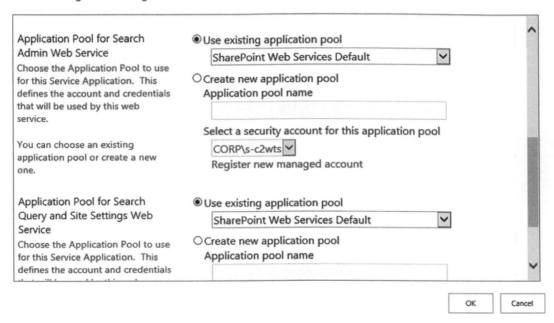

Figure 6-3. New Search Service Application Window

You can then click OK to create the Search Service Application. Once created, the Search Administration Page seen in Figure 6-4 will show the Search Server on which the Search Service Application activated the six components, as well as the Database Names, which have GUIDs in them because we have created this Service Application by using the user interface.

Search Application Topology

Server Name	Admin	Crawler	Content Processing	Analytics Processing	Query Processing	Index Partition 0
LSSPSR02	✓	✓	✓	✓	✓	✓

Database Server Name	Database Type	Database Name
spag.corp.learn-sp2016.com	Administration Database	Search_Service_Application_1_DB_b1bd05e8365e461287302dde324126c1
spag.corp.learn-sp2016.com	Analytics Reporting Database	Search_Service_Application_1_AnalyticsReportingStoreDB_0af24ca699e24df7b2b8dfb0204aef2e
spag.corp.learn-sp2016.com	Crawl Database	Search_Service_Application_1_CrawlStoreDB_4ba10d27f3ce43a3807edc340e33dfe8
spag.corp.learn-sp2016.com	Link Database	Search_Service_Application_1_LinksStoreDB_806690c02a6448ad8a0799259e824c21

Figure 6-4. Search Application Topology with GUID in Database Names

With the Service Application created from the User Interface, let's learn how to create it from PowerShell as well.

Creating a Search Service Application by Using PowerShell

Creating a Search Service Application by using PowerShell is as simple as creating it by the User Interface, and gives the SharePoint Administrator more control. To create a new Search Service Application, you need to open the SharePoint Management Shell as an Administrator, and use the New-SPEnterpriseSearchServiceApplication PowerShell cmdlet. The cmdlets will have to be run from a server that is configured in the Search MinRole, or a server that runs the Custom MinRole. Note that when creating a Search Service Application via PowerShell, it will not have an initial topology as it did when creating it by the User Interface, so it will not be usable until we modify the Search Service Application Topology, which we will cover a bit later in this chapter.

```
$sa = New-SPEnterpriseSearchServiceApplication -Name "<Service Application Name>"
-DatabaseName "<Search Database Name Prefix>" -ApplicationPool "<Name of existing Service
Application Pool>" -AdminApplicationPool "<Name of existing Service Application Pool>"
```

In order to create a Service Application with the same settings as we did through the User Interface a bit earlier in the chapter, we would run the following PowerShell cmdlet.

```
$sa = New-SPEnterpriseSearchServiceApplication -Name "Search Service Application"
-DatabaseName "SearchDB" -ApplicationPool "SharePoint Web Services Default"
-AdminApplicationPool "SharePoint Web Services Default"
```

After the Search Service Application is created, we need to create the Search Service Application proxy by running the New-SPEnterpriseSearchServiceApplicationProxy cmdlet. In the following cmdlet we will create a proxy named "Search Service Application Proxy" for the Search Service Application we created previously, that we saved a reference to in the $sa variable.

```
New-SPEnterpriseSearchServiceApplicationProxy -Name "Search Service Application Proxy"
-SearchApplication $sa
```

After both cmdlets finish running, we can navigate in our new Search Service Application via the User Interface, and you will notice that the Database Names do not have GUIDs in them anymore. However, since creating a Search Service Application by the User Interface does not also create an initial topology, the Search Application Topology is unable to be displayed as seen in Figure 6-5.

Search Application Topology

Unable to retrieve topology component health states. This may be because the admin component is not up and running.

Database Server Name	Database Type	Database Name
spag.corp.learn-sp2016.com	Administration Database	SearchDB
spag.corp.learn-sp2016.com	Analytics Reporting Database	SearchDB_AnalyticsReportingStore
spag.corp.learn-sp2016.com	Crawl Database	SearchDB_CrawlStore
spag.corp.learn-sp2016.com	Link Database	SearchDB_LinksStore

Figure 6-5. *Search Service Application created by PowerShell*

With the Service Application created, we will need to modify the Search Service Application topology to fit our needs.

Modifying the Search Service Application Topology

Modifying the Search Service Application topology can be done in a number of cases. You will need to do it when first creating your Search Service Application, as well as any time you need to change what components run on each server. Something to be aware of when modifying the Search Service Application topology using the following method is that the Index needs to be empty when changing the Search Service Application Topology. Later in this section we will learn how to change the Search Service Application Topology in a Service Application that already has items in the index.To change the Search Topology, we first need to get the Search Service Application and save it into a variable.

```
$sa = Get-SPEnterpriseSearchServiceApplication
```

Next, we need to get the Search Service Instance of our first Search Server, called LSSPSR01, and save it into a variable.

```
$si = Get-SPEnterpriseSearchServiceInstance | ?{$_.Server -match "LSSPSR01"}
```

If you want to use a server running the Custom MinRole to host one of the Search Components, you will first have to start the Enterprise Search Service Instance. This is done by running the Start-SP EnterpriseSearchServiceInstance cmdlet. To start the instance, we would run the following cmdlet:

```
Start-SPEnterpriseSearchServiceInstance -Identity $si
```

You will then need to validate that the Service Instance is online by running the Get-SPEnterpriseSearchServiceInstance cmdlet. When running the following cmdlet and replacing LSSPSR01 with your server name, the status should be 'Online.'

```
Get-SPEnterpriseSearchServiceInstance | ?{$_.Server -match "LSSPSR01"}
```

We then need to create a new variable, which will be a clone of the current Active Topology in our Search Service Application. The Search Service Application can have multiple topologies; however, only one of them can be active. When modifying our topology, we will first create a clone of the active one, and after we specify its properties, we will set it to Active.

```
$clone = $sa.ActiveTopology.Clone()
```

We can then decide what components we want to enable on our first server. Here are the cmdlets for each Search Service Application Component:

- Admin:New-SPEnterpriseSearchAdminComponent
- Crawl:New-SPEnterpriseSearchCrawlComponent
- Content Processing:New-SPEnterpriseSearchContentProcessingComponent
- Index: New-SPEnterpriseSearchIndexComponent
- Query: New-SPEnterpriseSearchQueryProcessingComponent
- Analytics: New-SPEnterpriseSearchAnalyticsProcessingComponent

For all the components, we will need to give a SearchTopology parameter, which specifies the search topology we want to add this component to; in our case, it will be the search topology that is currently in the $clone variable. We also need to give it a Search Instance, specifying on what server we want to enable this Search Component. In our case, we will specify the $SI variable in which we saved the Search Service Instance of server LSSPSR01. To add all the components on Search Server LSSPSR01, we would run the following PowerShell code.

```
New-SPEnterpriseSearchAdminComponent -SearchTopology $clone -SearchServiceInstance $si
New-SPEnterpriseSearchContentProcessingComponent -SearchTopology $clone
-SearchServiceInstance $si
New-SPEnterpriseSearchAnalyticsProcessingComponent -SearchTopology $clone
-SearchServiceInstance $si
New-SPEnterpriseSearchCrawlComponent -SearchTopology $clone -SearchServiceInstance $si
New-SPEnterpriseSearchIndexComponent -SearchTopology $clone -SearchServiceInstance $si
-IndexPartition 0
New-SPEnterpriseSearchQueryProcessingComponent -SearchTopology $clone -SearchServiceInstance
$si
```

Note that by default, the Index location is on the C drive at C:\Program Files\Microsoft Office Servers\16.0\Data\Office Server\Applications. This may impact performance as Search can have a significant Disk I/O requirement. An additional impact may be the size of the index, which has the potential to cause the disk to run out of available space. In order to create your index file on a different drive, you need to specify the RootDirectory parameter to the New-SPEnterpriseSearchIndexComponent cmdlet, like we will do in the following. The folder must be empty as the cmdlet will fail otherwise.

```
New-SPEnterpriseSearchIndexComponent -SearchTopology $clone -SearchServiceInstance $si
-IndexPartition 0 -RootDirectory F:\SearchIndex\0
```

We have added all the Search components on our first Search Server, so now it's time to add them on our second Search Server. The first thing we need to do is get the Search Service Instance of the second server, and save it into a variable called $si2.

```
$si2 = Get-SPEnterpriseSearchServiceInstance | ?{$_.Server -match "LSSPSRO2"}
```

■ **Note**   If the server is running the Custom Role, you will need to start the Search Service Instance as we learned earlier in this section.

We will then add a new search component of each type on the second search server as well.

```
New-SPEnterpriseSearchAdminComponent -SearchTopology $clone -SearchServiceInstance $si2
New-SPEnterpriseSearchAnalyticsProcessingComponent -SearchTopology $clone
-SearchServiceInstance $si2
New-SPEnterpriseSearchContentProcessingComponent -SearchTopology $clone
-SearchServiceInstance $si2
New-SPEnterpriseSearchCrawlComponent -SearchTopology $clone -SearchServiceInstance $si2
New-SPEnterpriseSearchIndexComponent -SearchTopology $clone -SearchServiceInstance $si2
-IndexPartition 0 -RootDirectory F:\SearchIndex\0
New-SPEnterpriseSearchQueryProcessingComponent -SearchTopology $clone -SearchServiceInstance
$si2
```

Lastly, we need to set the $clone topology, as the active topology in order to see the results in our Search Service Application. This is done with the following PowerShell cmdlet.

```
$clone.Activate()
```

After the clone finishes activating, when navigating to the Search Administration page the topology will show all components on both servers with a green checkbox, meaning they are healthy as seen in Figure 6-6.

Search Application Topology

Server Name	Admin	Crawler	Content Processing	Analytics Processing	Query Processing	Index Partition 0
LSSPSRO1	✓	✓	✓	✓	✓	✓
LSSPSRO2	✓	✓	✓	✓	✓	✓

Figure 6-6. *Search Service Application Topology*

As your search topology changes with your usage of the environment, the Search Service Application keeps a history of those topologies as Inactive. You can view them by running the following PowerShell cmdlet:

```
Get-SPEnterpriseSearchTopology -SearchApplication $sa
```

And as seen in Figure 6-7, our current Service Application has two topologies.

This can cause confusion when trying to manage the Search Service application later on, so we can run the following PowerShell cmdlet that will loop through all the existing topologies, and will delete all the inactive ones.

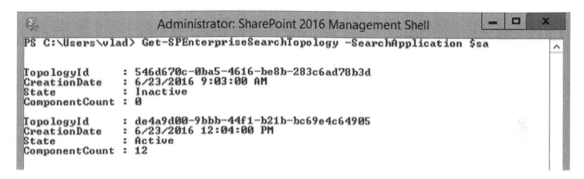

Figure 6-7. *Multiple Search Topologies in our Search Service Application*

```
foreach($topo in (Get-SPEnterpriseSearchTopology -SearchApplication $sa |
?{$_.State -eq "Inactive"}))
{
Remove-SPEnterpriseSearchTopology -Identity $topo -Confirm:$false
}
```

When modifying a topology that already has items in the index, we need to be a bit more careful. To move your index component to another server, you first need to add the second index component to your topology, wait for the index to be replicated to the new server, and then remove the old index component. To remove a component of the Search Service Application topology, we first need to get the active topology and create a clone by using the New-SPEnterpriseSearchTopology cmdlet. The following is an example of the cmdlets.

```
$sa = Get-SPEnterpriseSearchServiceApplication
$active = Get-SPEnterpriseSearchTopology -SearchApplication $sa -Active
$clone = New-SPEnterpriseSearchTopology -SearchApplication $sa -Clone -SearchTopology
$active
```

We then need to find out the ComponentId of the Search Component that we want to remove. To see all the Component IDs, we need to run the following cmdlet:

```
Get-SPEnterpriseSearchComponent -SearchTopology $clone
```

PowerShell will output a list of all the components, and of the components will have a ComponentId. In the following example, the IndexComponent2 running on server LSSPSR02 has the ComponentId '801d0307-e004-4f33-9eae-ade59db71afa'.

```
IndexPartitionOrdinal : 0
RootDirectory         :
ComponentId           : 801d0307-e004-4f33-9eae-ade59db71afa
TopologyId            : ffbc7d22-fd50-4a07-bbd2-05dbc98b04b0
ServerId              : c8309775-dcf3-44ea-8598-8185139eb90b
Name                  : IndexComponent2
ServerName            : LSSPSR02
ExperimentalComponent : False
```

Now that we know the ID, we can run the Remove-SPEnterpriseSearchComponent cmdlet and then activate our new topology. Remove the component that we targeted previously, we would run the following PowerShell cmdlets:

```
Remove-SPEnterpriseSearchComponent -Identity '801d0307-e004-4f33-9eae-ade59db71afa'
-SearchTopology $clone
```

$clone.Activate() The Index Component from server LSSPSR02 will then be removed from the topology. You can then run the PowerShell cmdlets we saw earlier in this chapter to clean up the inactive Search Topologies.

To further scale out your Search Service Application, you might also want to add extra Crawl or Link databases. If we want to add another Crawl Database, we can use the New-SPEnterpriseSearchCrawlDataba se cmdlet, and give it the Search Application and name for the new database.

```
New-SPEnterpriseSearchCrawlDatabase -SearchApplication $sa -DatabaseName SearchDB_
CrawlStore_2
```

We could also add extra Link databases using theNew-SPEnterpriseSearchLinksDatabase cmdlet, and giving the same set of parameters as we did for the crawl database.

```
New-SPEnterpriseSearchLinksDatabase -SearchApplication $sa -Da
tabaseName  SearchDB_LinksStore_2
```

Those databases will then appear on the on the Search Administration page on Central Administration, under the topology as seen in Figure 6-8.

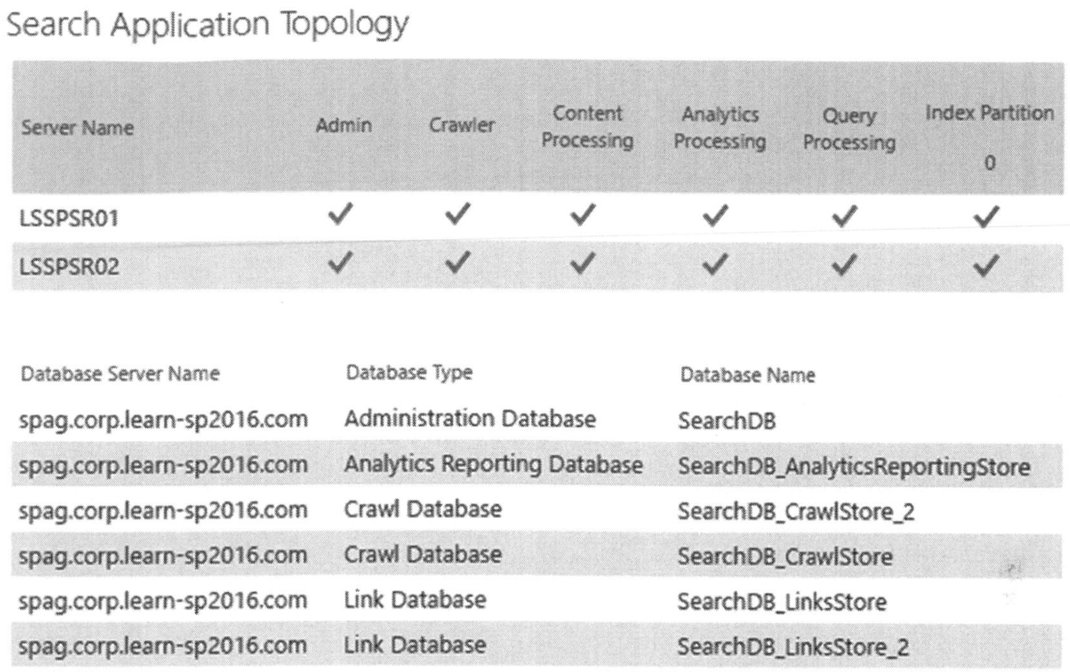

Search Application Topology

Server Name	Admin	Crawler	Content Processing	Analytics Processing	Query Processing	Index Partition 0
LSSPSR01	✓	✓	✓	✓	✓	✓
LSSPSR02	✓	✓	✓	✓	✓	✓

Database Server Name	Database Type	Database Name
spag.corp.learn-sp2016.com	Administration Database	SearchDB
spag.corp.learn-sp2016.com	Analytics Reporting Database	SearchDB_AnalyticsReportingStore
spag.corp.learn-sp2016.com	Crawl Database	SearchDB_CrawlStore_2
spag.corp.learn-sp2016.com	Crawl Database	SearchDB_CrawlStore
spag.corp.learn-sp2016.com	Link Database	SearchDB_LinksStore
spag.corp.learn-sp2016.com	Link Database	SearchDB_LinksStore_2

Figure 6-8. Multiple databases in our Search Service Topology

With our topology and databases all created, it's now time to configure the Search Service Application Settings.

Configuring Search Settings

The possibilities to customize your Search Service Application to your needs are endless. In this section we will focus on the settings that you need to do when first creating your Search Service Application.

Configuring the Default Content Access Account

The first thing you need to do after creating your Search Service Application is to configure your Search default content access account. This is the service account that the Crawl Component will use to access SharePoint content. This crawl account will have read access to all your SharePoint Web Applications, so it is important to keep the credentials in a safe location. By default, when creating the Search Service Application, SharePoint will set the default content access account to the service that runs the SharePoint Search Windows Service. In order to change it, simply click the username currently in the Default Content Access account row, as seen in Figure 6-9. A window will open prompting for the username and password of this account.

System Status

Administrative status	Running
Crawler background activity	None
Recent crawl rate	0.00 items per second
Searchable items	0
Recent query rate	0.00 queries per minute
Default content access account	CORP\s-svc
Contact e-mail address for crawls	sharepoint@learn-sp2016.com
Proxy server for crawling and federation	None

Figure 6-9. *Change Default Content Access Account*

The default content access account can also be configured via PowerShell with the following cmdlet.

```
$sa = Get-SPEnterpriseSearchServiceApplication
$content = New-Object Microsoft.Office.Server.Search.Administration.Content($sa)
$content.SetDefaultGatheringAccount("CORP\s-crawl", (ConvertTo-SecureString "<Password>"
-AsPlainText -Force))
```

Where corp\s-crawl is the account you want to use as default content access account. Since this account has read access to all the SharePoint content, we recommend having a dedicated service account for this purpose stated in Chapter 2.

As mentioned previously, the account will be added in the User Policy of the Web Application with Full Read permissions as seen in Figure 6-10.

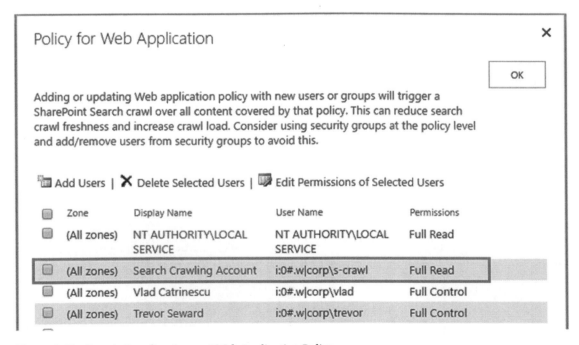

Figure 6-10. *Search Crawling Account Web Application Policy*

The default content access account must also have the "Retrieve People Data for Search Crawlers" right on the User Profile Service Application, as seen in Figure 6-11. To get to the "Administrators for User Profile Service Application" page, from the Manage Service Applications page, select the User Profile Service Application, and click the Administrators button in the ribbon. This will allow the crawl account to crawl the user profiles and return this information in search.

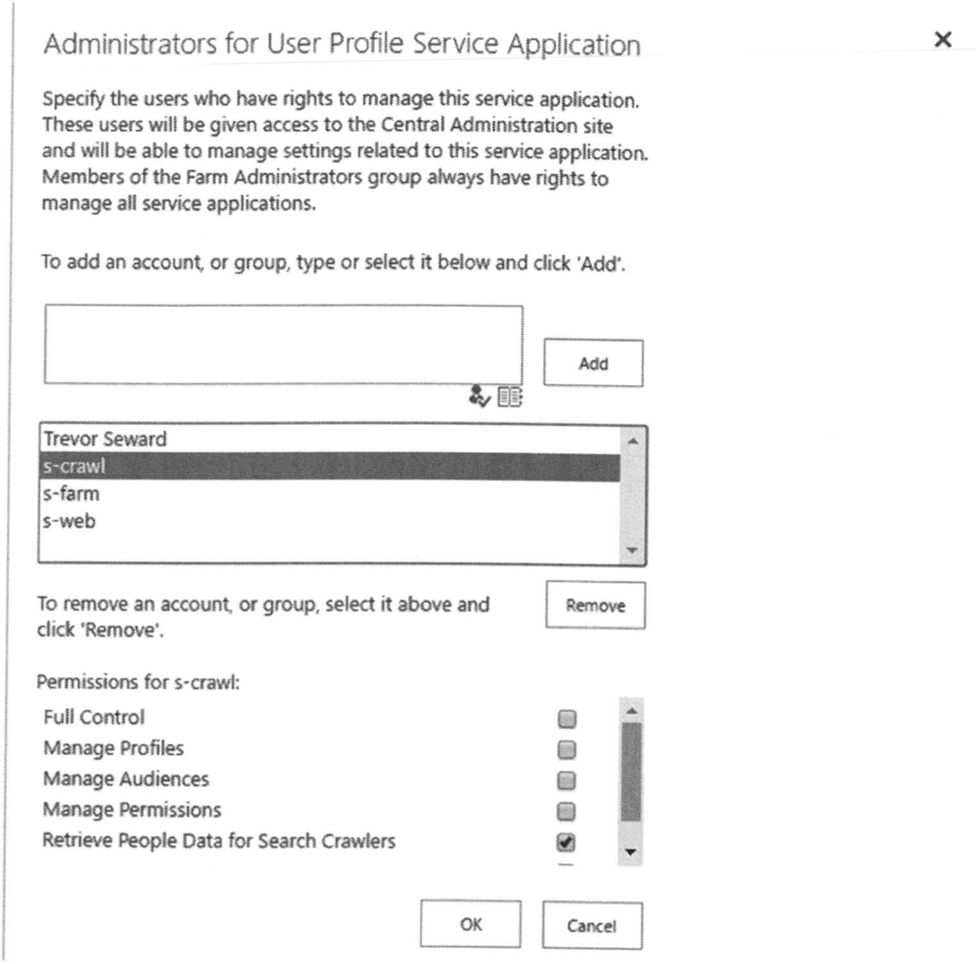

Figure 6-11. *Retrieve People Data for Search Crawlers permissions*

With the default content access account configured, it's now time to create our Content Sources.

Creating Content Sources

The next step to get our Search Service Application up and running is to create our content sources. When creating a Search Service Application, SharePoint creates a content source called *Local SharePoint sites* which contains all the Web Applications in our farm as seen in Figure 6-12.

Search Service Application: Edit Content Source

Use this page to edit a content source.

* Indicates a required field

Name

Type a name to describe this content source.

Name: *

Local SharePoint sites

Content Source Details

This shows the current status of the Content Source.

Content Source Type:	SharePoint Sites
Current Status:	Idle
Continuous Crawl Status:	
Last crawl type:	N/A
Last crawl began:	N/A
Last crawl duration:	N/A
Last crawl completed:	N/A

View Crawl History

Start Addresses

Type the URLs from which the search system should start crawling.

Type start addresses below (one per line): *

https://lsspap01
https://sharepoint.learn-sp2016.com
https://sharepoint-my.learn-sp2016.com

Figure 6-12. *Local SharePoint Sites Content Source*

You might want to split those Web Applications into different Content Sources if you want to set different crawl schedules, or create custom results based on only one Web Application. To create a Content Source, navigate to the Search Administration Page in the Central Administration, and afterward in the Content Sources settings page. From the Manage Content Sources page, click the "New Content Source" page seen in Figure 6-13.

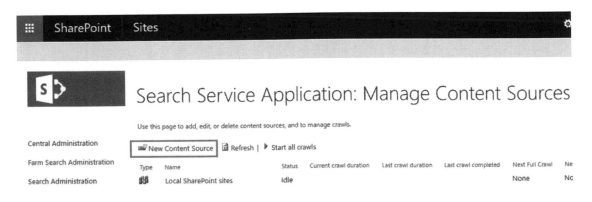

Figure 6-13. *Manage Content Sources page*

A window will open in which you can specify all the settings for the content source. First you will need to enter a name, in our example seen in Figure 6-14, the name is "SharePoint MySites." Next, we need to select what type of content is included in this Content Source. Depending on the choice of content, the available configurations later in the process will be different. Since the type of item we want to crawl in this Content Source is a SharePoint site, we have selected "SharePoint Sites."

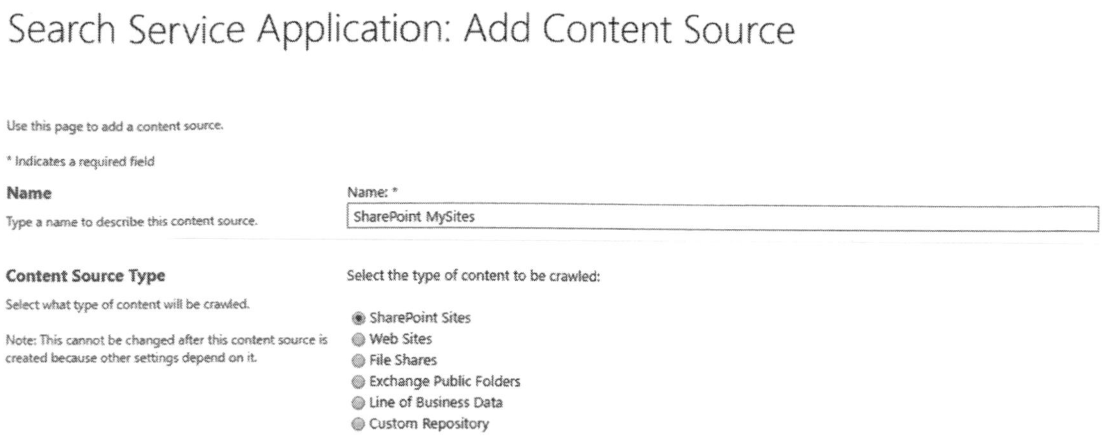

Search Service Application: Add Content Source

Use this page to add a content source.

* Indicates a required field

Name

Type a name to describe this content source.

Name: *

SharePoint MySites

Content Source Type

Select what type of content will be crawled.

Note: This cannot be changed after this content source is created because other settings depend on it.

Select the type of content to be crawled:

- ● SharePoint Sites
- ○ Web Sites
- ○ File Shares
- ○ Exchange Public Folders
- ○ Line of Business Data
- ○ Custom Repository

Figure 6-14. *Add a Content Source*

The content you enter in the Start Address will depend on the crawl Settings you select in the following checkbox. The easiest to manage solution, is to enter the root of the Web Application in the Start Address, and select to "Crawl everything under the hostname for each start address" as we did in Figure 6-15. This way, SharePoint will crawl all the Site Collections in that Web Application, and as new Site Collections get added, they will get automatically included in this content source. If you are using Host Named Site Collections, you only need to include the root Site Collection of the Web Application and SharePoint will be able to identify the other Site Collections in the same Web Applications. We will learn more about Host Named Site Collections in Chapter 13.

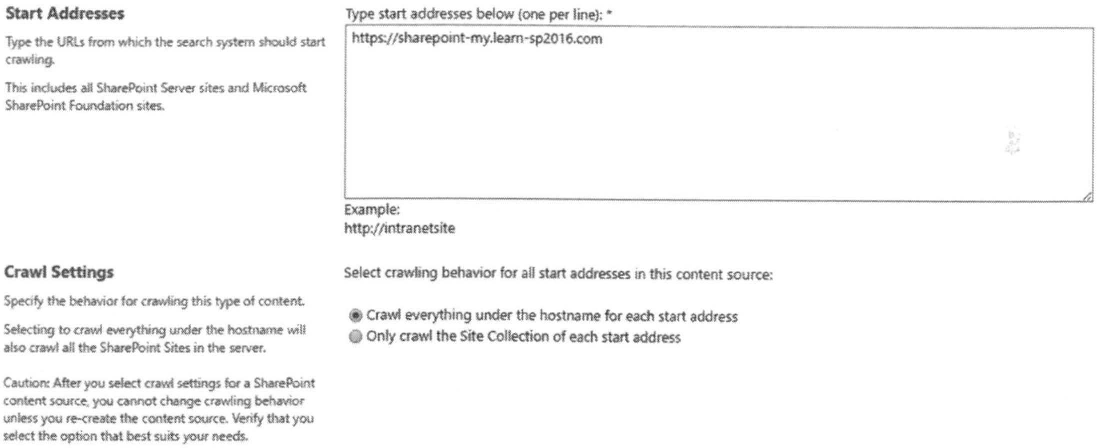

Start Addresses

Type the URLs from which the search system should start crawling.

This includes all SharePoint Server sites and Microsoft SharePoint Foundation sites.

Type start addresses below (one per line): *

https://sharepoint-my.learn-sp2016.com

Example:
http://intranetsite

Crawl Settings

Specify the behavior for crawling this type of content.

Selecting to crawl everything under the hostname will also crawl all the SharePoint Sites in the server.

Caution: After you select crawl settings for a SharePoint content source, you cannot change crawling behavior unless you re-create the content source. Verify that you select the option that best suits your needs.

Select crawling behavior for all start addresses in this content source:

- ● Crawl everything under the hostname for each start address
- ○ Only crawl the Site Collection of each start address

Figure 6-15. *Content Source Start Addresses and Crawl Settings*

If you want to have different Crawl Schedules between Site Collections in the same Web Application, you need to select "Only crawl the Site Collection of each start address" in the Crawl Settings, and manually enter each Site Collection URL in the Start Addresses.

Lastly, you will have the options to select your crawl schedule for this content source. Your crawl schedule will depend on your business requirements as well as your search capabilities. There are two different types of schedule for your content. The first one which has been there for the last few SharePoint versions is the Incremental and Full Crawl. The second type of crawl schedule is the Continuous Crawl, which was introduced in SharePoint Server 2013. Let's take a look at the different types of crawls:

- **Full Crawl**

  The Full Crawl is a crawl that will crawl the entire content of your content source whether the item already exists in the index or not. The Full Crawl will not only crawl content, but also process any changes in Managed Properties, iFilters, as well as the Content Enrichment Web Service, which is a Search Feature developers can use to customize SharePoint Search. Because the Full Crawl crawls all the content of a content source, it takes longer to finish, and it's usually run less often than the Incremental Crawl. A Full Crawl might never be scheduled, and only ran manually to process changes to the preceding customizations. You can minimize the number of times a Full Crawl is needed by using the built-in "Reindex Site" functionality, available in the Site Settings page of every site, under *Search and Offline Availability*. This will run a full crawl only on that specific site, and not on your whole content source, and can be useful when simply needing to update your Managed Properties or mapping of Crawled Properties.

- **Incremental Crawl**

  The Incremental Crawl is a crawl that will only index the contents that have been modified since the last time a crawl was done. The length of this crawl will directly depend on how many items were modified since you last did a crawl, and is usually a lot shorter in duration than a full crawl. This crawl is usually scheduled multiple times during a day, and can also be manually started.

- **Continuous Crawl**

  Continuous Crawl is a new type of crawl implemented since SharePoint Server 2013 that aims to keep the content as fresh as possible. Similar to the Incremental Crawl, the Continuous Crawl will only crawl items that have changed since the last crawl is finished. The main difference between Continuous Crawl and Incremental Crawl is that in Continuous Crawl mode, a crawl will start every 15 minutes, even if the last Crawl did not finish. If you want, you could customize the 15-minute crawl interval by running the following PowerShell cmdlet:

```
$sa = Get-SPEnterpriseSearchServiceApplication
$sa.SetProperty("ContinuousCrawlInterval",<TimeInMinutes>)
```

Where <TimeInMinutes> is the interval, in minutes, of how often crawls should be started. Be aware that Continuous Crawl, even with the default 15-minute delay can place a very big load on your SharePoint Infrastructure. Continuous Crawl is often used for search-based sites, where the activity of the site is highly dependent on a fresh index.

For the Content Source we created in this example, we have selected to use Continious Crawl as seen in Figure 6-16.

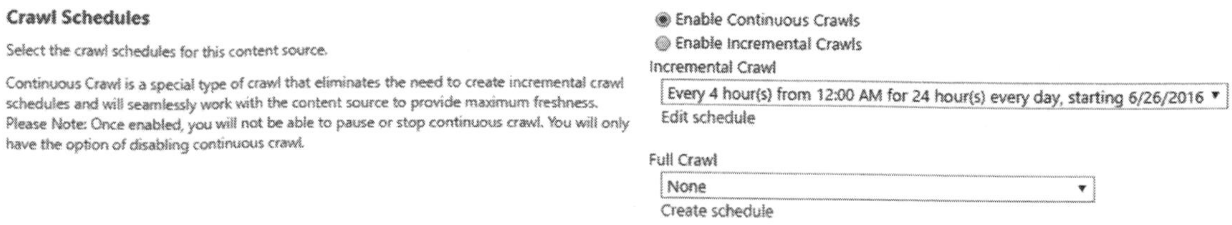

Crawl Schedules

Select the crawl schedules for this content source.

Continuous Crawl is a special type of crawl that eliminates the need to create incremental crawl schedules and will seamlessly work with the content source to provide maximum freshness. Please Note: Once enabled, you will not be able to pause or stop continuous crawl. You will only have the option of disabling continuous crawl.

⦿ Enable Continuous Crawls
⦾ Enable Incremental Crawls
Incremental Crawl

> Every 4 hour(s) from 12:00 AM for 24 hour(s) every day, starting 6/26/2016 ▾

Edit schedule

Full Crawl

> None ▾

Create schedule

Figure 6-16. *Crawl Schedules*

To create a schedule for the Full Crawl, click the Create Schedule link under the dropbox, and a pop-up window will open allowing you to create a new schedule. As an example, we have created a schedule in Figure 6-17, where the full crawl will happen every Saturday at 2 AM.

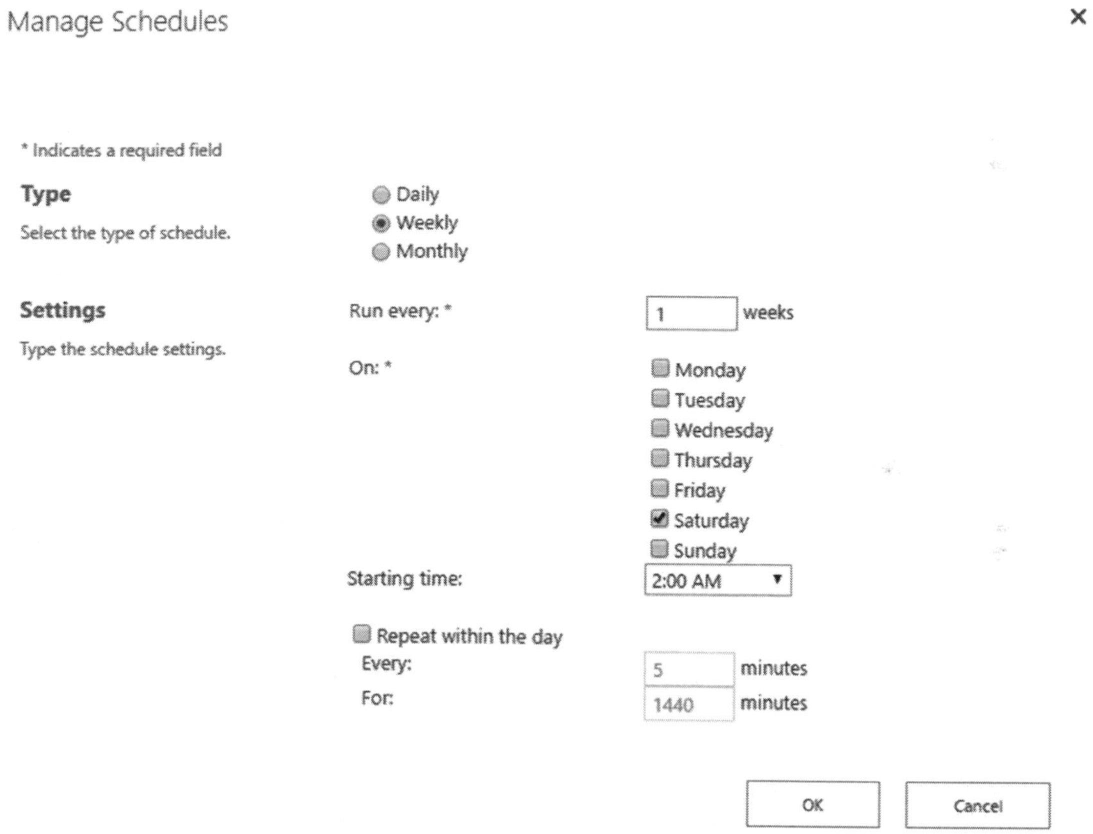

Manage Schedules   ✕

* Indicates a required field

Type

Select the type of schedule.

⦾ Daily
⦿ Weekly
⦾ Monthly

Settings

Type the schedule settings.

Run every: *   `1` weeks

On: *
☐ Monday
☐ Tuesday
☐ Wednesday
☐ Thursday
☐ Friday
☑ Saturday
☐ Sunday

Starting time: `2:00 AM ▾`

☐ Repeat within the day
Every: `5` minutes
For: `1440` minutes

| OK | Cancel |

Figure 6-17. *Full Crawl Schedule*

While most Full Crawls only run very rarely, Incremental crawls probably run multiple times every day. To set a crawl schedule to repeat during the day, you need to check the "Repeat within the day" checkbox. You will then need to enter how often the crawl must be repeated and for how long. In the example in Figure 6-18, we start a crawl every 30 minutes, for 1440 minutes (24h). Therefore, every day the crawl will run every 30 minutes.

Figure 6-18. Incremental Schedule every 30 minutes

Some companies that are located on only one time zone might only want the incremental crawls to happen during business hours, since there is usually no activity during off-hours. By changing the Start time and duration, you could set your Incremental Crawls to run every 30 minutes, from 6 AM to 6 PM, as seen in Figure 6-19. By setting the *For* field at 720 minutes (12 hours), no crawl will start after 6 PM, and the next incremental crawl will start at 6 AM the following day.

Manage Schedules   ✕

* Indicates a required field

Type   ⦿ Daily
Select the type of schedule.   ○ Weekly
                                  ○ Monthly

Settings   Run every: *   [1   ] days
Type the schedule settings.
                                  Starting time: [6:00 AM   ▾]

                                  ☑ Repeat within the day
                                  Every: [30   ] minutes
                                  For: [720   ] minutes

                                            [OK   ]   [Cancel   ]

Figure 6-19. *Incremental Crawl Schedule between 6 AM and 6 PM*

In our example in Figure 6-20, we have chosen to enable continuous crawl, and do a full crawl every Saturday, starting at 1 AM.

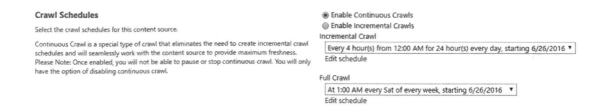

Figure 6-20. *Crawl Schedule*

After the crawl schedule is configured, simply press on OK and your new Content Source will be created. If you chose to enable Continuous Crawl, the crawl will start right away, and if you chose Incremental & Full, the crawl will start in the next scheduled period. You can always manually start the crawl from the Content Source menu as seen in Figure 6-21.

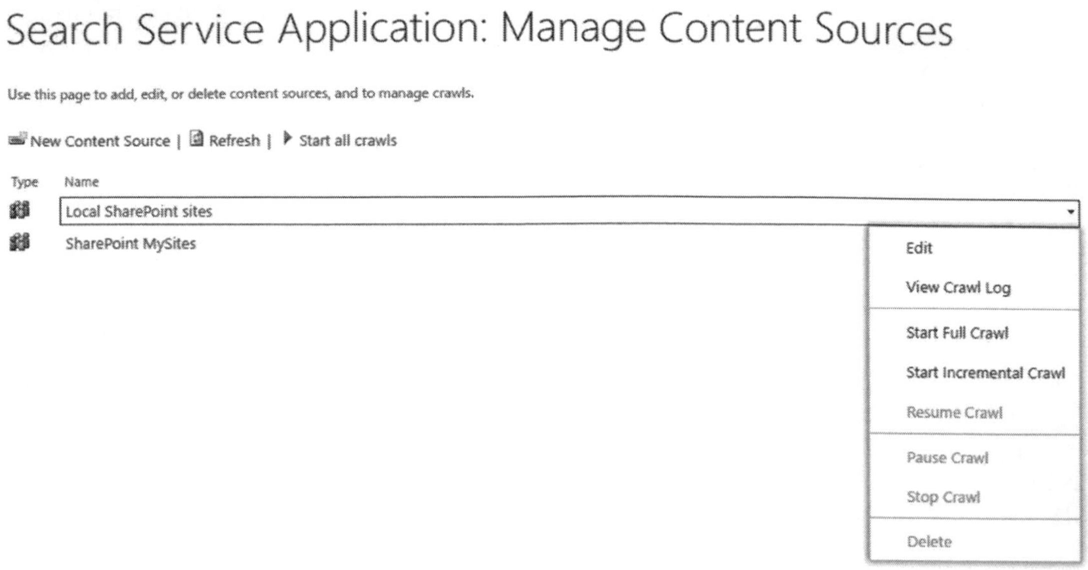

Search Service Application: Manage Content Sources

Use this page to add, edit, or delete content sources, and to manage crawls.

Figure 6-21. *Content Source Menu*

If Continuous Crawl is enabled, the menu will only allow you to disable Continuous crawl as seen in Figure 6-22. You will not be able to manually trigger incremental or full crawls.

Figure 6-22. *Content Source Menu with Continuous Crawl enabled*

Another popular type of content source you might want to create is a content source to crawl the User Profiles of users, that way important information such as names, departments, skills, and past projects will show up in the search. We have already given permission to the crawl account on the User Profile Service; we now need to create a content source to crawl People data. The content source type will still be "SharePoint Sites" as the previous example; however, what is a bit different is the Start Address we have to enter. The Start Address for People Search needs to be under the following format:

```
sps3://<MySites URL>
```

Where <MySites URL> is the URL of your MySites host. If your MySites host Web Application runs on HTTPS, you will need to start it with *sps3s* instead of *sps3* as seen in the following.

```
sps3s://<MySites URL>
```

In both cases, you do not have to enter the http:// or https:// in front of the host name.

In the environment for this book, we would enter `sps3s://sharepoint-my.learn-sp2016.com` as our Start Address as seen in Figure 6-23.

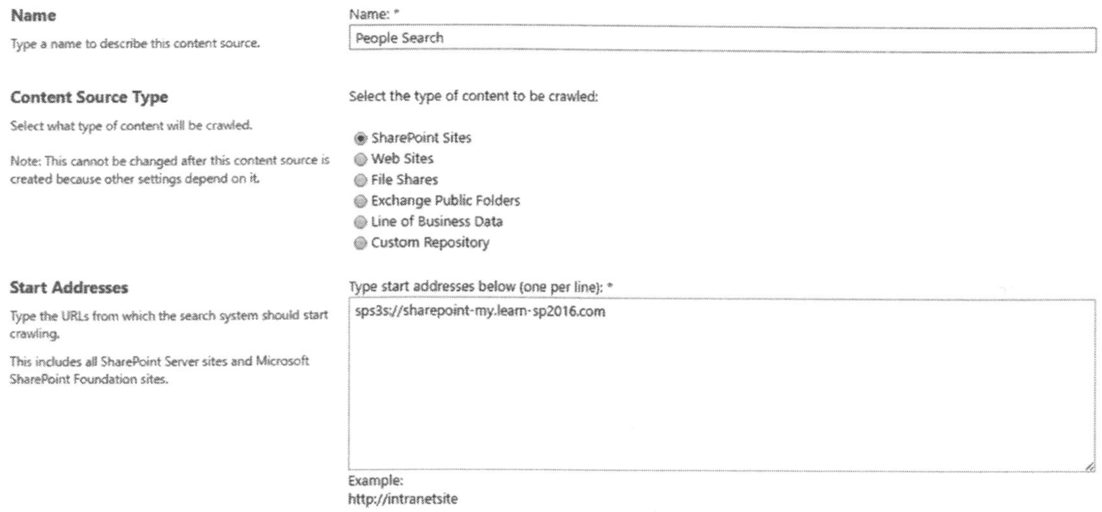

Name
Type a name to describe this content source.

Name: *
People Search

Content Source Type
Select what type of content will be crawled.

Note: This cannot be changed after this content source is created because other settings depend on it.

Select the type of content to be crawled:

- ◉ SharePoint Sites
- ○ Web Sites
- ○ File Shares
- ○ Exchange Public Folders
- ○ Line of Business Data
- ○ Custom Repository

Start Addresses
Type the URLs from which the search system should start crawling.

This includes all SharePoint Server sites and Microsoft SharePoint Foundation sites.

Type start addresses below (one per line): *

sps3s://sharepoint-my.learn-sp2016.com

Example:
http://intranetsite

Figure 6-23. Configuring People Search

With our content sources created, it's recommended to create an Enterprise Search Center where users can search across the whole SharePoint farm.

SharePoint Security and Search Performance

SharePoint Security and Search are highly connected because of the fact that SharePoint search results are security trimmed. This means that users will only see search results that they are allowed to access, and will not see any search results that they do not have permissions to. Whenever permissions change on an item, the SharePoint search engine will have to perform a crawl of that item in order to process the new permissions and calculate the Access Control List (ACL) of that item.

There are two major strategies of assigning permissions to a SharePoint site. The first one is by adding each user individually in a SharePoint group when they need access, and the second way is giving access to an Active Directory Security Group directly to the site, or placing it in a SharePoint group that has permissions on the site.

The big difference in search performance is that, each time you add a user directly to a SharePoint group, the crawler will have to do a security crawl on all the items that group has access to in order to recalculate the ACL of the site.

The first time you add an Active Directory group to a SharePoint Site, the behavior will be the same; however, when adding other users to that Active Directory group, SharePoint will not have to recalculate the ACL, since no users have been added directly in the SharePoint site. By not having to recrawl every item to recalculate the ACL, your crawls will take shorter and increase index freshness.

Lastly, when changing User Polices at the Web Application level, all the content in that Web Application will have to be recrawled for the preceding reasons. This is indicated at the top of the Policy for Web Application page seen in Figure 6-24.

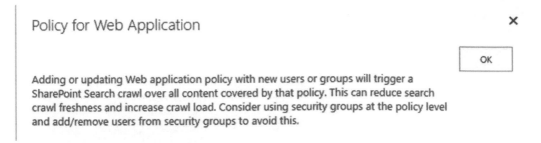

Figure 6-24. *Updating Web Application Policy will trigger a SharePoint Search Crawl*

Selecting the Search Center

Before selecting an Enterprise Search Center, you first need to create a Site Collection with the template "Enterprise Search Center," or if you create it by PowerShell, the SRCHCEN#0 template. Once that Site Collection is created, navigate to the Search Service Application Admin page and from the System Status click "Set a Search Center URL" as seen in Figure 6-25.

System Status

Administrative status	Running
Crawler background activity	None
Recent crawl rate	0.03 items per second
Searchable items	6,120
Recent query rate	0.00 queries per minute
Default content access account	CORP\s-crawl
Contact e-mail address for crawls	sharepoint@learn-sp2016.com
Proxy server for crawling and federation	None
Search alerts status	On Disable
Query logging	On Disable
Global Search Center URL	Set a Search Center URL

Figure 6-25. *Set a Search Center URL link*

A pop-up window will open similar to Figure 6-26, in which you have to enter the URL of your Enterprise Search Center Site collection that you created earlier, and add /pages at the end.

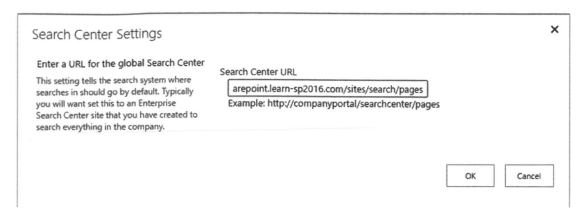

Figure 6-26. *Search Center URL*

You can also set the search center URL by using PowerShell and running the following cmdlet.

```
$ssa = Get-SPEnterpriseSearchServiceApplication
$ssa.SearchCenterUrl = "<Search Center URL>/pages"
$ssa.Update()
```

Where "`<Search Center URL>`" is the URL to your Site Collection using the Enterprise Search Center template.

With the Search Service Application configured, let's look at how to view what was crawled, and if there were any errors while crawling content.

Analyzing Crawl Logs

The Search Service Application displays the Crawl Logs directly in the Central Administration, allowing us to see if the Search is able to successfully crawl our content sources, and any errors that might stop content from getting to the index. This will be useful not only when setting up your Search Service Application the first time, but also as a check during regular maintenance. The Crawl logs can be accessed from the Search Administration page left navigation menu, in the Diagnostics category as seen in Figure 6-27.

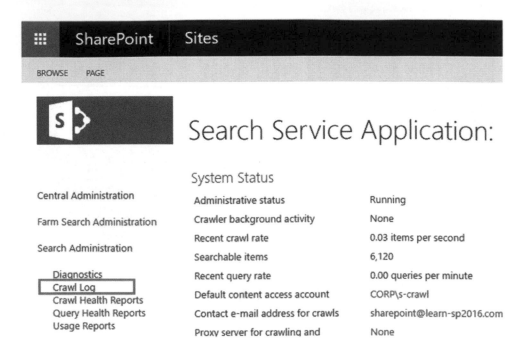

Figure 6-27. *Accessing the Crawl Log in the Search Administration Page*

The Crawl Log settings page default view seen in Figure 6-28 gives us a high-level overview of our Content Sources and the Successes and Warnings. The Successes are the number of items that have been successfully crawled, and moved to the index, while Warnings are items that could not be crawled, or were crawled, but due to certain reasons not placed in the index. The Error column includes how many individual items could not be placed in the index, while the Top Level Error column is only for critical errors that stop the crawl component from reaching an entire Content Source.

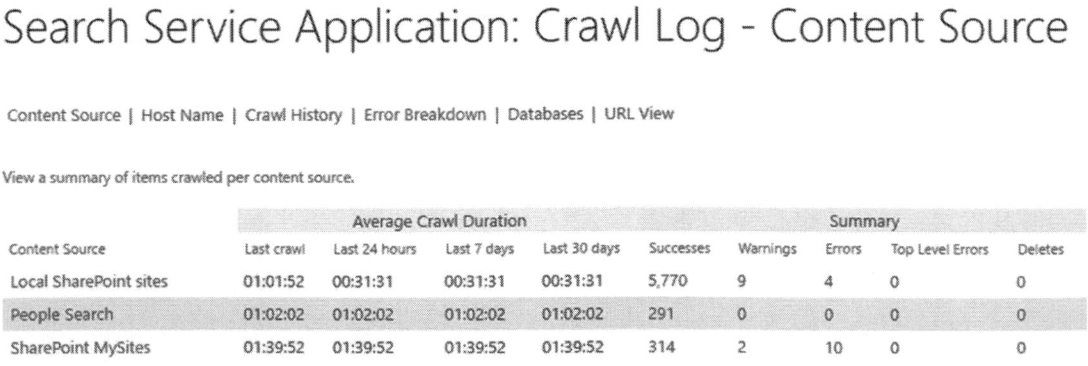

Search Service Application: Crawl Log - Content Source

Content Source | Host Name | Crawl History | Error Breakdown | Databases | URL View

View a summary of items crawled per content source.

Content Source	Average Crawl Duration				Summary				
	Last crawl	Last 24 hours	Last 7 days	Last 30 days	Successes	Warnings	Errors	Top Level Errors	Deletes
Local SharePoint sites	01:01:52	00:31:31	00:31:31	00:31:31	5,770	9	4	0	0
People Search	01:02:02	01:02:02	01:02:02	01:02:02	291	0	0	0	0
SharePoint MySites	01:39:52	01:39:52	01:39:52	01:39:52	314	2	10	0	0

Figure 6-28. *Crawl Logs page*

When clicking any of the numbers, SharePoint will show the message as well as URL for the items within that category. In Figure 6-29, we can see the three errors that we have in the SharePoint MySites content type, and how many items were affected by each error. This will allow us to easily fix errors, and get items in the index on the next crawl.

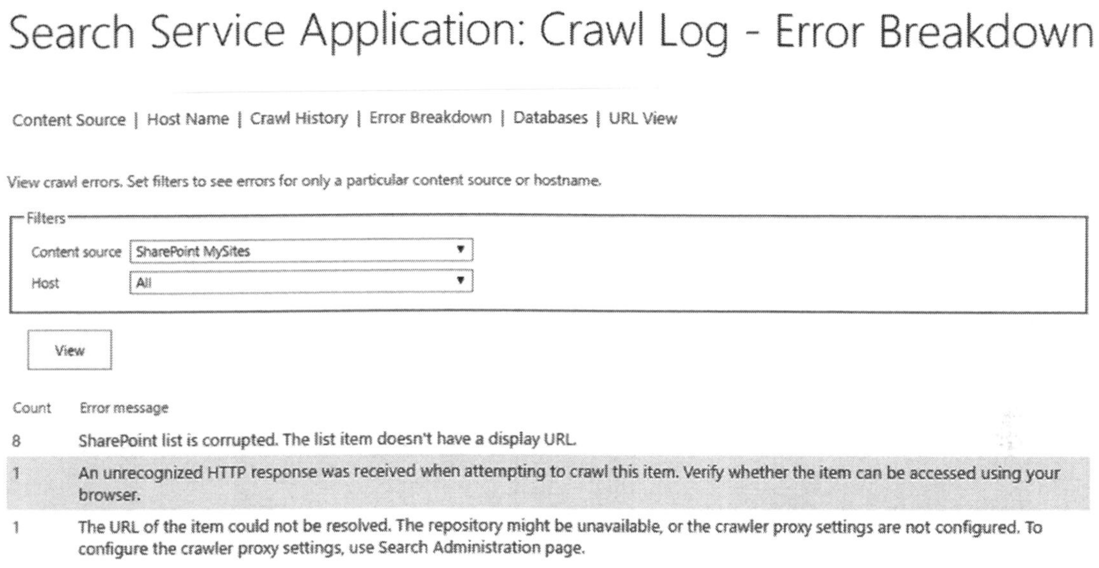

Search Service Application: Crawl Log - Error Breakdown

Content Source | Host Name | Crawl History | Error Breakdown | Databases | URL View

View crawl errors. Set filters to see errors for only a particular content source or hostname.

Filters

Content source	SharePoint MySites ▼
Host	All ▼

[View]

Count	Error message
8	SharePoint list is corrupted. The list item doesn't have a display URL.
1	An unrecognized HTTP response was received when attempting to crawl this item. Verify whether the item can be accessed using your browser.
1	The URL of the item could not be resolved. The repository might be unavailable, or the crawler proxy settings are not configured. To configure the crawler proxy settings, use Search Administration page.

Figure 6-29. *Crawl Log – Error Breakdown for the SharePoint MySites content source*

Accumulating a large number of errors over time will increase the size of your crawl database, since all those errors will be stored inside.

From the Crawl Logs page in the Central Administration, we can also search for specific items to find out if they have been crawled or not. This is useful when users report that their documents do not appear in search results, even if they uploaded them before the last crawl. To search the Crawl Logs, from the Crawl Log page, navigate to "URL View" in the top bar. From the URL View page, we can type an URL or hostname in the top bar and use wildcards to help us find the item we're looking for. Furthermore, we can use filters to only find the documents we are looking for. As you see in Figure 6-30, a Document in the library we searched for had a warning, and that could explain why it wouldn't appear in the search results.

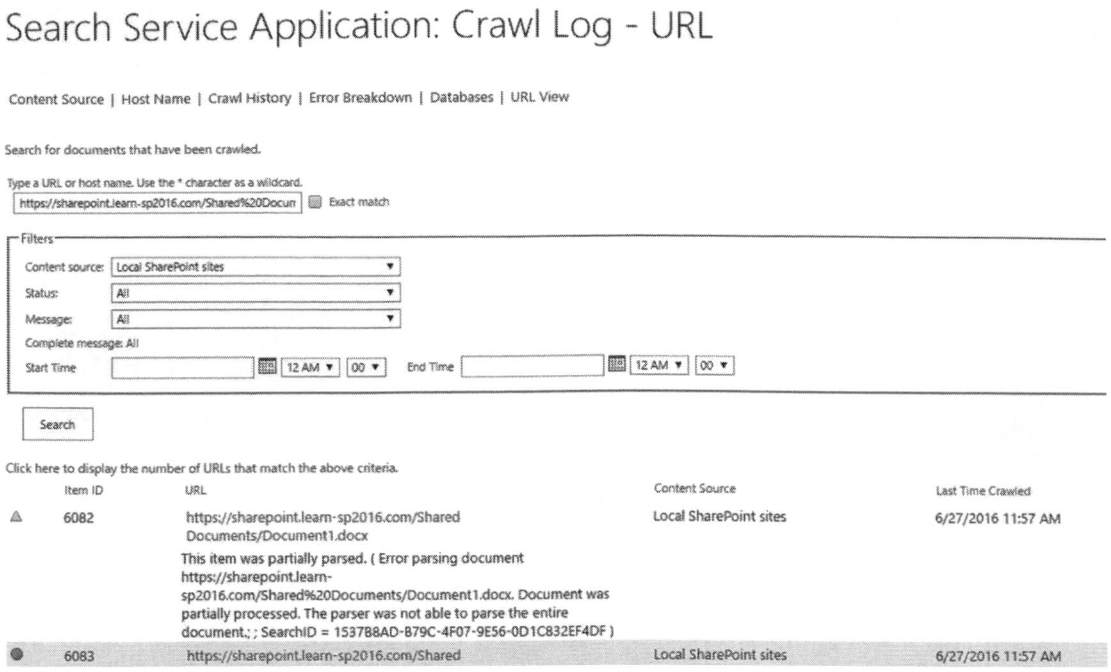

Search Service Application: Crawl Log - URL

Content Source | Host Name | Crawl History | Error Breakdown | Databases | URL View

Search for documents that have been crawled.

Type a URL or host name. Use the * character as a wildcard.

| https://sharepoint.learn-sp2016.com/Shared%20Docun | ☐ Exact match |

┌─ Filters ──
│ Content source: | Local SharePoint sites   ▼ |
│ Status: | All   ▼ |
│ Message: | All   ▼ |
│ Complete message: All
│ Start Time | | 🔲 | 12 AM ▼ | 00 ▼ | End Time | 🔲 | 12 AM ▼ | 00 ▼ |
└──

| Search |

Click here to display the number of URLs that match the above criteria.

	Item ID	URL	Content Source	Last Time Crawled
⚠	6082	https://sharepoint.learn-sp2016.com/Shared Documents/Document1.docx	Local SharePoint sites	6/27/2016 11:57 AM
		This item was partially parsed. (Error parsing document https://sharepoint.learn-sp2016.com/Shared%20Documents/Document1.docx. Document was partially processed. The parser was not able to parse the entire document.; ; SearchID = 1537B8AD-B79C-4F07-9E56-0D1C832EF4DF)		
●	6083	https://sharepoint.learn-sp2016.com/Shared	Local SharePoint sites	6/27/2016 11:57 AM

Figure 6-30. *Search Service Application Crawl Logs – URL View*

In some circumstances, to refresh our Search Results or to fix an error, we need to perform an Index Reset.

Resetting the Index

In some cases, the only way to "reset" our Search Service Application is to delete all the items in the index and recrawl all of the content sources. This is called an Index reset. To do an Index Reset, navigate to the Search Administration page, and from the left navigation menu click *Index Reset* as seen in Figure 6-31.

Search Service Application:

System Status

Central Administration	Administrative status
	Crawler background activity
Farm Search Administration	
	Recent crawl rate
Search Administration	Searchable items
Diagnostics	Recent query rate
Crawl Log	
Crawl Health Reports	Default content access account
Query Health Reports	Contact e-mail address for crawls
Usage Reports	Proxy server for crawling and federation
Crawling	Search alerts status
Content Sources	
Crawl Rules	Query logging
Server Name Mappings	Global Search Center URL
File Types	
Index Reset	
Pause/Resume	
Crawler Impact Rules	

Figure 6-31. *Index Reset Button*

After resetting the index, no search results will be available until those items have been recrawled; therefore, if you have a lot of content, or you have search-dependent sites, preferably run this during off-hours. Before resetting the index, you will have the option to disable Search Alerts, in order to not send alerts to your users because new items are added to the index. If you decide to disable Search Alerts during the recrawl, remember to manually activate them after the first Full Crawl is done.

When managing a large index, resetting the index trough the User Interface can cause it to time out. The easiest way to avoid a timeout is to do an index reset by using PowerShell. An index reset can be done with the following cmdlets:

```
$sa = Get-SPEnterpriseSearchServiceApplication
$sa.reset($true, $true)
```

Where the first $true parameter is to disable Alerts, and the second $true parameter is to ignore a timeout error.

To estimate how long the Full Crawl is going to take, you could calculate the Number of Items in your index (Searchable Items) divided by Recent Crawl Rate. While this won't be an exact measure, it's a good estimate. In Figure 6-32, we have 6141 items in our index, and a Recent Crawl Rate of 0.09 items per second.

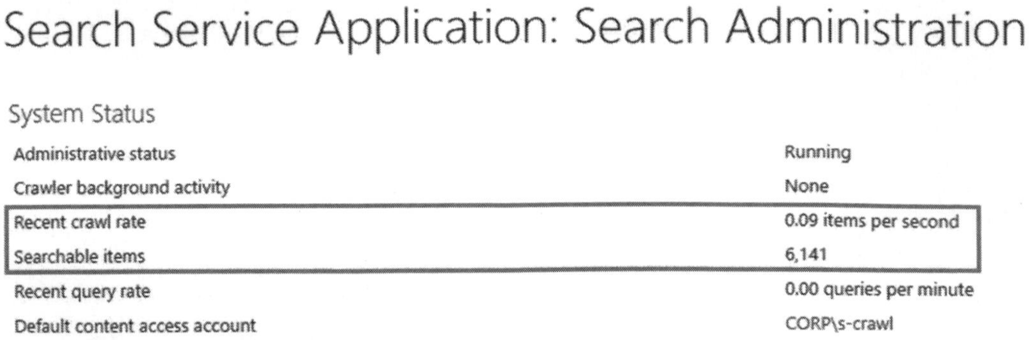

Search Service Application: Search Administration

System Status

Administrative status	Running
Crawler background activity	None
Recent crawl rate	0.09 items per second
Searchable items	6,141
Recent query rate	0.00 queries per minute
Default content access account	CORP\s-crawl

Figure 6-32. *Calculating Full Crawl Time*

Next Steps

With the Search Service Application created and our content crawled, in the next chapter we will learn how to configure the User Profile Service application.

CHAPTER 7

■ ■ ■

Configuring the User Profile Service

The User Profile Service is one of the core services in nearly all SharePoint Server deployments. This service provides information about users, OneDrive for Business, Social features, and Audiences, among other features. In this chapter, we will go through the options available for Active Directory synchronization, OneDrive for Business On-Premises setup, and Audiences configuration.

Initial Configuration

We performed an initial configuration of the User Profile Service Application in Chapter 3, where we created the User Profile Service Application and set up the MySite Host with a /personal/ wildcard Managed Path and enabled Self-Service Site Creation. We need to set up the User Profile Import from Active Directory into SharePoint. SharePoint only includes Active Directory Import (AD Import), unlike SharePoint Server 2010 and 2013, which included the User Profile Synchronization Service. AD Import has a few limitations, primarily that it is import only, which means no writing back of attributes to Active Directory, deletion of User Profiles for users who have been removed or disabled in Active Directory, and it does not import pictures. It also does not support multiforest scenarios. If any of these are a requirement, then Microsoft Identity Manager 2016 must be used, which we will discuss in further detail later in this chapter.

Unlike previous versions of SharePoint Server, the PowerShell cmdlet Add-SPProfileSyncConnection is supported to use with SharePoint Server 2016 On-Premises.

The User Profile Synchronization Service Account, in this case, CORP\s-sync, must have "Replicating Directory Changes" permission on the Active Directory domain we are synchronizing with. To grant this right, right-click the root of the domain in the Active Directory Users and Computers MMC, then proceed to start the Delegation Wizard. In the first step, add the synchronization account (CORP\s-sync), then create a Custom Task to Delegate. For the Active Directory Object Type, leave the default option of "This folder, existing objects in this folder, and creation of new objects in this folder." selected. In the last step, select the permissions named "Replicating Directory Changes," as shown in Figure 7-1. This completes the delegation process.

© Vlad Catrinescu and Trevor Seward 2016
V. Catrinescu and T. Seward, *Deploying SharePoint 2016*, DOI 10.1007/978-1-4842-1999-7_7

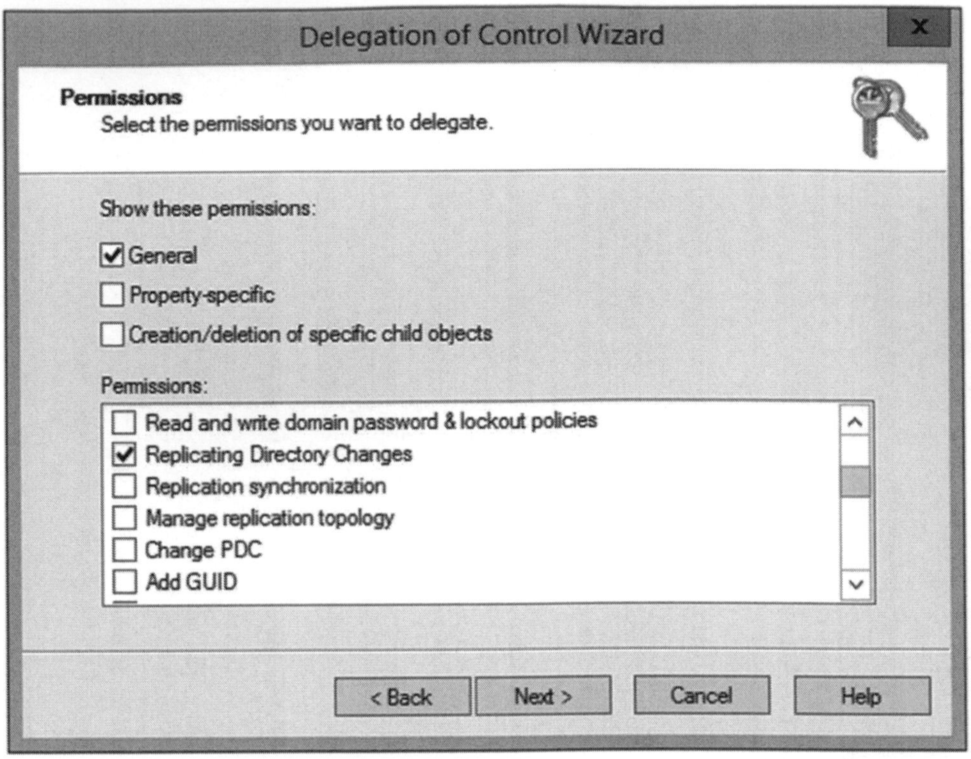

Figure 7-1. Adding the appropriate permissions in Active Directory for the synchronization account

If the NetBIOS domain name does not match the Fully Qualified Domain Name, that is, if the NetBIOS name was EXAMPLE while the Fully Qualified Domain Name was CORP.COMPANY.COM, an additional step is necessary using ADSI Edit (adsiedt.msc). While not the case for this environments domain, using ADSI Edit, connect to the Configuration Naming Context. As shown in Figure 7-2, right click the Configuration node (shown as "CN=Configuration,DC=CORP,DC=LEARN-SP2016,DC=COM"), and select Properties. From here, select the Security tab, add the synchronization account, and grant the same permissions, as shown in Figure 7-3.

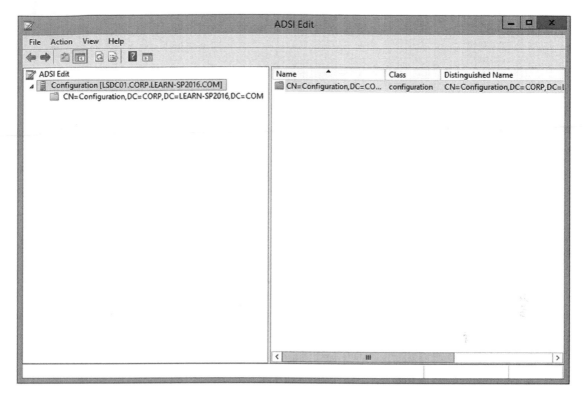

Figure 7-2. Using ADSI Edit while connected to the Configuration Naming Context

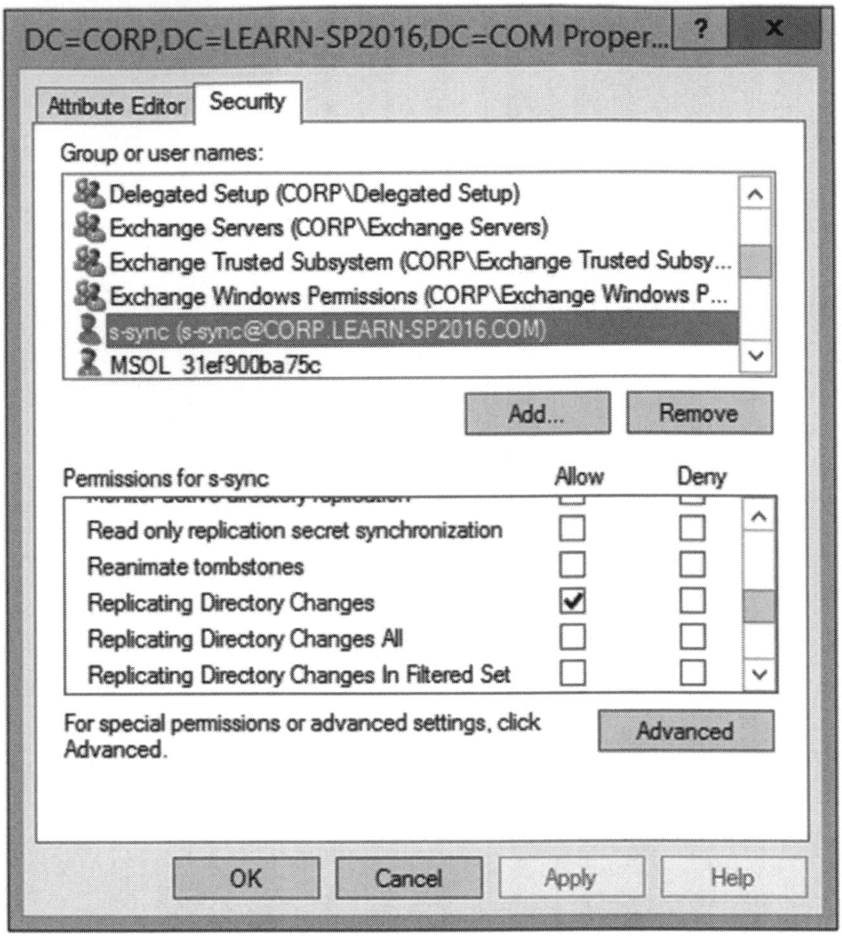

Figure 7-3. Adding the synchronization account with the "Replicating Directory Changes" permission

Once completed, we can continue creating the synchronization connection from SharePoint Central Administration.

Navigating in Central Administration to Manage Service Applications, click the User Profile Service Application previously created. Go into Configure Synchronization Connections and click Create New Connection. There should only be a single connection per Active Directory Forest. Provide a relevant Connection Name, such as the name of the Forest. You'll note the only available option for Type is now AD Import. Provide the fully qualified domain name for the root domain of the forest, and the account name in DOMAIN\Username format. Enter the password, and because we've deployed Active Directory Certificate Servers and our Domain Controller has a valid Server Authentication certificate, we will change the port number to 636 and check the Use SSL-secured connection. If the Domain Controllers do not have SSL certificates, leave the default port of 389 and Use SSL unchecked. We also do not want disabled users being imported, and will check that box as well. Add an LDAP filter if necessary; for example, to filter out Computer Objects, the filter would be as follows.

```
(!objectClass=computer)
```

The connection configuration is complete, as shown in Figure 7-4.

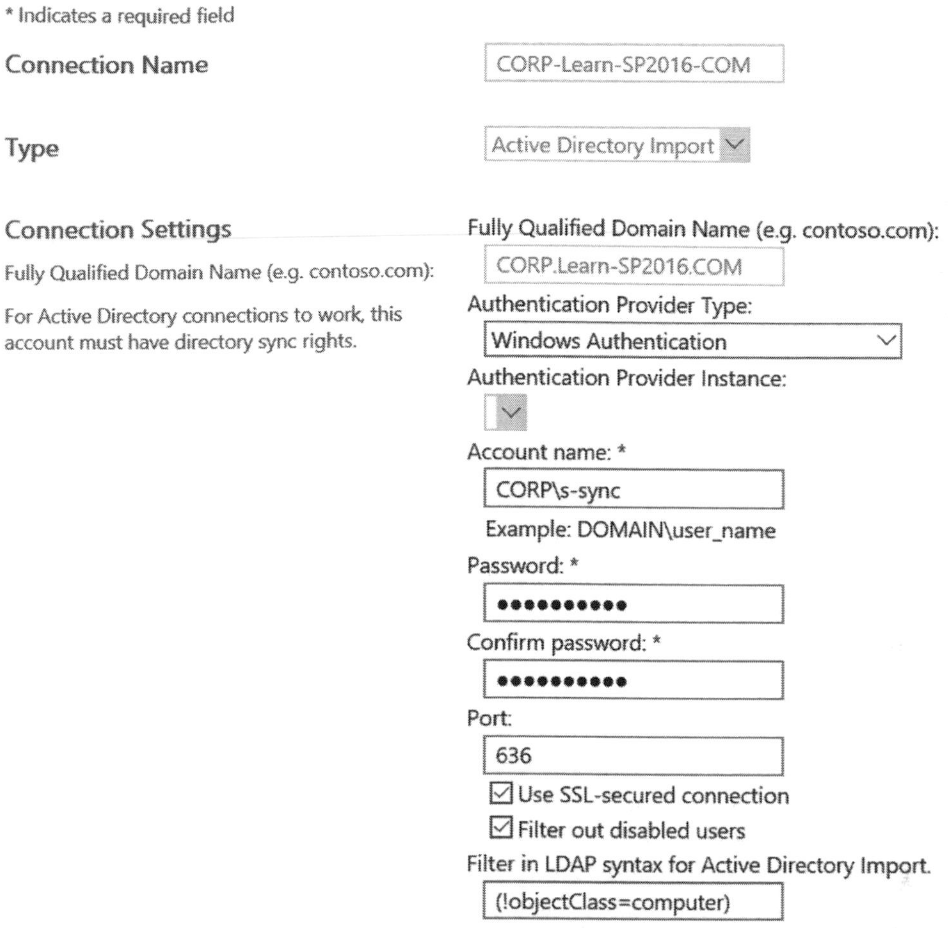

* Indicates a required field

Connection Name

CORP-Learn-SP2016-COM

Type

Active Directory Import ∨

Connection Settings

Fully Qualified Domain Name (e.g. contoso.com):

For Active Directory connections to work, this account must have directory sync rights.

Fully Qualified Domain Name (e.g. contoso.com):

CORP.Learn-SP2016.COM

Authentication Provider Type:

Windows Authentication ∨

Authentication Provider Instance:

∨

Account name: *

CORP\s-sync

Example: DOMAIN\user_name

Password: *

●●●●●●●●●●

Confirm password: *

●●●●●●●●●●

Port:

636

☑ Use SSL-secured connection

☑ Filter out disabled users

Filter in LDAP syntax for Active Directory Import.

(!objectClass=computer)

Figure 7-4. *The AD Import connection*

Click Populate Containers. Unlike the previous User Profile Synchronization Service import, AD Import will import all objects into the User Profile Service. It is recommended that you only select the specific containers you need, namely those containing Users and Groups. Groups will be imported for use in Audiences.

As our Organization Unit structure is not complicated, we will only be selecting a few containers as shown in Figure 7-5.

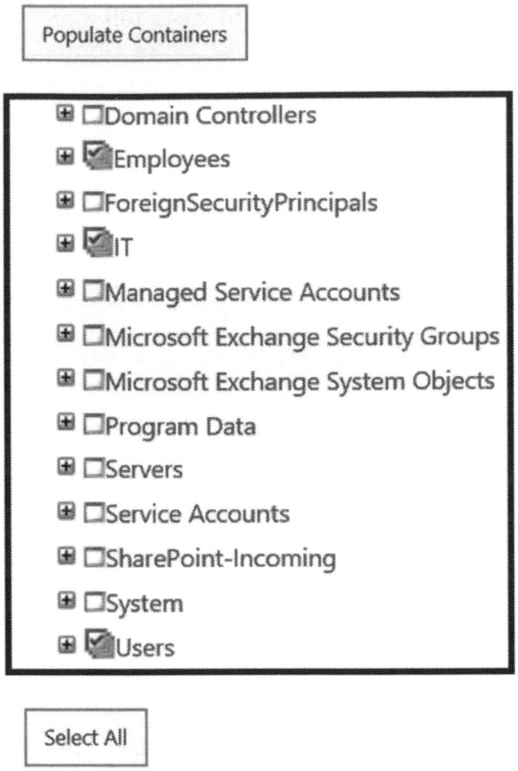

Populate Containers

⊞ ☐Domain Controllers

⊞ ☑Employees

⊞ ☐ForeignSecurityPrincipals

⊞ ☑IT

⊞ ☐Managed Service Accounts

⊞ ☐Microsoft Exchange Security Groups

⊞ ☐Microsoft Exchange System Objects

⊞ ☐Program Data

⊞ ☐Servers

⊞ ☐Service Accounts

⊞ ☐SharePoint-Incoming

⊞ ☐System

⊞ ☑Users

Select All

Figure 7-5. Selecting the Organization Units to import Users and Groups

Once the OU selection is complete, click OK and the Synchronization Connection will be created. Go back to the Manage Profile Service page, and click Start Profile Synchronization. Start a Full Synchronization. The time it takes for this import varies depending on the number of objects you are synchronizing. The synchronization will start shortly, and under the Synchronization Status on the right hand side, you will see it change to Synchronizing when refreshing your browser.

If you do not see additional profiles after the import process has completed, check the ULS logs on the server where the timer job ran. Using the SharePoint Management Shell, we can get the timer job and examine the history entries.

```
$job = Get-SPTimerJob | ?{$_.TypeName -like "*.UserProfileADImportJob"}
$job.HistoryEntries | Select -First 1
```

Here, examine the ServerName value for the last location the timer job ran on. Convert the Start and End time from UTC to your local time zone.

```
$historyEntry = $job.HistoryEntries | Select -First 1
$historyEntry.StartTime.ToLocalTime()
$historyEntry.EndTime.ToLocalTime()
```

Once you've gathered the appropriate ULS entries, examine them for "DirSync import failed." Here, you will see a stack trace that will contain the error message. For example:

```
ActiveDirectory Import: DirSync import failed: ScanDirSyncChanges: Exception thrown
by Dirsync request: page 0, LdapServer 'LSDCO1.CORP.LEARN-SP2016.COM:636', rootDn
'DC=CORP,DC=LEARN-SP2016,DC=COM', exception 'System.DirectoryServices.Protocols.
LdapException: The search filter is invalid.
```

In this particular case, we know that we must edit our LDAP filter as the syntax is incorrect. Other errors might include connectivity issues, such as timeouts or incorrect permissions. There are many free tools to validate LDAP syntax available on the Internet that you may want to use prior to adding a new filter.

Once the filter has been fixed, rerun your AD Import and validate the appropriate users are imported to the User Profile Service.

The synchronization connection may also be configured using PowerShell, with the Add-SPProfileSyncConnection cmdlet.

```
$sa = Get-SPServiceApplication | ?{$_.TypeName -eq "User Profile Service Application"}
Add-SPProfileSyncConnection-ProfileServiceApplication $sa -ConnectionForestName "CORP.
Learn-SP2016.COM" -ConnectionDomain "CORP" -ConnectionUserName "s-sync" -ConnectionPassword
(ConvertTo-SecureString "<Password>" -AsPlainText -Force) -ConnectionPort 636
-ConnectionUseSSL $true -ConnectionUseDisabledFilter $true -ConnectionSynchronizationOU
"OU=Employees,DC=CORP,DC=LEARN-SP2016,DC=COM"
```

This will create the same synchronization connection as shown in the preceding; however, if any additional Organization Units are needed, or an additional LDAP filter is required, add them through Central Administration. Note that the -ConnectionUserName parameter expects only the sAMAccountName, not the full DOMAIN\Username value.

With the AD Import configuration complete, let's take a look at the second option for importing User Profiles.

External Identity Manager Configuration

Configuring an external identity manager requires a significantly larger time investment. There is the Microsoft Identity Manager, which supports Active Directory and the SharePoint User Profile service, along with many other directory types and of course custom solutions.

The initial configuration requires changing the User Profile Service Application to use an External Identity Manager. This is set through the Configure Synchronization Settings in the User Profile Service Application, as shown in Figure 7-6. Select the "Enable External Identity Manager" option.

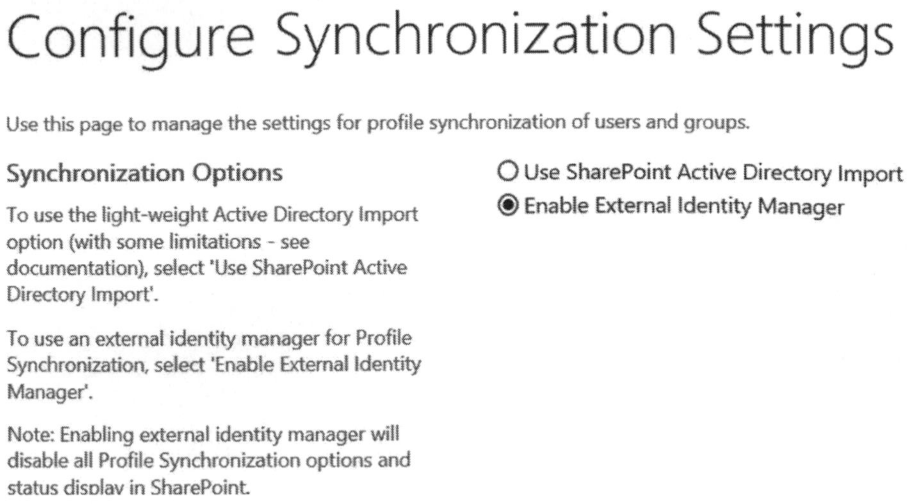

Configure Synchronization Settings

Use this page to manage the settings for profile synchronization of users and groups.

Synchronization Options

To use the light-weight Active Directory Import option (with some limitations - see documentation), select 'Use SharePoint Active Directory Import'.

To use an external identity manager for Profile Synchronization, select 'Enable External Identity Manager'.

Note: Enabling external identity manager will disable all Profile Synchronization options and status display in SharePoint.

○ Use SharePoint Active Directory Import

◉ Enable External Identity Manager

Figure 7-6. *Enabling External Identity Manager for SharePoint Server 2016*

When set, on the User Profile Service Application will display that it is now using an External Identity Manager, as shown in Figure 7-7.

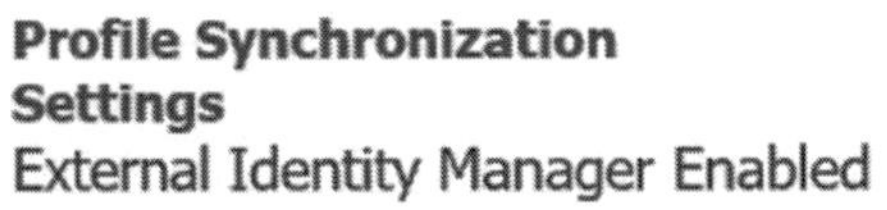

Profile Synchronization Settings
External Identity Manager Enabled

Figure 7-7. *The External Identity Manager is enabled for this User Profile Service Application*

In addition, due to a bug in the RTM version of SharePoint Server 2016, the following PowerShell is required in order to fully enable the External Identity Manager option.

```
$sa = Get-SPServiceApplication | ?{$_.TypeName -eq 'User Profile Service Application'}
$sa.NoILMUsed = $true
$sa.Update()
```

With Microsoft Identity Manager, we only need to install the Synchronization Service. This service provides inbound and outbound synchronization between many different directory and business data platforms.

Microsoft provides install documentation for Microsoft Identity Manager (MIM). MIM should be installed on a dedicated server, if possible.

■ **Note**   Documentation for the Microsoft Identity Manager 2016 installation is available from
http://aka.ms/UserProfileMIMSync

In order to install MIM on Windows Server 2012 R2 using the SQL Server 2012 AlwaysOn Failover Cluster Instance, the MIM server must first have the .NET 3.5 Framework and SQL 2008 R2 or 2012 Native Client installed. In addition, to support the SharePoint Connector, MIM must have at minimum build of 4.3.2064.0.

■ **Note**   Build 4.3.2064.0 is available from https://support.microsoft.com/kb/3092179

Install the Forefront Identity Manager Connector for SharePoint User Profile Store, available from `https://www.microsoft.com/en-us/download/details.aspx?id=41164`, on the MIM server. This is the Management Agent, which will connect to the SharePoint User Profile Service.

The User Profile Sync MIM solution includes a PowerShell Module, SharePointSync.psm1, to set up the Active Directory and SharePoint Management Agents. This will run on the MIM server.

■ **Note**   The User Profile Sync solution is available from `https://github.com/OfficeDev/PnP-Tools/tree/master/Solutions/UserProfile.MIMSync`

From an elevated PowerShell console, navigate to the extracted location of the module. To configure this will require two accounts, the account previously created with Replicate Directory Changes, as well as the Farm Administrator account to connect to the User Profile Service.

```
$syncCred = Get-Credential "CORP\s-sync"
$farmCred = Get-Credential "CORP\s-farm"
Import-Module C:\SharePointSync\SharePointSync.psm1
Install-SharePointSyncConfiguration -Path C:\SharePointSync -ForestDnsName "CORP.LEARN-
SP2016.COM" -ForestCredential $syncCred -OrganizationalUnit "OU=Employees,DC=CORP,DC=LEARN-
SP2016,DC=COM" -SharePointUrl https://ca.corp.learn-sp2016.com -SharePointCredential
$farmCred
```

Prior to running the synchronization, you must set the password for the synchronization account on the "ADMA" Management Agent. Using the Synchronization Service Manager, go to the Management Agents tab. Double-click the "ADMA" Management Agent. Click the "Connect to Active Directory Forest" section and enter the password for the synchronization account, as shown in Figure 7-8. Click OK to save the machines.

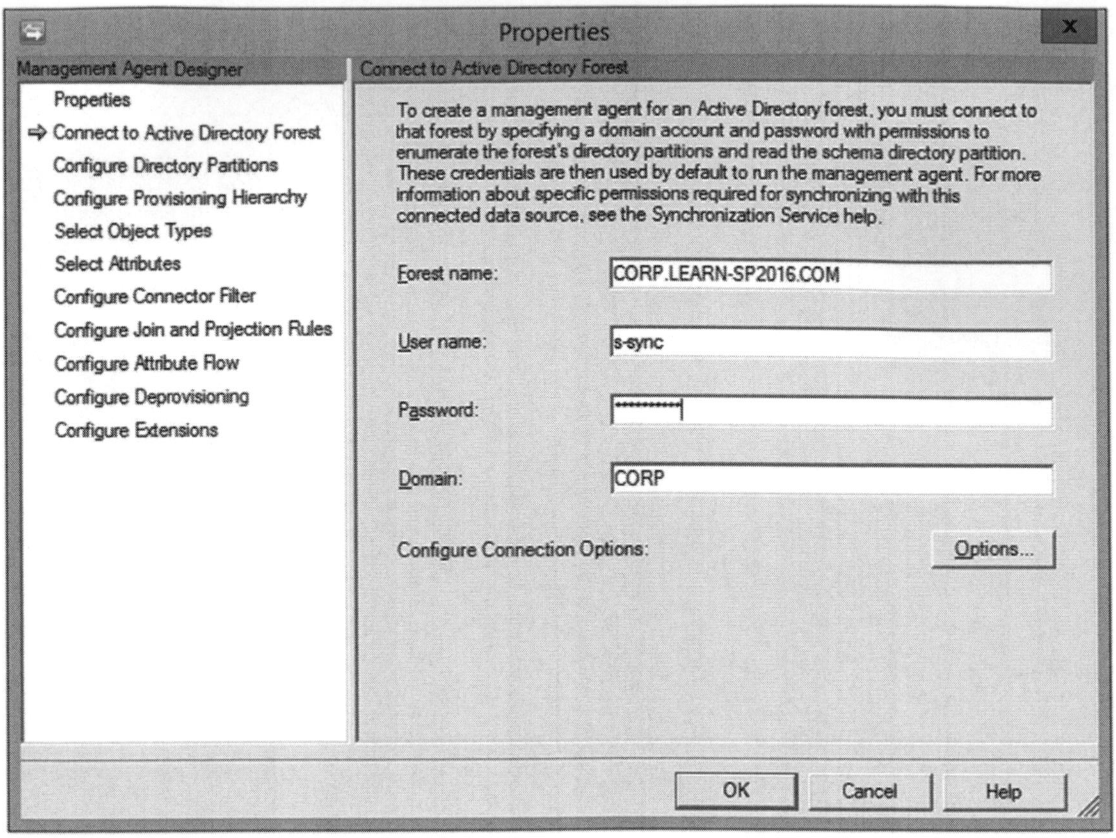

Figure 7-8. *Setting the password for the Active Directory synchronization account in the Active Directory Management Agent*

Once created, the synchronization can be run through PowerShell, again by importing the SharePointSync.psm1 file.

```
Start-SharePointSync -Confirm:$false
```

Monitoring the synchronization process can be done from the Synchronization Service Manager, which is installed at C:\Program Files\Microsoft Forefront Identity Manager\2010\Synchronization Service\UIShell\miisclient.exe. The Operations tab will show the progress of the two Management Agents, ADMA (Active Directory), and SPMA (SharePoint). Any errors will be notated in the Status column.

When a full synchronization has completed, you may then start using delta synchronization. Again, using the SharePointSync.psm1 module, run the following.

```
Start-SharePointSync -Delta -Confirm:$false
```

The delta process should be faster than the full synchronization. Note that, like the previous User Profile Synchronization Service, any changes to properties require a full synchronization to take place. In Figure 7-9, we see a Full Import process completed successfully and a subsequent Delta Import completing successfully.

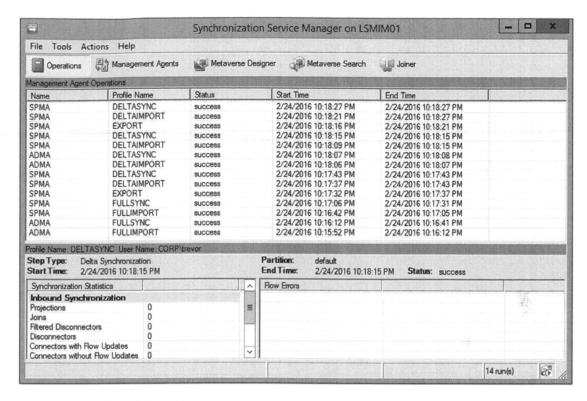

Figure 7-9. *A Full run followed by a Delta run*

While this process will import profile photos, the profile photos will need to be converted to the small, medium, and large photos. In order to do this, set up a Scheduled Task that runs the following cmdlet on the MySite Host. This must be run on a SharePoint server in the farm by a user who has administrative rights on the User Profile Service Application, as well as Shell Admin rights.

```
Add-PSSnapin Microsoft.SharePoint.PowerShell -EA 0
Update-SPProfilePhotoStore -MySiteHostLocation https://sharepoint-my.learn-sp2016.com
-CreateThumbnailsForImportedPhotos 1
```

This cmdlet may take some time to complete depending on the number of user profile photos that need to be converted.

Configuring Additional Import Properties

To configure additional import properties to import into SharePoint, it will require modification of the User Profile Service in SharePoint, the SharePoint Management Agent, and the Active Directory Management Agent in Microsoft Identity Manager. We will be creating a property named "Company" which pulls from the Active Directory attribute named "company."

In the User Profile Service Application, under Manage User Properties, create the property with the applicable settings, or in our case, a string with a 64-character limit. The limit of the value may be found in the Active Directory Schema Manager MMC. In order to view the Active Directory Schema, you must first register schmmgmt.dll.

```
regsvr32.exe C:\Windows\System32\schmmgmt.dll
```

From there, open mmc.exe and add the snap-in named "Active Directory Schema." In the Attributes node, find the target attribute, or company in this case. Viewing the attribute properties will tell you the constraints of the attribute, as shown in Figure 7-10.

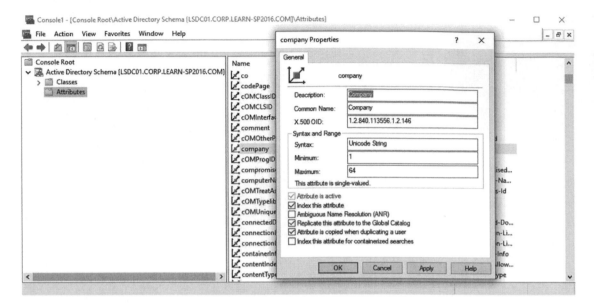

Figure 7-10. *Using the Active Directory Schema manager, showing the company attribute*

In the Microsoft Identity Manager Synchronization Service Manager, navigate to the Management Agents tab. Open up the Active Directory Domain Services Management Agent (named ADMA). Under Select Attributes, select the appropriate Active Directory attribute, or "company" in our case. The next step is to configure the Attribute Flow. Select the appropriate object type, or in this case, the Object Type of "user" which flows to the Object Type of "person," as shown in Figure 7-11.

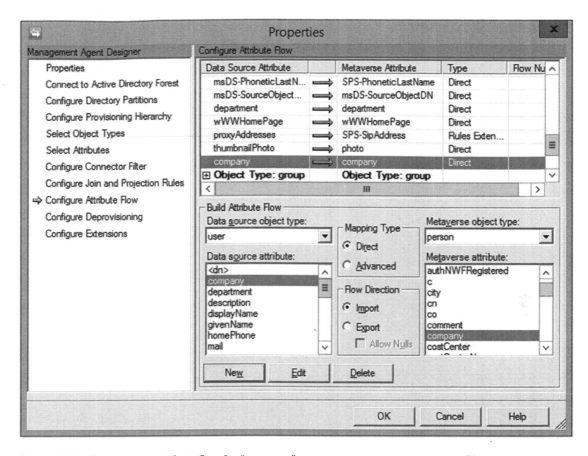

Figure 7-11. *Creating an attribute flow for "company"*

Once completed, the next step is to refresh the schema on the SharePoint Management Agent. Again, on the Management Agents tab, right-click the SharePoint Management Agent and select Refresh Schema. You will be prompted for the password of the user configured to connect to Central Administration. The schema update will take a few seconds to complete. At this point, it is time to edit the new Company attribute to import it into SharePoint, so edit the SharePoint Management Agent and navigate to Select Attributes. Select the new "Company" attribute, then move onto Configure Attribute Flow. We are modifying the Object Type user from the Object Type person. Add a new flow for Company as shown in Figure 7-12. Note that we must select "Allow Nulls" as this property may not have a value for each user in the directory.

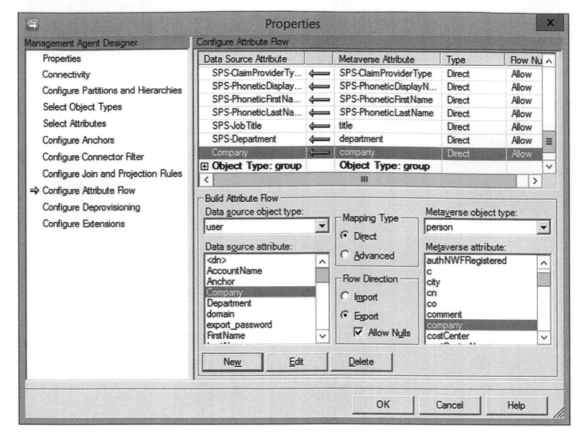

Figure 7-12. *Importing the company attribute into SharePoint*

Now, run a full import, and that's it! The new Company attribute will be populated for users who have that property populated in Active Directory.

Configuring Export Properties

To *export* properties, we'll allow users to enter their own Home Phone number. We need to create a new User Profile Service property of a string, with a length of 256 characters, which matches the value of the homePhone attribute as viewed through the Active Directory Schema Manager. As we want to write this attribute, we must provide our synchronization service account, CORP\s-sync, with the ability to write back this particular attribute to user accounts in Active Directory. For this, we will again start the Delegation Control Wizard via Active Directory Users and Computers, choosing the synchronization service account and a custom task to delegate. We will only delegate control to User objects, and the right to write to the Home Phone attribute, as shown in Figure 7-13.

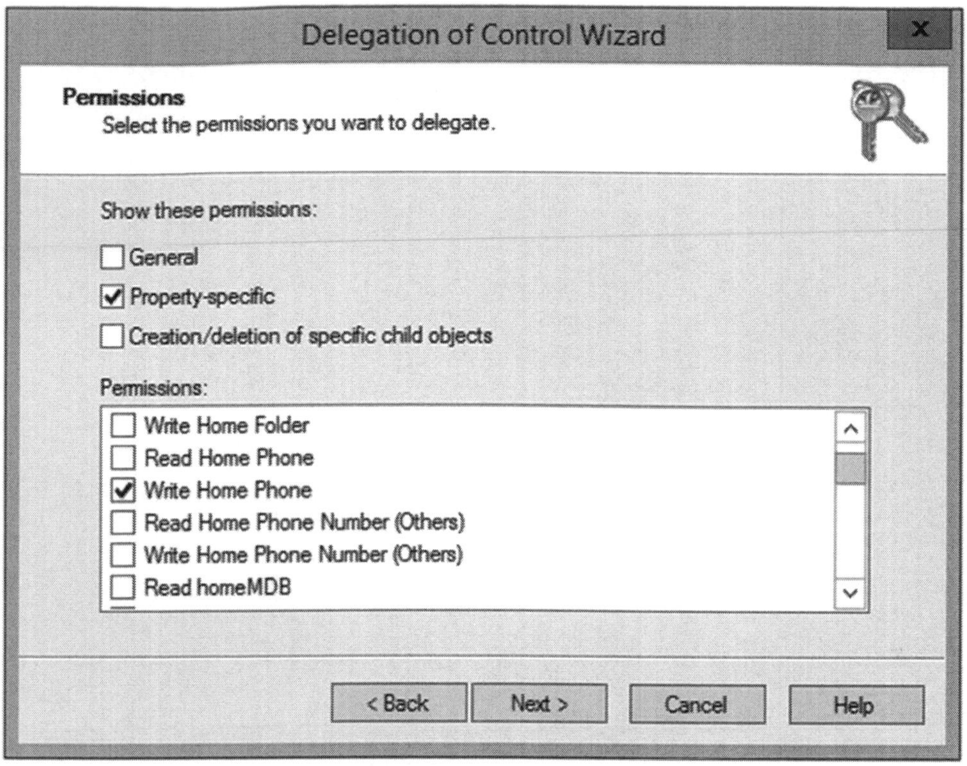

Figure 7-13. *Granting CORP\s-sync with Write access to the Home Phone attribute*

Working backward, in the Microsoft Identity Manager Synchronization Service Manager, modify the SharePoint Management Agent. Select the HomePhone attribute under Select Attribute, then configure an attribute flow to *import* the attribute HomePhone from SharePoint to the metaverse for user objects, as shown in Figure 7-14. The directional arrow points from the SharePoint Management Agent into the Microsoft Identity Manager metaverse.

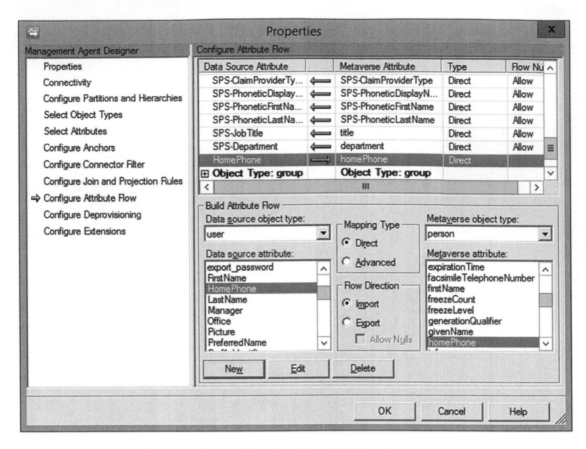

Figure 7-14. *Importing the HomePhone attribute from SharePoint into the metaverse*

■ **Tip** If you created a custom User Profile Property, refresh the SharePoint Management Agent Schema, otherwise it will not appear in the Select Attributes list.

Moving onto the Active Directory Management Agent, again select the homePhone attribute from Select Attributes. Under Configure Attribute Flows, for the Object Type of user, *export* the homePhone attribute from the metaverse into the homePhone attribute in Active Directory, allowing for nulls (as not all users may have populated the field), as shown in Figure 7-15.

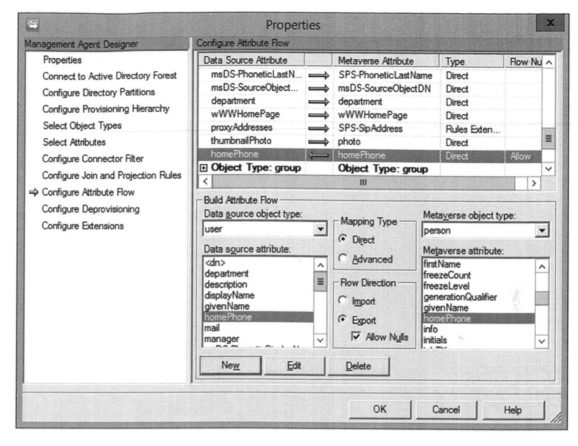

Figure 7-15. *Exporting homePhone from the metaverse into Active Directory*

The setup of the Management Agents does not create an *Export* attribute flow for Active Directory. This means, by default, we cannot write attributes in Active Directory. To configure an Export run profile, under the Management Agents tab, highlight the Active Directory Management Agent and select Configure Run Profiles. Create a new profile named Export and for the Step type, select Export. Complete the run profile. When you click Run for the Active Directory Management Agent, Export is now an option. Run the export, and if the permissions are configured correctly, the homePhone attribute will be written with the value inputted by a user from their User Profile in SharePoint.

The ADMA Export run profile may also be started with PowerShell by importing the SharePointSync. psm1 and using Start-ManagementAgent.

```
Import-Module .\SharePointSync.psm1
Start-ManagementAgent -Name ADMA -RunProfile Export
```

Now that we know how to import and export profiles from and to SharePoint Server, let's take a look at custom properties that may not exist within the metaverse.

Custom Properties

In order to support custom properties from either Active Directory or the SharePoint User Profile Service, it may be necessary to create a new attribute within the Microsoft Identity Manager metaverse. This can be accomplished under the Metaverse Designer. The object type will most likely be "person." When highlighting person, the existing attributes belonging to that object type in the metaverse will appear below. From here, it is possible to add additional attributes to the metaverse, or create *new* attributes within the metaverse, as seen in Figure 7-16. Once the attribute has been added to the metaverse, it is treated like any other attribute in terms of synchronization to and from the Management Agents.

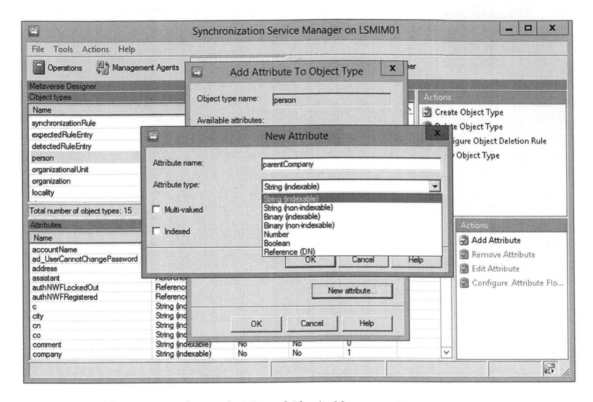

Figure 7-16. *Adding a new attribute to the Microsoft Identity Manager metaverse*

With our custom property in Microsoft Identity Manager created, take a brief look at Audiences and how to configure them within SharePoint.

Audiences

Audiences are used to scope certain content, such as SharePoint WebParts, to a certain set of users. Audiences are powerful in that they allow a variety of rules to be created to define who should belong to them. One caveat with audiences is that they are not security boundaries. Content hidden by an audience is still viewable by a client. Audiences, by default, are also only compiled once per week on Saturday at 1 AM. This can be adjusted to be more frequent, although was set specifically to one day per week for performance considerations.

In order to configure an audience, the audience is created under Manage Audiences within the User Profile Service Application. Here you will define the rules that scope the audience to specific users. In this example, as seen in Figure 7-17, we are creating a Project Managers audience containing all users who have a job title of "Project Manager."

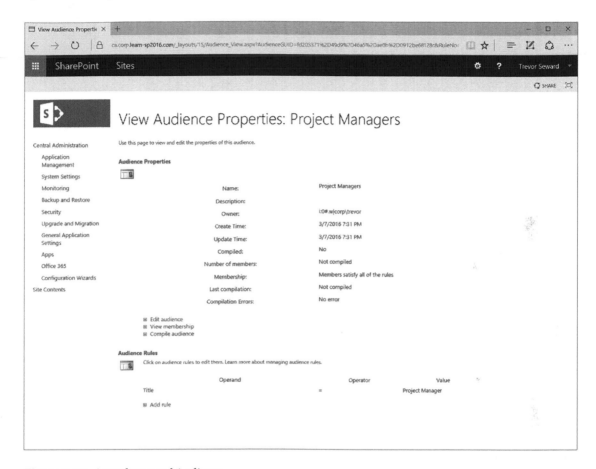

Figure 7-17. *A newly created Audience*

When compiled, as shown in Figure 7-18, the number of members will be displayed that match the rule(s) along with any errors that occurred during audience compilation. At this point, the audience can be used on SharePoint content to scope the content to the specific set of users.

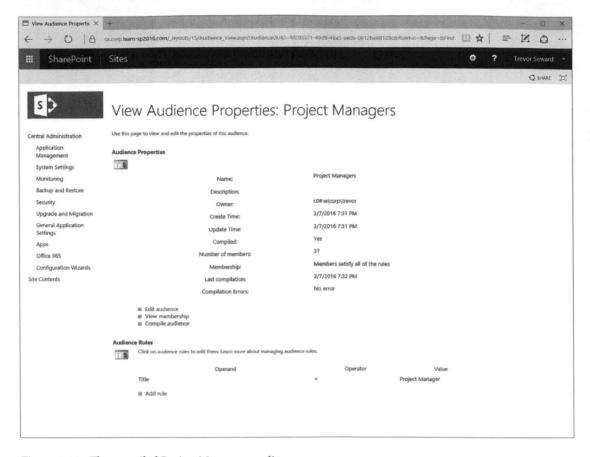

Figure 7-18. *The compiled Project Managers audience*

OneDrive for Business

OneDrive for Business, also known as a MySite, is a location where the user can upload documents to for personal use and limited sharing. This is also a location where the user can update their User Profile, share via the SharePoint Newsfeed, and create posts within their blog. One notable feature no longer available is Tasks, or the task aggregation feature available in SharePoint Server 2013 as the Work Management Service Application is no longer available.

The MySite settings were configured in Chapter 3, but can be further adjusted from the User Profile Service Application under Setup My Sites. For example, you may add a Preferred Search Center or change the Site Naming Format. Note that changing the Site Naming Format will cause all MySite Site Collections to migrate to the new naming format, which may be a disk I/O heavy operation.

Recently Shared Items is a new feature for SharePoint On-Premises that displays the items recently shared with you. It can only be enabled through the SharePoint Management Shell. The URL specified in this cmdlet is the MySite Host URL.

```
Enable-SPFeature "RecentlySharedItems" -Url https://sharepoint-my.learn-sp2016.com
```

Next Steps

In this chapter, we covered the User Profile Service Application, including how to manage AD Import as well as working with Microsoft Identity Manager. For the next chapter, we will be looking at productivity Service Applications, such as Access Services, Managed Metadata, and others.

■ ■ ■

CHAPTER 8

Configuring Productivity Service Applications

In previous chapters, we have already learned how to configure some Service Applications such as Search and User Profile as well as the App Management and Subscription Service Applications.

SharePoint Server 2016 includes other Service Applications that add many other features to SharePoint Server 2016 which can increase your users' productivity.

In this chapter, we will learn to configure the Managed Metadata Service Application, Business Connectivity Services, Word Automation Services, PowerPoint Automation Service, Visio Graphics Service, Machine Translation Services, and lastly Access Services.

Managed Metadata Service Application

The Managed Metadata Service Application is one of the most popular Service Applications that are deployed with SharePoint. This Service Application makes it possible to use managed metadata and share content types across site collections and Web Applications. Managed Metadata is a central repository that stores your information taxonomy in a hierarchical view. There are two ways to create this Service Application, Central Administration or PowerShell.

To create the Managed Metadata Service Application using the Central Administration, from the Manage Service Applications Page, click New on the ribbon, then select Managed Metadata Service Application. A window will open similar to Figure 8-1, in which you have to enter the name of your Managed Metadata Service Application as well as the database server and Database name you want to deploy it on.

© Vlad Catrinescu and Trevor Seward 2016
V. Catrinescu and T. Seward, *Deploying SharePoint 2016*, DOI 10.1007/978-1-4842-1999-7_8

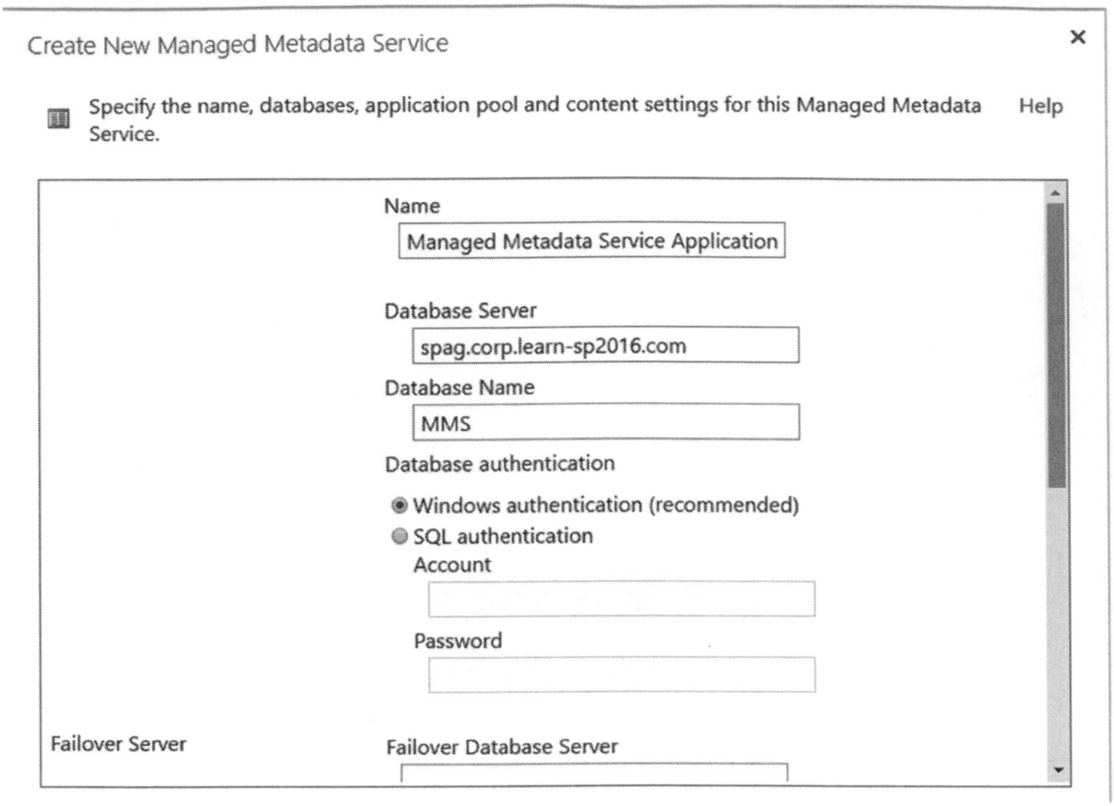

Figure 8-1. *Create New Managed Metadata Service Part 1*

Scrolling down to the end of the New Managed Metadata Service window seen in Figure 8-2, we need to select which Application Pool to host this Service Application on. Unless you have business requirements requiring this Service Application to be isolated from others, we recommend putting it in the same Service Application Pool as the rest of your Service Applications for a better resource management and server performance. In our environment, this application pool is named SharePoint Web Services Default. Lastly, you can optionally enter the Content Type hub URL. The Content Type Hub is a central location where you can manage and publish your content types. Other Site Collections can subscribe to this hub, and pull down the published content types and even receive updates when you update Content Types in the Content Type Hub. There is no special Site Collection template for the Content Type hub, and it's usually a Team Site template which is used for the Content Type Hub. The Content Type hub can also be configured after the Managed Metadata Service Application has been created. The *Report Syndication import errors from Site Collections using this service application* will report import errors in the Content type publishing error log, accessible from the Site Collection Site Settings page.

Create New Managed Metadata Service   ✕

▦ Specify the name, databases, application pool and content settings for this Managed Metadata   Help
   Service.

Application Pool   ● Use existing application pool

Choose the Application Pool to use | SharePoint Web Services Default   ▼ |
for this Service Application. This
defines the account and credentials   ○ Create new application pool
that will be used by this web   Application pool name
service. | |

You can choose an existing   Select a security account for this application pool
application pool or create a new
one. | CORP\s-c2wts ▼ |
                                        Register new managed account

                                        Content Type hub
Enter the URL of the site collection | |
(Content Type hub) from which this
service application will consume   ☑ Report syndication import errors from Site Collections using this
content types.   service application.

                                        ☑ Add this service application to the farm's default list.

                                                                    | OK | | Cancel |

Figure 8-2. *Create a New Managed Metadata Service Application Part 2*

Lastly, you can click OK and the Service Application will be created. The Managed Metadata Service
Application can also be created by PowerShell using the New-SPMetadataServiceApplication cmdlet. To
create the Service Application with the same settings used when we created it using Central Administration,
we would run the following cmdlet in an elevated SharePoint Management Shell.

```
$sa = New-SPMetadataServiceApplication -Name "Managed Metadata Service" -DatabaseName "MMS"
-ApplicationPool "SharePoint Web Services Default" -SyndicationErrorReportEnabled
```

When creating the Service Application by the UI, SharePoint will also create the Service Application
Proxy automatically; however, that is not the case by PowerShell. The next step will be to create the Service
Application proxy by using the New-SPMetadataServiceApplicationProxy cmdlet. In our example we would
run the following PowerShell cmdlet

```
New-SPMetadataServiceApplicationProxy -Name "Managed Metadata Service Proxy"
-ServiceApplication $sa -DefaultProxyGroup -ContentTypePushdownEnabled
-DefaultKeywordTaxonomy -DefaultSiteCollectionTaxonomy
```

We have added the -DefaultProxyGroup switch to specify that this Service Application Proxy will be part of the default proxy group for the farm. Next, the -ContentTypePushdownEnabled switch specifies that existing instances of changed content types in subsites and libraries will be updated. The -DefaultKeywordTaxonomy switch specifies that Enterprise Keywords will be stored in this service application, and lastly the -DefaultSiteCollectionTaxonomy switch specifies that when users create Managed Metadata Columns in a Site Collection, the term will be saved in this Service Application.

■ **Note** The preceding options are not in the form when creating the Managed Metadata Service Application using the Central Administration. To access those options from the Central Administration, select the Managed Metadata Service Proxy from the Manage Service Application Page, and click Properties as seen in Figure 8-3.

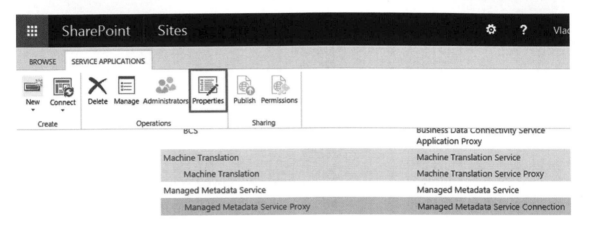

Figure 8-3. *Manage Metadata Service Proxy Properties*

For both options of creating the Service Application, if you are running a farm that uses the MinRole model, the Managed Metadata Service will be automatically started on all the servers running the Web Front End, or Application Roles. If you are running in a Custom mode farm, make sure to manually start the Managed Metadata Web Service on at least one server in your farm.

With the Managed Metadata Service Application created, you can now create Managed Terms that users can use throughout your SharePoint farm. To configure the Content Type Hub, you can create a Site Collection with a team site template that will be used for this purpose. We have created it using the following PowerShell cmdlet

```
New-SPSite -Url https://sharepoint.learn-sp2016.com/sites/ContentTypeHub -Template STS#0
-Name "Content Type Hub " -OwnerAlias "CORP\vlad"
```

Afterward, run the Set-SPMetadataServiceApplication to specify the Content Type Hub URL with the -HubUri parameter.

```
Set-SPMetadataServiceApplication -Identity "Managed Metadata Service" -HubUri https://
sharepoint.learn-sp2016.com/sites/ContentTypeHub
```

With the Managed Metadata Service Application configured, we will configure the Business Connectivity Service Application Next.

Business Data Connectivity Service

The Business Data Connectivity Service, often referred to as BCS, is a Service Application that allows SharePoint Administrators to display data from other data sources directly into SharePoint Server 2016. By using SharePoint Designer users can connect to an external data source such as a SQL Server database, and expose that information as an External List in SharePoint. Developers can also create External Content Types in Visual Studio that connect to more types of data sources, such as an OData Source. A Business Data Connectivity Service Application can be created either from the Central Administration, or through PowerShell.

To create the Business Data Connectivity Service Application by the Central Administration, from the Service Applications Page, click New on the ribbon, and Business Data Connectivity Service Application. A window will open similar to Figure 8-4, in which you have to enter the name of your Business Data Connectivity Service Application as well as the database server and Database name you want to deploy it on.

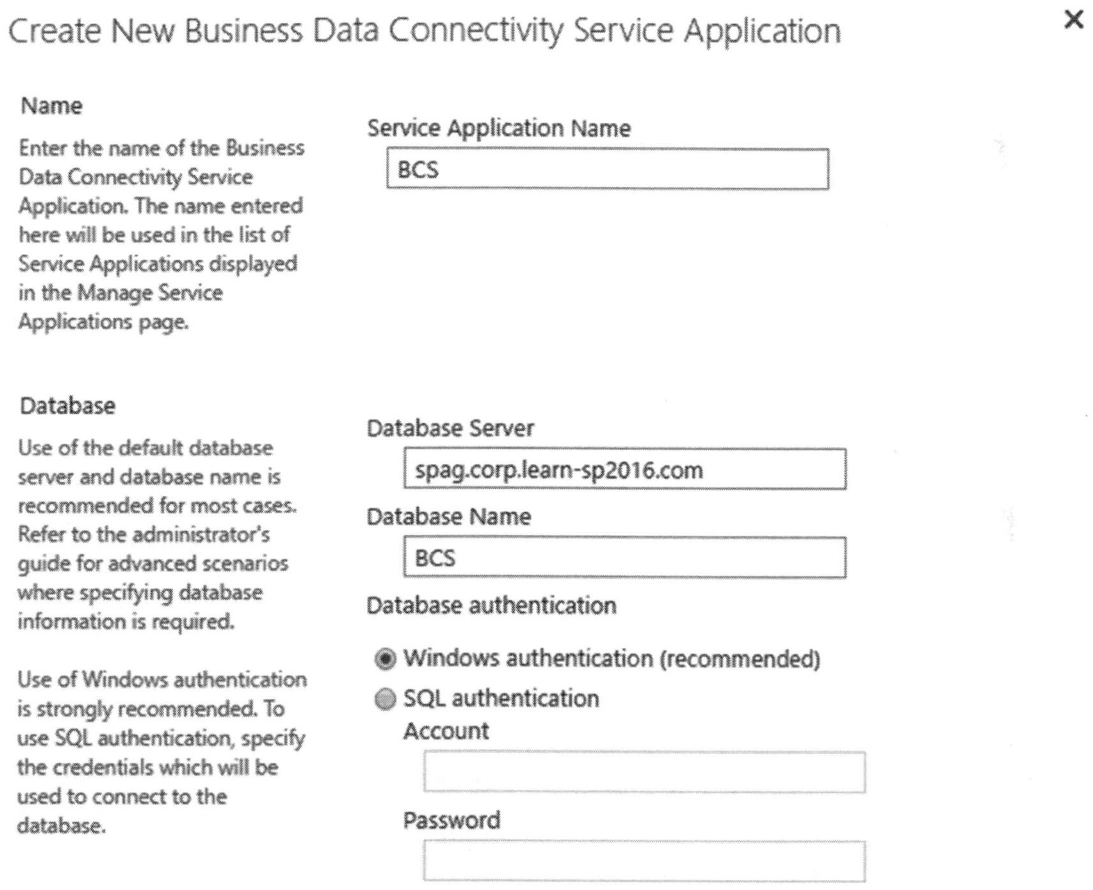

Create New Business Data Connectivity Service Application ✕

Name

Enter the name of the Business Data Connectivity Service Application. The name entered here will be used in the list of Service Applications displayed in the Manage Service Applications page.

Service Application Name

BCS

Database

Use of the default database server and database name is recommended for most cases. Refer to the administrator's guide for advanced scenarios where specifying database information is required.

Use of Windows authentication is strongly recommended. To use SQL authentication, specify the credentials which will be used to connect to the database.

Database Server

spag.corp.learn-sp2016.com

Database Name

BCS

Database authentication

◉ Windows authentication (recommended)

◯ SQL authentication

Account

Password

Figure 8-4. Create a New Business Data Connectivity Service Application

Scrolling down to the end of the New Business Data Connectivity Service Application window seen in Figure 8-5, we need to select which Application Pool to host this Service Application on. Unless you have business requirements requiring this Service Application to be isolated from others, we recommend putting it in the same Service Application Pool as the rest of your Service Applications for a better resource management and server performance. Simply press on OK to create the Service Application.

Application Pool

Choose the Application Pool to use for this Service Application. This defines the account and credentials that will be used by this web service.

You can choose an existing application pool or create a new one.

◉ Use existing application pool

SharePoint Web Services Default ▼

◉ Create new application pool
Application pool name

Select a security account for this application pool

CORP\s-c2wts ▼
Register new managed account

[OK]   [Cancel]

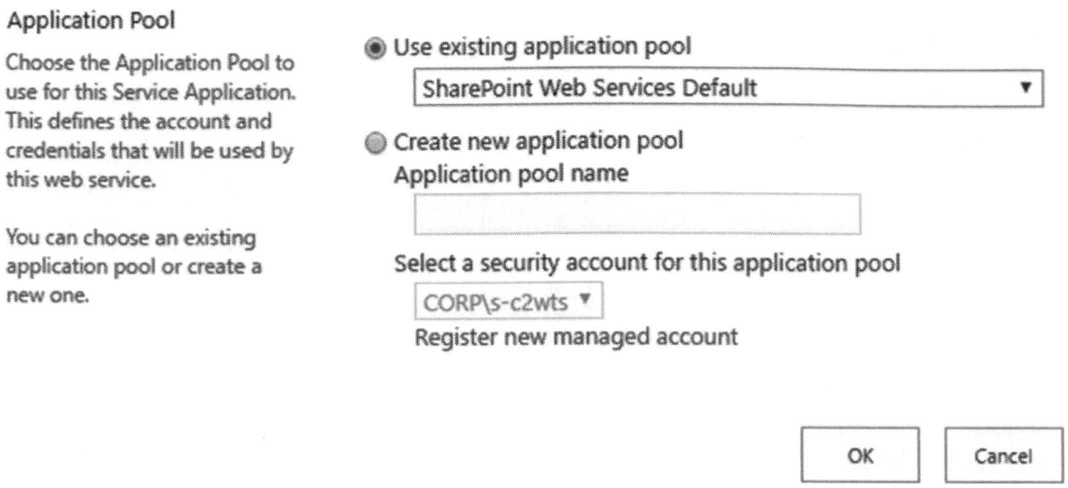

Figure 8-5. *Select an Application Pool for the Business Data Connectivity Service Application*

To create the Service Application by PowerShell, we need to use the `New-SPBusinessDataConnectivityServiceApplication` PowerShell cmdlet from an elevated SharePoint Management Shell. We need to specify the name of the Service Application, the Database name, and the Service Application Pool. To create a Service Application like the one we would have created by the User Interface, we would run the following PowerShell cmdlet:

```
New-SPBusinessDataCatalogServiceApplication -Name "BCS" -DatabaseName "BCS" -ApplicationPool
"SharePoint Web Services Default" If you are running SharePoint 2016 in a MinRole farm, the
Business Data Connectivity Service will be automatically started on all the servers running
the Web Front End or the Application roles. If you are running a farm using the Custom
MinRole, you will need to start the Business Data Connectivity Service on at least one
server in your SharePoint Server farm.
```

Your users can now create External Content Types by using SharePoint Designer to connect to external systems. For an example of how a developer can create an External Content Type by using an OData Service, you can refer to Chapter 14, the section on Hybrid Business Connectivity Services. Next, we will configure Word Automation Services.

Word Automation Services

The Word Automation Services Service Application is a Service Application that automatically converts documents supported by the Word client application into formats such as PDF and XPS. In a simpler way to explain it, the Word Automation Services takes the "Save As" functionality of the Word client, and replicates the functionality on SharePoint. A Word Automation Service Application can be created either through the User Interface, or through PowerShell.

To create a Word Automation Service Application, from the Central Administration on the Manage Service Applications page, click New on the Ribbon and select Word Automation Services. A window similar to Figure 8-6 will open in which you will have to enter the name and Application Pool, and select whether to add this Service Application to the farm default Proxy list. Similar to previous Service Applications, unless you have business requirements for this Service Application to be isolated from the rest, we recommend you to deploy it in the same Service Application Pool as the rest of your Service Applications. The Partitioned Mode checkbox must be checked only when you deploy the SharePoint farm in Multi-Tenant mode.

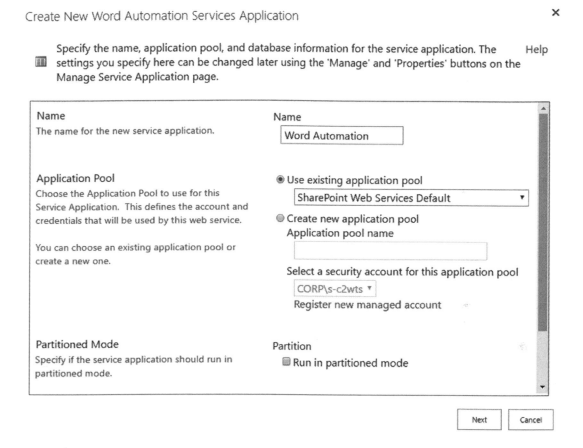

Figure 8-6. *Create a New Word Automation Services Application*

After clicking Next, SharePoint will ask you for the Database Server as well as the Database Name as seen in Figure 8-7.

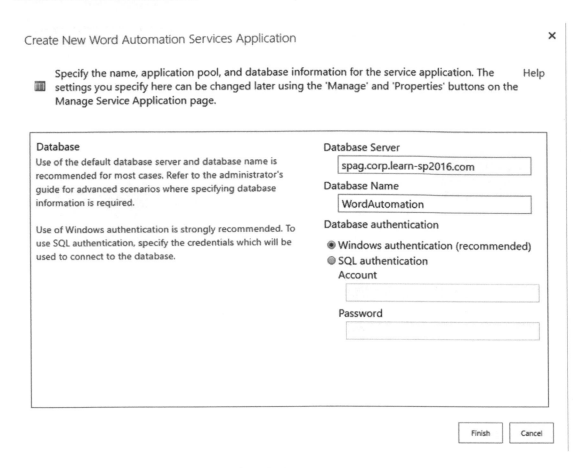

Figure 8-7. *Word Services Application Database Option*

After clicking OK, the Service Application will be created. To create a Word Automation Services Application with PowerShell, we will use the New-SPWordConversionServiceApplication cmdlet from an elevated SharePoint Management Shell. To create a Service Application like the one we would have created in the preceding screenshots, we would have used the following PowerShell cmdlet

```
New-SPWordConversionServiceApplication -Name "Word Automation" -DatabaseName
"WordAutomation" -ApplicationPool "SharePoint Web Services Default" -Default
```

The Word Automation Services can only be used via Code, and not by the User Interface; therefore, it is a bit trickier to test, but we can test it by calling functions directly from PowerShell. To test Word Automation Services, we have uploaded a document called "Document1.docx," which we want to convert to PDF with the name "Document1-Final.pdf." We will first load the assembly required to call Word Automation Services functions.

```
Add-Type -Path'C:\Windows\Microsoft.NET\assembly\GAC_MSIL\Microsoft.Office.Word.Server\
v4.0_16.0.0.0__71e9bce111e9429c\Microsoft.Office.Word.Server.dll'
```

We then create new Object of type ConversionJobSettings specifying the Output format is PDF.

```
$jobSettings = New-Object Microsoft.Office.Word.Server.Conversions.ConversionJobSettings
$jobSettings.OutputFormat = "PDF"
```

We then create a new object of type `ConversionJob` and give it our Service Application Proxy Name, in our case Word Automation, as well as the `$jobsettings` object. We then set the `$Job.Usertoken` to the SharePoint SPWeb where the document is stored.

```
$job = New-Object Microsoft.Office.Word.Server.Conversions.ConversionJob("Word Automation",
$jobSettings)
$job.UserToken = (Get-SPWeb https://sharepoint.learn-sp2016.com).CurrentUser.UserToken
```

Lastly, we add the properties for the file that we want converted. We give it the URL to the Word Document, as well as the URL to the future PDF document, which does not exist yet. We then Start the Job.

```
$job.AddFile("https://sharepoint.learn-sp2016.com/Shared%20Documents/Document1.docx",
"https://sharepoint.learn-sp2016.com/Shared%20Documents/Document1-Final.pdf")
$job.Start()
```

The Word Automation Services job runs asynchronous, meaning that we won't know when it will run directly from PowerShell; however, we can force the job to run right away by starting the Word Automation timer job.

```
Start-SPTimerJob  "Word Automation"
```

If we put it all together, the script looks like this:

```
Add-Type -Path 'C:\Windows\Microsoft.NET\assembly\GAC_MSIL\Microsoft.Office.Word.Server\
v4.0_16.0.0.0__71e9bce111e9429c\Microsoft.Office.Word.Server.dll'
$jobSettings = New-Object Microsoft.Office.Word.Server.Conversions.ConversionJobSettings
$jobSettings.OutputFormat = "PDF"
$job = New-Object Microsoft.Office.Word.Server.Conversions.ConversionJob("Word Automation",
$jobSettings)
$job.UserToken = (Get-SPWeb https://sharepoint.learn-sp2016.com).CurrentUser.UserToken
$job.AddFile("https://sharepoint.learn-sp2016.com/Shared%20Documents/Document1.docx",
"https://sharepoint.learn-sp2016.com/Shared%20Documents/Document1-Final.pdf")
$job.Start()
Start-SPTimerJob  "Word Automation"
```

To see the status of the job, run the following PowerShell cmdlet where "Word Automation" is the name of your Word Automation Services Application.

```
new-object Microsoft.Office.Word.Server.Conversions.ConversionJobStatus("Word Automation",
$job.JobId,$null);
```

Initially it will show as InProgress since we force started the Timer Job as seen in Figure 8-8.

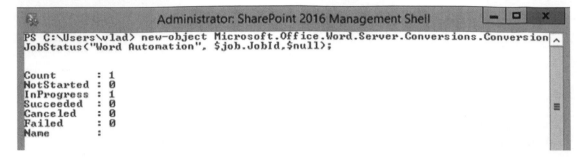

Figure 8-8. *Word Automation Job in Progress*

Once the job is completed, it will either show as Succeeded or Failed. If everything was configured correctly, it should show as Succeeded as seen in Figure 8-9, and you should see your PDF document in your document library.

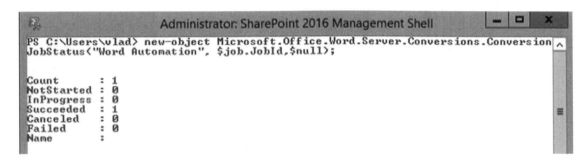

Figure 8-9. *Word Automation Job Succeeded*

In a MinRole farm configuration, the Word Automation Service will automatically be started on all the servers that have the Application Role. If you are running a farm using Custom Roles, you will need to start it manually on at least one server in the farm.

PowerPoint Automation Service

The PowerPoint Automation Service is very similar to the Word Automation Service that we just talked about, but it's for PowerPoint files instead of Word files. The PowerPoint Automation Service allows developers to create solutions that will convert PowerPoint Files to formats such as PDF, JPG, PNG, or XPS.

Unlike the Word Automation Service, the PowerPoint Automation Service can only be created via PowerShell, and not by the Central Administration. We will need to use the New-SPPowerPointConversion ServiceApplication cmdlet from an elevated SharePoint Management Shell. We need to give it a name, as well as the Service Application Pool in which it should be deployed.

```
$sa = New-SPPowerPointConversionServiceApplication -Name "PowerPoint Conversion Service"
-ApplicationPool "SharePoint Web Services Default"
```

After the Service Application is created, we will create a PowerPoint Conversion Service Application Proxy by using the New-SPPowerPointConversionServiceApplicationProxy cmdlet, and adding it to the default group with the -AddToDefaultGroup switch.

```
New-SPPowerPointConversionServiceApplicationProxy "PowerPoint Conversion Service Proxy"
-ServiceApplication $sa –AddToDefaultGroup
```

Your developers will then be able to use the PowerPoint Conversion APIs to convert PowerPoint files to supported formats.

■ **Note**   To learn more about the available APIs, check out the resources on MSDN: https://msdn.
microsoft.com/en-us/library/office/FP179894.aspx

Visio Graphics Service

The Visio Graphics Service Application allows user to visualize Visio diagrams directly in the browser, without needing the client application installed. Furthermore, users could consume those Visio files directly on their mobile devices. The Visio Service Application also makes it possible to automatically refresh drawings hosted on a SharePoint Site.

The Visio Graphics Service Application can either be created from the Central Administration, or from PowerShell. To create a Visio Graphics Service Application from the Central Administration, navigate to the Service Application Management page, click New in the Ribbon and select Visio Graphics Service Application. A window similar to Figure 8-10 will open, in which you will need to input the Service Application name, choose to create a new Application Pool or use an existing one, and finally create a Visio Graphics Service Application Proxy. We recommend using the same Service Application pool as the rest of the Service Application, unless you have a business requirement to isolate this Service Application from the rest.

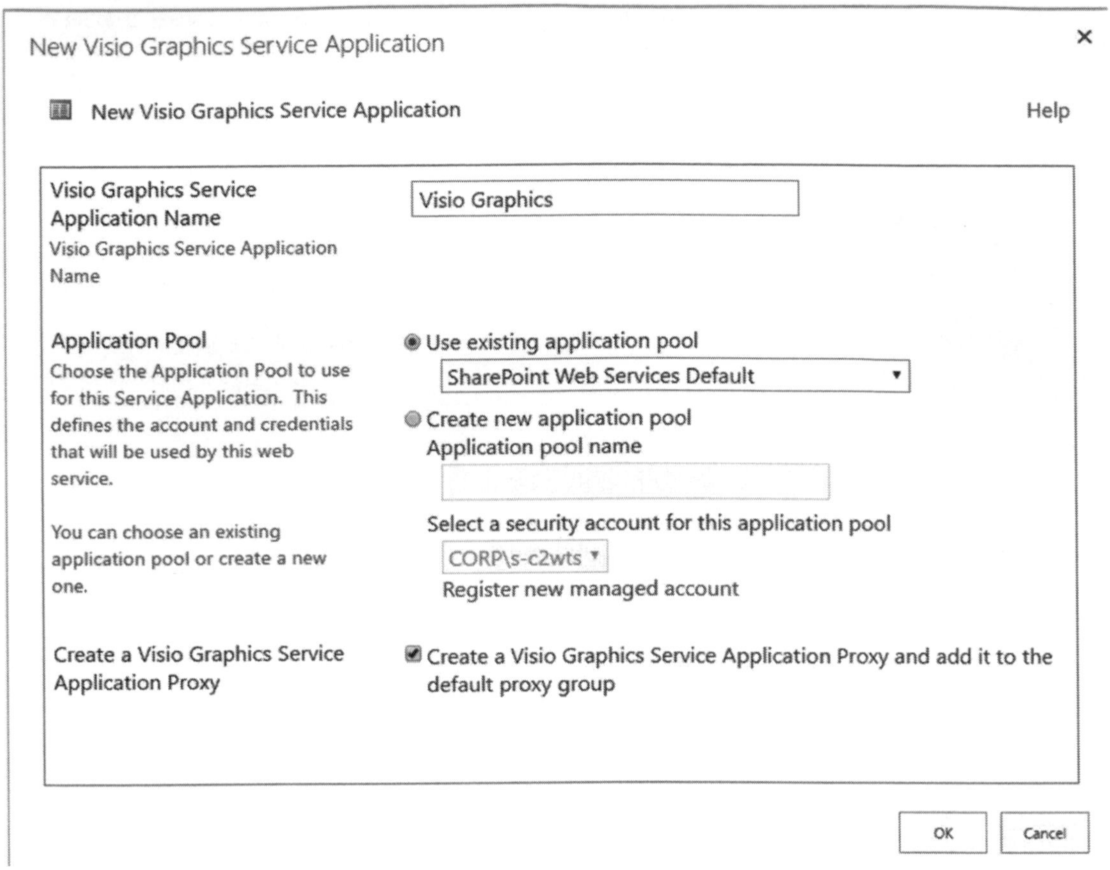

Figure 8-10. *New Visio Graphics Service Application*

The Visio Graphics Service Application can also be created by using the New-SPVisioServiceApplication cmdlet from an elevated SharePoint Management Shell. To create a Visio Graphics Service, we need to specify the Service Application name, Application Pool, and the switch to add it to the default Proxy group.

```
$sa = New-SPVisioServiceApplication -Name "Visio Graphics" -ApplicationPool "SharePoint Web Services Default" -AddToDefaultGroup
```

To test the Service Application, simply upload a Visio Diagram into SharePoint, and when clicking the document, it will open in the browser, instead of downloading it to the computer.

Machine Translation Services

The Machine Translation Services Service Application is a Service Application that allows users and developers to translate not only sites, but their content as well, to other languages. The Machine Translation Services is interacted through APIs, and the users do not have a "Translate Document" button, unless of course, their developers created a custom action for them.

Before creating the Machine Translation Service Application, you need to make sure the following Service Application exists in the SharePoint 2016 farm:

- App Management Service Application (seen in Chapter 5)
- A User Profile Service Application Proxy in the Default Group of the Farm
- The SharePoint Farm has access to the Internet

The Machine Translation Service Application can be created either from the Central Administration or by PowerShell. To create the machine Translation Service Application via the Central Administration, navigate to the Manage Service Application page, from the Ribbon click New, and select Machine Translation Service.

A Window will open similar to Figure 8-11, in which you will have to enter the Name of the Service Application as well as selecting whether to create a new Service Application pool or not. We recommend using the same Application pool as for the previous service applications, unless there is a business requirement to isolate this Servicer Application.

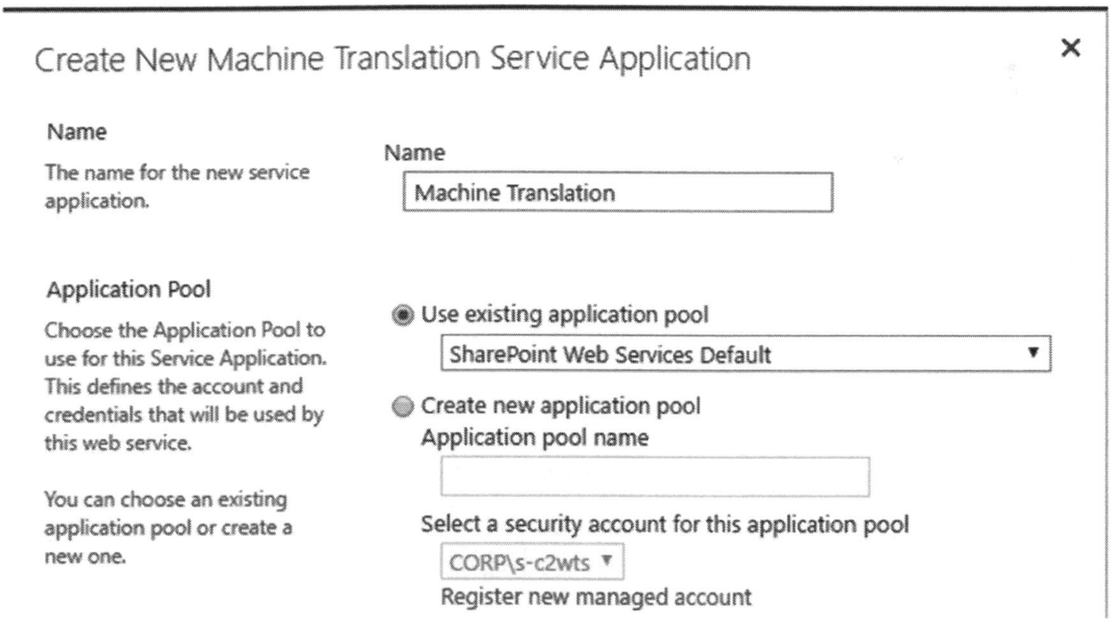

Figure 8-11. *New Machine Translation Service Application Name and Application Pool*

We then need to select whether to run the Machine Translation Service Application in Partitioned Mode, as well as whether you want to add it to the Default Proxy List. The Partitioned Mode checkbox must be checked only when you deploy the SharePoint farm in Multi-Tenant mode. This is an edge case, and is generally something you should not do, unless you have a specific requirement for Multi-Tenancy in your organization. Finally we must enter the Database Server and name for our Machine Translation database as seen in Figure 8-12.

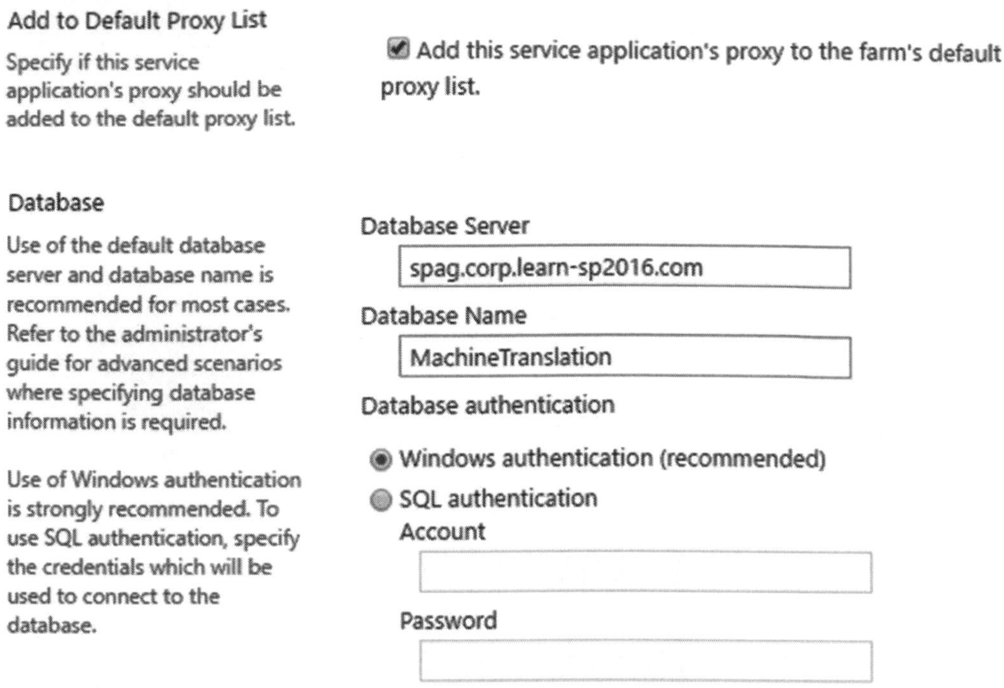

Add to Default Proxy List

Specify if this service
application's proxy should be
added to the default proxy list.

☑ Add this service application's proxy to the farm's default
proxy list.

Database

Use of the default database
server and database name is
recommended for most cases.
Refer to the administrator's
guide for advanced scenarios
where specifying database
information is required.

Use of Windows authentication
is strongly recommended. To
use SQL authentication, specify
the credentials which will be
used to connect to the
database.

Database Server

> spag.corp.learn-sp2016.com

Database Name

> MachineTranslation

Database authentication

◉ Windows authentication (recommended)

◉ SQL authentication

Account

Password

Figure 8-12. *New Machine Translation Service Application*

To create the Machine Translation Service Application via PowerShell, you must use the
`New-SPTranslationServiceApplication` cmdlet from an elevated SharePoint Management Shell. To create
the Machine Translation Service Application with the same settings as in the preceding screenshot, we
would run the following PowerShell command.

```
New-SPTranslationServiceApplication -Name "Machine Translation" -DatabaseName
"MachineTranslation" -ApplicationPool "SharePoint Web Services Default" -Default
```

To test the Machine Translation Service Application works properly, you can run a PowerShell script
that uses CSOM to call the required functions. We have created the following sample script:

```
$siteUrl = "https://sharepoint.learn-sp2016.com"
$loginname = "corp\vlad"
$language = "fr-fr"
$input = "https://sharepoint.learn-sp2016.com/Shared%20Documents/DocumentToTranslate.docx"
$output = "https://sharepoint.learn-sp2016.com/Shared%20Documents/DocumentFR.docx"
Add-Type -Path 'C:\Program Files\Common Files\Microsoft Shared\Web Server Extensions\15\
ISAPI\Microsoft.SharePoint.Client.dll'
Add-Type -Path 'C:\Program Files\Common Files\Microsoft Shared\Web Server Extensions\15\
ISAPI\Microsoft.SharePoint.Client.Runtime.dll'
Add-Type -Path 'C:\Program Files\Common Files\Microsoft Shared\Web Server Extensions\15\
ISAPI\Microsoft.Office.Client.TranslationServices.dll'
Write-Host "Please enter password for $($siteUrl):"
$pwd = Read-Host -AsSecureString
```

```
$ctx = New-Object Microsoft.SharePoint.Client.ClientContext($siteUrl)
$ctx.Credentials = New-Object System.Net.NetworkCredential($loginname, $pwd)

$job = New-Object Microsoft.Office.Client.TranslationServices.SyncTranslator($ctx, $language)

$job.OutputSaveBehavior = [Microsoft.Office.Client.TranslationServices.SaveBehavior]::Appen
dIfPossible

$job.Translate([string]$input, [string]$output);
$ctx.ExecuteQuery()
```

Where the $SiteUrl variable is the Site Collection where the document you want translated is stored. The $loginname is your username, and the $language is the language that you want the document translated into. The $input variable is the original document you want translated into another language, and the $output variable is the path where Machine Translation Services will create the document. The $input variable must be a valid URL to a document, while the $output variable will be the future URL where the translated document will be.

With the Machine Translation Service Application created, your developers can now create code that uses the Machine Translation Service.

■ **Tip**   To learn more about the Machine Translation Services APIs, visit the page on MSDN: `https://msdn.microsoft.com/en-us/library/office/jj163145.aspx`

Access Services 2010

SharePoint Server 2016 includes two different Access service applications. The first one is called "Access Services 2010," while the second one is "Access Services 2013". Access Services 2010 has been around since SharePoint 2010 and is present for compatibility purposes, while Access Services 2013 is a more advanced Service Application about which we will talk a bit later in this chapter. Access Services 2010 is a Service Application that allows users to modify and publish in SharePoint 2016, an access Web Database that was previously created in SharePoint 2010. Users can view the published web database without having Access installed locally; however, they need the Office application in order to modify the database structure.

To create the Access Services 2010 Service Application from Central Administration, navigate to the Manage Service Applications page, click New in the Ribbon, and select Access Services 2010. As seen in Figure 8-13, you will have to enter a name for the Service Application, select the Service Application Pool we created earlier for those Service Applications, and select whether this Service Application will be in the default proxy list.

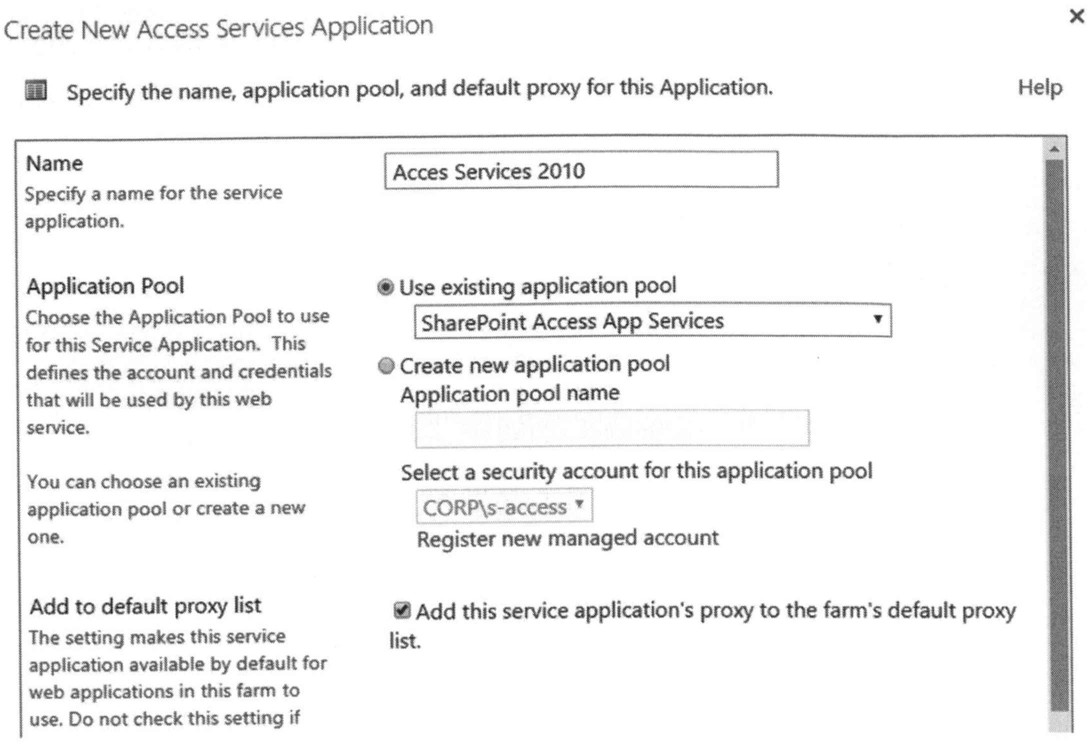

Figure 8-13. *New Access Services 2010 Service Application*

This can also be done by PowerShell with the `New-SPAccessServiceApplication` cmdlet from an elevated SharePoint Management Shell. In order to create a Service Application with the same parameters as before, we would run the following cmdlet.

```
New-SPAccessServiceApplication -Name "Access Services 2010" -ApplicationPool "SharePoint Web
Services Default" –Default
```

With the Access 2010 Service Application created, let's look at the Access App Services 2013 version.

Access Services 2013

Access Apps for SharePoint are a type of database that you build in Access, and use and share with others as an app in SharePoint directly in the browser. Access Services 2013 is a more advanced Service Application that allows you to create Access apps and track data such as contacts, orders, and so on. Access Services 2013 is a bit more complicated to configure compared to the other Service Applications, and will require installing extra prerequisites.

Before starting to configure Access Services, the following Service Applications need to be configured:

- Secure Store Service
- App Management Service
- Microsoft SharePoint Foundation Subscription Settings Service
- Access Services 2010

Your App environment must also be configured as we covered in Chapter 5.

First, since the account running Access Services 2013 requires more SQL permissions than the other Service Applications, we will create a new service account dedicated for this service application. In our environment, the account we created has the username CORP\s-access. Since this account will be used to run an Application Pool, we will register it as a managed account by running the following PowerShell cmdlet.

```
$cred = Get-Credential -UserName "CORP\s-access" -Message "Managed Account"
New-SPManagedAccount -Credential $cred
```

We will then create a new Service Application called "SharePoint Access App Services" in which we will run the Service Application.

```
New-SPServiceApplicationPool -Name "SharePoint Access App Services" -Account
(Get-SPManagedAccount "CORP\s-access")
```

After the Service Application is created, we need to modify a setting in IIS that will be unique to this Service Application. Navigate to the IIS Application Pools, and from Advanced Settings, change "Load User Profile" to True, as seen in Figure 8-14.

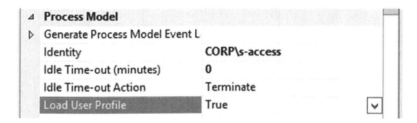

Figure 8-14. *Load User Profile Setting in IIS*

■ **Note**   Remember to make this change on all the servers where the App Pool is Present

---

Next we need to make sure our new Service Account has rights to the other content databases, since that is where the Access Apps will be created. This is done by the following PowerShell cmdlets:

```
$w = Get-SPWebApplication https://sharepoint.learn-sp2016.com
$w.GrantAccessToProcessIdentity("CORP\s-access")
$w.Update()
```

Remember to repeat this step for every Web Application where you wish to host Access Apps. Lastly, the service account must have Read/Write permission to the config cache folder located at C:\ProgramData\ Microsoft\SharePoint\Config on every server.

After those permissions are done, we need to install prerequisites from the SQL Server Feature Pack on our SharePoint servers. This is only required on the servers on which you will run the Access Services SharePoint service; however, we recommend installing those prerequisites on all the servers in your farm. This will make your farm more flexible if you decide to change roles in the future. In a MinRole configuration, Access Services are automatically started on all the servers running the Web Front End role. The Prerequisites are:

- Microsoft SQL Server Local DB (SQLLocalDB.msi)

  - SQL 2014: `https://www.microsoft.com/en-ca/download/details.aspx?id=42299`

  - SQL 2016: `https://www.microsoft.com/en-us/download/details.aspx?id=52679`

- Microsoft SQL Server Data-Tier Application Framework (Dacframework.msi)

  - SQL 2014: `https://www.microsoft.com/en-us/download/details.aspx?id=46898`

  - SQL 2016: `https://www.microsoft.com/en-us/download/details.aspx?id=46898`

- Microsoft SQL Server Native Client (sqlncli.msi)

  - SQL 2014: `https://www.microsoft.com/en-us/download/details.aspx?id=29065`

  - SQL 2016: `https://www.microsoft.com/en-us/download/details.aspx?id=29065`

- Microsoft SQL Server Transact-SQL ScriptDom (SQLDOM.MSI)

  - SQL 2014: `https://www.microsoft.com/en-ca/download/details.aspx?id=42295`

  - SQL 2016: `https://www.microsoft.com/en-us/download/details.aspx?id=52676`

- Microsoft System CLR Types for Microsoft SQL Server (SQLSysClrTypes.msi)

  - SQL 2014: `https://www.microsoft.com/en-ca/download/details.aspx?id=42295`

  - SQL 2016: `https://www.microsoft.com/en-us/download/details.aspx?id=52676`

After the prerequisites are installed, we need to configure SQL Server for Access Services. The SQL Server you use needs to have the following Instance features:

- Database Engine Services
- Full-Text and Semantic Extractions for Search
- Client Tools Connectivity

If those features weren't installed when originally creating the Instance, you can add them afterward from the SQL Server Installation Center. To install them using the command line, use the following command.

```
Setup.exe /IACCEPTSQLSERVERLICENSETERMS /Action=Instal /FEATURES=FullText,Conn
```

Next we need to create a new login in your SQL Server from SQL Server Management Studio as seen in Figure 8-15.

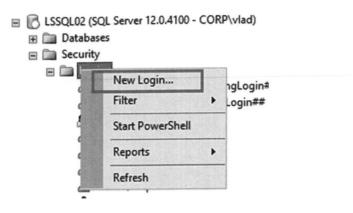

Figure 8-15. *New Login in SQL Server*

On the General Tab, write the username of the Access service account, and from the *Server Roles* tab, select *dbcreator* as well as *securityadmin* as seen in Figure 8-16.

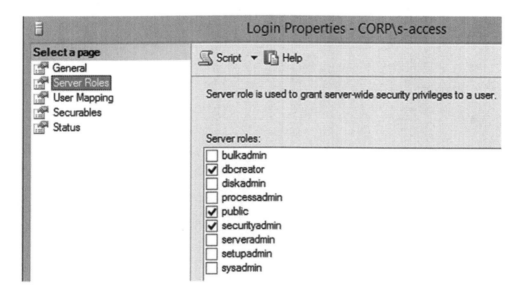

Figure 8-16. *Access Service Account Server Roles*

Since this account will also have to run some stored procedures on the Configuration database, in the User Mapping tab, give this account the *SPDataAccess* permission as seen in Figure 8-17.

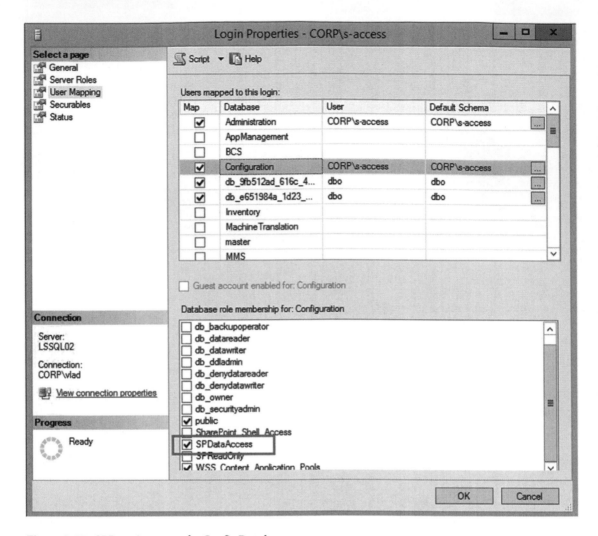

Figure 8-17. *SPDataAccess on the Config Database*

We then need to go to the SQL Server Properties, and from the Security Tab, enable mixed authentication mode (SQL Server and Windows) as seen in Figure 8-18.

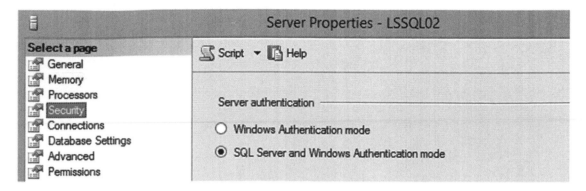

Figure 8-18. *Mixed SQL Authentication mode*

Afterward, from the Advanced Tab, we need to change the "Enable Contained Databases" and "Allow Triggers to Fire Others" to True, and set the Default Language to English as seen in Figure 8-19.

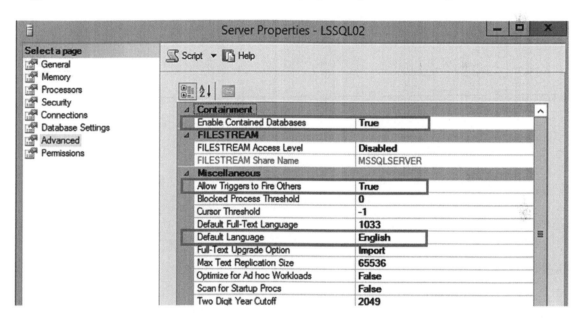

Figure 8-19. *Advanced SQL Server properties*

Lastly, we need to configure SQL Server protocols. Both the TCP/IP and Named Pipes protocols must be enabled. This can be done from the SQL Server Configuration Manager as seen in Figure 8-20.

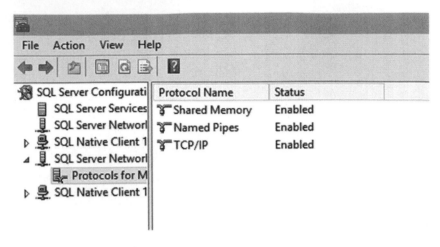

Figure 8-20. *Protocols for SQL Server*

For those changes to take effect, you need to restart the SQL Server Engine Service.

After SQL Server is configured, you must enable the following ports through the firewall:

- TCP 1433

- TCP 1434

- UDP 1434

With all the prerequisites configured, it's time to create the Access Service Application.

To create the Access Services 2013 Service Application we would use the New-SPAccessServicesApplication cmdlet, notice the extra s in Services compared to Access 2010. To create a Service Application with the name Access App Services in our Service Application pool dedicated for Access Services, we would run the following cmdlet:

```
New-SPAccessServicesApplication -Name "Access App Services" -ApplicationPool "SharePoint
Access App Services" –Default
```

The last step is to navigate to the Central Administration, into the Access App Services 2013 Service Application. At the bottom of the configuration window, open the New Application Database Server configuration group, and type the SQL Server that you want to use for the Access Services App Databases as seen in Figure 8-21.

◢ New Application Database Server

This database server is used to create new application databases.

We strongly recommend using Windows Authentication. If you want to use SQL authentication, specify the credentials which will be used to connect to the database.

Application Database Server

    spag.corp.learn-sp2016.com

Application Database Authentication

⦿ Windows authentication (recommended)

◯ SQL authentication

    Account

    Password

☐ Validate the application database server (recommended)

Figure 8-21. *New Application Database Server*

■ **Note** While the checkbox "Validate the application database server" is recommended, at the moment of writing this book it generated an error if selected. This error is documented by Microsoft in KB3153957 at https://support.microsoft.com/en-ca/kb/3153957

After the Application Database Server is configured, we can test the Service Application from a client that has Access 2016 installed. From Access, create a new Custom Web App as seen in Figure 8-22.

Figure 8-22. *New Custom Web App*

When prompted, enter the URL of a Site Collection to which you have contribute access. In our example seen in Figure 8-23, we have created an Access App by using the default Orders template.

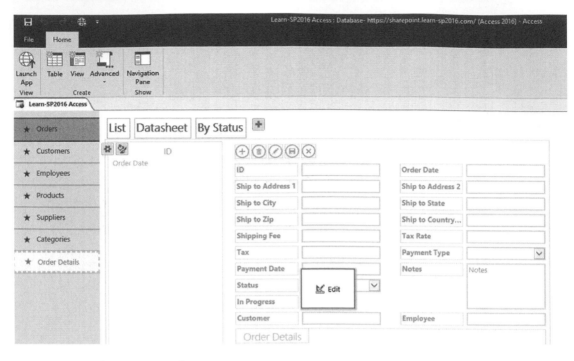

Figure 8-23. *Orders Access Database*

When ready to publish, click "Launch App" from the Ribbon, and the App should open in SharePoint 2016 as seen in Figure 8-24.

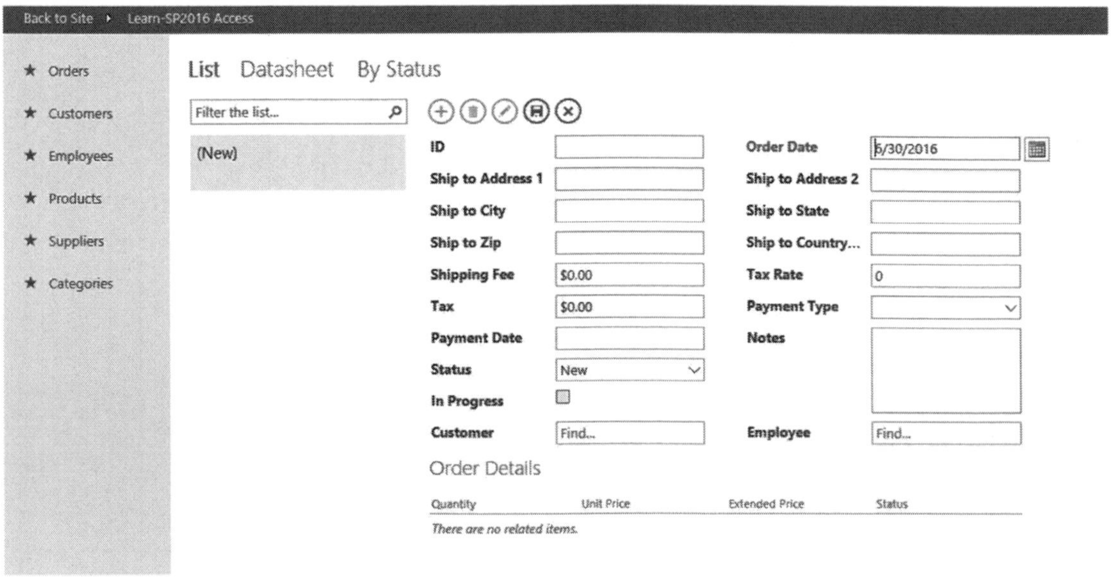

Figure 8-24. *Access App in SharePoint*

Access Services has successfully been configured. As a SharePoint Admin, it's important to understand that each App creates its own database in SQL Server; therefore, it's important to make sure new App databases are added to your SQL Maintenance plan and to your SQL AlwaysOn availability group or mirroring.

Next Steps

In this chapter, we learned how to deploy the productivity Service Applications in SharePoint Server 2016 both by the Central Administration, and by using PowerShell. In the next chapter, we will look at how to install and configure Office Online Server to allow our users to view, edit, and create Office documents directly in the browser.

■ ■ ■

CHAPTER 9

Configuring Office Online Server for SharePoint

Office Online Server, previously named Office Web Apps, is a server that allows users to view and edit Office documents such as Word, Excel, PowerPoint, and OneNote directly from the browser. Office Online Server also allows users to view PDF documents in the browser, and convert Office documents to PDF.

It's important not to get confused in Microsoft's choice of name for the product. Even if it's called Office *Online* Server, the product is fully On-Premises, and does not require a connection to Office 365 or any Office 365 licenses.

Furthermore, Office Online Server isn't only for SharePoint! Office Online Server can add features to Exchange Server 2013 / 2016 as well as Skype for Business Server 2015 or Lync Server 2013. We will not cover those features, or how to enable them in this book; however, it is important to know that the investments you make in Office Online Server aren't only for SharePoint, but for Exchange and Skype for Business as well.

There are multiple reasons to deploy Office Online Server other than the ability to view and edit Office documents from the browser. With Excel Services gone in SharePoint Server 2016, you need Office Online Server in order to view Excel and PowerPivot Dashboards. Furthermore, Office Online Server enables new features such as Durable Links and Modern Cloud attachments.

Office Online Server Architecture Overview

Before we get start configuring Office Online Server 2016, it's important to understand the Office Online Server 2016 architecture in order to understand what we will install and configure in this chapter.

Office Online Server is in a way similar to SharePoint Server as we need one or more Office Online Servers to create an Office Online Server Farm. This farm can serve one, or multiple SharePoint, Exchange and Skype for Business deployments. In Figure 9-1, we can see an Office Online Server farm consisting of three servers that serve two different SharePoint Farms as well as an Exchange deployment and a Skype for Business deployment.

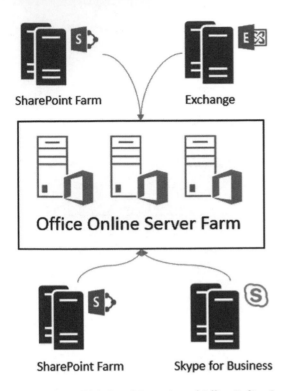

Figure 9-1. *High-Level Overview of Office Online Server Architecture*

An Office Online Server Farm can be made accessible through two different URLs. We call the first one the Internal URL, and the second one the External URL as seen in Figure 9-2. The URLs can be either HTTP or HTTPS, and at least the one of the URLs is mandatory. Office Online Server allows you to configure either the Internal URL, the External URL, or both. When configuring the Internal and External URLs, you have the choice to configure them either on HTTP or HTTPS. Since our SharePoint Server will use HTTPS, we will configure Office Online Server to use HTTPS as well. Securing your Office Online Server with SSL is extremely important, since the OAuth token is passed in a packet on the request, and you could be subject to a man-in-the-middle attack if that token is not secured. You can set up Office Online Server on HTTPS even if your SharePoint sites are running on HTTP.

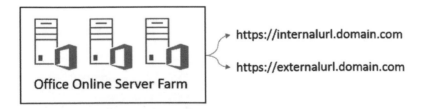

Figure 9-2. *Office Online Server Internal and External URL*

Office Online Server uses only three ports to communicate between servers and with SharePoint, Exchange, and Skype for Business. Those ports are described in Table 9-1.

Table 9-1. *Office Online Server Ports*

Port	Function
80	HTTP traffic
443	HTTPS traffic
809	Traffic between Office Online Servers

To enhance security, you can block the ports that you do not use. For example, if your Office Online Server farm will be only made of one server and be accessible via SSL, you only need port 443.

The minimum hardware requirements for Office Online Server are the same as for SharePoint Server 2016 and outlined in Table 9-2.

Table 9-2. *Office Online Server Minimum Requirements*

CPU	RAM	Disk
64-bit, 4 cores	12 GB	80 GB for system drive

The supported Operating System for Office Online Server is Windows Server 2012 R2 64 bit and the following Prerequisites are required:

- NET Framework 4.5.2
  (http://go.microsoft.com/fwlink/p/?LinkId=510096)

- Visual C++ Redistributable for Visual Studio 2015
  (http://go.microsoft.com/fwlink/p/?LinkId=620071)

- Microsoft Identity Extensions (Only required when using BI functions)
  (http://go.microsoft.com/fwlink/p/?LinkId=620072)

From a networking perspective, all the servers in an Office Online Server Farm must be in the same forest, and in order to use Business Intelligence Features, they must be in the same forest as the users who will use them.

Office Online Server must be installed on its own dedicated server. It can run on both Physical as well as in a Virtual Machine running on Hyper-V or VMware. Office Online Server cannot be installed on the same machine as Exchange, SharePoint, and Skype for Business, SQL, Domain Controller, or any server that has Office installed.

■ **Note** At the time of writing this book, the Office Online Server license prohibits enterprises installing Office Online Server on physical hardware they do not own, therefore making it impossible to use Office Online Server in Azure, AWS, or any other provider. Check with your Microsoft Licensing Expert before deploying Office Online Server on any machines you do not own.

If you plan to have more than one Office Online Server in your farm, you will need a load balancer that supports the following features:

- SSL Offloading or SSL Bridging

- Enabling client affinity or front-end affinity

- Layer 7 routing

Furthermore, if you plan to open Office Online Server to the Internet for SharePoint or Exchange, you will also need a reverse proxy in order to securely make it available to external users.

If you plan to use SSL, the certificate must come from a trusted Certificate Authority and include the fully qualified domain name (FQDN) of your Office Online Server farm URL in the SAN (Subject Alternative Name). Furthermore, the FQDN of every server in your Office Online Server farm must be in the SAN of the certificate. The certificate we used in our book can be seen in Figure 9-3 and has *office.learn-sp2016.com* as the Issued To, which is both our Internal and External URL, and also has servers *LSOOS1*, *LSOOS2*, and *LSOOS3* in the SAN in their FQDN format.

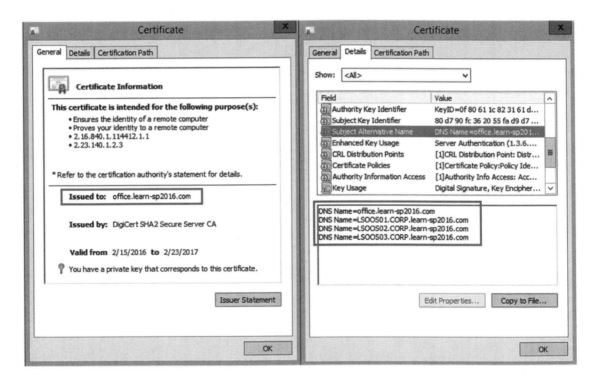

Figure 9-3. *Office Online Server Certificate*

Installing Office Online Server 2016

Now that we know the Office Online Server architecture, let's start installing it. We first need to install the following prerequisites.

- NET Framework 4.5.2

- Visual C++ Redistributable for Visual Studio 2015

Afterward, we need to activate the required Windows Server Features and Roles. This can be achieved with the following PowerShell script, which **will require a reboot.**

```
Add-WindowsFeature Web-Server,Web-Mgmt-Tools,Web-Mgmt-Console,Web-WebServer,Web-Common-
Http,Web-Default-Doc,Web-Static-Content,Web-Performance,Web-Stat-Compression,Web-Dyn-
Compression,Web-Security,Web-Filtering,Web-Windows-Auth,Web-App-Dev,Web-Net-Ext45,Web-
Asp-Net45,Web-ISAPI-Ext,Web-ISAPI-Filter,Web-Includes,InkandHandwritingServices,NET-
Framework-Features,NET-Framework-Core,NET-HTTP-Activation,NET-Non-HTTP-Activ,NET-WCF-HTTP-
Activation45,Windows-Identity-Foundation
```

After the reboot, the following prerequisites need to be installed:

- Microsoft.IdentityModel.Extention.dll

After all prerequisites are successfully installed, you can open the Office Online Server Setup.exe from the binaries you got either from MSDN or the Volume Licensing Center.

After accepting the terms, select where you want to install the Office Online Server binaries as seen in Figure 9-4.

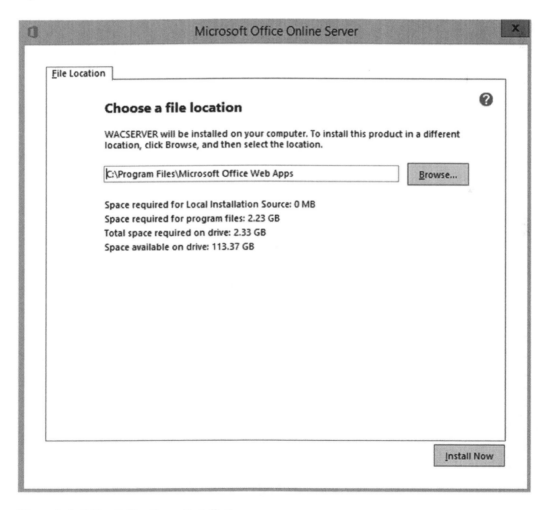

Figure 9-4. *Office Online Server Installation*

Location of the log files as well as cache location can be specified later when creating the Office Online Server farm. Click Next, until you get a screen similar to Figure 9-5 indicating that the installation has finished.

Figure 9-5. *Office Online Server Installation Confirmation*

With the installation of the Office Online Server binaries complete, it's now time to install any Language Packs that you might want to offer to you users. For the Multilanguage UI to work, the language pack must be installed both on the Office Online Server, as well as on your host (SharePoint, Exchange, or Skype for Business).

Since our farm is not created at this point, installing Public Updates or Language Packs is as simple as starting the installer, and clicking Next until it's done. As Public Updates also include updates for the Language Packs, make sure to install the base Language Packs before installing Public Updates. By installing the base Language Packs before the Public Updates, all the language related updates in the Public Updates will be applied.

After your Office Online Server(s) are on the update level you want and have the required Language Packs for your business, it's now time to create the Office Online Server farm.

Creating the Office Online Server Farm

Unlike most Microsoft products, Office Online Server does not have a user interface at all and the only way to manage it is by Windows PowerShell. Furthermore, unlike other Office Server products such as SharePoint, there is no "Office Online Management Shell" that you will find on your computer; the required module manage Office Online Server will be loaded by default every time you open PowerShell.

To create the farm, we need to run the New-OfficeWebAppsFarm PowerShell cmdlet. Office Web Apps is the old name of Office Online Server in the 2013 suite of Office Servers. You will see that most of the PowerShell cmdlets to manage Office Online Server still refer to Office Web Apps.

■ **Note**   Make sure to always run PowerShell as an administrator when changing Office Online Server configurations.

Before running the PowerShell to create our farm, there are a few things we need to plan. The first item to plan is what the URL will be that the consuming services (SharePoint, Exchange, or Skype for Business) will use to connect to the Office Online Server farm. From a SharePoint-only point of view, you could only have one URL if you want, since SharePoint can only use one of them, but not both. If you also plan to connect Skype for Business and Exchange to your Office Online Server Farm, they will sometimes need the External URL. A good example is when doing a Skype for Business meeting and sharing a PowerPoint presentation. Skype for Business will connect external users to the external URL of your office Online Server Farm. Something to consider is that to enable full functionality, the External URL must be accessible from the Internet. Some of the features are Document Previews from Outlook on the Web (formerly known as Outlook Web App), Skype for Business PowerPoint Presentations with external users, and document previews in Office 365 Search Results when using Cloud Hybrid Search.

Publishing both the Internal and External URL by using Secure Sockets Layers (SSL) is highly recommended for security reasons; both SharePoint and Exchange server can consume Office Online Server via HTTP. The only reasons that make it mandatory for you to publish it under SSL are as follows:

1. You have at least one SharePoint site that will be using HTTPS. If your SharePoint sites are using HTTPS, you will need it for your Office Online Server as well.

2. You plan to connect Office Online Server to Skype for Business. Skype for Business only connects to Office Online Server if the latter is using https.

While in this book we recommend SSL Bridging for security, Office Online Server also supports SSL Offloading. SSL Offloading is not recommended because the traffic between the Load Balancer and your Office Online Server will not be encrypted, and you can be subject to a man-in-the-middle attack. If you plan to use SSL up to the Office Online Server, either by using pass through or SSL bridging on your Network Load Balancer, make sure to import the certificate into IIS on every server of your Office Online Server Farm. Make sure the certificate has a Friendly Name in IIS, as that's what we will need to use in our PowerShell cmdlet.

■ **Note**   It is mandatory that the certificate have a Friendly Name, and this Friendly Name *cannot* contain an asterisk.

This certificate must also be trusted by the SharePoint Server Farm. If the certificate is from a Certification Authority such as DigiCert that is included by default in the Root Certification Authorities in Windows, it will work without doing any special configurations. However, if using a Self-Signed Certificate or an authority that is not in the root authority cert store by default, make sure to add it as a trusted certificate in the SharePoint Central Admin ➤ Security ➤ Manage Trust. Make sure to add the root certificate and not the end Certificate. You can view an example in Figure 9-6.

Establish Trust Relationship   ✕

General Setting

The name for this trust relationship.

Learn about trusts.

Name:

| Office Online Server Certificate |

Root Certificate for the trust relationship

This is mandatory regardless of whether you want to provide to or consume trust from the other farm. Please add the Root Certificate for the other farm with which you want to establish a trust relationship.

Learn about certificates.

Root Authority Certificate

| C:\Users\vlad\Downloads\ooscert.cer | Browse... |

Figure 9-6. Establish Trust Relation in the SharePoint 2016 Central Administration

You could also do this by running the following PowerShell cmdlets from an elevated SharePoint Management Shell.

```
$trustCert = Get-PfxCertificate <C:\Certs\OOSRootCert.cer>
New-SPTrustedRootAuthority "OOSRootCert" -Certificate $trustCert
```

The following is the cmdlet we used in our environment to create the Office Online Server Farm:

```
New-OfficeWebAppsFarm -InternalUrl "https://office.learn-sp2016.com" -ExternalUrl
"https://office.learn-sp2016.com" -CertificateName "office.learn-sp2016.com" -EditingEnabled
```

Where

InternalURL is the Internal URL of the farm

ExternalURL is the External URL of the farm, and as you see, you can select the same URL for both Internal and External URLs. This is what we did in our lab.

CertificateName is the Friendly Name of my Certificate in IIS

EditingEnabled is a switch that tells Office Online Server that users are allowed not only to view documents with it, but also to create and modify documents in SharePoint directly in the browser. As soon as you choose this switch, you will be prompted to approve that you have the right licenses.

■ **Note**   If you plan to use Office Online Server on HTTP you need to add the `-AllowHttp` switch. If you plan to use SSL Offloading, you need to pass the `-SSLOffloaded` switch.

The `New-OfficeWebAppsFarm` cmdlet has many parameters that are important to select the features you want to activate in your Office Online Server Farm. You can view those features on TechNet at the following link: `https://technet.microsoft.com/en-ca/library/jj219436.aspx` or by running the following PowerShell cmdlet

```
Get-Help New-OfficeWebAppsFarm -Online
```

After running the command, PowerShell will configure everything needed to get the farm configured. To validate the configuration was successful, point your DNS A record or host file to the server you just configured the farm on, and navigate to the Internal or `External URL` + `/hosting/discovery`. In this case that URL would be `https://office.learn-sp2016.com/hosting/discovery/`. If everything works as planned, you should see an XML file similar to Figure 9-7.

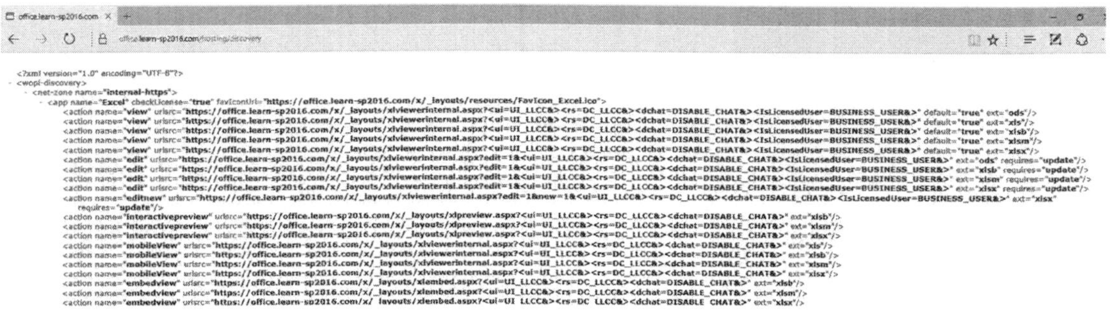

Figure 9-7. *Discovery XML File*

After we successfully configured our first machine in the Office Online Server farm, you need to install the same binaries on all the other machines in the Office Online Server farm, and if using an SSL Certificate, make sure you also import that into IIS. After the binaries are installed, simply run the following cmdlet.

```
New-OfficeWebAppsMachine -MachineToJoin LSOOS01.corp.learn-sp2016.com
```

Where in the MachineToJoin Parameter, you give it the FQDN of the first Office Online Server in the farm. In our case, that FQDN is LSOOS01.Corp.Learn-sp2016.com.

Repeat the New-OfficeWebAppsMachine cmdlet on all the servers you want to join to the Office Online Server Farm. After you finish adding all the servers in the farm, run the following cmdlet to validate their health status.

```
(Get-OfficeWebAppsFarm).Machines
```

The output should be all the servers in your Office Online Server farm, with a health status of healthy.

SSL Configuration

As we have enforced the use of TLS 1.2 for SharePoint, we must enable strong crypto as outlined in Microsoft Security Advisory 2960358. Per the advisory, it may be necessary to enable TLS 1.2 support on Windows Server 2012 R2 via a registry entry. Save the following text as a UseStrongCrypto.reg and import it into each Office Online Server. Once imported, restart each Office Online Server in your farm.

```
Windows Registry Editor Version 5.00

[HKEY_LOCAL_MACHINE\SOFTWARE\Microsoft\.NETFramework\v4.0.30319]
"SchUseStrongCrypto"=dword:00000001
```

Connecting Office Online Server with SharePoint 2016

After our Office Online Server Farm is up and running, we need to connect it to SharePoint Server 2016. The Process is pretty straightforward. From any SharePoint Server in the farm, run the following cmdlet to create the binding from SharePoint 2016 to Office Online Server.

```
New-SPWOPIBinding -ServerName office.learn-sp2016.com
```

If you are using Office Online Server on HTTP, you would need to add the –AllowHTTP switch, as in the following example.

```
New-SPWOPIBinding -ServerName office.learn-sp2016.com –AllowHTTP
```

Furthermore, if you use Office Online Server over HTTP, you also need to configure the Security Token Service to allow connections over HTTP. You can do this by running the following PowerShell Script.

```
$config = (Get-SPSecurityTokenServiceConfig)
$config.AllowOAuthOverHttp = $true
$config.Update()
```

The Server name you need to give is the FQDN of the URL you want SharePoint Server to use to access Office Online Server, without any http, or https in front. After that successfully finished, we will need to tell SharePoint how to correctly call this URL. SharePoint Server knows 4 WOPI Zones.

- Internal-http
- Internal-https (default)
- External-http
- External-https

The difference between the zones is the way that SharePoint calls the Office Online Server URL we gave it. In the Internal Zone, SharePoint will do a call on the short name. Since the default is internal-https, it would call our Office Online Server on *https://office*; however, we might have errors because our certificate SAN is *https://office.learn-sp2016.com*. That is why we need to set it to external-https by using the following cmdlet:

```
Set-SPWOPIZone -zone "external-https"
```

Lastly, you need to enable the Excel SOAP API for scheduled data refresh with Excel Online. To enable the Excel SOAP API, run the following Windows PowerShell cmdlet and replace the URL with your Office Online Server farm URL.

```
$Farm = Get-SPFarm
$Farm.Properties.Add("WopiLegacySoapSupport", "https://office.learn-sp2016.com /x/_vti_bin/
ExcelServiceInternal.asmx")
$Farm.Update()
```

To test that the connection was successfully configured, navigate to any SharePoint Site, and open an Office document. That document should open in the browser and you should be able to go through the entire document. Test Office Online Server with all of the supported Office document types, including editing functionality, if enabled.

One of the features of Office Online Server is document previews directly in the search results, as seen in Figure 9-8.

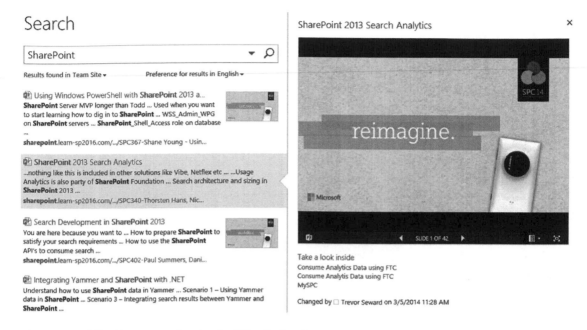

Figure 9-8. *Office Documents Preview in Office Online Server*

In order to enable this functionality, you will need to do a Full Crawl on your Content Sources and the previews will work afterward. With everything setup, let's learn how to maintain Office Online server, and how to debug it in case something goes wrong.

Office Online Server Maintenance

As a SharePoint Administrator, you might also be tasked with debugging and patching Office Online Server. Luckily, Office Online Server allows us to use tools we are already used to, since Office Online Server also has a ULS Log, and it works almost exactly the same as the SharePoint one. To find out the location of your Office Online simply run the following PowerShell cmdlet.

```
(Get-OfficeWebAppsFarm).LogLocation
```

■ **Note** By default, the Office Online Server log location is at C:\ProgramData\Microsoft\OfficeWebApps\Data\ Logs\ULS.

ULS log viewing tools such as UlsViewer will also work with Office Online Server as seen in Figure 9-9.

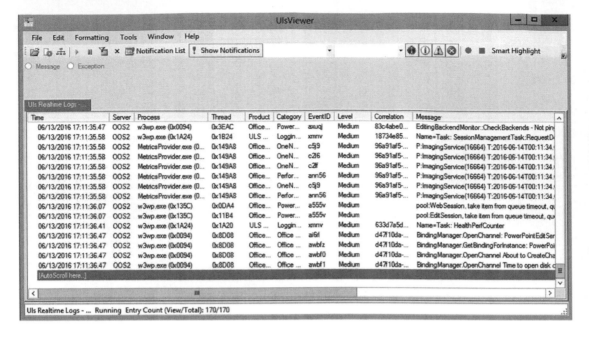

Figure 9-9. *Viewing ULS logs with UlsViewer*

You can also get more details in the ULS log files by changing the Log Verbosity. The Lowest level is VerboseEX, which will output everything, and the highest level is Unexpected, which will only show critical errors. To change the Log Verbosity in your Office Online Server farm, run the following cmdlet:

```
Set-OfficeWebAppsFarm -LogVerbosity Verbose
```

■ **Note**   A reboot of every machine in the Office Online Server farm is required for the Log Verbosity to be changed.

Patching Office Online Server

Patching Office Online server is very different from patching SharePoint Server. In order to apply patches to an Office Online Server machine, it needs to be removed from the Office Online Server farm it is part of. If you are patching a Single Server Office Online Server Farm, you simply have to remove the server from the farm by using the following PowerShell cmdlet:

```
Remove-OfficeWebAppsMachine
```

After the machine is removed, you can apply the patch, and then recreate the Office Online Server farm by using the `New-OfficeWebAppsFarm` and the same parameters that you initially used to create this Office Online Server Farm.

Patching a Multi-Server Office Online Server Farm adds an extra layer of complexity. In order to keep Office Online Server availability, you must first remove one of the servers from the load balancer pool, and afterward remove it from the Office Online server farm by using the `Remove-OfficeWebAppsMachine` cmdlet.

■ **Note**   You cannot start by removing the Office Online Server Master Machine as this can only be removed when there are no other machines left in the farm. To find out what server is your Master Machine, simply run the `Get-OfficeWebAppsMachine | Select MasterMachineName` cmdlet on any server in your Office Online Server farm.

Once you remove a server from the farm, apply the patches on it, and then recreate the farm by using the `New-OfficeWebAppsFarm` cmdlet and the same parameters that you initially used to create this Office Online Server Farm. Point the Load Balancer only to this server, so users will use the server with the patched version of Office Online Server.

Remove the other Office Online Servers from the old farm, apply the patches, and then join them to this server by running the `New-OfficeWebAppsMachine` cmdlet.

Finally, add the remaining servers in the load balancer to load balance the charge.

Next Steps

With Office Online Server successfully configured, in the next chapter we will learn how to configure Workflow Manager in order to provide modern workflows in SharePoint 2016.

■ ■ ■

CHAPTER 10

Workflow Manager

Workflow Manager is an external system to SharePoint Server, but is leveraged for advanced workflows created through SharePoint Designer 2013 or Visual Studio. Workflow Manager is designed to run in a separate Workflow Manager "farm," although it can be colocated on SharePoint.

Initial Setup

In our topology design, Workflow Manager 1.0 will be installed on LSWFM01, LSWFM02, and LSWFM03 for a highly available farm. Workflow Manager supports an architecture of one or three servers in a Workflow Manager farm. No other farm configuration is valid.

The SharePoint farm will consume Workflow Manager via the DNS name "workflow.corp.learn-sp2016.com," which is a virtual IP on a load balancer in front of the three Workflow Manager servers. A trusted SSL certificate, in this case a wildcard certificate, is used during the Workflow Manager configuration. This certificate must either have the SANs of the Workflow Manager servers and the URL used to connect to Workflow Manager, or a wildcard for the DNS name of the Workflow Manager servers. The certificate must also be trusted by the SharePoint farm. Workflow Manager 1.0 supports SQL Server 2008 R2 and SQL Server 2012. This installation will be using SQL Server 2012 with the AlwaysOn Listener of "gensql.corp.learn-sp2016.com."

Workflow Manager is installed via the Web Platform Installer (WebPI), which is run on each of the Workflow Manager servers.

■ **Tip** WebPI requires an Internet connection in order to download the applicable products. Not covered in this chapter is an Offline Installation of Workflow Manager. Microsoft has Offline Installation instructions at https://msdn.microsoft.com/en-us/library/jj906604.aspx.

In this installation, we will be starting with Service Bus 1.1 and the Service Bus 1.1 KB2972621. The Service Bus 1.1 installation will also include the Service Bus 1.1 KB3086798, which is an update for .NET 4.6 Framework compatibility. Search for 'Service Bus' and select 'Windows Azure Pack: Service Bus 1.1' and 'Windows Azure Pack: Security Update for Service Bus 1.1 (KB2972621),' as shown in Figure 10-1.

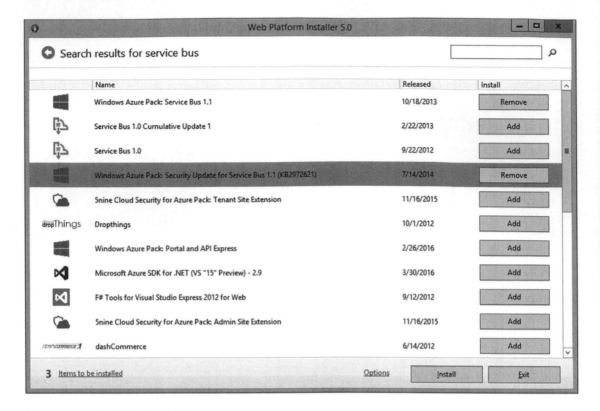

Figure 10-1. *Installing Service Bus 1.1*

Once the installation of the Service Bus 1.1 components has completed, search for 'Workflow Manager' in the Web Platform Installer. Find and select 'Workflow Manager 1.0 Refresh (CU2),' as shown in Figure 10-2.

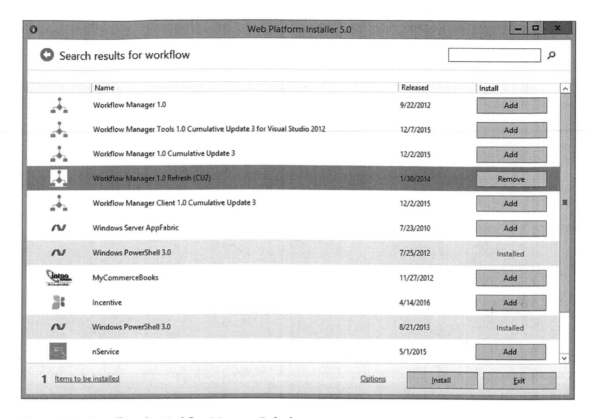

Figure 10-2. *Installing the Workflow Manager Refresh*

Once the Workflow Manager 1.0 Refresh (CU2) package has completed installing, you may be asked to run the Workflow Manager wizard. Instead, close out the wizard and then close and reopen the Web Platform Installer. This is done in order for the Web Platform Installer to detect that Service Bus 1.1 and Workflow Manager 1.0 are installed.

Again, search for 'Workflow Manager.' Find and select 'Workflow Manager 1.0 Cumulative Update 3,' as shown in Figure 10-3, and install it. Close the Workflow Manager wizard, if prompted, as well as the Web Platform Installer.

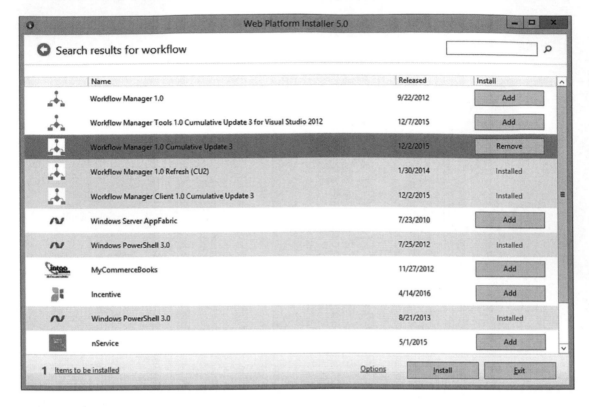

Figure 10-3. *Workflow Manager 1.0 CU3*

During the installation process, the Windows Fabric V1 RTM and IIS components will also be installed automatically.

Repeat the installation steps for the remaining two Workflow Manager servers.

Prior to deploying Workflow Manager, add the Service Account as a Local Administrator to each Workflow Manager server.

To create the Workflow Manager farm, we will be using the following PowerShell script, CreateWFMFarm.ps1.

```
$ErrorActionPreference = "Stop"
$ra = ConvertTo-SecureString "Password1!" -AsPlainText -Force
$certThumbprint = '3CF5BA40F795373E77A63A76F89C972EB7D6B81D'
$admins = 'BUILTIN\Administrators'
$svcAcct = 's-wfm@CORP'
$mgUsers = 's-wfm@CORP','trevor@CORP','vlad@CORP'
$baseConnectionString = 'Data Source=gensql.corp.learn-sp2016.com;Integrated Security=True;E
ncrypt=False;Initial Catalog='
$sbConnString = $baseConnectionString + 'SbManagementDB;'
$sbGateConnString = $baseConnectionString + 'SbGatewayDatabase;'
$sbMsgConnString = $baseConnectionString + 'SBMessageContainer01;'
$wfConnString = $baseConnectionString + 'WFManagementDB;'
$wfInstConnString = $baseConnectionString + 'WFInstanceManagementDB;'
$wfResConnString = $baseConnectionString + 'WFResourceManagementDB;'
```

The variables that must be adjusted in this script for your particular deployment are as follows:

- `$ra`
  - This variable contains the password of the RunAs account. Note this script uses the same RunAs account for the Service Bus and Workflow Manager farms.
- `$certThumbprint`
  - This contains the certificate thumbprint from the valid SSL certificate in use by the Workflow Manager farm.
- `$svcAcct`
  - This is the RunAs, or Service Account of the Service Bus and Workflow Manager farms. Note this script uses a single account to run both services.
- `$mgUsers`
  - This is a comma separated list of users in the format of username@DOMAIN that will have administrative rights over the Service Bus and Workflow Manager farms.
- `$baseConnectionString`
  - This variable contains the SQL Server AlwaysOn Availability Group fully qualified domain name. Alternatively, it can be adjusted to use a SQL Alias or SQL Server Name, as well as Instance Name if required.

All other variables may be left as they are.

```
Add-Type -Path "C:\Program Files\Workflow Manager\1.0\Workflow\Artifacts\Microsoft.ServiceBus.dll"

Write-Host -ForegroundColor Yellow "Creating Service Bus farm..."
New-SBFarm -SBFarmDBConnectionString $sbConnString `
    -InternalPortRangeStart 9000 -TcpPort 9354 -MessageBrokerPort 9356 -RunAsAccount
    $svcAcct -AdminGroup $admins `
    -GatewayDBConnectionString $sbGateConnString -FarmCertificateThumbprint $certThumbprint `
    -EncryptionCertificateThumbprint $certThumbprint -MessageContainerDBConnectionString
    $sbMsgConnString
```

New-SBFarm creates the ServiceBus farm and ServiceBus databases.

```
Write-Host -ForegroundColor Yellow "Creating Workflow Manager farm..."
New-WFFarm -WFFarmDBConnectionString $wfConnString `
    -RunAsAccount $svcAcct -AdminGroup $admins -HttpsPort 12290 -HttpPort 12291 `
        -InstanceDBConnectionString $wfInstConnString `
    -ResourceDBConnectionString $wfResConnString -OutboundCertificateThumbprint $certThumbprint `
        -SslCertificateThumbprint $certThumbprint `
    -EncryptionCertificateThumbprint $certThumbprint

Write-Host -ForegroundColor Yellow "Adding host to Service Bus farm..."
Add-SBHost -SBFarmDBConnectionString $sbConnString -RunAsPassword $ra -EnableFirewallRules $true
```

Likewise, New-WFFarm creates the Workflow Manager farm and databases. The next step, Add-SBHost, adds this particular server to the ServiceBus farm.

```
Try
{
    New-SBNamespace -Name 'WorkflowDefaultNamespace' -AddressingScheme 'Path' -ManageUsers $mgUsers
    Start-Sleep -s 90
}
Catch [system.InvalidOperationException] {}

$SBClientConfiguration = Get-SBClientConfiguration -Namespaces 'WorkflowDefaultNamespace'

Write-Host -ForegroundColor Yellow "Adding host to Workflow Manager Farm..."
Add-WFHost -WFFarmDBConnectionString $wfConnString -RunAsPassword $ra -EnableFirewallRules $true `
    -SBClientConfiguration $SBClientConfiguration
Write-Host -ForegroundColor Green "Completed."
$ErrorActionPreference = "Continue"
```

These last pieces of the script create the ServiceBus namespace along with add this particular server to the Workflow Manager farm.

Once the farm is created, one at a time, we will add the remaining two Workflow Manager servers to the farm using the ConnectWFMFarm.ps1 script. For these two servers, the PowerShell script is slightly shorter. The script adds the server to the ServiceBus farm and then to the Workflow Manager farm.

```
$ErrorActionPreference = "Stop"
$ra = ConvertTo-SecureString "Password1!" -AsPlainText -Force
$certThumbprint = '3CF5BA40F795373E77A63A76F89C972EB7D6B81D'
$mgUsers = 's-wfm@CORP','trevor@CORP'
$baseConnectionString = 'Data Source=gensql.corp.learn-sp2016.com;Integrated Security=True; ↵
                         ncrypt=False;Initial Catalog='
$sbConnString = $baseConnectionString + 'SbManagementDB;'
$wfConnString = $baseConnectionString + 'WFManagementDB;'

Add-Type -Path "C:\Program Files\Workflow Manager\1.0\Workflow\Artifacts\Microsoft.ServiceBus.dll"

Write-Host -ForegroundColor Yellow "Adding host to Service Bus Farm..."
Add-SBHost -SBFarmDBConnectionString $sbConnString -RunAsPassword $ra -EnableFirewallRules
           $true -Verbose;

$ErrorActionPreference = "Continue"

Try
{
    New-SBNamespace -Name 'WorkflowDefaultNamespace' -AddressingScheme 'Path' `
        -ManageUsers $mgUsers -Verbose;
    Start-Sleep -s 90
}
Catch [system.InvalidOperationException] {}

try
{
```

```
    $SBClientConfiguration = Get-SBClientConfiguration -Namespaces
'WorkflowDefaultNamespace' -Verbose;
}
Catch [system.InvalidOperationException] {}

Write-Host -ForegroundColor Yellow "Adding host to Workflow Manager Farm…"
Add-WFHost -WFFarmDBConnectionString $wfConnString -RunAsPassword $ra -EnableFirewallRules $true `
    -SBClientConfiguration $SBClientConfiguration -Verbose;
Write-Host -ForegroundColor Green "Completed."
$ErrorActionPreference = "Continue"
```

As with the CreateWFMFarm.ps1 script, the same variables are available to be adjusted, with the exception of $svcAcct. Note that when adding the second servers, it will stop and start the Service Bus and dependent services on the initial Workflow Manager server, and the final server will stop and start the Service Bus and dependent services on the first two servers.

Ultimately, the output of Get-SBFarm, in Figure 10-4, and Get-WFFarm, in Figure 10-5, will look similar to the following output.

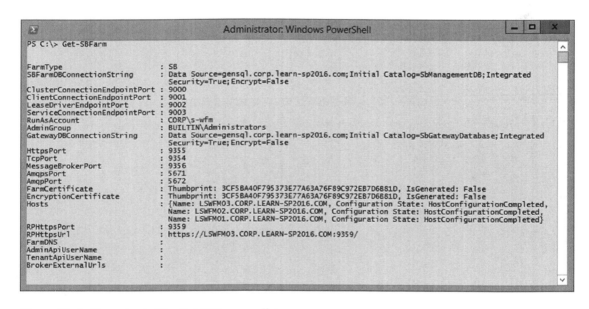

Figure 10-4. *The output of the Get-SBFarm cmdlet*

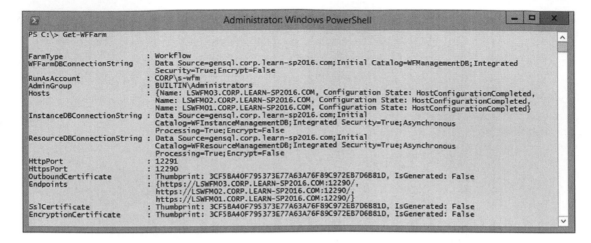

Figure 10-5. *The output of the Get-WFFarm cmdlet*

When the deploy has been completed, verify that the following services are running on each farm member.

- Service Bus Gateway

- Service Bus Message Broker

- Service Bus Resource Provider

- Windows Fabric Host Service

- Workflow Manager Backend

In addition, verify the status of the services via Get-SBFarmStatus, as shown in Figure 10-6, and Get-WFFarmStatus, as shown in Figure 10-7.

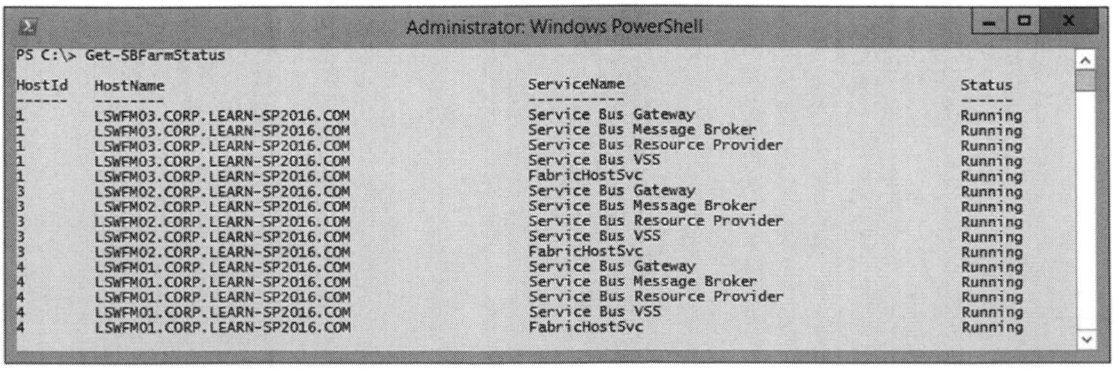

Figure 10-6. *The output of Get-SBFarmStatus*

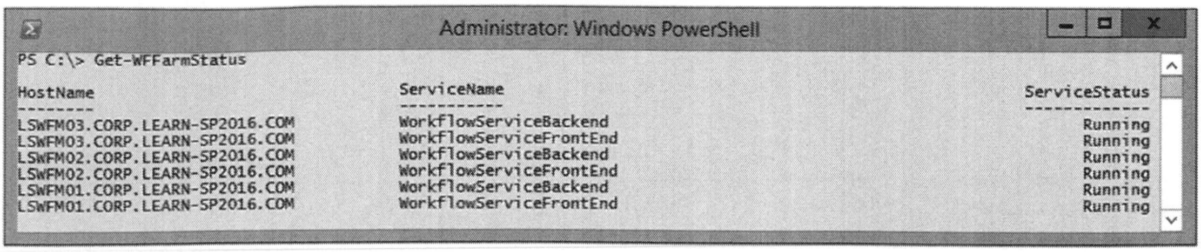

Figure 10-7. *The output of Get-WFFarmStatus*

The final step in the Workflow Manager configuration is to add the databases to the Availability Group on the SQL Server 2012 AlwaysOn Availability Group. Take a full backup of three Service Bus and three Workflow Manager databases.

- SbGatewayDatabase

- SbManagementDB

- SBMessageContainer01

- WFInstanceManagementDB

- WFManagementDB

- WFResourceManagementDB

Add the databases to the remaining replicas, and then add the Service Bus and Workflow Manager service account to the secondary node logins.

SSL Configuration

As we have enforced the use of TLS 1.2 for SharePoint, we must enable strong crypto as outlined in Microsoft Security Advisory 2960358. Per the advisory, it may be necessary to enable TLS 1.2 support on Windows Server 2012 R2 via a registry entry. Save the following text as a UseStrongCrypto.reg and import it into each Workflow Manager server. Once imported, restart each Workflow Manager server.

```
Windows Registry Editor Version 5.00

[HKEY_LOCAL_MACHINE\SOFTWARE\Microsoft\.NETFramework\v4.0.30319]
"SchUseStrongCrypto"=dword:00000001
```

Now that the Workflow Manager farm setup has been completed, we will move onto configuring and testing the SharePoint Server 2016 integration with Workflow Manager.

SharePoint Server Workflow Manager Integration

Prior to configuring the integration with Workflow Manager in the SharePoint farm, you must install the Workflow Manager Client. The client can be downloaded directly from Microsoft without the WebPI. The currently available version as of the publishing of this book is Workflow Manager Client Cumulative Update 3. This update may be installed without deploying previous versions of the Workflow Manager Client.

> ■ **Note** The Workflow Manager Client Cumulative Update 3 is available from https://www.microsoft.com/en-us/download/details.aspx?id=50043. Download the file WorkflowManagerClient_x64.msi.

As Workflow Manager will need to communicate with SharePoint via HTTPS requests, we must grant the Workflow Manager service account, CORP\s-wfm in this case, with Full Control over the SharePoint Web Applications where Workflow Manager will be used. Because we only have a single Web Application for Team, Publishing, and other sites, we will only grant this right on https://sharepoint.learn-sp2016.com. Using the SharePoint Management Shell, grant the service account Full Control via the User Policy.

```
$wa = Get-SPWebApplication https://sharepoint.learn-sp2016.com
$zp = $wa.ZonePolicies("Default")
$policy = $zp.Add("i:0#.w|CORP\s-wfm", "Workflow Manager")
$policyRole = $wa.PolicyRoles.GetSpecialRole("FullControl")
$policy.PolicyRoleBindings.Add($policyRole)
$wa.Update()
```

Workflow Manager may only be configured with SharePoint via the SharePoint Management Shell. From the SharePoint Management Shell, register Workflow Manager using the load balanced URL on port 12290 (default SSL port for Workflow Manager).

```
Register-SPWorkflowService -SPSite https://sharepoint.learn-sp2016.com -WorkflowHostUri
https://workflow.corp.learn-sp2016.com:12290
```

Note that while Register-SPWorkflowService needs a validate SharePoint site to register against, once Workflow Manager has been registered successfully, it will be registered for the entire farm, not just the specified Site Collection.

> ■ **Note** It may be necessary to restart the SharePoint servers in order to fully register the Workflow Manager binaries.

Now that Workflow Manager has been integrated into SharePoint, the next step will be to perform a simple test with SharePoint Designer 2013.

Testing Workflow Manager with SharePoint Designer 2013

For testing Workflow Manager with SharePoint Designer 2013, provision a new Site Collection using the Team Site template. If using an existing site, make sure the Site Feature "Workflow Task Content Type Feature" has been enabled.

On the site, create a new List named WorkflowTest. No additional configuration on the List needs to be performed for this test.

Using SharePoint Designer 2013 from a client computer, connect to the Site Collection and create a new List Workflow. Given the workflow a name and select the SharePoint 2013 Workflow under Platform Type as shown in Figure 10-8.

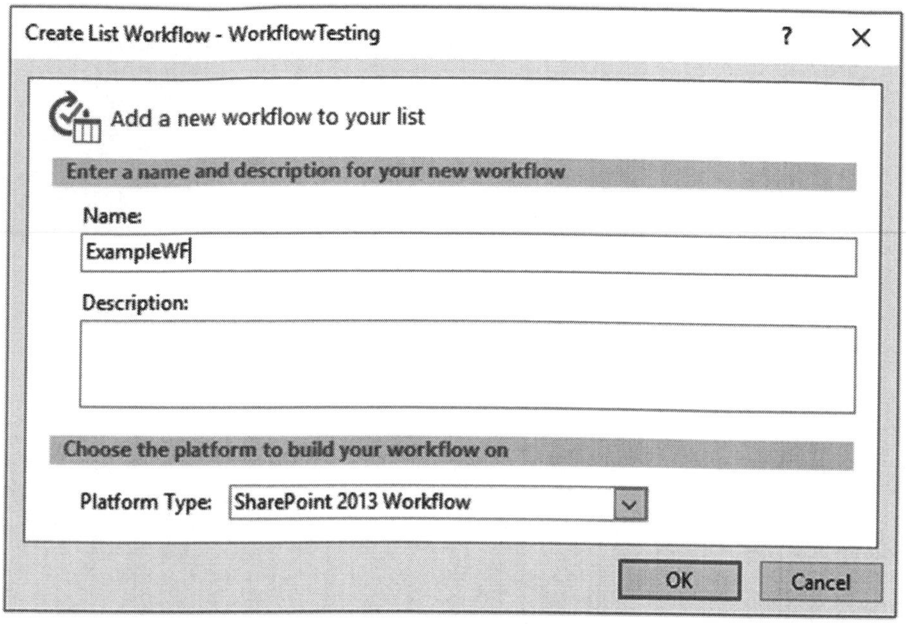

Create List Workflow - WorkflowTesting   ?   ✕

Add a new workflow to your list

Enter a name and description for your new workflow

Name:

ExampleWF

Description:

Choose the platform to build your workflow on

Platform Type: SharePoint 2013 Workflow   ▾

OK   Cancel

Figure 10-8. Creating a new SharePoint 2013 Workflow for testing

Insert an Action of "Log to History List" and add text to the action. Under Transition to Stage, select End of Workflow. In Figure 10-9, the Log to History List text is "Workflow Testing."

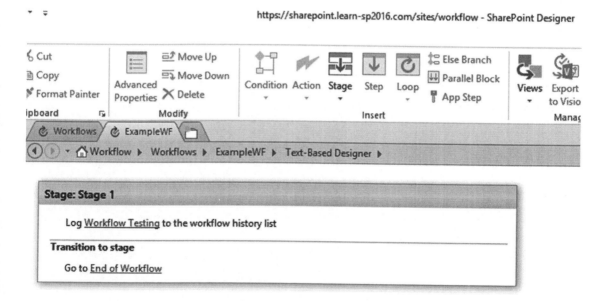

Figure 10-9. The steps in the example workflow

Under Workflow Settings, check the box next to "Start this workflow automatically when an item is created" as shown in Figure 10-10. When we create an entry on the new List, it will automatically start the workflow for us. Click the Publish button to publish the workflow to SharePoint.

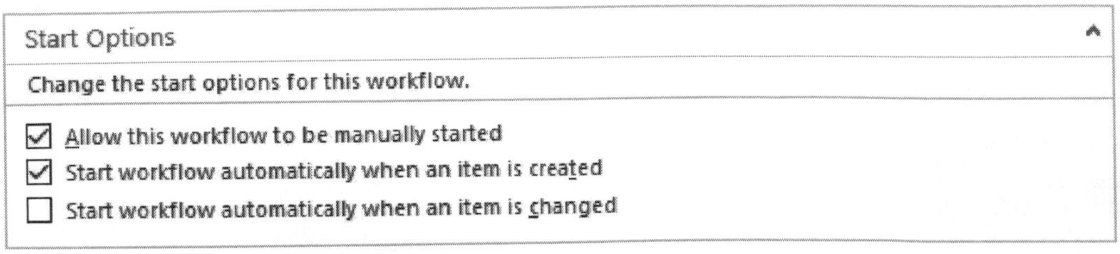

Start Options	⌃
Change the start options for this workflow.	

☑ Allow this workflow to be manually started
☑ Start workflow automatically when an item is created
☐ Start workflow automatically when an item is changed

Figure 10-10. *Enabling the workflow to automatically start when a new item is created*

From SharePoint, navigate to the custom List. Create a new item, specifying any value for the title. The workflow will automatically start. Monitor the status by clicking the ellipsis next to the List Item and navigate to Advanced ➤ Workflows. This page will display the workflow status, along with allowing you to manually start it if needed, as shown in Figure 10-11.

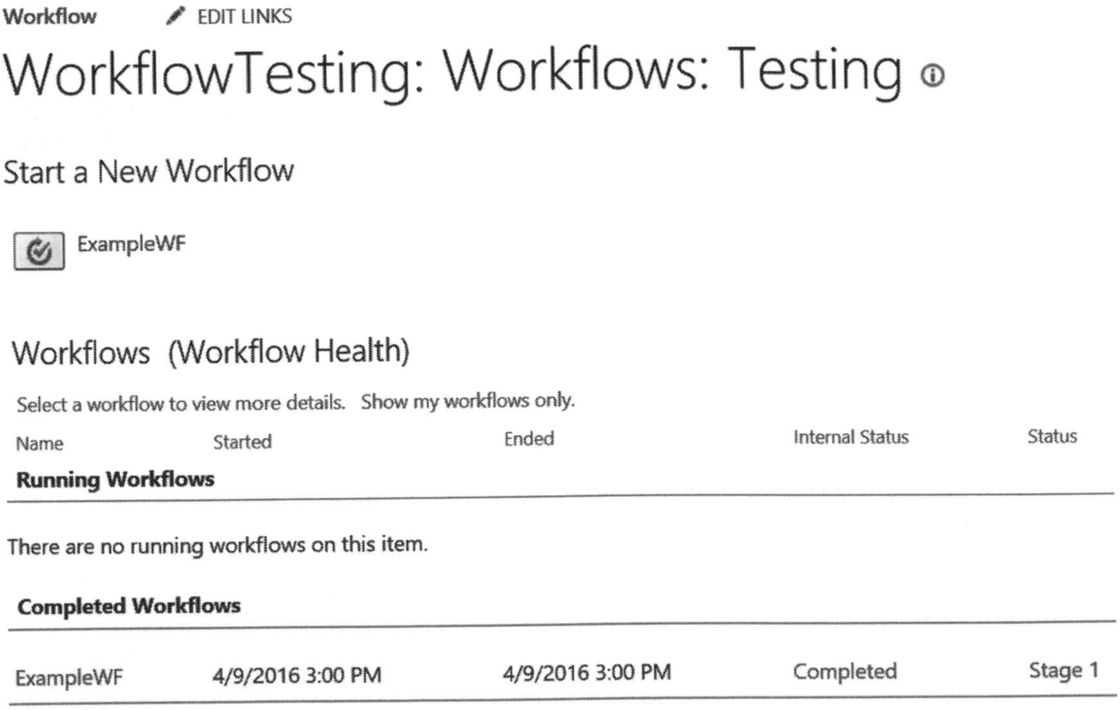

Workflow   ✏ EDIT LINKS

WorkflowTesting: Workflows: Testing ⓘ

Start a New Workflow

ExampleWF

Workflows (Workflow Health)

Select a workflow to view more details.   Show my workflows only.

Name	Started	Ended	Internal Status	Status
Running Workflows				

There are no running workflows on this item.

Name	Started	Ended	Internal Status	Status
Completed Workflows				
ExampleWF	4/9/2016 3:00 PM	4/9/2016 3:00 PM	Completed	Stage 1

Figure 10-11. *The workflow completed without errors*

Clicking the ExampleWF link in Figure 10-11 will provide additional details about the workflow, including any potential errors during execution. Figure 10-12 displays a successful workflow execution, but if there were an error, an informational icon would be displayed next to the Internal Status. Hovering over the icon will display a pop-out with the error encountered.

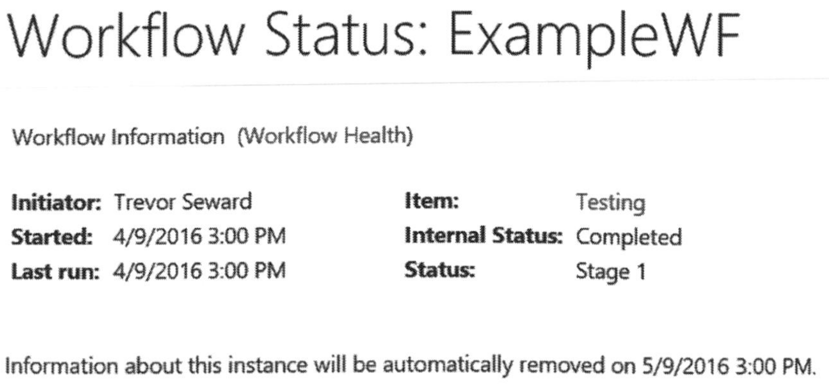

Workflow Status: ExampleWF

Workflow Information (Workflow Health)

Initiator: Trevor Seward   **Item:**   Testing
Started: 4/9/2016 3:00 PM   **Internal Status:** Completed
Last run: 4/9/2016 3:00 PM   **Status:**   Stage 1

Information about this instance will be automatically removed on 5/9/2016 3:00 PM.

Figure 10-12. *Details about the successful execution of the workflow*

It may also be helpful to monitor the ULS logs across the farm. Using Microsoft's ULSViewer, filter to the category "Workflow Services," which will provide detailed information regarding any potential errors. Errors are also logged in the Workflow Manager WFInstanceManagementDB database. Using SQL Server Management Studio, connect to the SQL Server instance that hosts the WFInstanceManagementDB. Run the following query to retrieve the additional information which will primarily be contained within the Message column.

```
Use [WFInstanceManagementDB]
SELECT * FROM DebugTraces (NoLock)
ORDER BY CreationTime DESC
```

This completes the deployment of the Workflow Manager and SharePoint Server 2016 integration. With working SharePoint 2013 Workflows, it is now possible to allow users to create modern workflows for their sites.

Next Steps

With working SharePoint 2013 Workflows, the next chapter will look at SharePoint Server 2016 and Exchange Server 2016 integration.

■ ■ ■

CHAPTER 11

SharePoint and Exchange Integration

While SharePoint Server 2016 alone provides great value to each and every company that decides to install it, it can offer more features when integrated with other servers from the Office suite such as Exchange Server 2016.

By integrating Exchange Server 2016 with SharePoint Server 2016, you enable features such as the Site Mailbox and Modern Attachments. As noted in the first chapter of this book, the Work Management Service from SharePoint 2013 does not exist in SharePoint Server 2016.

Site Mailbox Overview

The Site Mailbox was first introduced in Exchange 2013 / SharePoint 2013 and aims to increase collaboration as well as user productivity when dealing with both documents and e-mails for the same task. Traditionally, e-mails are stored in Exchange Server and consumed in Outlook, while documents are stored and consumed in SharePoint. This creates two different silos where users need to check for information. By implementing the Site Mailbox, you can create an Exchange Mailbox for specific SharePoint Sites, allowing your users to consume both SharePoint documents and Exchange e-mails from the same place.

After successfully being configured, the Site Mailbox will become an app (like a List or Document Library) that can be added in the Site Collection as seen in Figure 11-1.

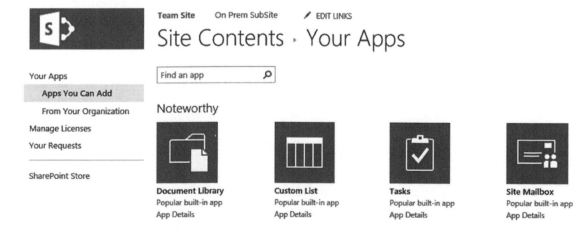

Figure 11-1. Add a Site Mailbox to a SharePoint Site

© Vlad Catrinescu and Trevor Seward 2016

V. Catrinescu and T. Seward, *Deploying SharePoint 2016*, DOI 10.1007/978-1-4842-1999-7_11

It's important to know that only one Site Mailbox can be added per SharePoint Site. Once created, the Site Mailbox will be assigned an e-mail address following the following naming convention: SM-SiteName@domain.tld. The Site Mailbox we created in a Site called "Team Site" is named "Team Site" and can be e-mailed at "SM-TeamSite@learn-sp2016.com." The Site Mailbox can be accessed from the browser as seen in Figure 11-2.

Figure 11-2. *Viewing the Site Mailbox in the browser*

The Site Mailbox can also be accessed directly from Outlook. When a user has access to a Site Mailbox, it will automatically be added to that user's Outlook client as seen in Figure 11-3.

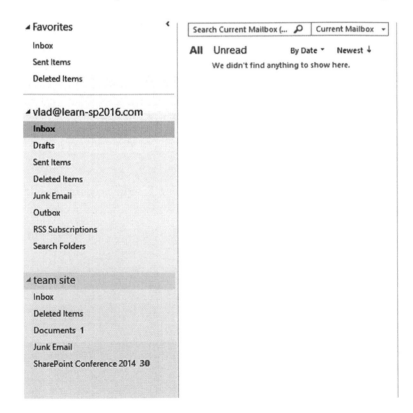

Figure 11-3. *The 'Team Site' Site Mailbox in Outlook 2016*

Another advantage of the Site Mailbox is that document libraries that are displayed in the Quick Launch will also be available as a folder in your Outlook client. Users will be able to quickly open documents in their client applications, as well as drag and drop documents in Outlook, which will automatically be uploaded to their SharePoint document library. Figure 11-4 shows the "SharePoint Conference 2014" document library inside Outlook 2016.

Figure 11-4. *A Document Library inside Outlook 2016*

Now that we know what a Site Mailbox is, in the next section we will learn how to configure it.

Configure SharePoint Server 2016 Site Mailbox

The process to configure the SharePoint Server 2016 Site Mailbox is pretty straightforward. We will first need to install the Exchange Web Services (EWS) Managed API 2.2 on all the servers in our farm. This will install the required tools that SharePoint will use to communicate with Exchange Server 2016. The next step will then be to create a trust between our SharePoint Server 2016 and Exchange Server 2016 so they can securely exchange information. Lastly, we will need to enable the Site Mailbox feature on the sites we want to use this feature on.

It's important to know that Site Mailboxes will only work on Web Applications that use SSL on their default Zone. Furthermore, in order for Site Mailboxes to work, the User Profile Service Application needs to work and users need to be synchronized from Active Directory. Lastly, the App Management Service Application should be configured. We covered both those requirements in previous chapters.

Installing Exchange Web Services Managed API

To get our SharePoint Servers ready, we will need to download the Exchange Web Services (EWS) Managed API on every server in our SharePoint Server Farm. You can download EWS Managed API 2.2 from the Microsoft Download Center:

- Microsoft Exchange Web Services Managed API 2.2 (`https://www.microsoft.com/en-ca/download/details.aspx?id=42951`)

Once downloaded, run the following cmd either from an elevated Command Prompt or PowerShell Window:

`msiexec /i EwsManagedApi.msi addlocal="ExchangeWebServicesApi_Feature,ExchangeWebServicesApi_Gac"`

After the install finishes successfully, you will have to do an IIS Reset on every server in the farm. With the Prerequisites configured, it's time to configure SharePoint 2016 to trust the Exchange Server.

Establish OAuth Trust and Permissions on SharePoint

In this section, we will configure our Exchange Server as a new SP Trusted Security Token Issuer, as well as add a property in the Web Application Property Bag. We will do this by using PowerShell scripts provided by Microsoft. There are two scripts that we need to create on any one of our SharePoint Servers. The first script is named `Set-SiteMailboxConfig.ps1` and can be found in **Appendix A** of the book. The Second Script is called `Check-SiteMailboxConfig.ps1` and it can also be found in **Appendix A**.

■ **Note**   Both scripts can be downloaded from TechNet at the following link: https://technet.microsoft.com/library/jj552524(office.15).aspx.

The Set-SiteMailboxConfig script is the script that will configure everything, while the Check-SiteMailboxConfig.ps1 will simply verify that the configuration is valid before enabling the CollaborationMailbox Farm Feature.

To run the Set-SiteMailboxConfig, open SharePoint Management Shell as an administrator, and run the following cmdlet:

```
.\Set-SiteMailboxConfig.ps1 -ExchangeSiteMailboxDomain <Domain Name>
-ExchangeAutodiscoverDomain <Exchange Server FQDN>
```

Where the `<Domain Name>` is the Domain Name that your Exchange Mailbox addresses should be created in, and the `<ExchangeAutodiscoverDomain>` is the FQDN of your Exchange Server. Here is the cmdlet that we ran in our environment.

```
.\Set-SiteMailboxConfig.ps1 -ExchangeSiteMailboxDomain learn-sp2016.com
-ExchangeAutodiscoverDomain LSEXCH01.CORP.LEARN-SP2016.COM
```

If you only want to enable it on a certain Web Application, you can add the –WebApplication parameter to the script, for example:

```
.\Set-SiteMailboxConfig.ps1 -ExchangeSiteMailboxDomain learn-sp2016.com -ExchangeAutodiscoverDomain
LSEXCH01.CORP.LEARN-SP2016.COM –WebApplication https://sharepoint.learn-sp2016.com/
```

The script will add the Exchange Server and Mailbox domain in the Web App properties as seen in Table 11-1.

Table 11-1. *Web Application Property Bag for Site Mailboxes*

Property Name	Value
ExchangeAutodiscoverDomain	LSEXCH01.CORP.LEARN-SP2016.COM
ExchangeTeamMailboxDomain	learn-sp2016.com

With everything configured on the SharePoint side, we need to configure Exchange Server as well.

Configure Exchange Server 2016 for Site Mailboxes

The last part of the Site Mailbox configuration is to configure Exchange Server 2016 for Site Mailboxes. The scripts required for the configuration are included with ever Exchange Server installation, and you will find them at the following path: 'C:\Program Files\Microsoft\Exchange Server\V15\Scripts'

As we have enforced the use of TLS 1.2 for SharePoint, we must enable strong crypto as outlined in Microsoft Security Advisory 2960358. Per the advisory, it may be necessary to enable TLS 1.2 support on Windows Server 2012 R2 via a registry entry. Save the following text as a UseStrongCrypto.reg and import it into each Office Online Server. Once imported, restart each Office Online Server in your farm.

```
Windows Registry Editor Version 5.00
[HKEY_LOCAL_MACHINE\SOFTWARE\Microsoft\.NETFramework\v4.0.30319]
"SchUseStrongCrypto"=dword:00000001
```

After the reboot, open Exchange Management Shell as an Administrator and make sure you are in that script location and run the following PowerShell cmdlet:

```
.\Configure-EnterprisePartnerApplication.ps1 -ApplicationType Sharepoint -AuthMetadataUrl
https://<SP Site Collection>/_layouts/15/metadata/json/1
```

Where <SP Site Collection> is the Root Site Collection of the Web Application where you enabled Site Mailbox. In our environment, the cmdlet we ran was

```
.\Configure-EnterprisePartnerApplication.ps1 -ApplicationType Sharepoint -AuthMetadataUrl
https://sharepoint.learn-sp2016.com/_layouts/15/metadata/json/1
```

The Script should output that the Configuration has succeeded. To test the Site Mailbox feature, navigate to a SharePoint Site and try to add a new Site Mailbox from the "Add an app" page. After adding the Site Mailbox, SharePoint will display a note that it might take up to 30 minutes for the Site Mailbox to be created as seen in Figure 11-5.

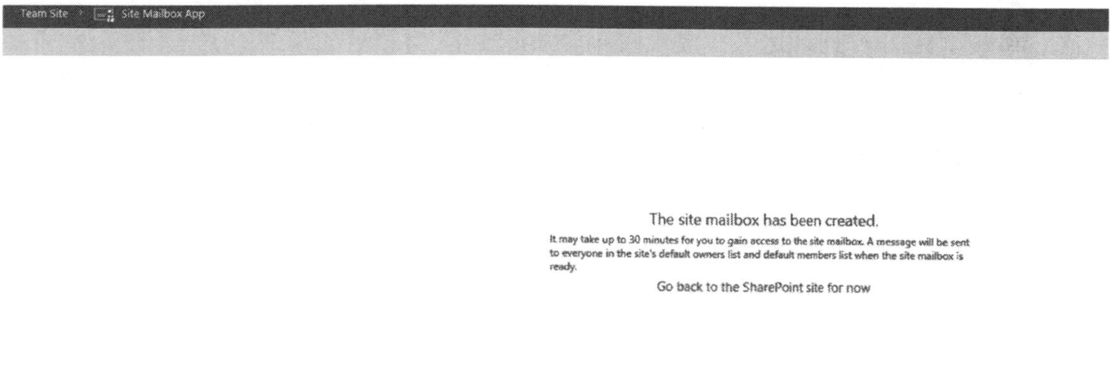

The site mailbox has been created.

It may take up to 30 minutes for you to gain access to the site mailbox. A message will be sent to everyone in the site's default owners list and default members list when the site mailbox is ready.

Go back to the SharePoint site for now

Figure 11-5. *Site Mailbox has been created*

Once the Site Mailbox is ready to use, every Site Owner will receive an e-mail notifying them of the Site Mailbox e-mail address as well as a link to learn more about what a Site Mailbox is. An example of this welcome e-mail can be seen in Figure 11-6.

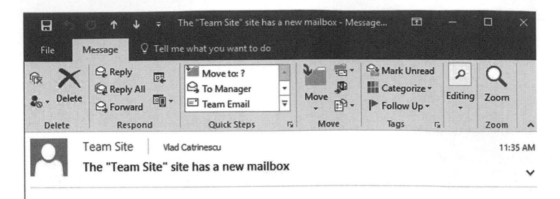

Figure 11-6. Site Mailbox Welcome E-mail

By default, all the Site Owners and Site Members will have access to the Site Mailbox and will be able to view and send e-mails.

With the Site Mailbox configured, another feature we can enable by integrating SharePoint Server and Exchange Server together is Exchange Photo Synchronization.

Exchange Photo Synchronization

The User Profile Service is capable of synchronizing photos from Exchange Server 2013 or Exchange Server 2016 instead of the `thumbnailPhoto` attribute in Active Directory. This provides significantly higher-quality pictures.

As we've already performed the preceding prerequisites by installing the Exchange Web Services API on SharePoint and configuring OAuth between Exchange Server and SharePoint using the Configure. EnterprisePartnerApplication.ps1 script, those steps will not be repeated here. Instead, only the necessary steps for Exchange Photo Synchronization will be present.

First, validate the Autodiscovery domain for Exchange Server. This can be done using the Exchange Management Console. In this example, the Exchange Server name is LSEXCH01.

```
(Get-AutodiscoverVirtualDirectory -Server LSEXCH01).InternalUrl.AbsoluteUri
```

This will provide the full path for the Autodiscovery URL.

On SharePoint, using the SharePoint Management Shell, configure the Security Token Service, setting the `HybridStsSelectionEnabled` property to true.

```
$sts=Get-SPSecurityTokenServiceConfig
$sts.HybridStsSelectionEnabled = $true
$sts.AllowMetadataOverHttp = $false
$sts.AllowOAuthOverHttp = $false
$sts.Update()
```

The next step is to retrieve the Exchange Trusted Security Token Issuer and apply the App Principal to our MySite Host. In this farm, the MySite Host is `https://sharepoint-my.learn-sp2016.com`.

```
$exchange = Get-SPTrustedSecurityTokenIssuer -Identity "Exchange"
$app = Get-SPAppPrincipal -Site https://sharepoint-my.learn-sp2016.com -NameIdentifier
$exchange.NameId
$site = Get-SPSite https://sharepoint-my.learn-sp2016.com
Set-SPAppPrincipalPermission -AppPrincipal $app -Site $site.RootWeb -Scope SiteSubscription
-Right FullControl -EnableAppOnlyPolicy
```

Continuing to use the SharePoint Management Shell, place the MySite Web Application into a variable, set the ExchangeAutodiscoverDomain property to the Autodiscovery URL, the photo expiration properties, and finally enable the user photo import.

```
$wa.Properties["ExchangeAutodiscoverDomain"] = https://autodiscover.learn-sp2016.com
$wa.UserPhotoErrorExpiration = 1
$wa.UserPhotoExpiration = 12
$wa.UserPhotoImportEnabled = $true
$wa.Update()
```

Once this is completed, each user must visit the About Me page to establish the OAuth session between Exchange and SharePoint to import the picture into the MySite host.

There can be a variety of errors present in the ULS log for picture import. To filter to just the specific errors, set the Category to "Exchange Integration." This will narrow the scope to the import process when a user visits their About Me page.

As previously mentioned, pictures are imported when a user visits their own About Me (profile) page. If the import process runs into an error, SharePoint will not retry for the number of hours specified in UserPhotoErrorExpiration. Likewise, if the photo import is successful, SharePoint will not look for a new photo for the number of hours specified in UserPhotoExpiration. The value for when the last import took place is the timestamp of the photo in the MySite Host. This includes the generic person image when a photo import fails.

When a photo has been successfully imported, it will be displayed for that user. If you search for the user's profile in the User Profile Service Application, as shown in Figure 11-7, the picture cannot be changed by the administrator via editing the User Profile.

| Picture: | You can't change this person's photo because it is synchronized with Microsoft Exchange. | Everyone |

Figure 11-7. *The Picture property when a user's profile photo is synchronized from Exchange*

Additionally, if the user edits their own profile via the MySite Host to change their picture, they will be redirected to Outlook on the Web.

Next Steps

With the integration between Exchange and SharePoint now completed, in the next chapter we will learn how to deploy Business Intelligence Services in SharePoint 2016.

CHAPTER 12

■ ■ ■

Business Intelligence Service Applications

SharePoint is the Microsoft's recommended platform to publish Business Intelligence reports On-Premises. SharePoint allows us to publish PowerPivot and Power View reports, and this give users a very powerful platform to mold and slice their data as they need. Businesses can also install SQL Server Reporting Services (SSRS) in Integrated Mode with SharePoint to provide static reports that users can easily view. SharePoint Server 2016 brings some major changes to the Business Intelligence architecture as Excel Services is no longer included in SharePoint. The capabilities of Excel Services have been replaced by Excel Online in Office Online Server. We have learned how to deploy Office Online Server in Chapter 9. In this chapter, we will learn how to enable Excel Services capabilities in SharePoint 2016 and how to deploy PowerPivot and SSRS.

SharePoint Server 2016 Business Intelligence Architecture

In previous versions of SharePoint, there was a service application called Excel Services. Excel Services allowed users to display reports in Excel as well as use PowerPivot and Power View. Office Web Apps Server also offered users the ability to view Excel documents in the browser, but was not able to display reports. Managing two tools that almost did the same things, each with their strengths and weaknesses, caused headaches for SharePoint Administrators. With SharePoint Server 2016, Microsoft decided to eliminate Excel Services from SharePoint and shift the functionality to Office Online Server.

While this will make life easier for administrators, there are some architecture changes to keep in mind when deploying SharePoint Business Intelligence Services. As we learned in Chapter 9, Office Online Server must be deployed on a server other than SharePoint; therefore, a highly available Business Intelligence setup would require two extra servers over what it did in the past. Furthermore, since Excel Services is now on the Office Online Server, we have an extra hop between the SharePoint Server and our SQL Server Analysis Services (SSAS) server. Therefore, for some scenarios, it will be mandatory to enable Kerberos Constrained Delegation (KCD). Some scenarios such as displaying Excel workbooks connected to SSAS Data Sources can still be done by using the EffectiveUserName; however, displaying Excel workbooks that connect to Windows Authentication SQL Server Data Sources will need to have KCD configured. EffectiveUserName is a SSAS connection string property that contains the name of the user who is accessing a report or dashboard. This allows you to specify the appropriate level of data access for a given user on the OLAP cube itself, without the need to configure Kerberos delegation. Something to take into consideration is that PowerPivot works only with Windows Claims–based Web Applications, and will not work with SAML-based authentication.

It is also important to know that while SharePoint Server 2016 supports both SQL 2014 and SQL 2016 for its databases, you need to have a SQL 2016 SSAS instance to have the full functionality. Features such as Excel Services and Power Query will not work with SQL 2014. Furthermore, none of the four MinRole roles is configured to support SSRS; therefore, you must have at least one SharePoint Server with the Custom MinRole in your SharePoint 2016 farm to run SSRS.

© Vlad Catrinescu and Trevor Seward 2016

V. Catrinescu and T. Seward, *Deploying SharePoint 2016*, DOI 10.1007/978-1-4842-1999-7_12

If you wish to configure PowerPivot to use an unattended account to access certain data sources, you will also need to create a service account for this purpose. For this book we have created an account with the username s-PowerPivot that will serve as the PowerPivot Unattended Service Account.

Installing SSAS in PowerPivot Mode

Excel Online requires an Analysis Services instance deployed in PowerPivot mode in order to load and query data models. As previously stated in this chapter, this instance needs to be a SQL Server 2016 Analysis Services instance since SQL 2014 is not supported for the BI Stack. It is recommended that the SSAS instance that you deploy is on a server separate from the rest of your databases; however, for testing and development purposes with a smaller load, it can be hosted on the same SQL Server as your databases.

Before starting the SQL Server installation, you will need to enable the .NET Framework 3.5 on the Windows Server that will be hosting the SSAS instance. Once you start the SQL Server 2016 Setup Wizard and get to the Feature Selection Page, select "Analysis Services" as seen in Figure 12-1.

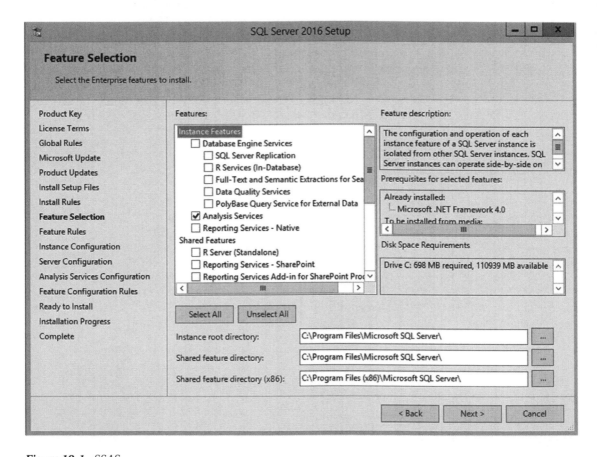

Figure 12-1. SSAS

On the Instance Configuration name, make sure to use a Named Instance and not the default instance. In past versions of SharePoint this instance was always named PowerPivot, but that is not mandatory anymore. In our environment, we will name it PowerPivot2016 as seen in Figure 12-2.

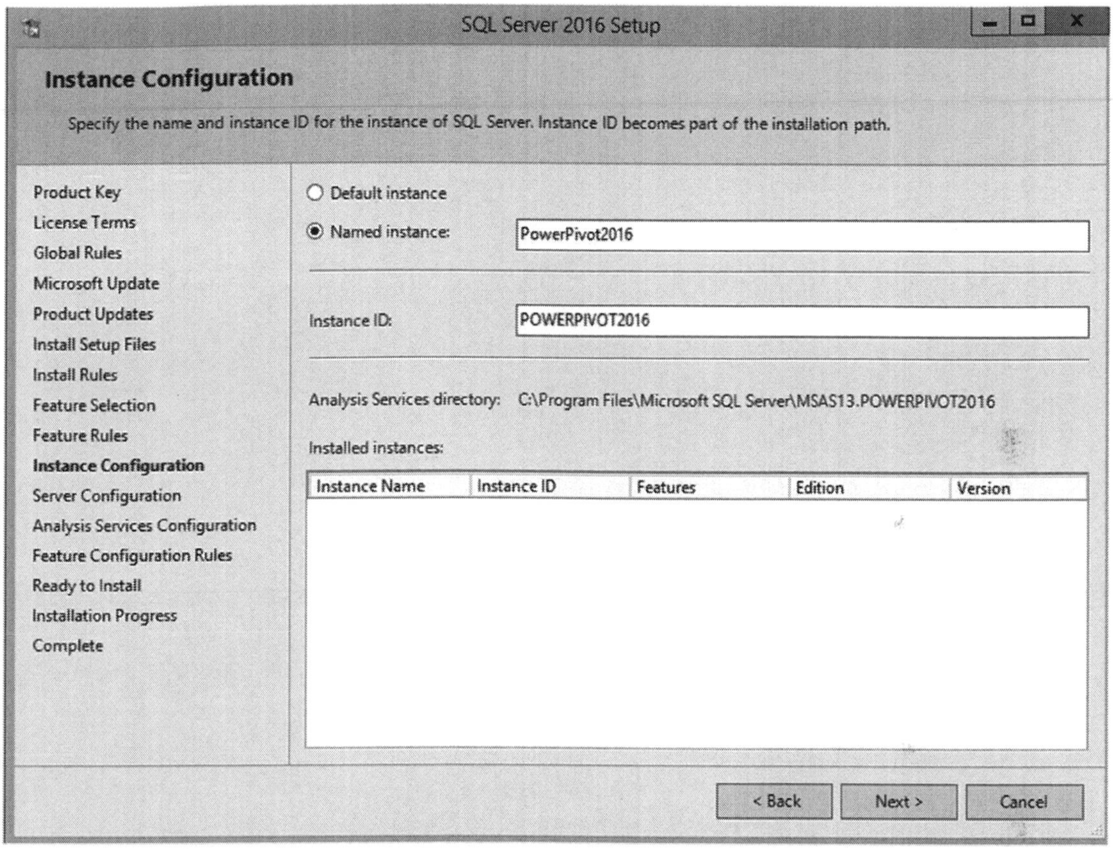

Figure 12-2. SQL Server Instance Configuration

On the Analysis Services Configuration screen, make sure to select the Power Pivot Mode in the Server Mode section, and add the required administrators with permissions to your SSAS instance as seen in Figure 12-3.

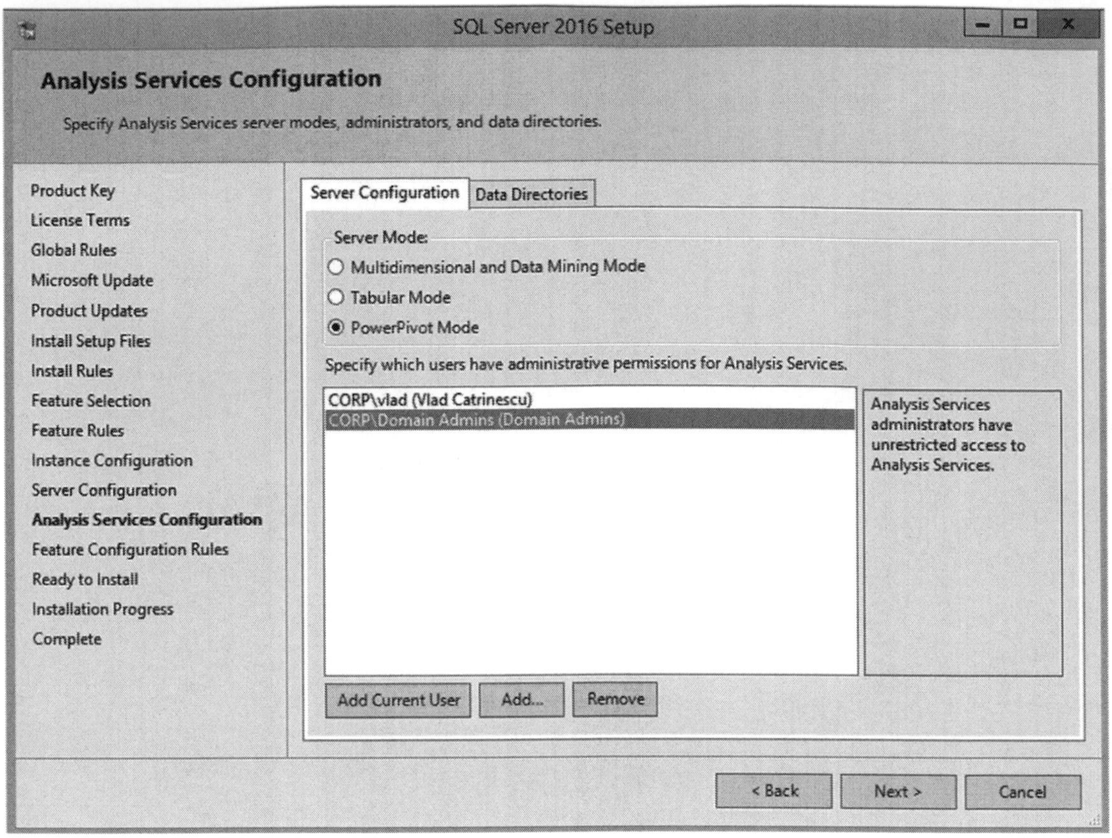

Figure 12-3. *Analysis Services Configuration*

After this step, you will need to confirm the features and finally click the Install button to proceed with the installation. With the Instance installed, we will need to open port TCP/2382 for the SQL Browser, as well as open the SSAS port on the Program in order to enable dynamic ports. TCP/2382 is used by the SQL Browser service to listen for SSAS instances.

```
New-NetFirewallRule -DisplayName "Allow Inbound SSAS" -Direction Inbound -Program "C:\
Program Files\Microsoft SQL Server\MSAS13.POWERPIVOT2016\OLAP\bin\msmdsrv.exe"  -Action
Allow
New-NetFirewallRule -DisplayName "SQL Browser Inbound" -Direction Inbound -Protocol TCP -
LocalPort 2382 -Action allow
```

Do not forget to change the -Program parameter to match the path to the instance name you have created. With the SSAS Instance created, it is time to configure the Office Online Server for Business Intelligence.

Configuring Office Online Server for BI

Office Online Server is an important part of configuring Business Intelligence functionality in SharePoint Server 2016, and without a configured Office Online Server farm you cannot go forward. If you did not install and configure Office Online Server yet, follow Chapter 9 to get it configured. The first thing we have to do on Office Online Server is to make sure that it can reach our SSAS instance. Use the following PowerShell script and change the Connection String with your instance name to validate that your Office Online Server can query the SSAS Instance. You need to be logged in as a user that has access to the SSAS Instance in order for the script to work.

```
$ssasConnection = New-Object System.Data.OleDb.OleDbConnection
$ssasConnection.ConnectionString = "Provider=MSOLAP;Data Source=LSSASS01\PowerPivot2016"
$ssasConnection.Open()

$guid = New-Object System.Guid "3444B255-171E-4cb9-AD98-19E57888A75F"
$restrictionList = @($null, $null, $null, $null, $null, $null, $null, "Administrators")
$schemaTable = $ssasConnection.GetOleDbSchemaTable($guid, $restrictionList);
[xml]$admins = $schemaTable.METADATA

$ssasConnection.Close()

$admins.Role.Members.Member
```

■ **Note** If you have multiple servers in your Office Online Server Farm, validate access on all the servers in the farm.

If the Office Online Server can access the SSAS Instance, the PowerShell script will display all the administrators of the instance as seen in Figure 12-4.

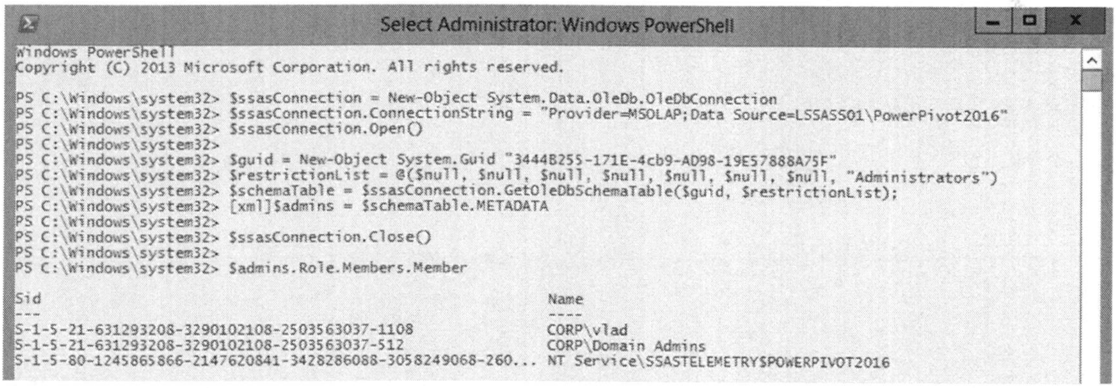

***Figure 12-4.** Validating Office Online Server access to SSAS*

Next, we need to give access to the Office Online Server machines to the SSAS Instance. Since the Office Online Server service runs under the Network Service account, the computer account needs to be an administrator of the SSAS Instance. From the SSAS Instance Properties in SQL Server Management Studios, go the Security and add a new Administrator. Make sure to select Computer Objects and the Entire Directory as location. Enter the name of all your servers from your Office Online Server farm as seen in Figure 12-5, and click OK.

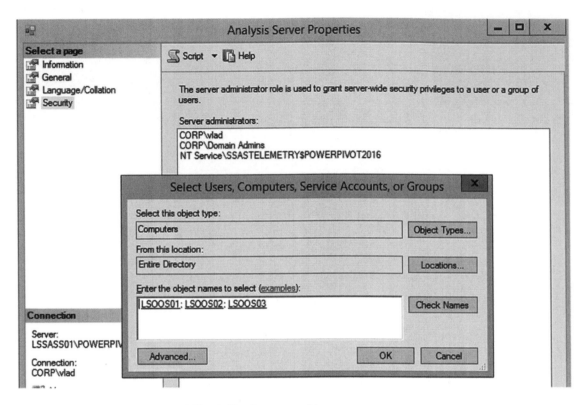

Figure 12-5. *Granting access to Office Online Server machines*

The next step is to configure this Office Online Server to use the SSAS Instance. This is done by PowerShell on any Office Online Server in the farm. Run the following cmdlet and change the ServerID with your server and instance name.

```
New-OfficeWebAppsExcelBIServer –ServerId LSSASS01\PowerPivot2016
```

Since this is a farm-level change, it needs to be done only on one server in the Office Online Server Farm. Next we need to enable the Claims to Windows Token Service on the Office Online Server. By using notepad as an administrator, open the c2wtshost.exe.config file located at `C:\Program Files\ Windows Identity Foundation\v3.5\c2wtshost.exe.config` and remove the comment tags around `<add value="NT AUTHORITY\Network Service" />` as seen in Figure 12-6.

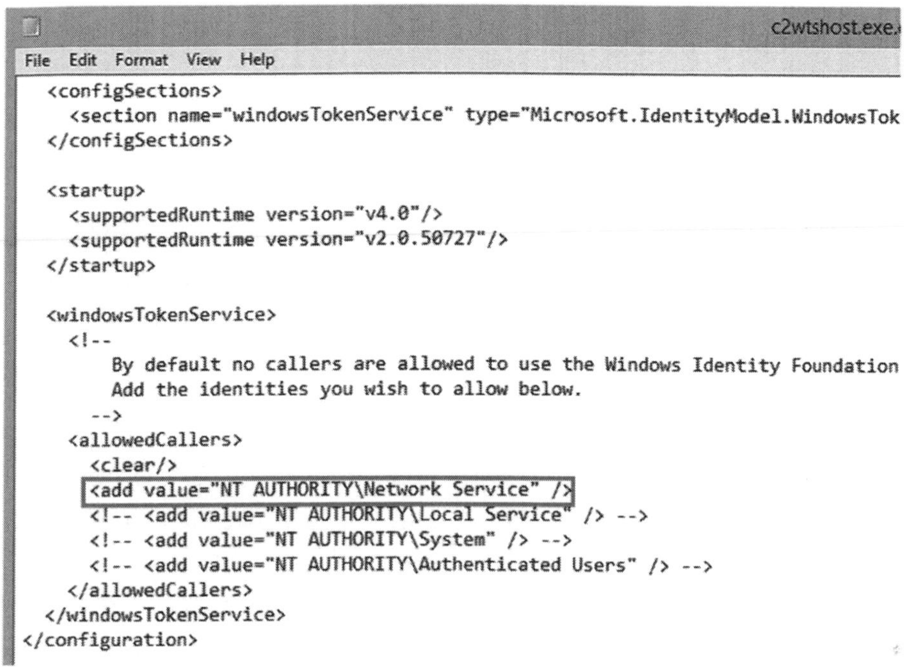

```
                                                                   c2wtshost.exe.
File  Edit  Format  View  Help
  <configSections>
    <section name="windowsTokenService" type="Microsoft.IdentityModel.WindowsTok
  </configSections>

  <startup>
    <supportedRuntime version="v4.0"/>
    <supportedRuntime version="v2.0.50727"/>
  </startup>

  <windowsTokenService>
    <!--
        By default no callers are allowed to use the Windows Identity Foundation
        Add the identities you wish to allow below.
    -->
    <allowedCallers>
      <clear/>
      <add value="NT AUTHORITY\Network Service" />
      <!-- <add value="NT AUTHORITY\Local Service" /> -->
      <!-- <add value="NT AUTHORITY\System" /> -->
      <!-- <add value="NT AUTHORITY\Authenticated Users" /> -->
    </allowedCallers>
  </windowsTokenService>
</configuration>
```

Figure 12-6. *Claims to Windows Token Service Configuration*

Afterward, you will need to set the Claims to Windows Token Service to start up automatically with Windows, and start it right away. This is done with the following PowerShell cmdlets:

```
Set-Service -Name C2WTS -startuptype "automatic"
Start-Service -Name C2WTS
```

▪ **Note**   This must be done on every Office Online Server in the farm.

With Excel services enabled in Office Online Server, we now need to configure PowerPivot.

Configuring PowerPivot Services

The next step to configure the BI stack on SharePoint Server 2016 is to configure PowerPivot. The first step will be to install the PowerPivot Add-in on all the SharePoint Servers in the farm. This will allow any server to display PowerPivot reports when requested from a user. Download the PowerPivot Add-in from the following link:

- Microsoft SQL Server 2016 PowerPivot for Microsoft SharePoint 2016 (https://www.microsoft.com/en-us/download/details.aspx?id=52675)

After the PowerPivot Add-in is installed on all the servers in the farm, on the server that you want to run PowerPivot, run the PowerPivot for SharePoint 2016 Configuration. When opening the tool you might get an error specifying that "The user is not a farm administrator" as seen in Figure 12-7. You might get this error even if this user is a farm administrator.

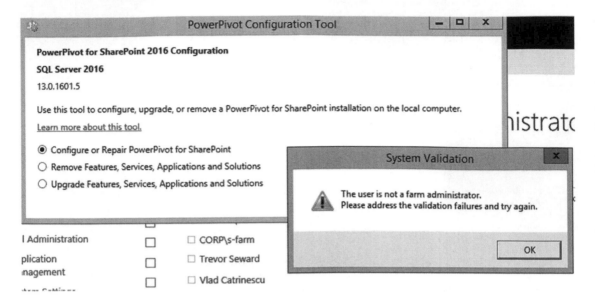

Figure 12-7. *The user is not a farm administrator*

In order to get around this error, you need to configure your current user as a Site Collection Administrator on the Central Administration as seen in Figure 12-8.

Figure 12-8. *Central Administration Site Collection Administration*

Reopen the PowerPivot Configuration tool and select to Configure or Repair PowerPivot for SharePoint as seen in Figure 12-9.

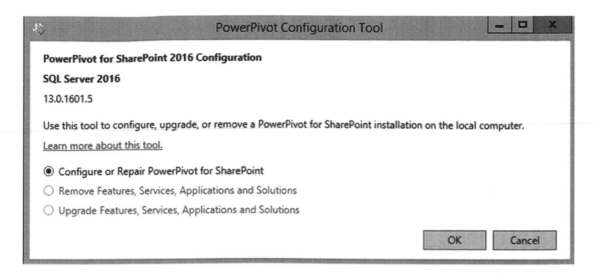

Figure 12-9. *Configure or repair PowerPivot for SharePoint*

There are some settings you need to configure in the PowerPivot Configuration tool. First, you will need to enter the "Default Account Username" and password, which is an account that needs to be a farm administrator, be able to deploy farm solutions and activate features on a Site Collection we will select later. In Figure 12-10 I have chosen to run the install with my own account, and selected the default database server.

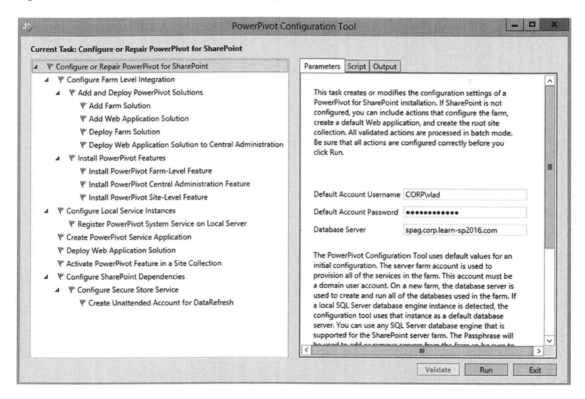

Figure 12-10. *PowerPivot Configuration Tool Default Account Username*

On the next screen that accepts parameters seen in Figure 12-11, we need to enter the Service Application Name as well as the database name.

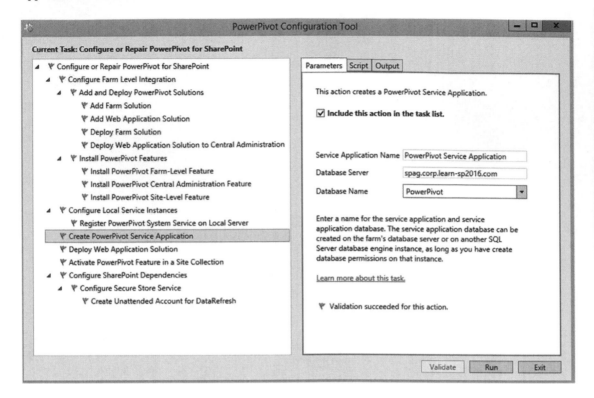

Figure 12-11. *PowerPivot Configuration Tool Service Application Configuration*

The PowerPivot Configuration Tool will enable the PowerPivot on one Site Collection by default and you can choose this site collection in "Activate PowerPivot feature in a Site Collection" seen in Figure 12-12. If you don't want to activate this feature yet, simply uncheck the box "Include this action in the task list"

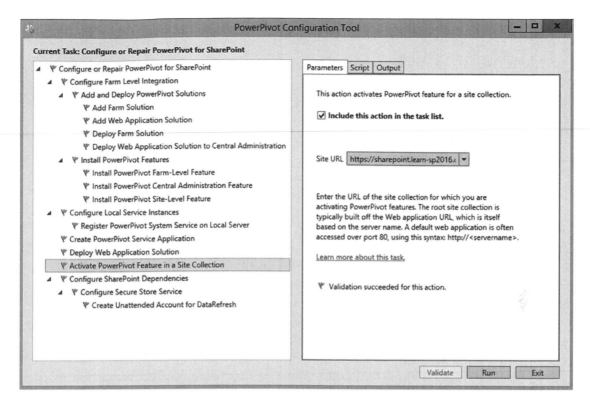

Figure 12-12. *PowerPivot Configuration Tool Site Collection to Activate Feature*

In the last configuration screen seen in Figure 12-13, we have to specify the TargetApplicationID, Friendly Name and the unattended account username and password for the Secure Store Target ID the PowerPivot Configuration Tool creates.

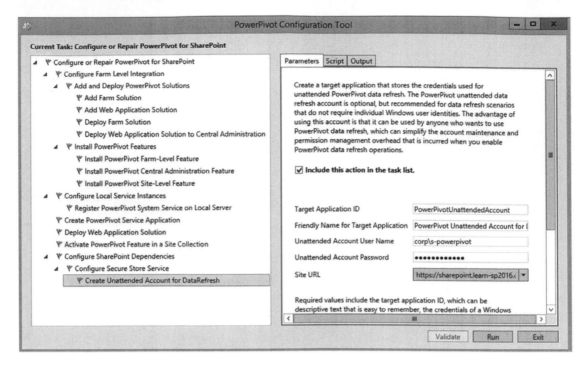

Figure 12-13. *PowerPivot Configuration Tool Unattended Account*

After clicking Validate, and then Run, the configuration tool will deploy the farm solutions and activate them if you have selected to do so. As deploying farm solutions causes an IIS Reset, make sure to do this outside business hours to avoid service disruption. Next, you will also need to give admin permissions to the SSAS instance to the account running the Service Application pool of the PowerPivot Service Application, which in our case is CORP\s-services.

In order to allow the use of Workbook as a Data Source, we will need to enable KCD. The first thing we need is to configure our Web Application to use Kerberos, and we have covered this in Chapter 3. We then need to allow the computer account for the Office Online servers to delegate credentials to the account running the Web Application Pool of the SharePoint Web Application. You will need to run this PowerShell script either from a Domain Controller, or from a computer that has the Active Directory Management Tools installed. We have created a variable called $allowedPrincipals, in which we will get the computer property for all the Office Online Servers in our farm. In our case, we added the three servers and then ran the Set-ADUser cmdlet to apply the change in the Active Directory.

```
$allowedPrincipals = @()
$allowedPrincipals += Get-ADComputer -Identity LSOOS01
$allowedPrincipals += Get-ADComputer -Identity LSOOS02
$allowedPrincipals += Get-ADComputer -Identity LSOOS03
Set-ADUser s-web -PrincipalsAllowedToDelegateToAccount $allowedPrincipals
```

To verify the Kerberos configuration, run the setspn -l cmdlet, on the account running the Web Application pool, in our case corp\s-web.

```
SetSPN -l corp\s-web
```

If everything is configured correctly, you should see the Web Application where you have configured Kerberos. In our case, it's the sharepoint.learn-sp2016.com Web Application.

```
HTTP/sharepoint
HTTP/sharepoint.learn-sp2016.com
```

We also need to make sure that we have some SPNs set on each Office Online Server. Run the `Setspn -l <OOS Server Name>` cmdlet for each office Online Server, and validate that you see the `HOST\<Server Name>` and `HOST\<FQDN>` in the list of SPNs. Those entries are highlighted in Figure 12-14.

```
PS C:\Windows\system32> setspn -l LSOOS01
Registered ServicePrincipalNames for CN=LSOOS01,OU=OOS,OU=Servers,DC=CORP,DC=LEARN-SP2016,DC=COM:
        TERMSRV/LSOOS01
        TERMSRV/LSOOS01.CORP.LEARN-SP2016.COM
        WSMAN/LSOOS01
        WSMAN/LSOOS01.CORP.LEARN-SP2016.COM
        RestrictedKrbHost/LSOOS01
        HOST/LSOOS01
        RestrictedKrbHost/LSOOS01.CORP.LEARN-SP2016.COM
        HOST/LSOOS01.CORP.LEARN-SP2016.COM
```

Figure 12-14. *Validating Office Online Server SPN*

Finally we need to install the Analysis Services OLE DB Provider on Office Online Server. The Analysis Services OLE DB Provider can be downloaded from the SQL Server 2016 Feature Pack from the Microsoft Download Center at the following link: https://www.microsoft.com/en-us/download/details.aspx?id=52676; the download name is <Language>\X64\SQL_AS_OLEDB.msi. You will need to install it on every Office Online Server in your farm. Furthermore, you need to update the registry with information about the OLE DB Provider. Save the following text in a file named MSOLAP.5.Update.reg and run it on every Office Online Server in the farm.

```
Windows Registry Editor Version 5.00
[HKEY_CLASSES_ROOT\MSOLAP.5]
@="MSOLAP 13.0 OLE DB Provider"
[HKEY_CLASSES_ROOT\MSOLAP.5\CLSID]
@="{FBE7F3BD-C550-490E-B38C-A8661E420070}"
```

A reboot will be required after performing the installation and registry edit.

Before testing the PowerPivot functionality, make sure that the "PowerPivot Feature Integration for Site Collections" is activated as seen in Figure 12-15.

PowerPivot Feature Integration for Site Collections
Extends the capabilities of site collections using PowerPivot for SharePoint

Deactivate Active

Figure 12-15. *PowerPivot Feature Integration for Site Collections*

Once you validate that feature is activated, add a new library of type PowerPivot Gallery as seen in Figure 12-16.

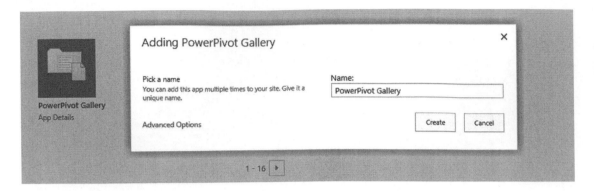

Figure 12-16. *New PowerPivot Gallery*

You will now be able to upload and test PowerPivot Business Intelligence reports in SharePoint. You can use the PowerPivot sample files provided in the "Verify a Power Pivot for SharePoint Installation" article on MSDN at https://msdn.microsoft.com/en-CA/library/hh231684.aspx.

Configuring SSRS

The last part of our Business Intelligence configuration is to configure SSRS in SharePoint integrated mode. The SSRS instance must be installed on a SharePoint server running the Custom MinRole, since none of the other roles will allow you to run the SSRS Service.

You will first need to have the SQL installation media on your SharePoint Server running the Custom MinRole, and on the Feature Selection screen shown in Figure 12-17, choose Reporting Services – SharePoint.

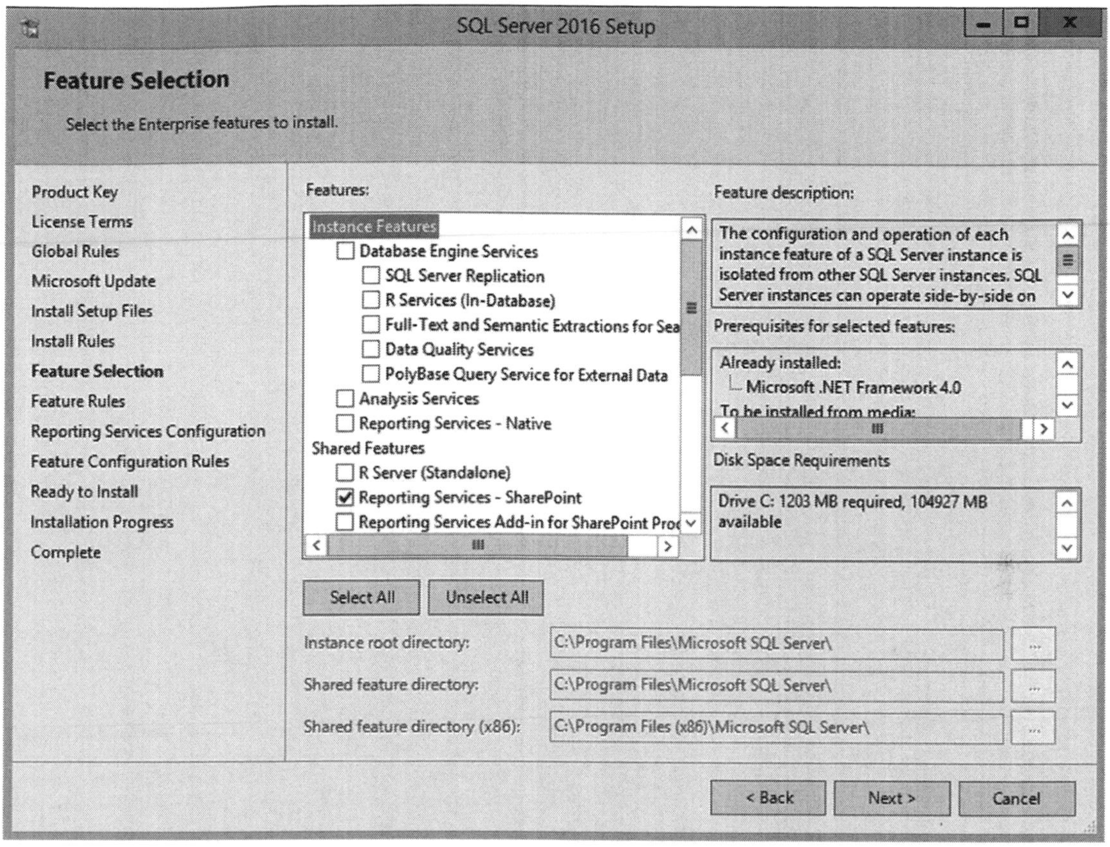

Figure 12-17. Reporting Services – SharePoint Feature Selection

On the Reporting Services Configuration page, select the Install Only option, and then click Install. Once the install is done, we will need to install the Reporting Services Add-in for SharePoint Products on all the servers in the farm. This can be downloaded from the following link:

- Microsoft SQL Server 2016 Reporting Services Add-in for Microsoft SharePoint
  https://www.microsoft.com/en-us/download/details.aspx?id=52682

The minimum requirements are that this Add-in must be installed on all the Web Front Ends in the SharePoint farm; however, we recommend installing it on all the servers in the farm for convenience, should the server role be changed in the future. When the installation is done, from the Central Administration, navigate to the Service Applications page, and create a new Service Application of type SSRS Application. Enter the name, Application Pool as well as Database, and what Web Applications you want to deploy the SSRS functionality to. In our environment, we have configured the SSRS Service Application to use the same Service Application Pool as our other Service Applications as seen in Figure 12-18.

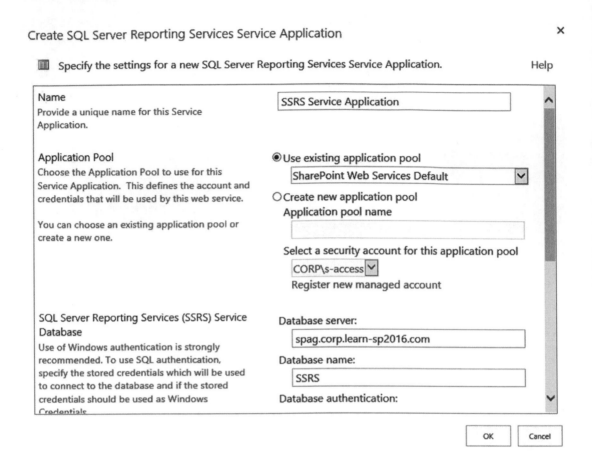

Figure 12-18. New SSRS Service Application

After the Service Application is created, navigate to the Services on Server page, and validate that the SSRS service is started. Make sure to select the server running the Custom role on the top right of the page. If the service is not started, start it manually.

You can then deploy a simple report using SQL Server Report Builder, and validate that everything is working. The first step is to download SQL Server Report Builder from the Microsoft Download Center.

- Microsoft SQL Server 2016 Report Builder (`https://www.microsoft.com/en-us/download/details.aspx?id=52674`)

We can then either create a new document library, or use an existing one, and add the "Report Builder Report" and "Report Data Source" Content Types to your library as seen in Figure 12-19.

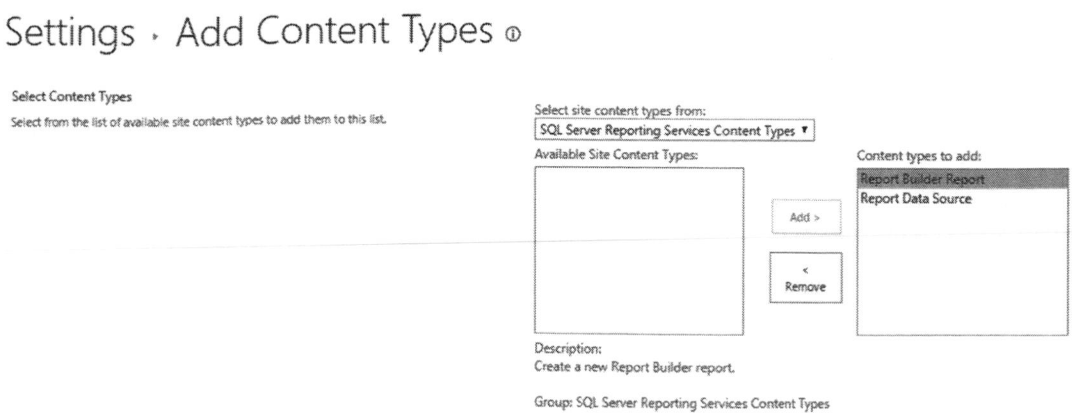

Settings · Add Content Types ⓘ

Select Content Types
Select from the list of available site content types to add them to this list.

Select site content types from:
SQL Server Reporting Services Content Types ▼

Available Site Content Types:

Content types to add:
Report Builder Report
Report Data Source

Add >

< Remove

Description:
Create a new Report Builder report.

Group: SQL Server Reporting Services Content Types

Figure 12-19. *SSRS Content Types*

Use the New button, and select Report Builder Report as seen in Figure 12-20.

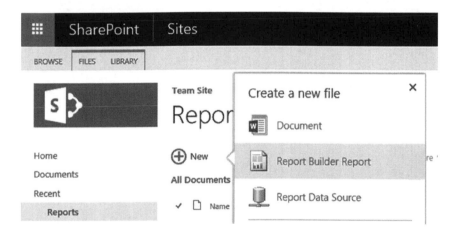

Figure 12-20. *New Report Builder Report*

The SQL Server Report Builder will open as seen in Figure 12-21, and you can then follow a wizard to create to connect to a database and display data from that database in a simple report.

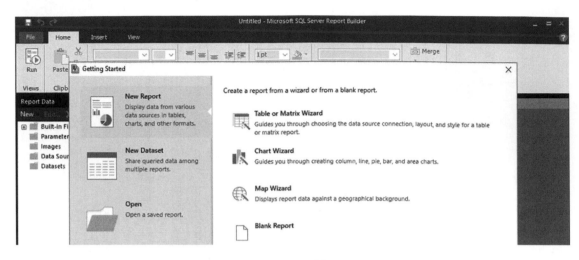

Figure 12-21. *Getting Started with SQL Server Reports Builder*

In Figure 12-22, we simply created a report of the Inventory database, used in Chapter 14.

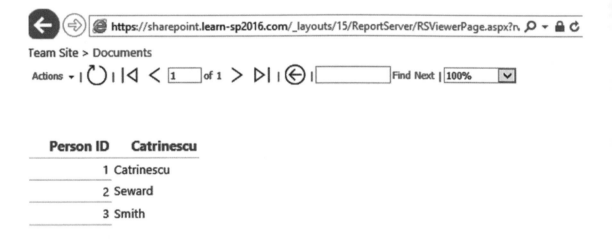

Figure 12-22. *Testing SSRS*

Next Steps

In this chapter, we have deployed the SharePoint 2016 BI Service Applications such as PowerPivot and SSRS, allowing our developers to publish reports on SharePoint 2016. In the next chapter, we will learn how to create Web Applications and Site Collections.

■ ■ ■

CHAPTER 13

Creating Web Applications and Site Collections

In previous chapters, we have learned how to create Service Applications in order to enable additional functionality for our users. In this chapter, we will learn how to create Web Applications and Path-based as well as Host Named Site Collections, and how to customize Alternate Access Mappings, create Content Databases for our Site Collections, and enable Fast Site Collection Creation, a new feature in SharePoint Server 2016.

SharePoint Web Architecture

When talking about SharePoint sites, we usually talk about three different levels: Web Applications, Site Collections, and Webs. The first two are actually simply containers; as there is no content stored directly in the Web Application and Site Collection, all the content is stored in the actual Web, which can be the root Web of your Site Collection.

The Web Applications can only be created by SharePoint Administrators who have Farm Administrator privileges as well as Local Administrator permissions on the SharePoint Servers. Creating a Web Application will create a new site in IIS on every server running the Microsoft SharePoint Foundation Web Application service, as well as a new database in SQL. While two SharePoint Web Applications can be hosted in the same IIS Application Pool, they cannot have the same URL or be hosted in the same database. A Web Application can have one, or many Content Databases attached to it. All the Site Collections created in that Web Application will go to one of those Content Databases. Every Web Application needs to have a root Site Collection, which is a Site Collection with the same URL as the Web Application. This is not created automatically, but is a requirement for supportability and stability of your SharePoint system. A Site Collection can be placed into its own Content Database, and can be moved between content databases that are attached in the same Web Application. Under the site collection, we find Webs. Those Webs can either be at the root of the Site Collection, meaning they have the same URL as the Site Collection, or they can be a subsite of the Root Web. Those Webs cannot be moved in a different Content Database individually; they all reside in the same Site Collection container. In Figure 13-1, you can see en example SharePoint Web Architecture.

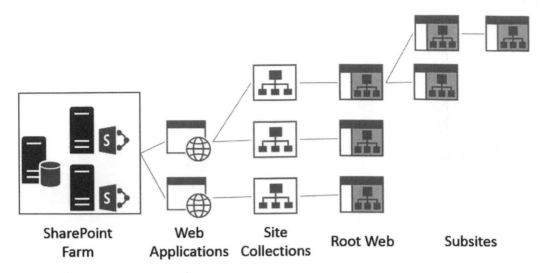

SharePoint Farm   **Web Applications**   **Site Collections**   **Root Web**   **Subsites**

Figure 13-1. *SharePoint Web Architecture*

Not that we know a bit more of the architecture behind, let's start creating Web Applications in SharePoint 2016.

Web Applications

Web Applications in SharePoint 2016 can be created either from the SharePoint Central Administration, or by PowerShell. Before creating a Web Application, you need to know the business requirements for creating that Web Application, and have that information ready. Since Web Applications consume significant resources on the SharePoint server, it is recommended to keep the number of Web Applications to a minimum. According to the Software boundaries and limits for SharePoint Server 2016, there is a supported limit of 20 Web Applications per SharePoint farm.

You will first need the information for the IIS Site seen in Figure 13-2.

- **URL of the Web Application**

  This will be the host header of the web application, for example intranet. company.com. This information should be taken from the business requirements, and can be changed later if needed.

- **Port**

  The port that the site will be accessed on. Usually port 80 for sites on HTTP and port 443 for sites using HTTPS. While it's possible to choose any port, we recommend keeping either 80 or 443 for an improved user experience, as users won't have to specify the port when entering the URL when using those two. You can have multiple Web Applications using the same port.

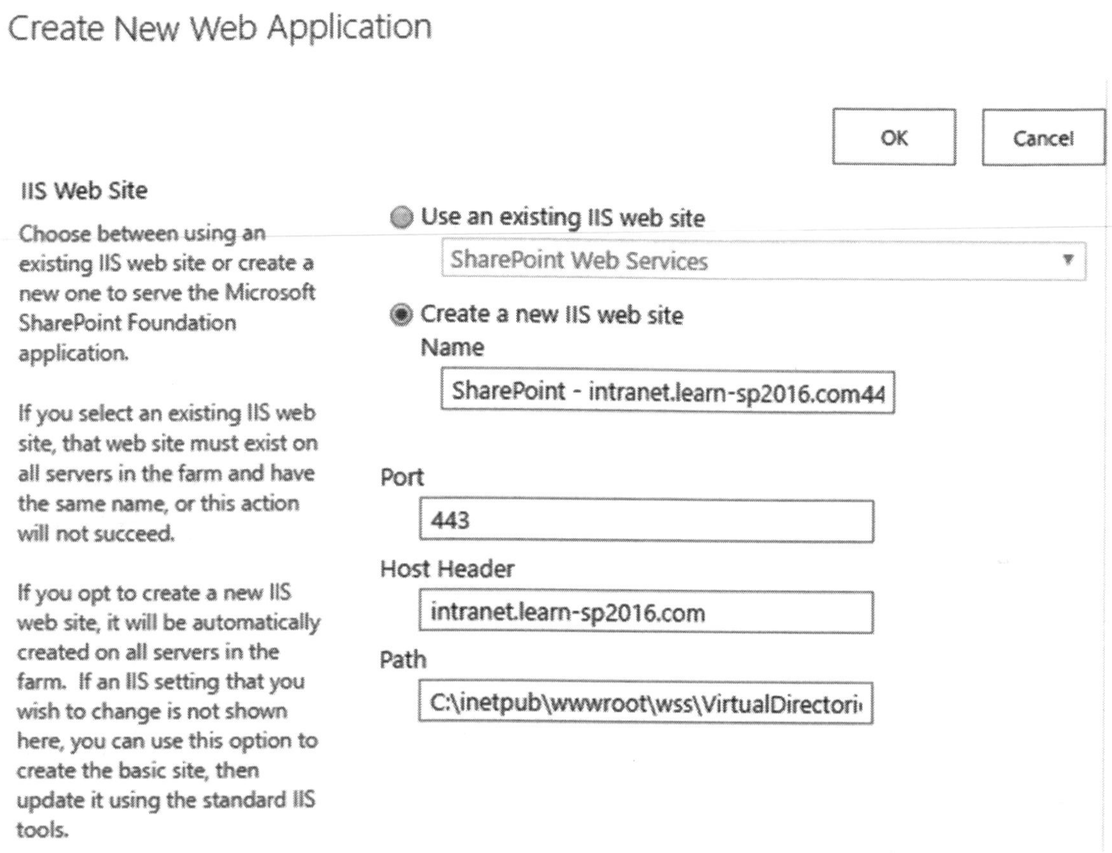

Create New Web Application

| | OK | Cancel |

IIS Web Site

Choose between using an existing IIS web site or create a new one to serve the Microsoft SharePoint Foundation application.

If you select an existing IIS web site, that web site must exist on all servers in the farm and have the same name, or this action will not succeed.

If you opt to create a new IIS web site, it will be automatically created on all servers in the farm. If an IIS setting that you wish to change is not shown here, you can use this option to create the basic site, then update it using the standard IIS tools.

○ Use an existing IIS web site

    SharePoint Web Services   ▼

◉ Create a new IIS web site

Name

    SharePoint - intranet.learn-sp2016.com44

Port

    443

Host Header

    intranet.learn-sp2016.com

Path

    C:\inetpub\wwwroot\wss\VirtualDirectori·

Figure 13-2. IIS Web Site Information when creating a new Web Application

In the next portion of the Web Application creation process, you will need to enter the information on the Security and Authentication of the Web Application as seen in Figure 13-3.

- **Allow Anonymous**

    Select Yes if you want this Web Application to serve a public Internet site, where users will not have to log in to see information.

- **Use Secure Sockets Layer (SSL)**

    Select Yes if your Web Application will use HTTPS

- **Claims Authentication Types**

    This is the authentication method that your users will use to authenticate to SharePoint. Those possibilities have been explained in **Chapter 4.**

■ **Note**   We recommend using SSL throughout on every Web Applications that you create to increase the security of your SharePoint deployment.

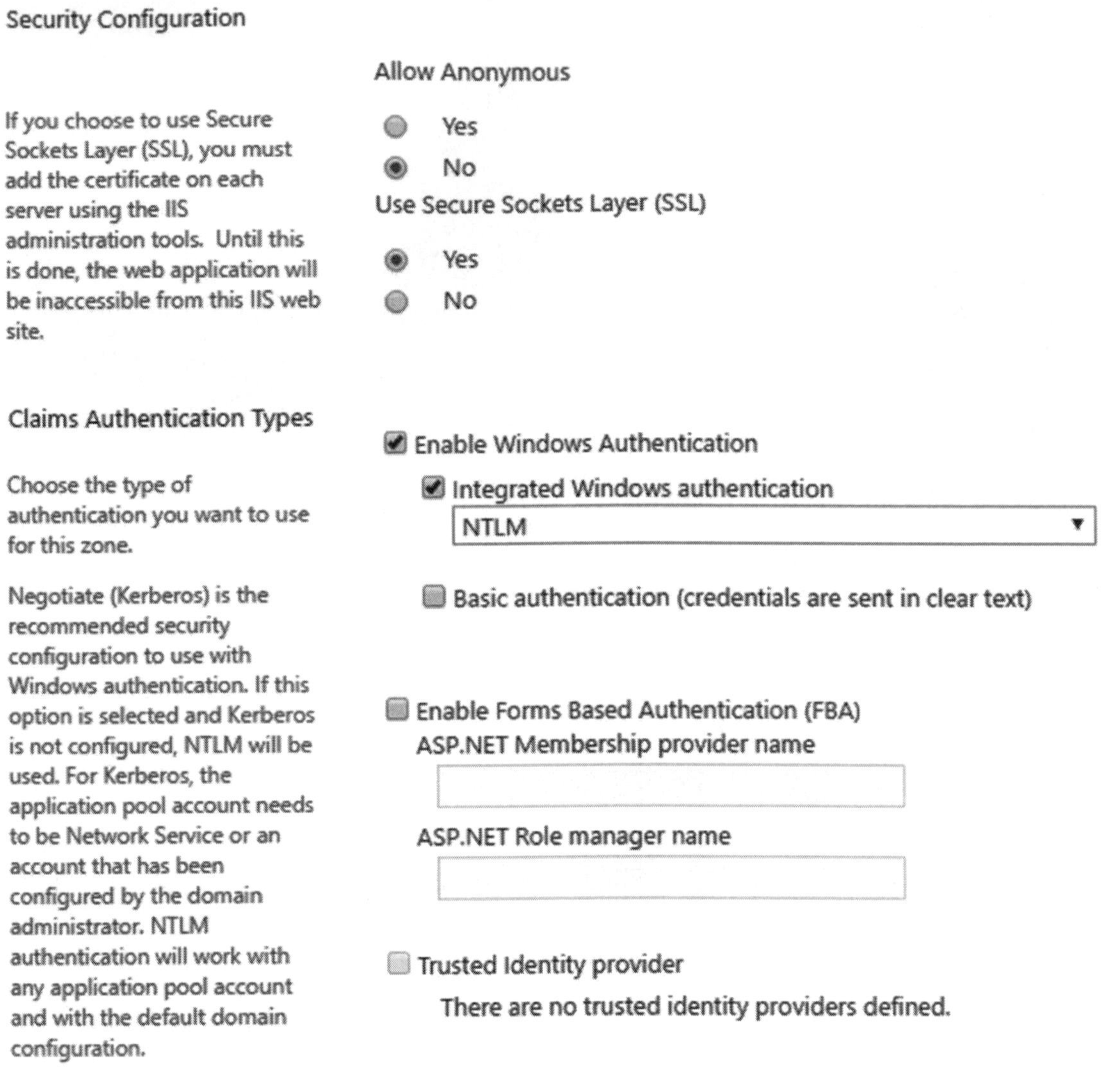

Security Configuration

Allow Anonymous

If you choose to use Secure Sockets Layer (SSL), you must add the certificate on each server using the IIS administration tools. Until this is done, the web application will be inaccessible from this IIS web site.

○ Yes

◉ No

Use Secure Sockets Layer (SSL)

◉ Yes

○ No

Claims Authentication Types

Choose the type of authentication you want to use for this zone.

Negotiate (Kerberos) is the recommended security configuration to use with Windows authentication. If this option is selected and Kerberos is not configured, NTLM will be used. For Kerberos, the application pool account needs to be Network Service or an account that has been configured by the domain administrator. NTLM authentication will work with any application pool account and with the default domain configuration.

☑ Enable Windows Authentication

☑ Integrated Windows authentication

| NTLM | ▼ |

☐ Basic authentication (credentials are sent in clear text)

☐ Enable Forms Based Authentication (FBA)
ASP.NET Membership provider name

ASP.NET Role manager name

☐ Trusted Identity provider

There are no trusted identity providers defined.

Figure 13-3. *Security Configuration Information when creating a new Web Application*

On the next part of the Web Application creation process, we need to specify the Sign in Page URL as well as the Public URL as seen in Figure 13-4. The Sign in Page URL would be changed when creating a custom login page for your users, for example an Extranet, and you want them to use this personalized page rather than the Out-of-the-Box SharePoint login page. The Public URL will be automatically populated from the Host Header you specified earlier, as well as the SSL checkbox.

Sign In Page URL

When Claims Based
Authentication types are
enabled, a URL for redirecting
the user to the Sign In page is
required.

Learn about Sign In page
redirection URL.

◉ Default Sign In Page
◉ Custom Sign In Page

Public URL

The public URL is the domain
name for all sites that users will
access in this SharePoint Web
application. This URL domain
will be used in all links shown
on pages within the web
application. By default, it is set
to the current servername and
port.
http://go.microsoft.com/fwlink/?
LinkId=114854

URL

https://intranet.learn-sp2016.com:443

Zone

Default ▾

Figure 13-4. Sign in Page URL and Public URL

We will then need to select if we create a new Web Application Pool for this Web Application, or use an existing one. Unless you have specific business or security requirements to create a new application pool, we suggest using the same one as the rest of your Web Applications. In Figure 13-5, we selected the existing *SharePoint* Application pool, which runs under the *Corp\S-Web* account.

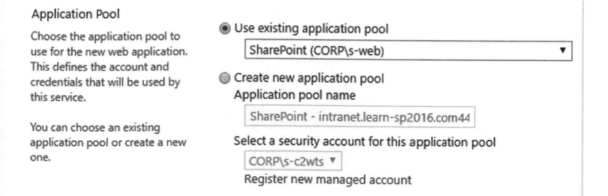

Application Pool

Choose the application pool to
use for the new web application.
This defines the account and
credentials that will be used by
this service.

You can choose an existing
application pool or create a new
one.

◉ Use existing application pool
SharePoint (CORP\s-web) ▾

◉ Create new application pool
Application pool name
SharePoint - intranet.learn-sp2016.com44

Select a security account for this application pool
CORP\s-c2wts ▾
Register new managed account

Figure 13-5. Application Pool Selection

The Next Step is to enter the information about the Database Server, and database name as seen in Figure 13-6. The Database Server will be automatically populated with your main SQL Server from your farm configuration. The Failover Server is only required when using SQL Mirroring, and not required when using AlwaysOn Availability Groups or SQL Server Clustering. In both AlwaysOn Availability Groups and Mirroring, you must manually add the database to the secondary replica or Availability Group after it has been created.

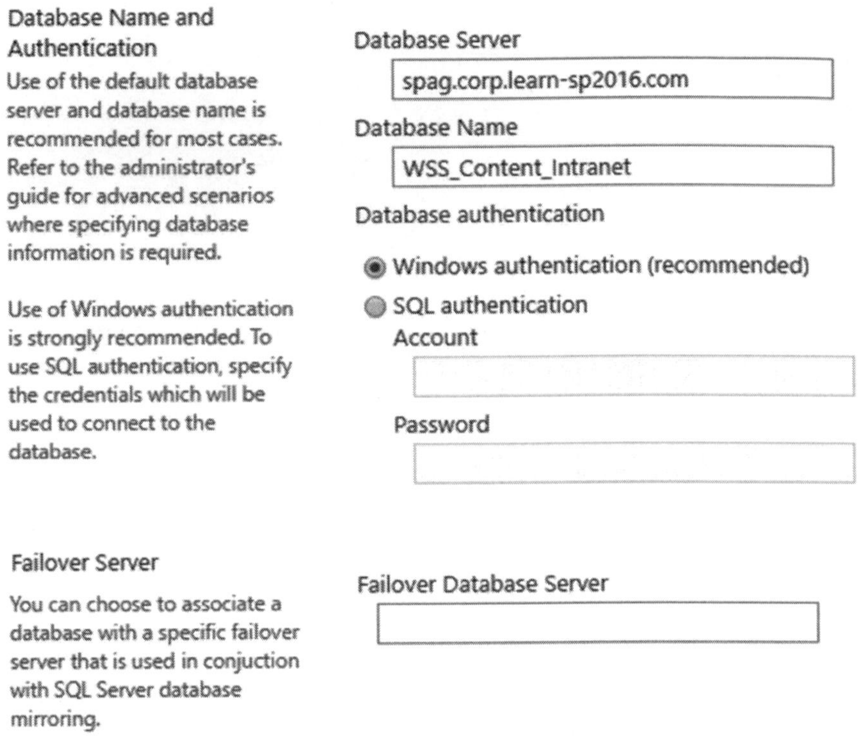

Database Name and Authentication

Use of the default database server and database name is recommended for most cases. Refer to the administrator's guide for advanced scenarios where specifying database information is required.

Use of Windows authentication is strongly recommended. To use SQL authentication, specify the credentials which will be used to connect to the database.

Database Server

spag.corp.learn-sp2016.com

Database Name

WSS_Content_Intranet

Database authentication

◉ Windows authentication (recommended)

◉ SQL authentication

Account

Password

Failover Server

You can choose to associate a database with a specific failover server that is used in conjuction with SQL Server database mirroring.

Failover Database Server

Figure 13-6. Database Information for the Web Application

The Final step to create the Web Application is to select the Service Application Connections. Those are what Service Applications will serve this Web Application. By default, the Web Application will be connected to the Default proxy group; however, you can select custom, and only select the Service Applications you want for this Web Application as seen in Figure 13-7.

Service Application Connections

Choose the service applications that this Web application will be connected to. A Web application can be connected to the default set of service applications or to a custom set of service applications. You can change the set of service applications that a Web application is connected to at any time by using the Configure service application associations page in Central Administration.

Edit the following group of connections: [custom] ▼

	Name	Type
☐	App Management Service Application Proxy_66bd1f94-e0c5-4f64-bdaa-61265850ba1a	App Management Service Application Proxy
☐	ACS	Azure Access Control Service Application Proxy
☑	BCS	Business Data Connectivity Service Application Proxy
☐	Machine Translation	Machine Translation Service Proxy
☐	Managed Metadata Service Proxy	Managed Metadata Service Connection
☐	PowerPoint Conversion Service Proxy	PowerPoint Conversion Service Application Proxy
☑	Search Service Application Proxy	Search Service Application Proxy
☑	Secure Store Service Application	Secure Store Service Application Proxy

Figure 13-7. Service Application Connections

After clicking OK, the Web Application will be created. The Web Application can also be created by using PowerShell. To create a Web Application via PowerShell, we need to use the New-SPWebApplication cmdlet from an elevated SharePoint Management Shell. To create the Intranet Web Application, we would first need to create a New Authentication Provider in order to create a Claims Web Application.

```
$ap = New-SPAuthenticationProvider
```

■ **Note**   While it is still possible to create Web Application in classic authentication mode in SharePoint 2016, this mode has been deprecated and not recommended.

We then need to create the Web Application and give it the Name, HostHeader, URL, Port, Application Pool and Database name as we did in the User Interface. We also specify the $ap provider we created just before, and use the SecureSocketsLayer switch to specify that it will run on SSL.

```
New-SPWebApplication -Name "Learn SP2016 Intranet" -HostHeader "intranet.learn-
sp2016.com" -URL "https://intranet.learn-sp2016.com" -Port 443 -ApplicationPool
"SharePoint"  -AuthenticationProvider $ap  -DatabaseName "WSS_Content_Intranet"
-SecureSocketsLayer
```

Since we have created a Web Application that uses SSL, we need to go to IIS, and select the certificate for this Web Application. If this certificate is not imported into IIS yet, you will need to import it first, and afterward from the IIS Site, Edit Bindings, and select the SSL Certificate in the drop-down as seen in Figure 13-8. Depending of your configurations, you might need to enable the "Require Server Name Indication" checkbox. Server Name Indication allows you to host sites with multiple SSL Certificates, on the same IP.

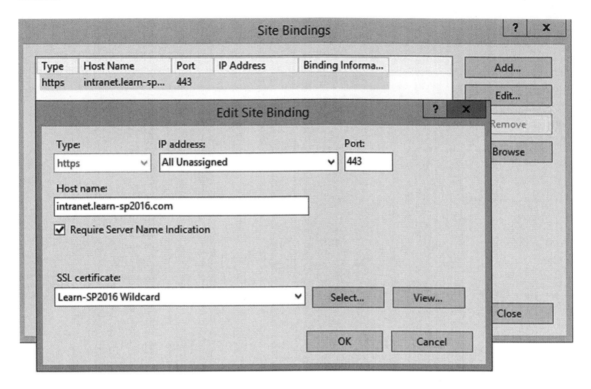

Figure 13-8. *Edit Bindings in IIS*

■ **Note** This needs to be done on all the servers running the Foundation Web Application Service. In a MinRole Farm configuration, this service runs on all the roles except Search.

Furthermore, if you haven't already, make sure to add this new entry to your company DNS as well as configure your load balancer if you have multiple Web Front Ends. With our Web Application created, let's see how we can add other URLs to this Web Application.

Alternate Access Mappings

SharePoint includes a feature called Alternate Access Mappings which allows you to create multiple URLs for the same Web Application. An alternative to Alternate Access Mappings would be Host Named Site Collections, which we will cover later in this chapter. Common uses for Alternate Access Mappings are to allow users from the internal company network to access the intranet by simply using https://intranet, but forcing users accessing from the internet to use the FQDN, which is https://intranet.learn-sp2016.com. From a User Experience point of view, it's preferable to have the same URL from both inside and outside the organization.

To create an Alternate Access Mapping from Central Administration, navigate to the Application Management page, and choose "Configure Alternate Access Mappings." SharePoint will show you all the Alternate Access Mappings from all the Web Applications as seen in Figure 13-9. By using the top right drop-down, you can select only the Web Application that you wish to view.

Alternate Access Mappings

📝 Edit Public URLs | 📝 Add Internal URLs | 📝 Map to External Resource   Alternate Access Mapping Collection: Show All ▾

Internal URL	Zone	Public URL for Zone
https://sharepoint.learn-sp2016.com	Default	https://sharepoint.learn-sp2016.com
https://lsspap01	Default	https://lsspap01
https://intranet.learn-sp2016.com	Default	https://intranet.learn-sp2016.com
https://ca.corp.learn-sp2016.com	Default	https://ca.corp.learn-sp2016.com
https://sharepoint-my.learn-sp2016.com	Default	https://sharepoint-my.learn-sp2016.com

Figure 13-9. *Alternate Access Mappings*

There are two types of Alternate Access Mappings that we can add in SharePoint Server 2016:

- **Internal URL**

  The Internal URL is simply an alias for the same site. For example, you could call me Vlad, or Vlad Catrinescu, and I will answer to both names, since I know you are talking to me. However, it's the same person (Vlad Catrinescu) that will answer back to you. When creating an internal SharePoint URL, users will be able to access the SharePoint site by typing this URL in the browser; however, they will be redirected to the Public URL of the Web Application.

- **Public URL**

  A public URL is another URL for the Web Application. For example, I would have an identity Vlad Catrinescu and another one John Smith. Depending on what name you call, still the same person will answer; however, the identity displayed, in our case the URL, will be the one you called. Every URL that a user sees in his browser should be registered as a Public URL. An alternative to creating Public URLs, which will also allow us to change authentication modes is extending the Web Application, which we cover a bit later in this chapter.

  To create a new public URL or change existing ones, use the "Edit Public URLs" button at the top right. SharePoint offers five Zones for five different URLs. There is no technical difference between the Intranet, Internet, Custom and Extranet zones. The exception here is the Default zone, which is used internally by SharePoint. One example is Search, where in order to get results displayed with the correct URL, you absolutely need to crawl the Default Public URL of the Web Application. In Figure 13-10, we have added a second public URL `https://publishing.learn-sp2016.com` in the Intranet Zone.

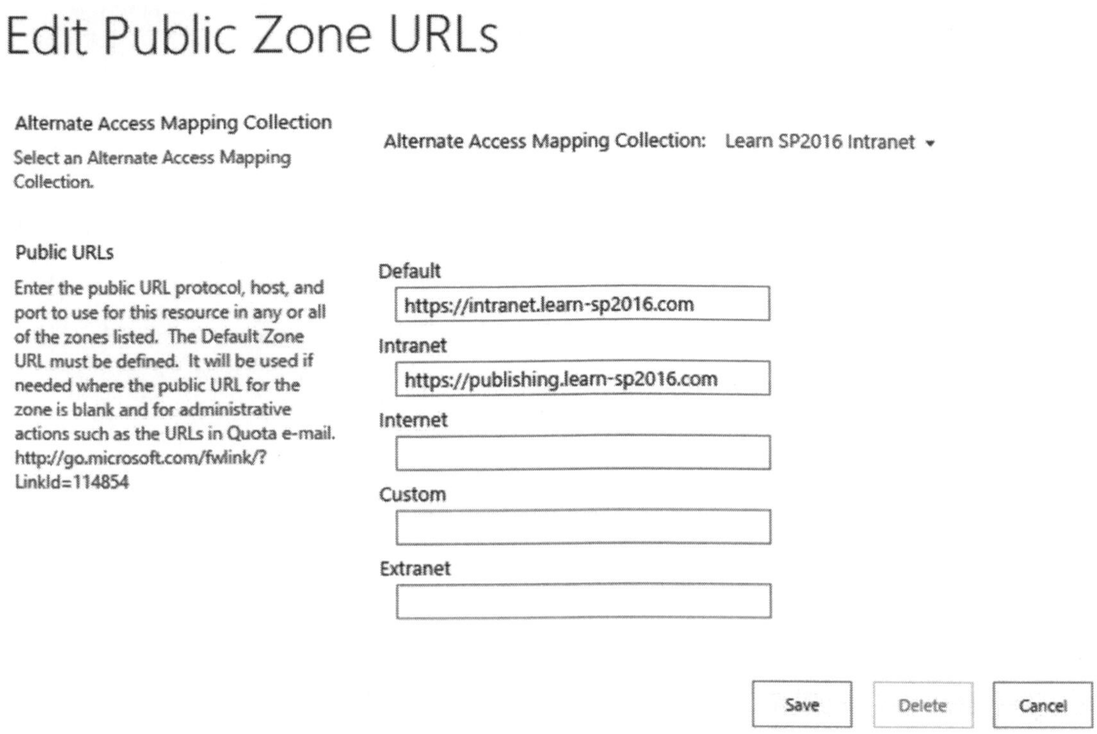

Edit Public Zone URLs

Alternate Access Mapping Collection

Select an Alternate Access Mapping Collection.

Alternate Access Mapping Collection: Learn SP2016 Intranet ▾

Public URLs

Enter the public URL protocol, host, and port to use for this resource in any or all of the zones listed. The Default Zone URL must be defined. It will be used if needed where the public URL for the zone is blank and for administrative actions such as the URLs in Quota e-mail. http://go.microsoft.com/fwlink/?LinkId=114854

Default

https://intranet.learn-sp2016.com

Intranet

https://publishing.learn-sp2016.com

Internet

Custom

Extranet

[Save]   [Delete]   [Cancel]

Figure 13-10. *New Public URL*

This can also be done by PowerShell by using the New-SPAlternateURL PowerShell cmdlet from an elevated SharePoint Management Shell. To create a new Public URL as we did in the preceding, we would run the following cmdlet:

```
New-SPAlternateURL -Url https://publishing.learn-sp2016.com -Zone "Intranet" -WebApplication
https://intranet.learn-sp2016.com
```

To create an Internal URL that would redirect https://intranet to https://intranet.learn-sp2016.com, we would still use the New-SPAlternateURL cmdlet, but add the -Internal switch.

```
New-SPAlternateURL -Url https://intranet -Zone "Default" -WebApplication https://intranet.
learn-sp2016.com -Internal
```

The result seen in Figure 13-11 will be that this SharePoint Web Application is able to be accessed by those three URLs.

Alternate Access Mappings

📝 Edit Public URLs | ✏️ Add Internal URLs | ✏️ Map to External Resource   Alternate Access Mapping Collection: Learn SP2016 Intranet ▾

Internal URL	Zone	Public URL for Zone
https://intranet.learn-sp2016.com	Default	https://intranet.learn-sp2016.com
https://intranet	Default	https://intranet.learn-sp2016.com
https://publishing.learn-sp2016.com	Intranet	https://publishing.learn-sp2016.com

Figure 13-11. *Alternate Access Mappings*

Alternate Access Mappings only apply to SharePoint, and any changes you make here do not automatically make changes to the Web Application in IIS. Furthermore, the new hostnames also need to be added in DNS. Figure 13-12 better explains where your new URL needs to be resolved, before a user can get to your SharePoint Site.

1. When requesting an URL, that URL must first be resolved in the Domain Name System (DNS). The DNS will tell the browser what IP or server it should go to. Depending on your topology, it will either directly to a SharePoint Server, or to a Load Balancer that will then forward the request to one of your Web Servers.

2. IIS receives the request and looks for a binding that matches. This is why it's important to always make sure to update your URLs not only in SharePoint but in IIS as well.

3. Once IIS matches the request to one of the sites, the request will go to SharePoint, which will match it against one of the Web Applications, and return the SharePoint site to the user.

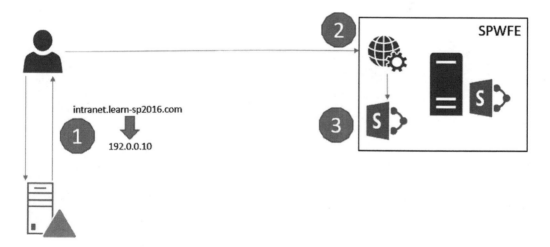

Figure 13-12. *SharePoint Site Resolution*

It's important to remember that whenever you add, or change an URL in SharePoint, the change must be done in all three places: DNS, IIS and SharePoint.

Extending a Web Application

In the previous section we saw how to add a new Public URL to our Web Application in order to allow users to access it under another name. A different way to achieve the same result, as well as provide more options is to extend the Web Application. When you extend a Web Application, not only you do have a new URL to access that Web Application, but the process also creates a different IIS site, as well as allowing you to set a different authentication method.

Take, for example, a Web Application used for an extranet that internal user's access with `http://extranet` and uses NTLM authentication. Since we don't want external users to have an AD account, we need to enable Form-Based Authentication. By extending the Web Application to `https://extranet.learn-sp2016.com` we are able to get the new URL, as well as enable another form of authentication, in our case Form-Based Authentication.

To extend a Web Application from the Central Administration, from the Web Applications page, select the Web Application you want to extend and click Extend as seen in Figure 13-13.

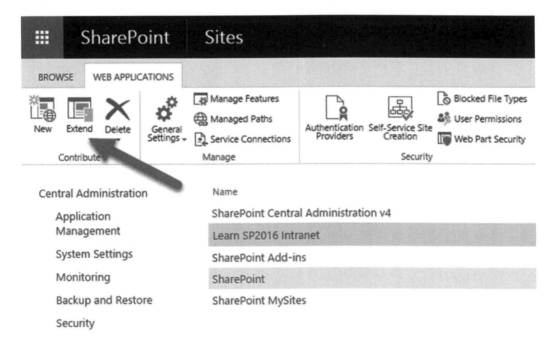

Figure 13-13. *Extend Web Application*

The Extend screen seen in Figure 13-14 is very similar to the new Web Application. We first need to enter the Port and Host header of the new IIS Web Site.

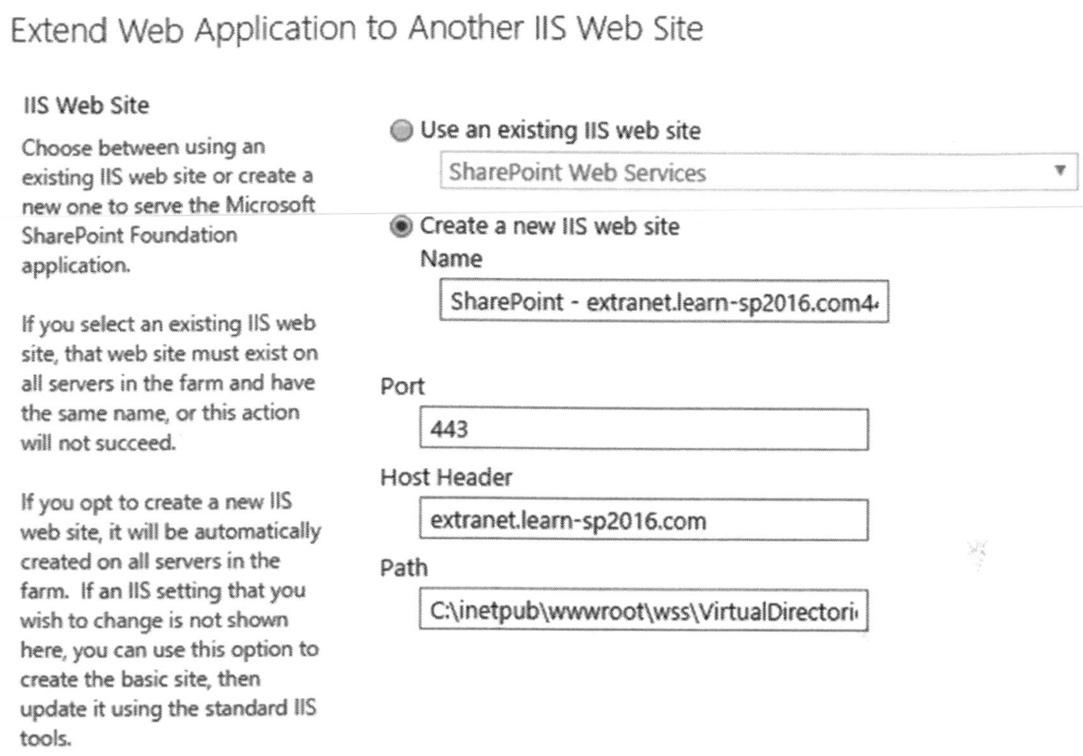

Extend Web Application to Another IIS Web Site

IIS Web Site

Choose between using an existing IIS web site or create a new one to serve the Microsoft SharePoint Foundation application.

If you select an existing IIS web site, that web site must exist on all servers in the farm and have the same name, or this action will not succeed.

If you opt to create a new IIS web site, it will be automatically created on all servers in the farm. If an IIS setting that you wish to change is not shown here, you can use this option to create the basic site, then update it using the standard IIS tools.

○ Use an existing IIS web site

SharePoint Web Services ▼

⦿ Create a new IIS web site

Name

SharePoint - extranet.learn-sp2016.com4·

Port

443

Host Header

extranet.learn-sp2016.com

Path

C:\inetpub\wwwroot\wss\VirtualDirectori·

Figure 13-14. *Extend Web Application to another IIS Web Site*

We then need to specify the Security Configuration as well as the Claims authentication types we want to use. In Figure 13-15 we selected to use SSL, and allow users to connect to the Web Application with both NTLM and FBA.

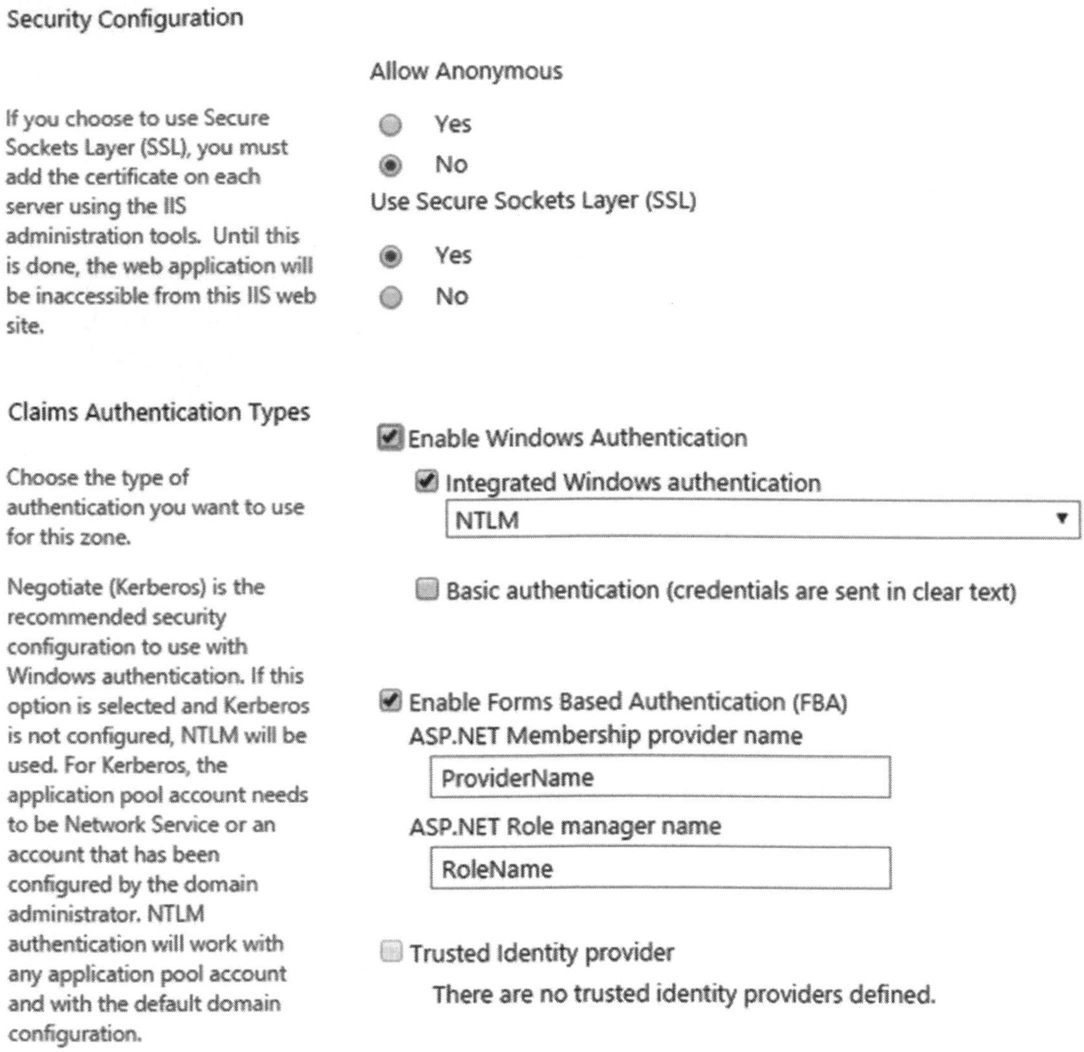

Security Configuration

If you choose to use Secure Sockets Layer (SSL), you must add the certificate on each server using the IIS administration tools. Until this is done, the web application will be inaccessible from this IIS web site.

Allow Anonymous

○ Yes
◉ No

Use Secure Sockets Layer (SSL)

◉ Yes
○ No

Claims Authentication Types

Choose the type of authentication you want to use for this zone.

Negotiate (Kerberos) is the recommended security configuration to use with Windows authentication. If this option is selected and Kerberos is not configured, NTLM will be used. For Kerberos, the application pool account needs to be Network Service or an account that has been configured by the domain administrator. NTLM authentication will work with any application pool account and with the default domain configuration.

☑ Enable Windows Authentication

  ☑ Integrated Windows authentication

    | NTLM ▼ |

  ☐ Basic authentication (credentials are sent in clear text)

☑ Enable Forms Based Authentication (FBA)
ASP.NET Membership provider name

  | ProviderName |

ASP.NET Role manager name

  | RoleName |

☐ Trusted Identity provider

    There are no trusted identity providers defined.

Figure 13-15. *Extend Web Application Security Configuration*

A new site will be created in IIS with the extranet.learn-sp2016.com binding already there; however, we need to set the certificate manually as well as enter it in the DNS. To extend a Web Application via PowerShell, we need to run the New-SPWebApplicationExtension cmdlet from an elevated SharePoint Management Shell. To extend our Intranet Web Application with the URL https://extranet.learn-sp2016.com on port 443 and using SSL, we would run the following cmdlet.

```
Get-SPWebApplication https://intranet.learn-sp2016.com | New-SPWebApplicationExtension
-Name "Extranet" -URL "https://extranet.learn-sp2016.com"  -SecureSocketsLayer -Zone
"Extranet" -HostHeader "extranet.learn-sp2016.com" -Port 443
```

Web Application User Policy

SharePoint allows us to give certain permissions to users, directly at the Web Application level. This is very useful for SharePoint Administrators who need access to all the Site Collections in a Web Application, but don't want to add themselves manually. SharePoint also uses Web Application policies to give certain accounts permissions to the Web Application. For example, the Search Crawl account has Full Read permissions on every Web Applications in the farm it needs to crawl. There are four available permissions at the Web Application level:

1. Full Control

    Full Control to all the Site Collections in the Web Application.

2. Full Read

    Can read all the content in the Web Application, but not modify or add content, unless given rights directly in the Site.

3. Deny Write

    This policy will not allow the user or group to modify or add any content in the Web Application, even if given rights directly in a SharePoint Site.

4. Deny All

    This policy will not allow the user or group to access any site in the Web Application, even if given rights directly in a SharePoint site in that Web Application.

You can also create custom policies in the Web Application Permission Policy; however, it's recommended to only use the default ones if possible.

To add users to the Web Application Policy, from the Web Application page in Central Administration, select the Web Application you want to apply the policy to, and select User Policy from the ribbon. A window similar to Figure 13-16 will open, displaying all the current policies for the Web Application.

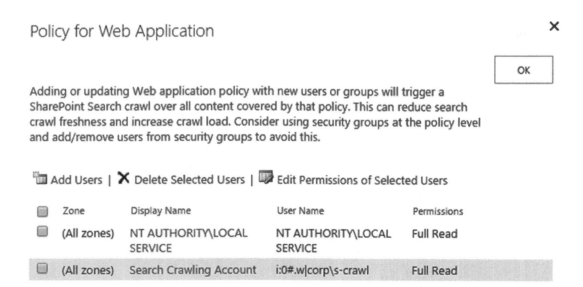

Figure 13-16. *Policy for Web Application*

As noted in Chapter 6, adding or deleting users from the Web Application policies will make the search engine crawl the whole content of the Web Application on the next crawl, in order to recalculate the item Access Control List.

To add a User to the Web Application Policy, click Add Users at the top left of the window and if the Web Application has more than one zone, select the zone you want to apply this policy to. On the next window seen in Figure 13-17, enter the users our groups that you wish to add to the Web Application policy, as well as what permissions you want to give them. The "Account operates as System" checkbox is only recommended for service accounts, as their actions will be marked as "System" in the logs, and not the actual username.

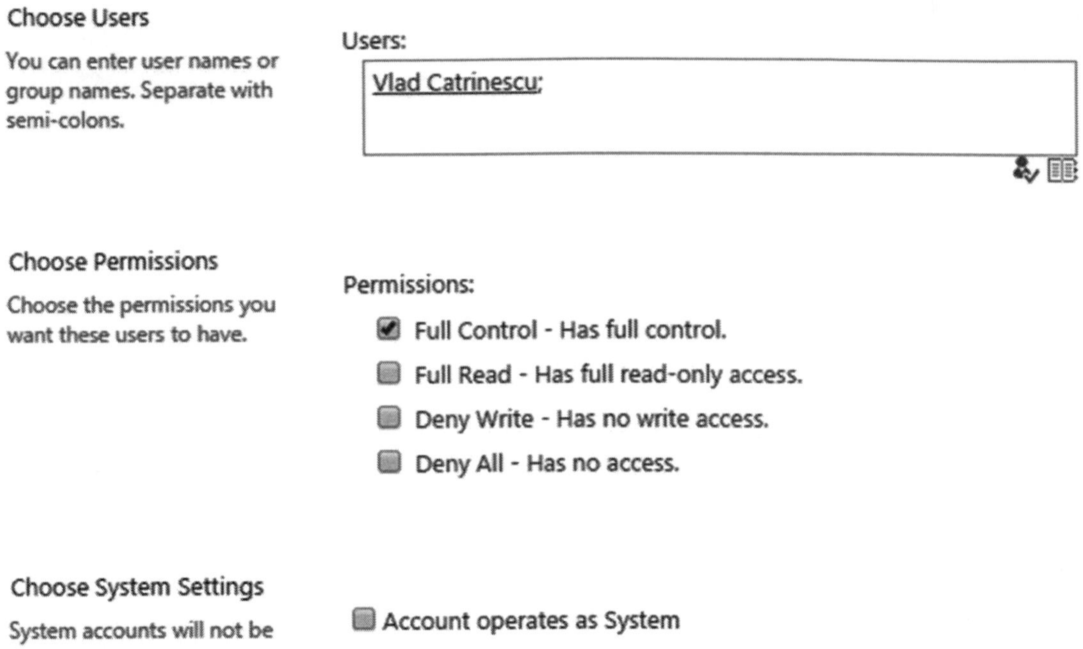

Choose Users

You can enter user names or group names. Separate with semi-colons.

Users:

Vlad Catrinescu;

Choose Permissions

Choose the permissions you want these users to have.

Permissions:

☑ Full Control - Has full control.

☐ Full Read - Has full read-only access.

☐ Deny Write - Has no write access.

☐ Deny All - Has no access.

Choose System Settings

System accounts will not be

☐ Account operates as System

Figure 13-17. *New Web Application Policy*

Click Finish to add the Policy. To add the same policy via PowerShell, we need to run the following cmdlets from an elevated SharePoint Management Shell.

```
$w = Get-SPWebApplication https://intranet.learn-sp2016.com/
$policy = $w.Policies.Add("i:0#.w|corp\vlad", "SharePoint Admin")
$policyRole = $w.PolicyRoles.GetSpecialRole([Microsoft.SharePoint.Administration.SPPolicyRole
Type]::FullControl)
$policy.PolicyRoleBindings.Add($policyRole)
$w.Update()
```

Where corp\vlad is the account we want to add, and SharePoint Admin is the display name that will appear in the Web Application Policy. The result of this cmdlet can be seen in Figure 13-18.

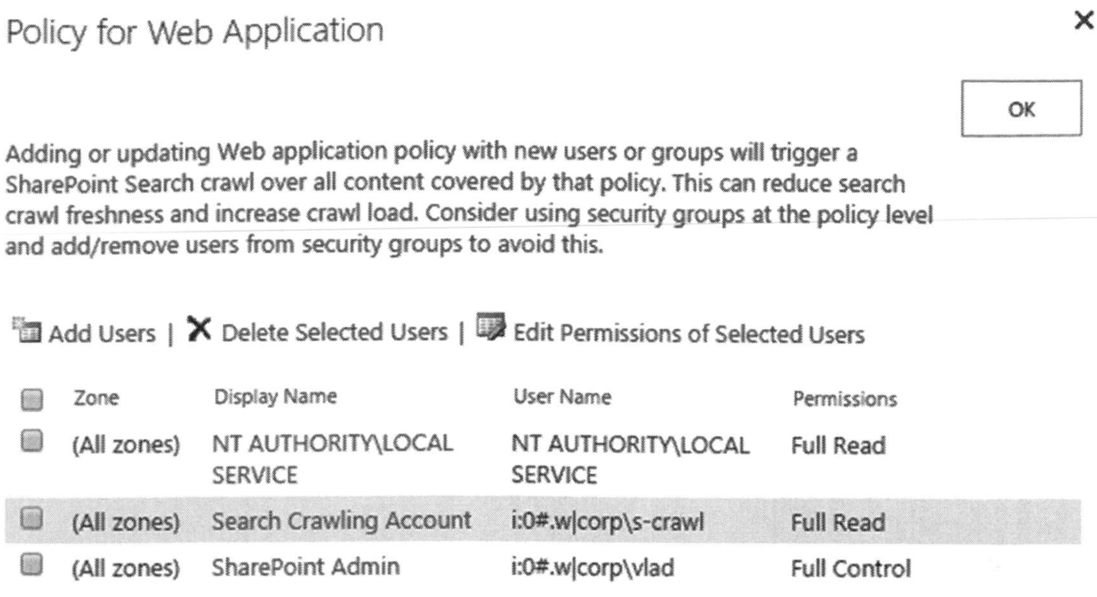

Policy for Web Application   ✕

OK

Adding or updating Web application policy with new users or groups will trigger a SharePoint Search crawl over all content covered by that policy. This can reduce search crawl freshness and increase crawl load. Consider using security groups at the policy level and add/remove users from security groups to avoid this.

▥ Add Users | ✗ Delete Selected Users | ▨ Edit Permissions of Selected Users

☐	Zone	Display Name	User Name	Permissions
☐	(All zones)	NT AUTHORITY\LOCAL SERVICE	NT AUTHORITY\LOCAL SERVICE	Full Read
☐	(All zones)	Search Crawling Account	i:0#.w|corp\s-crawl	Full Read
☐	(All zones)	SharePoint Admin	i:0#.w|corp\vlad	Full Control

Figure 13-18. *Add Web Application Policy via PowerShell*

Object Cache Accounts

SharePoint publishing sites use two Object Cache Accounts to improve page rendering speeds on publishing pages, and reduce load on the SQL Server. Those accounts are often referred to Portal Super User and Portal Super Reader accounts. The Portal Super User account will have Full Control on the Web Application, while the Portal Super Reader account will only have Full Read on the Web Application. SharePoint will use those cache accounts, to create two versions of the object cache, one with the Portal Super Reader account, which will only see published items, and one with the Portal Super User account, which will see both published items and drafts. When a user queries a publishing page, the object cache will check that user's permissions, and will return the appropriate cached object depending if he can see draft items or not. The Object Cache accounts are only needed for Web Applications that will run publishing sites, but there is no harm in setting them on all your Web Applications.

The Portal Super User and Portal Super Reader accounts must be two separate service accounts, and they must not be used to login on the site. We must first add them to the Web Application property bag by using the following cmdlets.

```
$wa = Get-SPWebApplication https://intranet.learn-sp2016.com/
$wa.Properties["portalsuperuseraccount"] = "i:0#.w|CORP\s-su"
$wa.Properties["portalsuperreaderaccount"] = "i:0#.w|CORP\s-sr"
$wa.Update()
```

Afterward, we must give them the required permissions. The Super User account needs to have full control at the Web Application level, while the Super Reader must have full read.

```
$w = Get-SPWebApplication https://intranet.learn-sp2016.com/
$policy = $w.Policies.Add("i:0#.w|CORP\s-su", "Portal Super User")
$policyRole = $w.PolicyRoles.GetSpecialRole([Microsoft.SharePoint.Administration.SPPolicyRole
Type]::FullControl)
```

259

```
$policy.PolicyRoleBindings.Add($policyRole)
$policy = $w.Policies.Add("i:0#.w|CORP\s-sr", "Portal Super Reader")
$policyRole = $w.PolicyRoles.GetSpecialRole([Microsoft.SharePoint.Administration.
SPPolicyRoleType]::FullRead)
$policy.PolicyRoleBindings.Add($policyRole)
$w.Update()
```

After running those scripts, the accounts will be seen in the Web Application properties as seen in Figure 13-19.

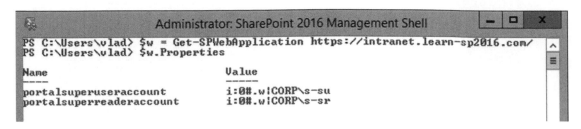

Figure 13-19. *Web Application Properties*

The two Object Cache accounts will also be seen in the Web Application Policy with the required permissions.

■ **Note**   In order for the Object Cache Accounts changes to take effect, you will need to perform an IISReset.

Content Databases

A Web Application can have one, or many Content Databases attached to it. By creating multiple content databases, you can isolate Site Collections from one another, making database management easier. To view or create databases from Central Administration, navigate to the Application Management Page, and then click Manage Content Databases. The page seen in Figure 13-20 will show all the databases attached to this Web Application, as well as how many Site Collections they have inside.

Content Databases ⓘ

🖼 Add a content database   Web Application: https://intranet.learn-sp2016.com/ ▾

Database Name	Database Status	Database Read-Only	Current Number of Site Collections	Site Collection Level Warning	Maximum Number of Site Collections	Preferred Timer Server
WSS_Content_Intranet	Started	No	0	2000	5000	

Figure 13-20. *Content Databases*

To create a new Content Database, click the "Add a Content Database" button on the top left. You will first need to enter the Database Server where to add the database as well as its name. In Figure 13-21 we kept our default database server, and named the database WSS_Content_Intranet_2

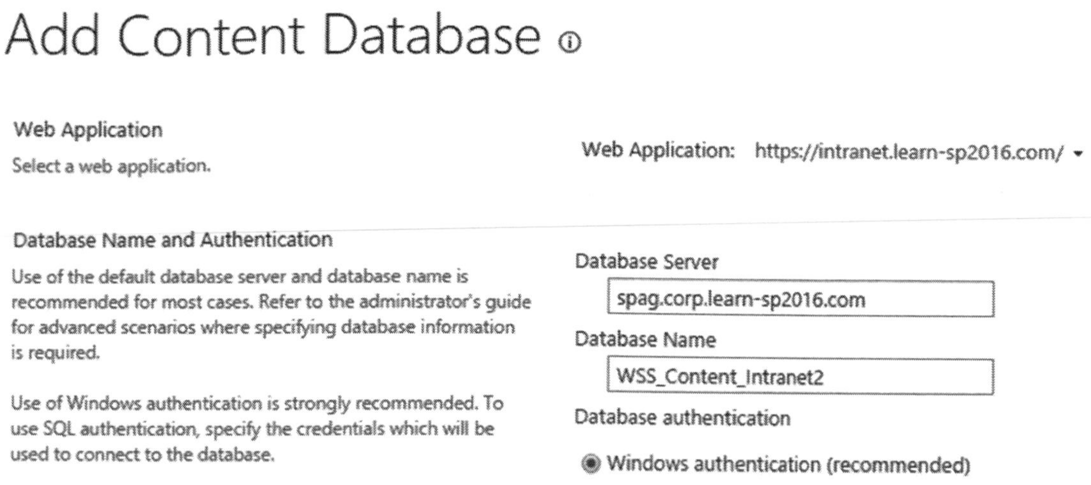

Add Content Database ⓘ

Web Application

Select a web application.

Web Application: https://intranet.learn-sp2016.com/ ▾

Database Name and Authentication

Use of the default database server and database name is recommended for most cases. Refer to the administrator's guide for advanced scenarios where specifying database information is required.

Use of Windows authentication is strongly recommended. To use SQL authentication, specify the credentials which will be used to connect to the database.

Database Server

    spag.corp.learn-sp2016.com

Database Name

    WSS_Content_Intranet2

Database authentication

⦿ Windows authentication (recommended)

***Figure 13-21.** New Content Database Server and Name*

We then need to enter the Failover Database Server if we are running SQL Mirroring. This is not required if you are running SQL Server AlwaysOn Availability groups, or SQL Server Clustering. Finally you will need to enter the maximum number of Site Collections that can be created in this database, as well as a number where a warning event will be generated in the event log. If you set this maximum to the current number of Site Collections in the Content Database, SharePoint will simply not create any more Site Collections in this Content Database. In Figure 13-22 we set the warning at 10, and maximum number at 15.

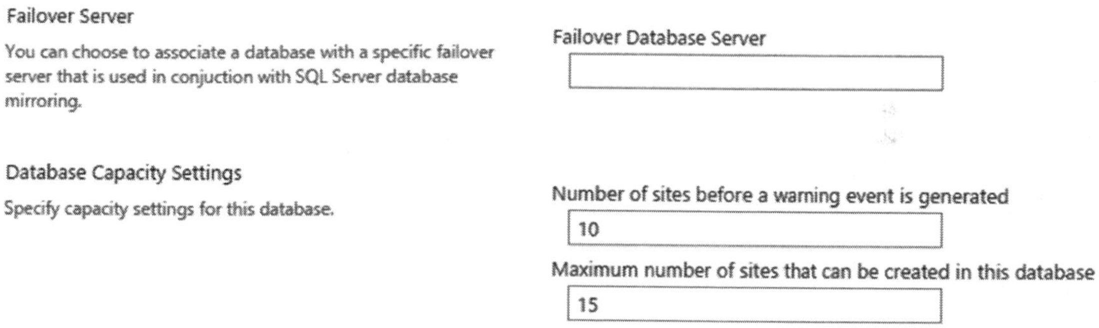

Failover Server

You can choose to associate a database with a specific failover server that is used in conjuction with SQL Server database mirroring.

Failover Database Server

Database Capacity Settings

Specify capacity settings for this database.

Number of sites before a warning event is generated

    10

Maximum number of sites that can be created in this database

    15

***Figure 13-22.** Database Capacity Settings*

Simply press on OK to create the Content Database. Make sure to add the database to your Availability group or to the secondary replica if you have High Availability at the SQL tier. The Content Database can also be created via PowerShell by using the New-SPContentDatabase cmdlet from an elevated SharePoint Management Shell. To create a database with the same parameters as the one before, we would run the following PowerShell cmdlet:

```
New-SPContentDatabase "WSS_Content_Intranet_3" -WebApplication https://intranet.learn-sp2016.com/ -WarningSiteCount 10 -MaxSiteCount 15
```

To Edit a Content Database, from the Database Management page, simply click the name and you will get to the Manage Content Database Settings. The Name and Server of the database cannot be changed; however, you can change the status of the database from *Ready* to *Offline* as seen in Figure 13-23. Changing the Database status to Offline, will not actually put the database offline, it will only tell SharePoint not to put any new Site Collections in this database. All the existing databases will work as before.

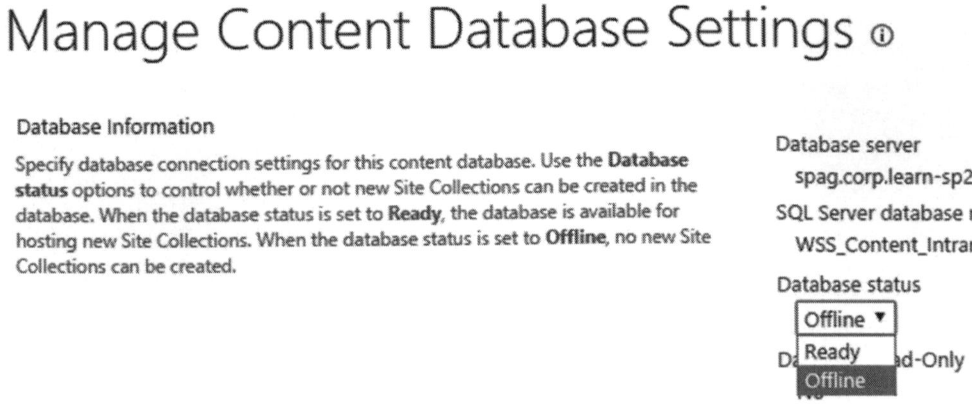

Manage Content Database Settings ⓘ

Database Information

Specify database connection settings for this content database. Use the **Database status** options to control whether or not new Site Collections can be created in the database. When the database status is set to **Ready**, the database is available for hosting new Site Collections. When the database status is set to **Offline**, no new Site Collections can be created.

Database server
    spag.corp.learn-sp2016.com

SQL Server database name
    WSS_Content_Intranet

Database status

Figure 13-23. Database Status

You can also change the Maximum Number of Site Collections in the database from this page. To Remove a Content Database, check the "Remove Content Database" checkbox seen in Figure 13-24. This will not delete the database, but it will simply detach it from the farm, and all the Site Collections in that database will not be available in the SharePoint farm anymore. The data will still be kept in the database, until you delete it from SQL Server.

Database Capacity Settings

Specify capacity settings for this database.

Number of sites before a warning event is generated

```
20
```

Maximum number of sites that can be created in this database

```
30
```

Remove Content Database

Use this section to remove a content database from the server farm. When you select the **Remove content database** check box and click **OK**, the database is no longer associated with this Web application. **Caution:** When you remove the content database, any sites listed in that content database are removed from the server farm, but the site data remains in the database.

☑ Remove content database

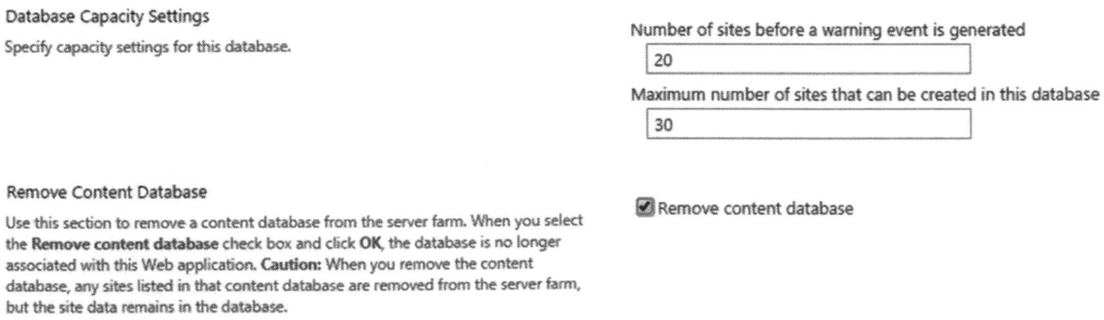

Figure 13-24. Remove Content Database

You can also detach a Content Database from SharePoint by using the `Dismount-SPContentDatabase` PowerShell cmdlet. To remove a Content Database from both SharePoint and delete it from SQL Server, you can use the `Remove-SPContentDatabase` PowerShell cmdlet.

When Site Collections are created without specifying a Content Database, SharePoint will create the Site Collection in the Content Database that is available and has the lowest number of Site Collections inside. With this algorithm, Content Database will grow evenly. You can also implement a custom Site Creation Provider by using custom code to analyze what type of Site Collection is being created and route it to a certain database.

Site Collections

With our Web Application created and ready, we now need to create Site Collections. There are two strategies to create Site Collections. The first one is called Path-Based Site Collection and is the traditional approach we have used since SharePoint 2010. A Path-Based Site Collection always has the same URL as the Web Application it is under. For example, if my Web Application URL is `https://intranet.learn-sp2016.com`, all my Site Collections in that Web Application will start with `https://intranet.learn-sp2016.com`. Therefore, if a team asks you to create a Site Collection that is at `https://communications.learn-sp2016.com`, you would need to create a new Web Application. Remember that for performance reasons, we should have a maximum of 20 Web Applications, so this approach can be very limited in scalability.

Since SharePoint 2013, Microsoft has encouraged the use of Host Named Site Collections. Host Named Site Collections do not necessarily share the same URL as the Web Application they are in, therefore I could have my Site Collection with the URL `https://communications.learn-sp2016.com` in my `https://intranet.learn-sp2016.com`.

But what is the problem with Web Applications? Web Applications consume a lot more resources on your Web Front End than a Site Collection. In the SharePoint 2016 Software Boundaries and Limits, Microsoft lists 20 as the maximum supported number of Web Applications per SharePoint farm. While having fewer Web Applications, and using Host Named Site Collections is definitely better for your server performance, creating and managing Host Named Site Collection is more difficult and a lot less user friendly. We will get more into details in the section covering Host Named Site Collections.

Path-Based Site Collections

Path-Based Site Collections are still the most common Site Collections across On-Premises SharePoint deployments because they are easier to create and manage. To create a Site Collection from Central Administration, navigate to the Application Management page and under Site Collections, click Create Site Collections. On the top of the screen, you need to select in which Web Application you want to create this site collection. You will have to first enter the Title of the Site Collection, and optionally the description as well. You then have to choose the URL of your Site Collection. Since our Web Application doesn't have any Site Collections at the root, meaning with the same URL as the Web Application, we can create either a Root Site Collection, or a site collection that is under /sites/url. The Sites part of the URL is what we call a managed path, and we are able to customize those to include sites after /teams/ for example, or even create a site collection that is the (Web Application URL)/HR, for example `https://intranet/HR`. We will look at Managed Paths later in this chapter. In our example seen in Figure 13-25, we will create a root Site Collection with the title Intranet Home.

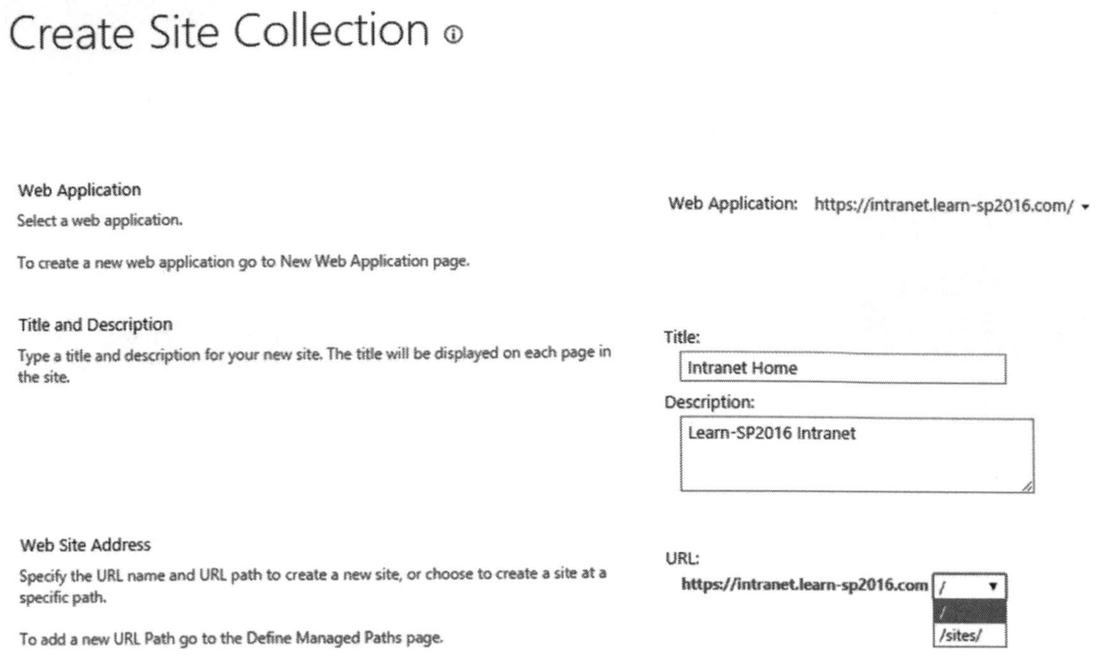

Create Site Collection ⓘ

Web Application

Select a web application.

To create a new web application go to New Web Application page.

Web Application: https://intranet.learn-sp2016.com/ ▾

Title and Description

Type a title and description for your new site. The title will be displayed on each page in the site.

Title:

Intranet Home

Description:

Learn-SP2016 Intranet

Web Site Address

Specify the URL name and URL path to create a new site, or choose to create a site at a specific path.

To add a new URL Path go to the Define Managed Paths page.

URL:

https://intranet.learn-sp2016.com / ▾

/

/sites/

Figure 13-25. *New Site Collection*

On the second part of the form, you need to select the Template, as well as the Primary and Secondary Site Collection Administrators as seen in Figure 13-26. If you have multiple language packs installed, you will also have a drop-down field where you can select the language of the site collection. Lastly, not seen in Figure 13-26 is the Quota Template selection. We will talk about Quota Templates a bit later in the chapter.

Template Selection

Select a template:

| Collaboration | Enterprise | Publishing | Custom |

Team Site
Blog
Developer Site
Project Site
Community Site

A place to work together with a group of people.

Primary Site Collection Administrator

Specify the administrator for this site collection. Only one user login can be provided; security groups are not supported.

User name:

Vlad Catrinescu;

Secondary Site Collection Administrator

Optionally specify a secondary site collection administrator. Only one user login can be provided; security groups are not supported.

User name:

Trevor Seward;

Figure 13-26. *New Site Collection Template and Site Collection Administrators*

To create the Site Collection, simply press on OK at the bottom of the screen. To create a Site Collection by PowerShell, we need to use the `New-SPSite` cmdlet from an elevated SharePoint Management Shell. By using the SharePoint Management Shell, we also have the possibility of selecting in which Content Database we want to put this Site Collection in. In the following cmdlet we specify the URL, name, and description of the Site Collection. We also pass the usernames of the first and secondary owners. Lastly, we specify the Team Site template ID (STS#0) and the Content Database in which we want to create the Site Collection.

```
New-SPSite -url "https://intranet.learn-sp2016.com/sites/team1" -Name "Team 1 Home"
-Description "Team 1 SharePoint Site" -OwnerAlias "corp\vlad" -SecondaryOwnerAlias "corp\
trevor" -Template "STS#0" -ContentDatabase WSS_Content_Intranet_3
```

> ■ **Note** When creating a Site Collections trough PowerShell, the default SharePoint groups will not be created.

If you do not specify a template, the Site Collection will be created without a Root Web, and SharePoint will ask you to select a template the first time you browse to the site as seen in Figure 13-27.

Figure 13-27. *Site Collection Template Selection*

Site Quotas

SharePoint allows administrators to specify a quota for each Site Collection. Quotas will not allow users to use more than a certain amount of storage, as well as limit the number of resources that can be consumed by Sandboxed Solutions. Once the quota is reached, a "No Free Space" message appears to users when they try to create new items in SharePoint, and a red bar is displayed at the top of the site. To create a new Site Quota by Central Administration, navigate to the Application Management page, and then, Specify Quota templates.

In Figure 13-28, I created a new Site Quota Template named "Bronze Team Site" with a limit of 500MB and a warning sent to the Site Collection Administrator at 300MB. I did not set a maximum for Sandboxed Solutions.

Template Name
 	
 Edit an existing quota template, or create a new template. For a new template, you can start from a blank template or modify an existing template.
	○ Edit an existing template
	    Template to modify
	    [Personal Site ▾]
	
	 ⦿ Create a new quota template
	    Template to start from
	    [[new blank template] ▾]
	
	    New template name:
	    [Bronze Team Site]

Storage Limit Values
 	
 Specify whether to limit the amount of storage available on a Site Collection, and set the maximum amount of storage, and a warning level. When the warning level or maximum storage level is reached, an e-mail is sent to the site administrator to inform them of the issue.
	☑ Limit site storage to a maximum of:
	    [500] MB
	
	 ☑ Send warning E-mail when Site Collection storage reaches:
	    [300] MB

Sandboxed Solutions With Code Limits Specifies whether sandboxed solutions with code are allowed for this site collection. When the warning level is reached, an e-mail is sent. When the maximum usage limit is reached, sandboxed solutions with code are disabled for the rest of the day and an e-mail is sent to the site administrator.	Limit maximum usage per day to: [0] points ☑ Send warning e-mail when usage per day reaches: [0] points

Figure 13-28. *New Quota Template*

266

The Quota Template can also be created via PowerShell. In the next script, we will create a quota named "Silver Team Site" with a 1024MB maximum storage limit, and a warning sent at 750MB. Notice the StorageMaximumLevel and StorageWarningLevel variables need to be in bytes.

```
$Template = New-Object Microsoft.SharePoint.Administration.SPQuotaTemplate
$Template.Name = "Silver Team Site"
$Template.StorageMaximumLevel = 1073741824
$Template.StorageWarningLevel = 786432000
$ContentService = [Microsoft.SharePoint.Administration.SPWebService]::ContentService
$ContentService.QuotaTemplates.Add($Template)
$ContentService.Update()
```

Assigning a Quota Template to a Site Collection can be done by using the Set-SPSite cmdlet and specifying the URL and name of the QuotaTemplate as seen in the following example.

```
Set-SPSite -Identity https://intranet.learn-sp2016.com/sites/team1 -QuotaTemplate
"Silver Team Site"
```

You can also use the Set-SPSite cmdlet to change the quota to another template later on.

Managed Paths

Managed Paths allow you to customize the URL of your sites in order to make them more user friendly and to align with your business requirements and to allow us to host multiple Site Collections in the same Web Application. Managed Paths are what is between the Web Application URL and the part of your URL you want to give to your Site Collection. By Default, every SharePoint Web Application contains the /sites/ Managed Path as well as the (root) Managed Path, allowing you to create the root Site Collection. There are two types of Managed Paths that you can create in SharePoint:

- Wildcard Inclusion

A Wildcard Inclusion is a managed math that allows you to create multiple Site Collections using the path you specify. For example, if you create a /teams/ managed path, you could create URLs like https://intranet.learn-sp2016.com/teams/engineering, https://intranet.learn-sp2016.com/teams/HR, https://intranet.learn-sp2016.com/teams/Marketing and so on. However, you cannot create a site with the URL https://intranet.learn-sp2016.com/teams. The default /sites Managed Path is of type Wildcard Inclusion.

- Explicit Inclusion

An Explicit Inclusion only allows you to create a Site Collection with the specified address. For example, we could create a /HR Managed path in Explicit Inclusion, you could only create a Site Collection at https://intranet.learn-sp2016.com/HR. You will not need to add anything after the HR as you would have to do with a Wildcard Inclusion. For performance reasons, Microsoft recommends a maximum of 20 Managed Paths per Web Application.

To create a Managed Path via Central Administration, navigate to the Web Application Management Page, and from the Ribbon click Managed Paths as seen in Figure 13-29.

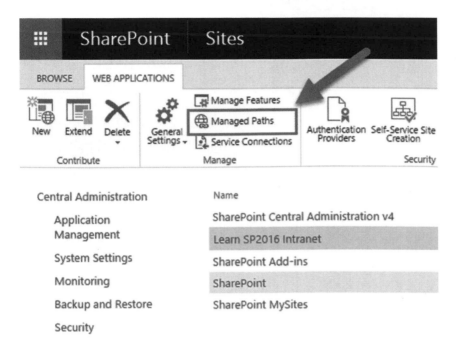

Figure 13-29. *Managed Paths*

Simply enter the path that you wish to create, as well as the Type from the drop-down, and click the "Add Path" button. After the path is added to the included paths, you can click OK to close the pop-up window. In Figure 13-30 we have created a Managed Path called "Teams" of type Wildcard.

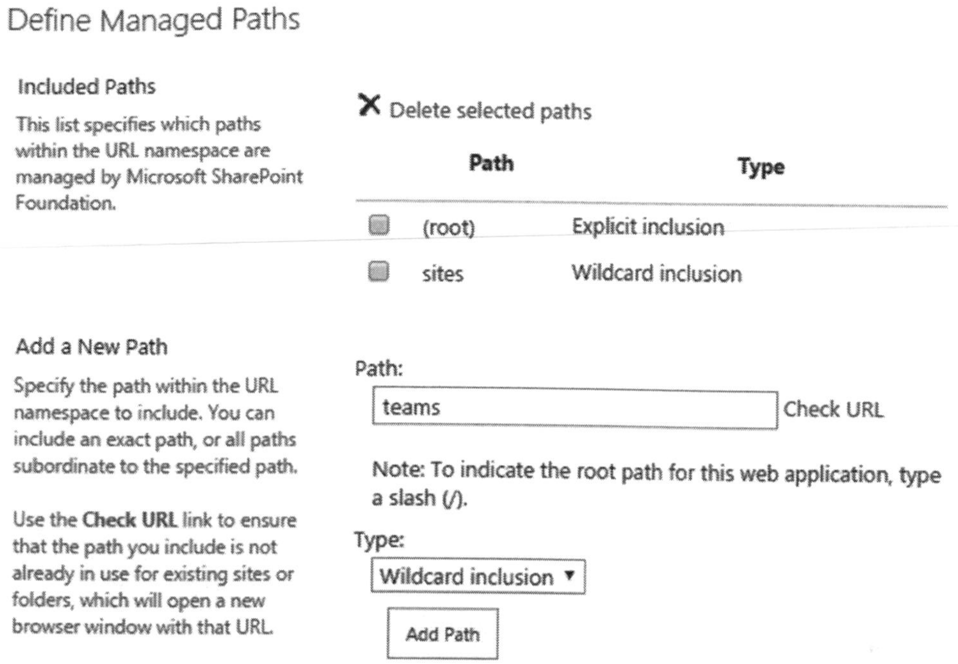

Define Managed Paths

Included Paths

This list specifies which paths within the URL namespace are managed by Microsoft SharePoint Foundation.

✖ Delete selected paths

	Path	Type
▢	(root)	Explicit inclusion
▢	sites	Wildcard inclusion

Add a New Path

Specify the path within the URL namespace to include. You can include an exact path, or all paths subordinate to the specified path.

Use the **Check URL** link to ensure that the path you include is not already in use for existing sites or folders, which will open a new browser window with that URL.

Path:

| teams | | Check URL |

Note: To indicate the root path for this web application, type a slash (/).

Type:

| Wildcard inclusion ▾ |

Add Path

Figure 13-30. *Teams Managed Path*

To create a Managed Path with PowerShell, we need to run the New-SPManagedPath PowerShell cmdlet from an elevated SharePoint Management Shell. For example, to create a new Wildcard inclusion Managed Path with the "department" path, we would run the following PowerShell cmdlet.

```
New-SPManagedPath "department" -WebApplication https://intranet.learn-sp2016.com
```

If we want to create an Explicit Managed Path, we need to add the - Explicit switch, as in the following example.

```
New-SPManagedPath "communications" -WebApplication "https://intranet.learn-sp2016.com" -
Explicit
```

If we go back to create a new Site Collection via Central Administration, we will see both the /teams Managed Path as seen in Figure 13-31 and the /communications Explicit Managed Path seen in Figure 13-32.

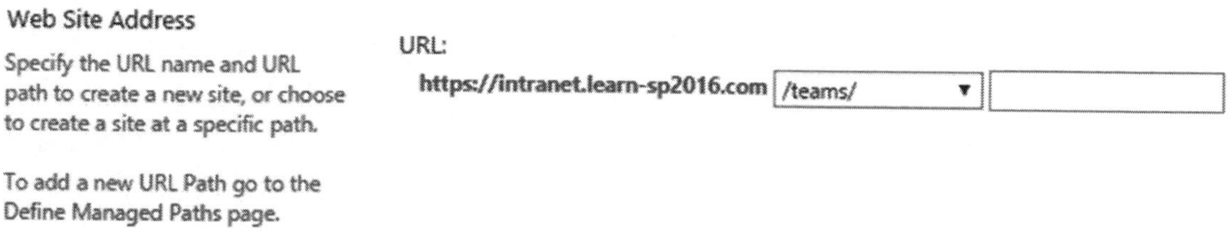

Web Site Address

Specify the URL name and URL path to create a new site, or choose to create a site at a specific path.

To add a new URL Path go to the Define Managed Paths page.

URL:

https://intranet.learn-sp2016.com | /teams/ ▾ | |

Figure 13-31. *Teams Wildcard Inclusion Managed Path*

Web Site Address

Specify the URL name and URL path to create a new site, or choose to create a site at a specific path.

To add a new URL Path go to the Define Managed Paths page.

URL:

https://intranet.learn-sp2016.com /communications ▼

Figure 13-32. *Communications Explicit Managed Path*

Now that we know how to create Path-Based Site Collections, let's take a look at Host Named Site Collections.

Host Named Site Collections

As discussed previously, Host Named Site Collections allow you to host multiple hostnames in the same Web Application. Although this approach is the best practice approach according to Microsoft, don't embark on a Host Named Site Collections journey without the proper planning. The Web Application in which you will create Host Named Site Collections will need to have an IIS Binding that answers to all the traffic on a specific port. For example, if we want to create Host Named Site Collections in the https://sharepoint. learn-sp2016.com Web Application, you need to add a binding that listens on *:443, which has a certificate assigned to it that is either a wildcard, or has all the Host Named Site Collection URLs in the SAN.

Since in Chapter 5 we have configured Add-ins to listen on *:443, we cannot have another site listen to the exact same binding, so we have configured another IP Address for our server. If you are running multiple Web Front Ends, you will need to configure an additional IP for every Web Front End in your farm. It is recommended to have an additional IP and correctly configure every server running the Microsoft SharePoint Foundation Web Application service in the farm. For every Web Application that you want to use for Host Named Site Collections, you will need to add another IP, since that one as well will need to listen on *:443, or *:80 if you do not use SSL.

To prepare our https://sharepoint.learn-sp2016.com we have added the binding in IIS that listens to all requests on the 172.16.0.110 IP address and port 443. We have also used the *.learn-sp2016.com wildcard certificate, which means all the Host Named Site Collections we will create will need to be in the learn-sp2016.com domain. The IIS Binding can be seen in Figure 13-33.

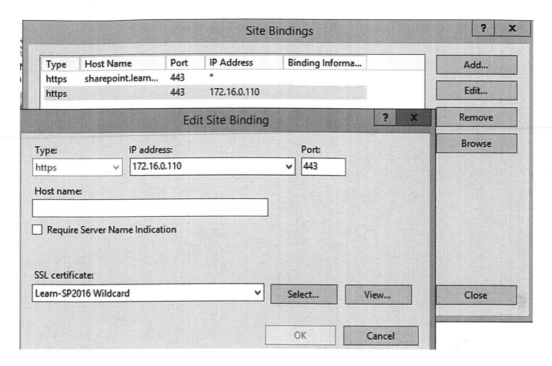

Figure 13-33. *Host Named Site Collection Binding*

With IIS Configured, we can now create our Host Named Site Collection. Unlike Path-Based Site Collections, we cannot use Central Administration to create them, so PowerShell is mandatory. We still use the New-SPSite cmdlet and most parameters are the same; however, when creating Host Named Site Collections, we need to specify the –HostHeaderWebApplication parameter, in order to tell SharePoint what Web Application to put it in.

```
New-SPSite https://Team1.learn-sp2016.com –OwnerAlias "corp\vlad" -HostHeaderWebApplication
https://sharepoint.learn-sp2016.com –Name "Team Site 1" -Template "STS#0"
```

The other difference with Host Named Site Collections are the Managed Paths. Managed Paths for Host Named Site Collections cannot be created by Central Administration, and can only be created with PowerShell. We need to use the same cmdlet, which is New-SPManagedPath, and we need to add the – HostHeader switch to make it available for Host Named Site Collections. To create a "Projects" Wildcard Inclusion Managed Path, we need to use the following PowerShell cmdlet:

```
New-SPManagedPath "projects" -HostHeader
```

■ **Note**   Managed Paths created using the –HostHeader switch are valid for all the Web Applications in the farm.

We could afterward create a Site Collection with the URL https://Team1.learn-sp2016.com/ Projects/Project1 by using the following PowerShell cmdlet.

```
New-SPSite https://Team1.learn-sp2016.com/Projects/Project1 –OwnerAlias "corp\vlad" –
HostHeaderWebApplication https://sharepoint.learn-sp2016.com –Name "Project Site 1"
-Template "STS#0"
```

Alternate Access Mappings also do not apply to Host Named Site Collections. Alternate URLs can be set individual to each Host Named Site Collection by using the Set-SPSiteUrl PowerShell cmdlet. To make our https://Team1.learn-sp2016.com Site Collection also accessible with the URL https://ProjectCenter.learn-sp2016.com we would run the following PowerShell cmdlets.

```
$site = Get-SPSite https://Team1.learn-sp2016.com
Set-SPSiteUrl $site -Url 'https://ProjectCenter.learn-sp2016.com' -Zone Intranet
```

Similar to how Alternate Access Mappings work, you will need to assign the URL to one of the five zones. To view all the current URLs for a Host Named Site Collection you need to use the Get-SPSiteURL cmdlet, and give the $site variable we saved earlier. In Figure 13-34 we can see the URLs we set for the Team1 Site Collection.

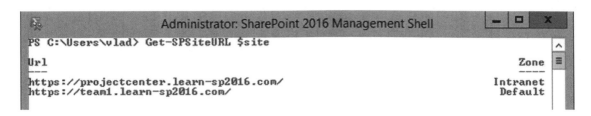

Figure 13-34. *Get-SPSiteURL*

While Host Named Site Collections are recommended by Microsoft and do have performance advantages over using multiple Web Applications, there are some disadvantages that stop companies from using them. First of all, there are no management tools for Host Named Site Collections in Central Administration. Also, mixing MySites and Content Site Collections in the same Web Application can cause disorganization in Content Database, since you will have both MySites Site Collections, as well as Content Site Collections in mixed Databases, and they might not all have the same requirement for backups and management. Lastly, you cannot create Host Named Site Collections using the built in Self Service Site Creation feature. Users will still be able to use the feature and create Path-Based Site Collections under an existing Managed Path.

Ultimately, the decision between Host Named Site Collections and Path-Based Site Collections will depend on your business requirements.

Fast Site Collection Creation

Fast Site Collection Creation is a new feature in SharePoint Server 2016 that allows administrators to create Site Collections faster than the traditional method. When creating a Site Collection, SharePoint creates a blank site, and activates all the features necessary to get to your desired template. With Fast Site Collection Creation, a copy of a template would be saved in the database, and every time you create a Site Collection with that template by using Fast Site Collection Creation, SharePoint will copy the site directly in the Content Database, making the site creation a lot faster. SharePoint enables this by default for the MySite template, and all the MySite Site Collections that SharePoint automatically creates use this method.

It's important to know that in order to benefit from Fast Site Collection Creation, you need to create sites trough PowerShell as the Site Collections that are created through Central Administration will not use this new engine.

The first thing we need to do is to enable the template for Fast Site Collection Creation by using the `Enable-SPWebTemplateForSiteMaster` PowerShell cmdlet. Throughout the examples, we will use CMSPUBLISHING#0, which is the Publishing Site Template. The cmdlet we will use is:

```
Enable-SPWebTemplateForSiteMaster -Template CMSPUBLISHING#0 -CompatibilityLevel 15
```

While '15' is usually associated with SharePoint 2013, SharePoint 2016 uses the same Compatibility level We then need to create the Site Master in the Content Database by using the New-SPSiteMaster cmdlet. You will need to do this for every Content Database that you wish to create those types of Site Collections in. In our case, the Content Database name is SharePoint_CDB1 and we ran the following cmdlet:

```
New-SPSiteMaster -ContentDatabase SharePoint_CDB1 -Template CMSPUBLISHING#0
```

With everything ready, we can now create our site using the `New-SPSite` PowerShell cmdlet as seen previously, but we need to add the `-CreateFromSiteMaster` switch in order to tell SharePoint to use Fast Site Collection Creation to create this Site Collection. An example cmdlet to create the Site Collection will be:

```
New-SPSite https://sharepoint.learn-sp2016.com/sites/Publishing1 -Template CMSPUBLISHING#0
-ContentDatabase SharePoint_CDB1 -CompatibilityLevel 15 -CreateFromSiteMaster -OwnerAlias
corp\vlad
```

To compare the speed of site provisioning side by side, we have created two Site Collections using the same template. The first one was created without the –CreateFromSiteMaster switch, while the second one was created with the switch. The results seen in Figure 13-35 show that the Site Collection provisioned using the traditional method took 134 seconds to create, while the Site Collection provisioned with Fast Site Collection creation took 41 seconds.

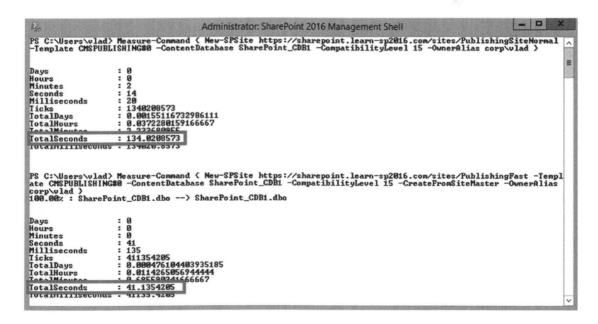

Figure 13-35. *Measuring Fast Site Collection Creation*

Depending on the site template you want to enable for Fast Site Collection, the increase in speed might not be noticeable. For example, Team Sites that do not have many features to activate can be created slower using Fast Site Collection than normal provisioning. Also, remember that Fast Site Collection can only be used by PowerShell or by code, and all the Site Collections created via Central Administration will use the standard provisioning engine.

Next Steps

In this chapter, we have learned how to create Web Applications, as well as Path-Based and Host Named Site Collections. We have also learned how to enable Fast Site Collection Creation for the templates that we use the most often. In the next chapter, we will cover how to implement a Hybrid SharePoint Infrastructure between SharePoint 2016 and Office 365.

CHAPTER 14

Hybrid Scenarios

Deploying a hybrid SharePoint infrastructure can provide great benefits to your enterprise and enable your business users to be more productive, wherever in the world they are.

In this chapter, we will look at how to deploy a hybrid SharePoint Server 2016 infrastructure from the requirements to the Hybrid Team Sites, Profile Redirection, OneDrive for Business, and the Cloud Search Service Application.

What Is a Hybrid Deployment?

Before going into technical details, let's first understand what a SharePoint hybrid deployment is. A hybrid SharePoint deployment is a link between a SharePoint Server farm and Office 365. The SharePoint Server farm can be hosted in our own datacenter, in a private cloud, or in a public cloud such as Azure or AWS.

There are multiple reasons to deploy a hybrid SharePoint Server 2016 Infrastructure. As you probably heard countless times already, Microsoft's vision is Cloud-First, Mobile-First, meaning that all the newest features come in the cloud first, and then make their way in the next On-Premises release. Furthermore, some features such as Delve and Office 365 Groups will not make it to the On-Premises version of SharePoint because of the way they are built.

At the same time, there are multiple reasons to keep using SharePoint On-Premises. Companies can easily customize SharePoint 2016 to fit their business requirements with farm solutions and timer jobs, as well as keeping control of all the SharePoint settings and configurations. Furthermore, due to legal, compliance, or security reasons, some companies simply cannot store some of their data in Office 365 as the data must be protected in certain ways.

This is why a Hybrid deployment is the best of both worlds. By using the right system for the right business need, your business users will be able to have the custom SharePoint solutions and control they need On-Premises, as well as the latest and greatest features in the cloud.

Authentication and Authorization

A big part of setting up a hybrid Microsoft environment is setting up the user synchronization between the On-Premises Active Directory and Azure Active Directory, which is the directory used by Office 365. Microsoft provides DirSync, now deprecated, Azure AD Connect, and a Microsoft Identity Manager Management Agent. Third parties also provide synchronization agents.

The next topic is providing Single Sign on (SSO). An SSO solution will make sure that your users only log in once on the local Active Directory and don't have to re-enter their credentials when trying to use a cloud service. Microsoft offers Active Directory Federation Services (ADFS) in order to achieve SSO and there are also multiple third-party solutions that offer the same functionality such as OKTA and OneLogin. Providing a SSO solution is optional for your user experience, and is not mandatory for setting up a hybrid SharePoint 2016 Infrastructure.

© Vlad Catrinescu and Trevor Seward 2016
V. Catrinescu and T. Seward, *Deploying SharePoint 2016*, DOI 10.1007/978-1-4842-1999-7_14

In this book we will not cover the differences between User Synchronization solutions and how to configure them since this action is typically implemented by a Domain Administrator, and not by the SharePoint Administrator. In the context of this book we have used Azure AD Connect to sync our On-Premises users to Office 365. Let's take a look at the high-level architecture of a hybrid SharePoint deployment.

Architecture Overview

In a Hybrid Infrastructure we have both a SharePoint 2016 On-Premises Farm as well as a SharePoint Online tenant. There is a Server-To-Server Authentication (S2S Trust) setup between the two different systems so that they could authenticate to each other and communicate securely.

For inbound features such as Hybrid BCS and Inbound Hybrid Federated Search, a Reverse Proxy is needed to secure inbound communication from SharePoint Online to our SharePoint On-Premises farm. This can be visualized in Figure 14-1.

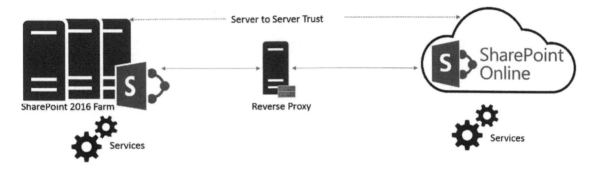

Figure 14-1. *Hybrid SharePoint 2016 Infrastructure high-level overview*

Hybrid Search Options

SharePoint Server 2016 offers us two options to integrate search between SharePoint On-Premises and SharePoint Online. The first option was there since the release of SharePoint Server 2013 and is called Federated Search. In a Federated Search setup, SharePoint Server 2016 can show results from SharePoint Online by making a Remote SharePoint query, and users can also search SharePoint On-Premises directly from SharePoint Online. What is important to understand is that in a Federated Search scenario, the index stays on the same system as the data. The SharePoint Server 2016 index remains On-Premises while the SharePoint Online index remains in the cloud.

The second option, which comes out of the box with SharePoint Server 2016, but can also be used with SharePoint Server 2013 September 2015 Public Update and later, is called the Cloud Hybrid Search. The Cloud Hybrid Search requires a different type of Search Service Application called the Cloud Search Service Application, and the main difference between Federated Search and Cloud Hybrid Search is that in a Cloud Hybrid Search scenario, SharePoint Server 2016 pushes the index of On-Premises items and documents to Office 365, where it's merged with the SharePoint Online index. By having the index of both On-Premises and Cloud documents merged in the cloud, your users will have access to Office 365–only features such as Delve and the Office Graph.

Hybrid Federated Search Overview

In a Hybrid Federated Search setup, the index of SharePoint On-Premises documents remains On-Premises, and all the SharePoint Online index remains in Office 365. When configuring Hybrid Federated Search, we have three possible topologies we can choose from.

One-Way Outbound Topology

In a One-Way Outbound Topology, SharePoint Server can query SharePoint Online; however, SharePoint Online cannot query SharePoint Server. Therefore, a user who logs on to SharePoint On-Premises and performs a search query will be able to retrieve both SharePoint On-Premises and SharePoint Online results. However, a user performing a query on SharePoint Online will not be able to get results from SharePoint On-Premises.

One-Way Inbound Topology

In a One-Way Inbound Topology, SharePoint Online can query SharePoint Server 2016; however, SharePoint On-Premises cannot query SharePoint Online. Therefore, a user that logs on to SharePoint Online and performs a query will be able to see results from both SharePoint Online and SharePoint On-Premises. However, a user performing a query in SharePoint On-Premises will only see results from SharePoint On-Premises and not SharePoint Online.

Two-Way (Bidirectional) Topology

In a Two-Way (Bidirectional) topology, we basically configure both the One-Way Inbound and One-Way Outbound topologies. In this topology, both systems can query each other and therefore return results from the other system.

Hybrid Cloud Search Overview

The main difference in the Hybrid Cloud Search topology is that the new SharePoint 2016 Cloud Search Service Application does not store the index on the SharePoint On-Premises; instead, it pushes it to Office 365. Out of the six Search components in the Search Service Application, only the Admin, Crawl and Query components are active. The Index, Content Processing and Analytics components do need to exist, but they are not used in a Hybrid Cloud Search scenario. All the Content Processing and Analytics are done in Office 365, where the Index is stored.

The Cloud Search Service Application can crawl the same type of Content Sources as a normal Search Service Application; therefore, you can push items from Remote SharePoint Sites, File Shares, BCS, and more in the SharePoint Online Index.

One of the disadvantages of the Hybrid Cloud Search topology is that you are limited to the Search customization options of SharePoint Online, since that is where the content processing is done and Index is stored. Therefore, some options like Custom Entity Extraction and Content Enrichment Web Service are not available. The big advantage of the Hybrid Cloud Search is having homogeneous results when doing a query, whether those results come from SharePoint Online or SharePoint On-Premises.

Which Option Should You Choose?

The choice between Federated Search and Hybrid Cloud Search will ultimately depend on your business requirements and on the regulation applicable to your data. In a Federated Search scenario, the index of your On-Premises documents remains On-Premises. In a Cloud Hybrid Search scenario, your index, and therefore the content of all your documents, will be in Office 365. Some regulations about the data and the documents might not allow your business to put the content of your documents in Office 365.

Furthermore, in a Cloud Hybrid Search topology, since the index is stored in the SharePoint Online, all your SharePoint users will have to be licensed in Office 365 even if they only want to search SharePoint On-Premises and never use SharePoint Online. With Hybrid Federated Search, users who are only licensed On-Premises can still search all the SharePoint On-Premises items.

Microsoft recommends using the Cloud Hybrid Search whenever possible since it will provide a better experience for your users, enable cloud-only features on On-Premises content, and save disk space and maybe even SharePoint Server 2016 licenses On-Premises, since you do not need to have an index component in your On-Premises SharePoint Server 2016 infrastructure.

Prerequisites

Before starting to configure different Hybrid features, there are a few requirements that you need to have.

SharePoint Server Prerequisites

In order to start configuring Hybrid, you need to configure the following Service Applications on your SharePoint Server 2016 Server:

1. Managed Metadata Service Application

2. User Profile Service Application

3. App Management Service

4. Subscription Settings Service Application

Furthermore, you also need to have MySites configured inside your User Profile Service Application. As we already covered how to create those service applications, we will not cover that again in this chapter. One important thing to note is that the *Work Email* user property needs to contain the e-mail address that you configured for the user in Active Directory, and the User Principal Name property must be mapped to the *userPrincipalName* attributed in Active Directory.

If you plan to use Inbound Hybrid Federated Search or Hybrid Business Connectivity Services, you will need to have a primary Web Application. There is nothing special to configure on this Web Application; however, it must be using SSL and all the users need read access to the root site. This Web Application needs to be using Claims – NTLM authentication.

Licensing Prerequisites

In order to be able to use hybrid functionalities your users must have licenses assigned in Office 365. By default when Azure AD Connect or DirSync synchronizes new users in Office 365, the users are synchronized but no licenses are assigned automatically. Creating a PowerShell script that runs every day in order to assign licenses to new users will be useful to make sure that all your users are licensed.

■ **Note**   If you plan to use the Cloud Search Service Application as well as the SharePoint 2016 Data Loss Prevention feature, you will need to synchronize and assign a license to the SharePoint Farm account as well.

Reverse Proxy Requirements

If you plan to implement hybrid Business Connectivity Services, or Inbound Federated Search, you will need to configure a reverse proxy so Office 365 can securely access your SharePoint 2016 On-Premises farm. The reverse proxy is also required to show document previews of On-Premises documents in SharePoint Online when using Cloud Hybrid Search if you are using Office Online Server. At the time of writing this book, there are four supported Reverse Proxy tools; however, more might be added in the future. The four supported ones by Microsoft are

- Windows Server 2012 R2 with Web Application Proxy

- Forefront Threat Management Gateway • TMG • 2010

- F5 BIG-IP

- Citrix NetScaler

■ **Note**   To view the up-to-date list of supported Reverse Proxies for a hybrid SharePoint infrastructure, visit the following TechNet article. https://technet.microsoft.com/en-us/library/dn607304.aspx#devices.

While the preceding Reverse Proxies are the recommended ones by Microsoft, you could make SharePoint work in hybrid mode with a reverse proxy that supports the following features:

- Support client certificate authentication with a wildcard or SAN SSL certificate.

- Support pass-through authentication for OAuth 2.0, including unlimited OAuth bearer token transactions.

- Accept unsolicited inbound traffic on TCP port 443 • HTTPS • .

- Bind a wildcard or SAN SSL certificate to a published endpoint.

- Relay traffic to an On-Premises SharePoint Server 2016 farm or load balancer without rewriting any packet headers.

Accounts Needed for Hybrid Configuration and Testing

In order to configure all the hybrid SharePoint 2016 features described in this chapter, you will need to have access to the following accounts:

- Office 365 Global Administrator

- SharePoint Farm Admin

Creating DNS entries, configuring ADFS, and the Reverse Proxy will require you to have elevated permissions in Active Directory. If you don't have those rights, you can simply request those entries to the team in your company who has access to them.

If you don't plan to deploy Hybrid SharePoint features to all the users in your organization, consider creating a Security Group in Active Directory with all the accounts that will have access to Hybrid Features. By creating a Security Group, we will easily be able to create an audience in the SharePoint User Profile Service Application and only offer Hybrid Features to those users, while the rest of the users will still be able to use features such as OneDrive for Business Fully On-Premises.

Domain User Requirements

You have to create an UPN domain suffix for your On-Premises users that matches the public domain you are using in Office 365. To give a concrete example, in our book we use the *corp.learn-sp2016.com* domain for all our users and computers; therefore, usernames are under the CORP\Username format. In order for the synchronization and user mapping to work, we set up our users to use the `username@learn-sp2016.com` format as well. This is done in the "User Logon Name" property as seen in Figure 14-2.

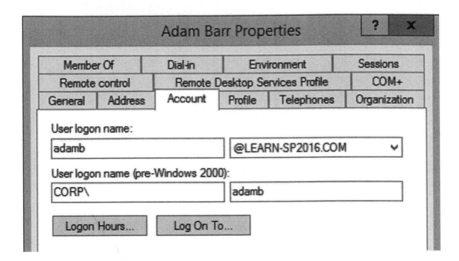

Figure 14-2. *User Logon Name is the same as our Office 365 domain.*

Certificate Requirements

To configure secure communication between your SharePoint 2016 On-Premises farm and SharePoint Online from Office 365, you will need to update your SharePoint Server Security Token Service (STS) certificate. This certificate is only used to configure Server-to-Server trust between SharePoint Online and your SharePoint 2016 Server farm. While both Self-Signed Certificates and certificates issued by a public certification authority such as DigiCert are accepted, Microsoft recommends using a certificate issued by a public certification authority for production environments in order to facilitate integration with other systems. It is recommended that this certificate contain the SAN of the server on which you will configure the Server-to-Server (S2S) trust. For this book we created a DigiCert SSL Certificate and included the name of our App Server inside, as seen in Figure 14-3.

Figure 14-3. SSL Certificate to configure Server-to-Server Authentication

---

■ **Note**   You will need both the PFX and the CER version of the certificate in order to complete the setup process.

If you plan to use Inbound Federated Search or Hybrid Business Connectivity Services you will also need to create a default Web Application that needs to be using SSL; therefore, a certificate will also be needed for that Web Application. Furthermore, a Wildcard SSL Certificate will be required on the Reverse Proxy to secure incoming communication from Office 365 to SharePoint On-Premises. In official Microsoft documentation this certificate is referred to as the Secure Channel SSL Certificate. You could use the same wildcard certificate for Server-to-Server authentication, Web Application as well the Secure Channel SSL Certificate if you wish.

Software

In order to set up the steps in this chapter, you will need to install the following tools on the Server on which you will configure Hybrid.

- Microsoft Online Services Sign-In Assistant (https://www.microsoft.com/en-us/download/details.aspx?id=41950)

- Azure Active Directory Module for Windows PowerShell (https://msdn.microsoft.com/en-us/library/azure/jj151815.aspx)

- SharePoint Online Management Shell (http://www.microsoft.com/en-us/download/details.aspx?id=35588)

Hybrid Features Required Configurations

Throughout this chapter, we will configure multiple requirements for various hybrid features. To give you a better preview and reference of what configuration is required for each feature, refer to Table 14-1.

Table 14-1. *Required Configurations for Each SharePoint Hybrid Feature*

	Hybrid OneDrive for Business	Hybrid Sites	Hybrid Federated Search (Outbound)	Hybrid Federated Search (Inbound)	Hybrid Cloud Search	Hybrid BCS
Synchronized Users	X	X	X	X	X	X
Service Applications	X	X	X	X	X	X
Server-to-Server Trust		X	X	X	X	X
Primary Web Application				X		X
Reverse Proxy				X		X

Now that we know what we have to configure, let's start with Server-to-Server authentication.

Configure Server-to-Server Authentication

Server-to-Server authentication, often called Server-to-Server Trust, is an important part of setting up your hybrid SharePoint Infrastructure. This is not required for OneDrive for Business; however, it is required for Hybrid Sites, Hybrid Search, and Hybrid Business Connectivity Services. When you set up Server-to-Server authentication, you will create a trust relationship between your SharePoint Online tenant, and your SharePoint Server 2016 farm. This trust will use Azure Active Directory as a trusted token signing service.

As noted previously, in a hybrid Federated Search, users can send requests from SharePoint On-Premises to SharePoint Online from your SharePoint 2016 Search Center. The Web Application in which the Search Center is must use NTLM authentication.

It is strongly recommended to use a Web Application over HTTPS for security reasons. If you decide to go with HTTP, you will need to run the following PowerShell cmdlets in your SharePoint 2016 Server farm in order to allow OAuth over HTTP.

```
$serviceConfig = Get-SPSecurityTokenServiceConfig
$serviceConfig.AllowOAuthOverHttp = $true
$serviceConfig.Update()
```

Now that we know the prerequisites, let's start with the first step, which is replacing the STS Certificate.

Replacing the Default STS Certificate

When you install SharePoint Server 2016, the STS creates a default certificate to validate all incoming requests. However, Azure Active Directory cannot use the default STS Certificate to act as a trusted token signing service for SharePoint. That is why we need to replace it using either a certificate from a public certification authority, or a self-signed certificate.

We can easily replace the default STS Certificate by using the following PowerShell script. You will need to replace the Path and Password variables with the path and password of your PFX certificate. This requires a reset of IIS, so this must be done off hours. Furthermore, after changing the STS Certificate some users might experience log in problems. This is due to a FedAuth cookie that is still valid, but since the signing certificate changed, it cannot be used anymore. To fix the problem, you can either delete the local cookies, or use In Private or Incognito browsing until the cookie expires.

■ **Note**   You need to run the following code on **ALL** the servers in your SharePoint Farm.

```
$pfxPath = "C:\certs\sts.pfx"
$pfxPass = "pass@word1"
$stsCertificate = New-Object System.Security.Cryptography.X509Certificates.X509Certificate2
$pfxPath, $pfxPass, 20
Set-SPSecurityTokenServiceConfig -ImportSigningCertificate $stsCertificate -confirm:$false
iisreset
net stop SPTimerV4
net start SPTimerV4
```

Do not forget to back up the STS Certificate as well as its password, because once it's changed, you cannot get it back! Now that the STS Certificate is replaced, we need to set up our Service Principal.

Upload the STS Certificate to SharePoint Online

Now that we have our certificate set up in our On-Premises SharePoint Server 2016 Farm, we need to upload it to SharePoint Online so both systems can connect and consume each other's service applications.

This step only needs to be done on one server, and this server needs to have the following prerequisite software installed:

- Microsoft Online Services Sign-In Assistant
- Azure Active Directory Module for Windows PowerShell
- SharePoint Online Management Shell

The first thing you need to do is open PowerShell as an Administrator, and load the required modules as well as connect to Office 365. Run the following PowerShell cmdlets to import the modules:

```
Add-PSSnapin Microsoft.SharePoint.PowerShell
Import-Module Microsoft.PowerShell.Utility
Import-Module MSOnline -force
Import-Module MSOnlineExtended -force
Import-Module Microsoft.Online.SharePoint.PowerShell -force
```

Afterward, we need to connect to Office 365. To do this step, you need to be an Office 365 Global Administrator. The following Get-Credential cmdlet will open a pop-up asking you to enter the username and password to connect to Office 365. Afterward, the Connect-MsolService cmdlet will establish the connection between your PowerShell session and your Office 365 tenant.

```
$cred = Get-Credential
Connect-MsolService -Credential $cred
```

■ **Note** Keep your PowerShell Window open with all the modules loaded for the duration of this section on Configuring Server-to-Server Authentication, since you will need the same modules.

The next thing you will need is to get the path and password to your .PFX file, which should be the same as the ones used previously when replacing the STS Certificate, as well as the .CER version of the certificate. First thing we need to do is declare our three certificate variables, which are only the paths to the certificates as well as the password.

```
$pfxPath = "C:\certs\sts.pfx"
$pfxPass = "pass@word1"
$cerPath = "C:\certs\stscer2.cer"
```

We also need to create a few more variables to have everything we need to set up the Server-to-Server trust. The first variable we need to create is the root domain name of your public domain name, with no protocol, with a wildcard mention in the front. Here is the variable we created with our learn-sp2016.com domain.

```
$spcn = "*.learn-sp2016.com"
```

The next variable is the URL of our On-Premises primary Web Application. This will be your external endpoint where requests from SharePoint Online will be received. This Web Application needs to use NTLM authentication, preferably be secured via HTTPS and accessible from the Internet.

```
$site = Get-SPsite "https://sharepoint.learn-sp2016.com"
```

The next variables we need to create already have preset values. The first one is the SharePoint Online Application Principal ID, which is always 00000003-0000-0ff1-ce00-000000000000. This value identifies all SharePoint Online Objects in your Office 365 tenant.

```
$spoappid = "00000003-0000-0ff1-ce00-000000000000"
```

The next variable is the ObjectID of your SharePoint Online tenant. This is the unique GUID that identifies your tenant.

```
$spocontextID = (Get-MsolCompanyInformation).ObjectID
```

Lastly, we need to create our Metadata Endpoint. The metadata endpoint is the URL that is used by the Azure AD proxy to connect to your Azure AD tenancy. It's built with the default URL and contains your SPO Context ID.

```
$metadataEndpoint = "https://accounts.accesscontrol.windows.net/" + $spocontextID + "/
metadata/json/1"
```

To put it all together, here is what the beginning of your script will look like:

```
Add-PSSnapin Microsoft.SharePoint.PowerShell
Import-Module Microsoft.PowerShell.Utility
Import-Module MSOnline -force
Import-Module MSOnlineExtended -force
Import-Module Microsoft.Online.SharePoint.PowerShell –force
```

```
$cred=Get-Credential
Connect-MsolService -Credential $cred

$pfxPath = "C:\certs\sts.pfx"
$pfxPass = "pass@word1"
$cerPath = "C:\certs\stscer2.cer"
$spcn = "*.learn-sp2016.com"
$site = Get-SPsite "https://sharepoint.learn-sp2016.com"
$spoappid = "00000003-0000-0ff1-ce00-000000000000"
$spocontextID = (Get-MsolCompanyInformation).ObjectID
$metadataEndpoint = "https://accounts.accesscontrol.windows.net/" + $spocontextID + "/
metadata/json/1"
```

With everything ready, the next step is to upload the STS certificate to SharePoint Online. We will use the variables created before, to create a new *MsolServicePrincipalCredential*.

```
$cer = New-Object System.Security.Cryptography.X509Certificates.X509Certificate2
-ArgumentList $pfxPath, $pfxPass
$cer.Import($cerPath)
$binCert = $cer.GetRawCertData()
$credValue = [System.Convert]::ToBase64String($binCert);
New-MsolServicePrincipalCredential -AppPrincipalId $spoappid -Type asymmetric -Usage Verify
-Value $credValue
```

With the certificate uploaded to SharePoint Online, it is now time to configure the Service Principal name for our public domain name in Azure.

Add a Service Principal Name to Azure Active Directory

The next step we need to do is add the Service Principal Name of our public domain in Azure AD. The SPN is used to support mutual authentication between SharePoint Server 2016, and our SharePoint Online tenant. The Service Principal Name is built of the SharePoint Online Application Principal ID and the URL of our company public DNS domain namespace. This will be expressed as a wildcard, even if we have a SAN-based certificate. The reason of using a wildcard value is so SharePoint Online can validate connections with any host in our domain. This will be useful if we ever want to change the SharePoint 2016 Primary Web Application in the future.

The SPN syntax will be similar to

00000003-0000-0ff1-ce00-000000000000/*.<public domain name>.com

Where *00000003-0000-0ff1-ce00-000000000000* is the SharePoint Online Application Principal ID we previously saved in the $spoappid variable, and the *.<public domain name>.com*, which we saved in the $spcn variable.

Use the following PowerShell cmdlets to create the Service Principal Name in Azure AD

```
$msp = Get-MsolServicePrincipal -AppPrincipalId $spoappid
$spns = $msp.ServicePrincipalNames
$spns.Add("$spoappid/$spcn")
Set-MsolServicePrincipal '
-AppPrincipalId $spoappid '
-ServicePrincipalNames $spns
```

To make sure everything worked, you can run the following PowerShell cmdlets to get a list of SPNs.

```
$msp = Get-MsolServicePrincipal -AppPrincipalId $spoappid
$spns = $msp.ServicePrincipalNames
$spns
```

The result should look similar to this, with one of the SPNs having your public domain inside.

```
00000003-0000-0ff1-ce00-000000000000/*.learn-sp2016.com
00000003-0000-0ff1-ce00-000000000000/*.sharepoint.com
00000003-0000-0ff1-ce00-000000000000
Microsoft.SharePoint
```

Once that is validated, the next step is to register the SPO Application Principal ID with the On-Premises SharePoint Application Management Service.

Register the SharePoint Online Application Principal

Registering the SPO Application Principal ID with your SharePoint 2016 Application Management Service allows SharePoint 2016 to authenticate to SharePoint Online using OAuth. This will be registered as a SPAppPrincipal on the root Site Collection of your Principal Web Application.

```
$spoapppprincipalID = (Get-MsolServicePrincipal -ServicePrincipalName $spoappid).ObjectID
$sponameidentifier = "$spoapppprincipalID@$spocontextID"
$appPrincipal = Register-SPAppPrincipal -site $site.rootweb '
-nameIdentifier $sponameidentifier -displayName "SharePoint Online"
```

Set the Authentication Realm

The next step is to set the authentication realm of the SharePoint Server 2016 farm to the context ID of your Office 365 Tenancy. Once you have configured the SharePoint Farm Authentication Realm, this value must always match the tenant context identifier. If you change this value, your hybrid configuration will stop working. Use the following PowerShell cmdlet to set the Authentication Realm.

```
Set-SPAuthenticationRealm -realm $spocontextID
```

To validate the configuration, you can run the following PowerShell cmdlets. If everything worked well, they should both return the same GUID.

```
$spocontextID
Get-SPAuthenticationRealm
```

■ **Note**   When changing the Authentication Realm, some Provider-hosted Add-ins might stop working. Make sure to verify with your developers if you are using those types of Add-ins in your SharePoint 2016 farm.

Configure the On-Premises Proxy for Azure AD

The last configuration step for Step for Server-to-Server trust is creating an Azure Active Directory Proxy Service in your SharePoint Server 2016 Farm. This will allow Azure Active Directory to become a Trusted Token Issuer that will sign and authenticate claims tokens from SharePoint Online. With the next PowerShell cmdlets we will create an Azure Access Control Service Application Proxy named "ACS" and put it in the Default Proxy Group. We will then add it as a new Trusted Security Token Issuer.

```
New-SPAzureAccessControlServiceApplicationProxy '
-Name "ACS" '
-MetadataServiceEndpointUri $metadataEndpoint '
-DefaultProxyGroup

New-SPTrustedSecurityTokenIssuer '
-MetadataEndpoint $metadataEndpoint '
-IsTrustBroker:$true '
-Name "ACS"
```

To validate the configuration, run the following PowerShell cmdlet.

```
Get-SPTrustedSecurityTokenIssuer | Select RegisteredIssuerName
```

The result should start with 00000001-0000-0000-c000-000000000000@ and end with your context ID. With Server-to-Server Trust Configured, it is now time to configure SharePoint 2016 Hybrid Features.

Hybrid OneDrive for Business

In this section, we are going to configure the Hybrid OneDrive for Business functionality. This functionality redirects users to their OneDrive in Office 365 when they click Office 365 in the SharePoint Server 2016 Farm.

The Prerequisites for Hybrid OneDrive for Business are as follows:

- Existing Office 365 Tenant with a Custom Domain and synchronized users

- SharePoint Server Services (User Profiles, App Management Service, MMS, Subscription Settings Service)

If you followed this chapter up until now, all those should already be done. To Configure hybrid OneDrive for Business you need to go in the SharePoint Server 2016 Central Administration in the **Office 365 ➤ Configure hybrid OneDrive and Sites features** section and you should reach a page similar to Figure 14-4.

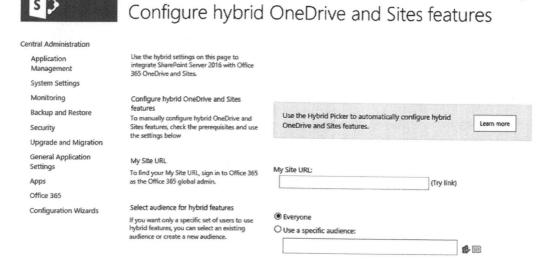

Figure 14-4. *Configure Hybrid OneDrive and Sites features in Central Administration*

In the My Site URL section, we need to enter the My Site URL of your SharePoint Online Tenant. This can be found in the SharePoint Online Admin Center, and is the one under the format `https://orgname-my.sharepoint.com`, which is the selected checkbox in Figure 14-5.

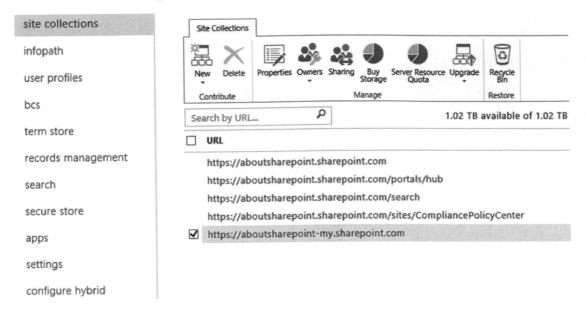

Figure 14-5. *The SharePoint Online MySites Site Collection*

In the Audience Picker you must select if either all your users will be Hybrid Enabled (Everyone), meaning that all your users must be synchronized to Office 365 and have an Office 365 license. If that is not the case, you can use the audience we created previously, in our case called "Hybrid Users." Figure 14-6 is what it should look like when both fields are filled.

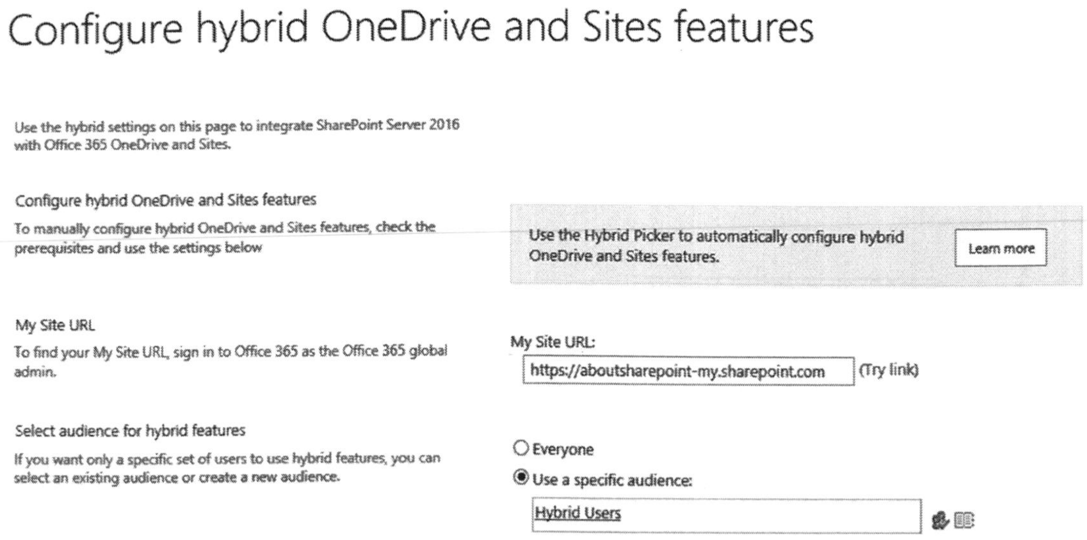

Configure hybrid OneDrive and Sites features

Use the hybrid settings on this page to integrate SharePoint Server 2016 with Office 365 OneDrive and Sites.

Configure hybrid OneDrive and Sites features

To manually configure hybrid OneDrive and Sites features, check the prerequisites and use the settings below

Use the Hybrid Picker to automatically configure hybrid OneDrive and Sites features.   [Learn more]

My Site URL

To find your My Site URL, sign in to Office 365 as the Office 365 global admin.

My Site URL:

https://aboutsharepoint-my.sharepoint.com   (Try link)

Select audience for hybrid features

If you want only a specific set of users to use hybrid features, you can select an existing audience or create a new audience.

○ Everyone
◉ Use a specific audience:

Hybrid Users

Figure 14-6. Configuring Hybrid OneDrive for Business Settings

In the next section of the page pictured in Figure 14-7, we have to choose what feature we want to activate. Our choices are

- OneDrive and Sites

- OneDrive only

- None

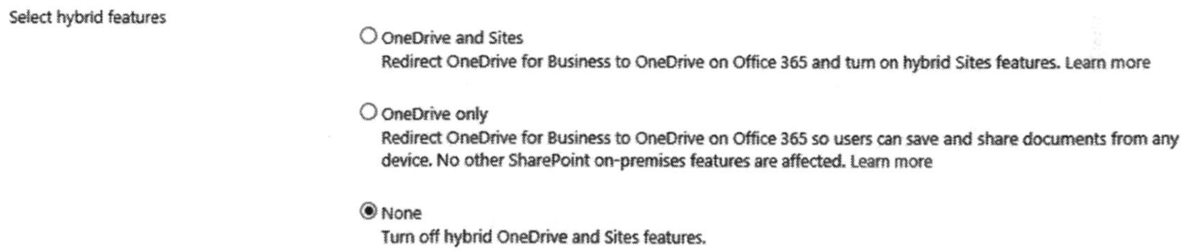

Select hybrid features

○ OneDrive and Sites
Redirect OneDrive for Business to OneDrive on Office 365 and turn on hybrid Sites features. Learn more

○ OneDrive only
Redirect OneDrive for Business to OneDrive on Office 365 so users can save and share documents from any device. No other SharePoint on-premises features are affected. Learn more

◉ None
Turn off hybrid OneDrive and Sites features.

Figure 14-7. Hybrid Feature Selection Radio Boxes

Choose the feature that you want to enable between those three. If you want to also enable sites, read the next section on Hybrid Sites before enabling.

After enabling the features, an IIS Reset is required to take effect for all the users immediately. To test the Hybrid OneDrive for Business functionality, log in as a user in the Hybrid Users audience, and in the App Launcher, when you click the "OneDrive" icon, you should be redirected to their OneDrive in Office 365. Furthermore, hybrid-enabled users will also see the Delve and Video in the App Launcher as seen in Figure 14-8.

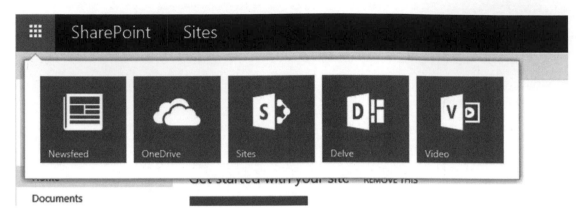

Figure 14-8. *Hybrid-Enabled App Launcher*

Users that are not in the Hybrid Users audience will see a Ribbon without the "Delve" and "Video" as seen in Figure 14-9.

Figure 14-9. *Out-of-the-box SharePoint 2016 App Launcher*

Furthermore, when they click the OneDrive icon, they will be redirected in their On-Premises OneDrive.

An important aspect to remember when configuring Hybrid OneDrive for Business is that if you had implemented OneDrive for Business On-Premises before and your users had already put documents in their SharePoint 2016 OneDrive for Business, those files will not be automatically migrated to Office 365. You will need to migrate those files manually, by using PowerShell or a third-party product. The original My Site and OneDrive are still accessible for your users if they access it by entering the URL in the browser. Make sure to educate your users to use the version in Office 365 for business after you have successfully migrated their content.

■ **Tip** If you want to avoid users having the "Welcome" screen and wait for their OneDrive for Business to be created in Office 365 on their first use, you can preprovision them by following this TechNet article: `https://technet.microsoft.com/en-us/library/dn800987.aspx`.

Hybrid Sites

In this section, we are going to configure the Hybrid Sites functionality. This functionality also enables the Profile Redirection as well as the Extensible App Launcher. The Profile Redirection feature makes hybrid-enabled users only have one profile, the one in Office 365.

The Extensible App Launcher brings Office 365 Video, Delve along with your custom Office 365 Apps in your SharePoint 2016 Ribbon.

The Prerequisite for Hybrid Sites are as follows:

- Existing Office 365 Tenant with a Custom Domain and synchronized users

- SharePoint Server Services (User Profiles, App Management Service, MMS, Subscription Settings Service)

- Server-to-Server Authentication

If you did all the steps in this chapter so far, you should have all of those ready, so the next step is to configure the Hybrid Sites. The Configuration is done via the SharePoint Server 2016 Central Administration in the **Office 365 ➤ Configure hybrid OneDrive and Sites features** section and you should reach a page similar to Figure 14-10.

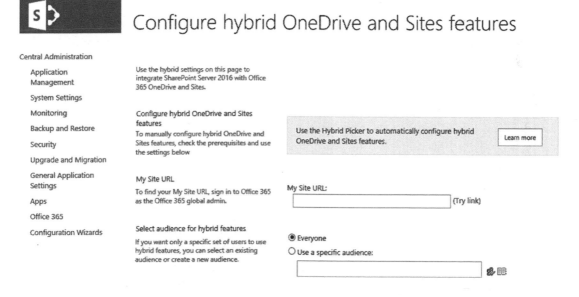

Figure 14-10. Configure hybrid OneDrive and Sites features in Central Administration

In the My Site URL section, we need to enter the My Site URL of your SharePoint Online Tenant. This can be found in the SharePoint Online Admin Center, and is the one under the format `https://orgname-my.sharepoint.com` and is checked in Figure 14-11.

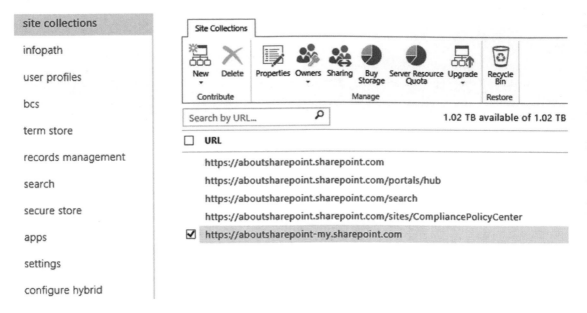

Figure 14-11. *The SharePoint Online MySites Site Collection in SharePoint Online*

In the Audience Picker you must select if either all your users will be Hybrid Enabled (Everyone), meaning that all your users must be synchronized to Office 365 and have an Office 365 license. If that is not the case, you can use the audience we created previously, in our case called "Hybrid Users." Figure 14-12 is what it should look like when both fields are filled.

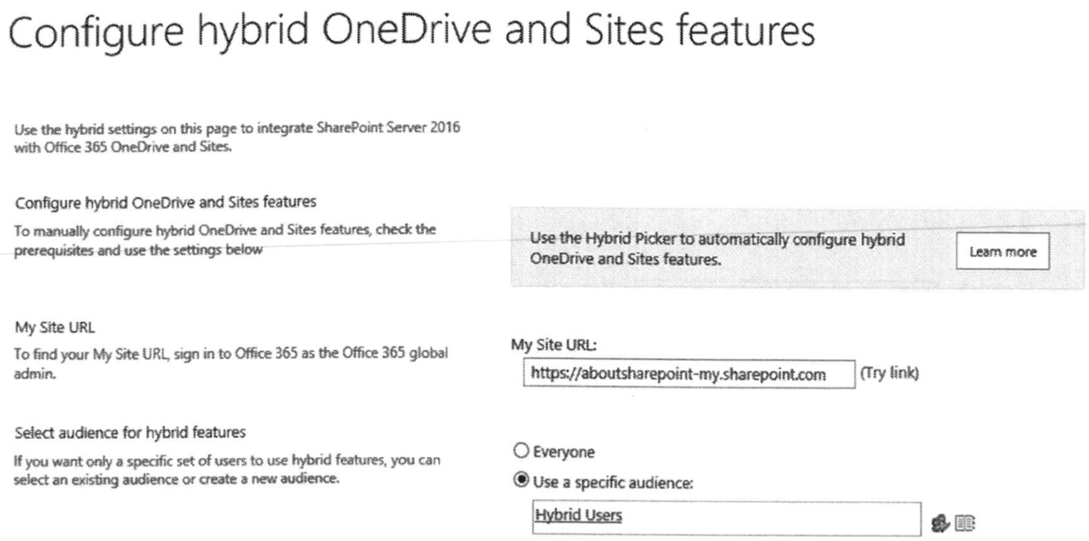

Configure hybrid OneDrive and Sites features

Use the hybrid settings on this page to integrate SharePoint Server 2016 with Office 365 OneDrive and Sites.

Configure hybrid OneDrive and Sites features

To manually configure hybrid OneDrive and Sites features, check the prerequisites and use the settings below

Use the Hybrid Picker to automatically configure hybrid OneDrive and Sites features.　[Learn more]

My Site URL

To find your My Site URL, sign in to Office 365 as the Office 365 global admin.

My Site URL:

https://aboutsharepoint-my.sharepoint.com　(Try link)

Select audience for hybrid features

If you want only a specific set of users to use hybrid features, you can select an existing audience or create a new audience.

○ Everyone
◉ Use a specific audience:

Hybrid Users

Figure 14-12.　Configuring Hybrid Sites features

In the next section of the page seen in Figure 14-13, we have to choose what feature we want to activate. Our choices are

- OneDrive and Sites

- OneDrive only

- None

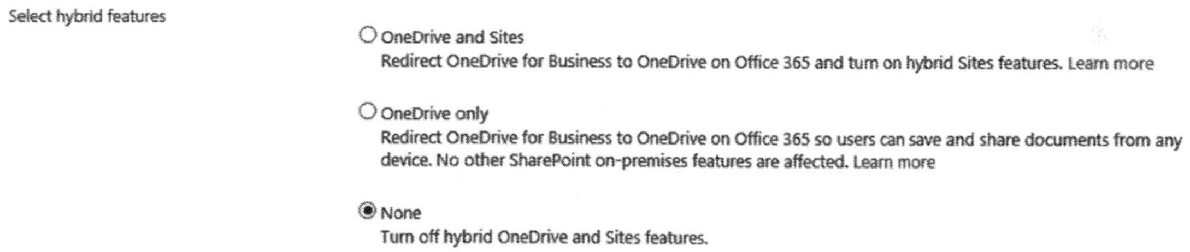

Select hybrid features

○ OneDrive and Sites
　Redirect OneDrive for Business to OneDrive on Office 365 and turn on hybrid Sites features. Learn more

○ OneDrive only
　Redirect OneDrive for Business to OneDrive on Office 365 so users can save and share documents from any device. No other SharePoint on-premises features are affected. Learn more

◉ None
　Turn off hybrid OneDrive and Sites features.

Figure 14-13.　Hybrid Features Selection Radio Buttons

You cannot enable Hybrid Sites without enabling Hybrid OneDrive for Business as well. After enabling the OneDrive and Sites hybrid functionality, an IIS Reset might be required to make the change visible for your users.

To test the functionality, log in as a member of the Hybrid Users audience, and follow an On-Premises Site by using the "Follow" button at the top right of a site seen in Figure 14-14.

Figure 14-14. *The Follow Site Button*

Afterward, when you go in the Ribbon and click the Sites icon, you should be redirected to the Sites section in Office 365.

On the Sites Page seen in Figure 14-15, you should see the site you just followed from your On-Premises SharePoint Server 2016 Farm. In our case, that site is called "On Prem SubSite" and you can see it in Office 365.

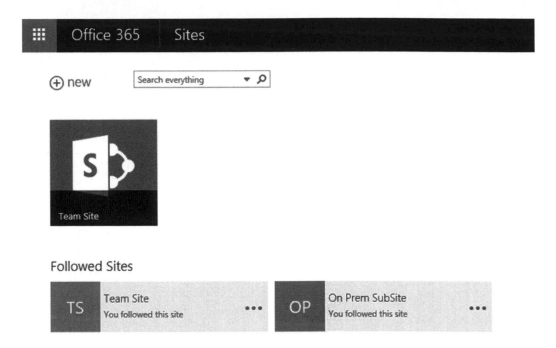

Figure 14-15. *On-Premises and SharePoint Online sites in the Office 365 Sites Page*

Hybrid Federated Search

In this section, we will enable Hybrid Federated Search between our On-Premises SharePoint 2016 Server Farm and SharePoint Online. There are three possible topologies to implement Hybrid Federated Search.

The first topology is called One-Way Outbound topology. In the One-Way Outbound topology, users that do a query from the SharePoint On-Premises Search Center will be able to retrieve results from SharePoint Online; however, users that do a Query in the SharePoint Online Search Center cannot query SharePoint On-Premises. This is the easiest topology to set up.

The second topology is called One-Way Inbound topology. In a One-Way Inbound topology, users that do a query from the SharePoint Online Search Center will be able to retrieve results from SharePoint On-Premises index; however, users from SharePoint On-Premises Search Center will not get any results from SharePoint Online. This topology requires additional configuration as well as a reverse proxy.

The third and last topology is called a Two-Way Hybrid Federated Search topology. This topology is basically a combination of both the One-Way Inbound and the One-Way Outbound topologies. Therefore, users from both systems can get results from the other system.

■ **Tip** To easily remember what inbound / outbound means, think at it from an On-Premises Point of view. In an Outbound topology, the user will go OUTBOUND to SharePoint Online to get results. In an Inbound topology, SharePoint Online does an INBOUND connection to SharePoint On-Premises to fetch the results.

Let's start by setting up the easiest one, the One-Way Outbound topology.

One-Way Outbound Federated Search

In a One-Way outbound Federated Search scenario, we need to configure our SharePoint On-Premises Search Service Application to query SharePoint Online. The Prerequisites for a One-Way Outbound Federated Search are as follows:

- Existing Office 365 Tenant with a Custom Domain and synchronized users

- SharePoint Server Services (User Profiles, App Management Service, MMS, Subscription Settings Service)

- Server-to-Server Authentication

If you followed the chapter in order until now, everything should already be set up, and we can start configuring Hybrid Federated Search in a One-Way Outbound topology. The first thing we need to do in order to configure Hybrid Federated Search with SharePoint Online is to create a Result Source. We could either create a Result Source at the Search Service Application level, Site collection level, or even site level. However, since we want to offer the functionality to all of the farm, we will create it at the Search Service Application level.

Navigate to the Central Administration ➤ Manage Service Applications and select your Search Service Application.

From the Search Service Application Administration Page, in the Queries and Results section, click Result Sources. On the Result Sources Page, click "New Result Source." Enter the following information as seen in Figure 14-16.

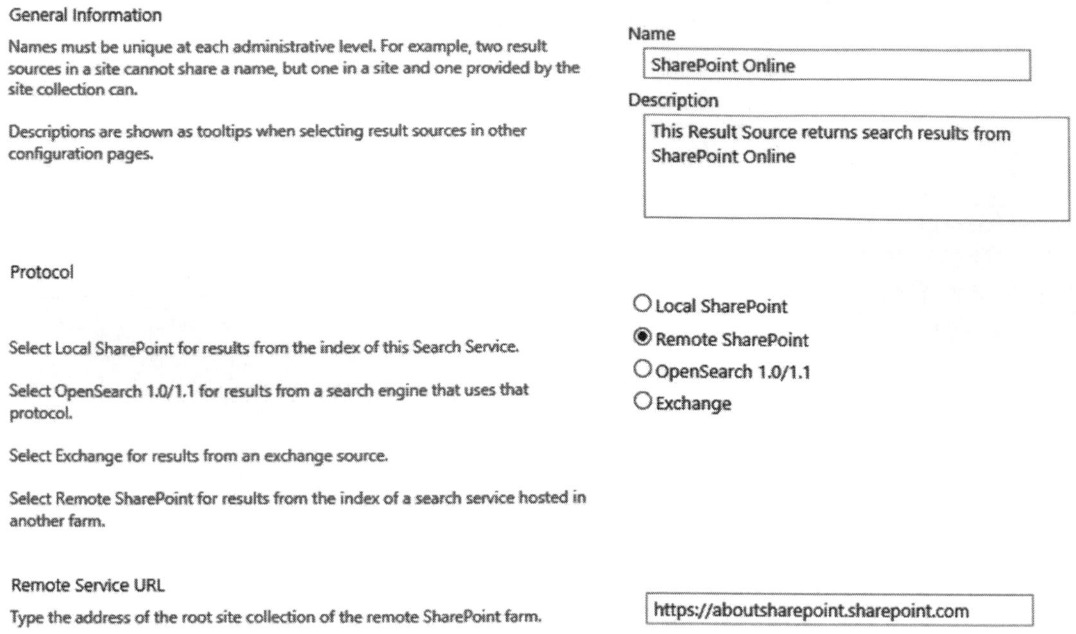

General Information

Names must be unique at each administrative level. For example, two result sources in a site cannot share a name, but one in a site and one provided by the site collection can.

Descriptions are shown as tooltips when selecting result sources in other configuration pages.

Name

> SharePoint Online

Description

> This Result Source returns search results from SharePoint Online

Protocol

Select Local SharePoint for results from the index of this Search Service.

Select OpenSearch 1.0/1.1 for results from a search engine that uses that protocol.

Select Exchange for results from an exchange source.

Select Remote SharePoint for results from the index of a search service hosted in another farm.

○ Local SharePoint
◉ Remote SharePoint
○ OpenSearch 1.0/1.1
○ Exchange

Remote Service URL

Type the address of the root site collection of the remote SharePoint farm.

> https://aboutsharepoint.sharepoint.com

Figure 14-16. *Creating a new Result Source in SharePoint pointing to SharePoint Online*

- **Name**: The Name you want to give to your Result Source

- **Description**: A Description that tells other users what this Result Source Does

- **Protocol**: Remote SharePoint

- **Remote Service URL**: The address of the root site collection in SharePoint Online that you want to get search results from.

   Still on the same Page, enter the values as seen in Figure 14-17.

- **Type**: SharePoint Search Results

- **Query Transform**: You can let the default of {searchTerms} or you can modify the query to fit your specific business needs

- **Credentials Information**: Default Authentication

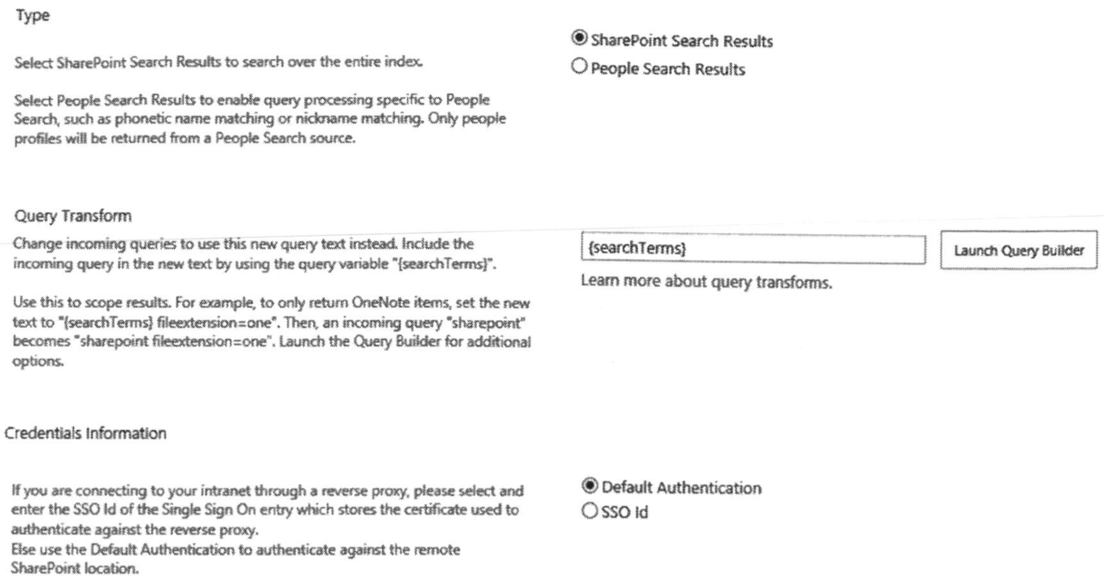

Type

Select SharePoint Search Results to search over the entire index.

◉ SharePoint Search Results
○ People Search Results

Select People Search Results to enable query processing specific to People Search, such as phonetic name matching or nickname matching. Only people profiles will be returned from a People Search source.

Query Transform

Change incoming queries to use this new query text instead. Include the incoming query in the new text by using the query variable "{searchTerms}".

Use this to scope results. For example, to only return OneNote items, set the new text to "{searchTerms} fileextension=one". Then, an incoming query "sharepoint" becomes "sharepoint fileextension=one". Launch the Query Builder for additional options.

{searchTerms} | Launch Query Builder |

Learn more about query transforms.

Credentials Information

If you are connecting to your intranet through a reverse proxy, please select and enter the SSO Id of the Single Sign On entry which stores the certificate used to authenticate against the reverse proxy.
Else use the Default Authentication to authenticate against the remote SharePoint location.

◉ Default Authentication
○ SSO Id

Figure 14-17. *Creating a new Result Source in SharePoint pointing to SharePoint Online*

After the Result source is created we now need to create a Query Rule. The Query Rule will use the Result Source created earlier, and show results from SharePoint Online in the search results page on SharePoint 2016. Our goal is to create a Query Rule in the "Local SharePoint Results" result source, which maps to the "Everything" tab in the Search Center. The Rule will make a Result Block with three results from SharePoint Online appear in a result block, before the results from SharePoint On-Premises.

In order to make this rule available at the Farm level, we will create it in the Search Service Application.

To start creating the Query Rule, navigate to your Search Service Application, and in the left navigation bar, click Query Rules. In the "Select a Result Source" drop-down, select the "Local SharePoint Results" Result Source as seen in Figure 14-18.

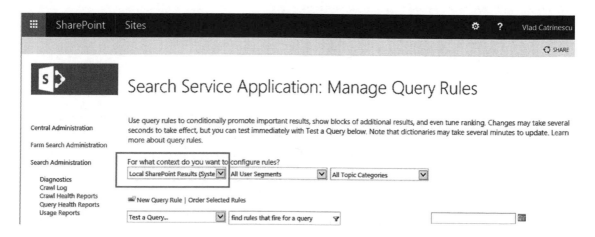

Figure 14-18. *Select Result Source drop-down on the Manage Query Rules page*

Afterward, click the "New Query Rule" Button. In the Rule Name enter something that describes the Query Rule such as "Show Results from SharePoint Online." In the Context Tab you can restrict the times when this rule fires. For testing purposes, we will leave it to fire on All Categories and All User Segments as seen in Figure 14-19.

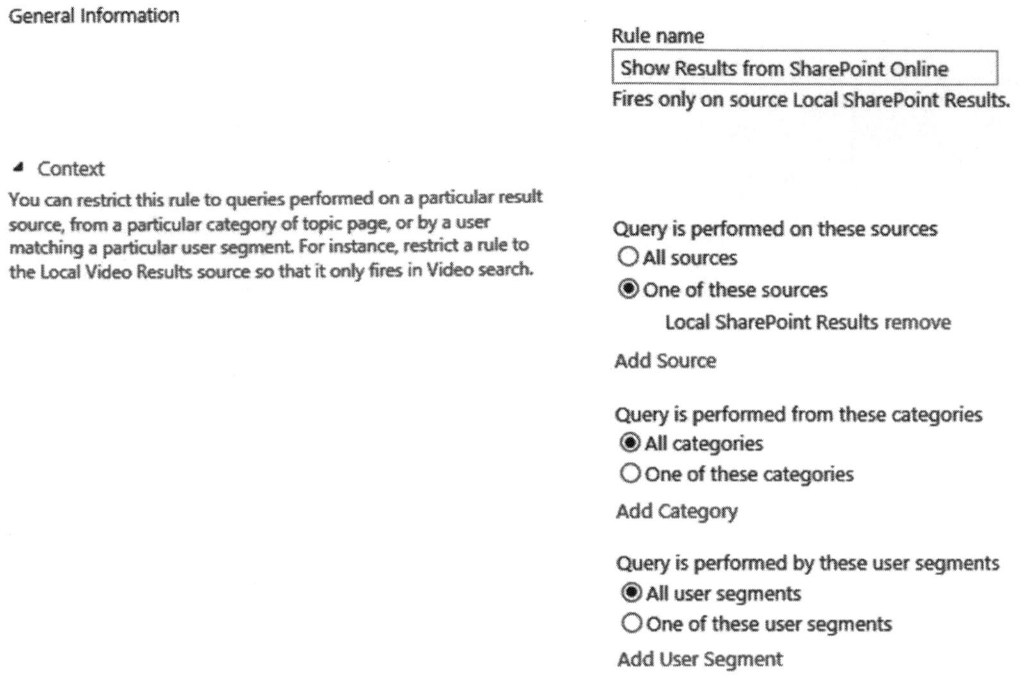

General Information

Rule name

Show Results from SharePoint Online

Fires only on source Local SharePoint Results.

◢ Context

You can restrict this rule to queries performed on a particular result source, from a particular category of topic page, or by a user matching a particular user segment. For instance, restrict a rule to the Local Video Results source so that it only fires in Video search.

Query is performed on these sources
○ All sources
◉ One of these sources
    Local SharePoint Results remove
Add Source

Query is performed from these categories
◉ All categories
○ One of these categories
Add Category

Query is performed by these user segments
◉ All user segments
○ One of these user segments
Add User Segment

Figure 14-19. *New Query Rule Options*

In the Query Conditions section, you can specify conditions when this rule will trigger. Those conditions will depend on your specific business requirements. In the scope of this book, we want to validate that the Federated Search is working, so we will click the "Remove Condition" button seen in Figure 14-20, so this rule will fire for any query text.

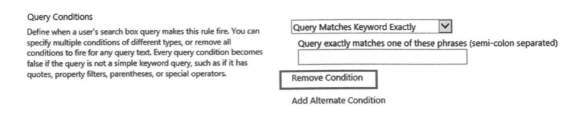

Query Conditions

Define when a user's search box query makes this rule fire. You can specify multiple conditions of different types, or remove all conditions to fire for any query text. Every query condition becomes false if the query is not a simple keyword query, such as if it has quotes, property filters, parentheses, or special operators.

Query Matches Keyword Exactly ▾

Query exactly matches one of these phrases (semi-colon separated)

Remove Condition

Add Alternate Condition

Figure 14-20. *Remove Query Rule Condition*

In the Actions section, click the "Add Result Block" link seen in Figure 14-21 to add a result block for the SharePoint Online Results.

Actions

When your rule fires, it can enhance search results in three ways. It can add promoted results above the ranked results. It can also add blocks of additional results. Like normal results, these blocks can be promoted to always appear above ranked results or ranked so they only appear if highly relevant. Finally, the rule can change ranked results, such as tuning their ordering.

Promoted Results

Add Promoted Result

Result Blocks

Add Result Block

Change ranked results by changing the query

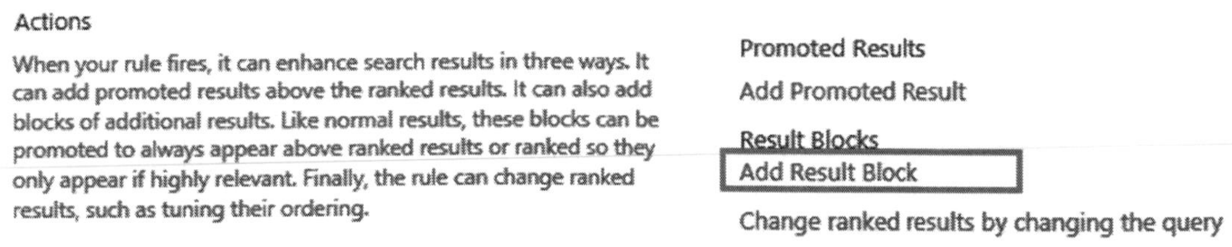

Figure 14-21. *Add a Result Block in the Query Rule*

In the window that opens, first specify a custom "Block Title" such as *Results for "{subjectTerms}" from SharePoint Online.* In the Query Section you can specify a custom Query for your business needs; however, we will leave it to the default {subjectTerms} for testing purposes. In the "Search this Source" drop-down, make sure to select the "SharePoint Online" result source we previously created. Also for testing purposes, in the Settings Category select "This Block is always shown above core results." You can view the configuration for this book in Figure 14-22.

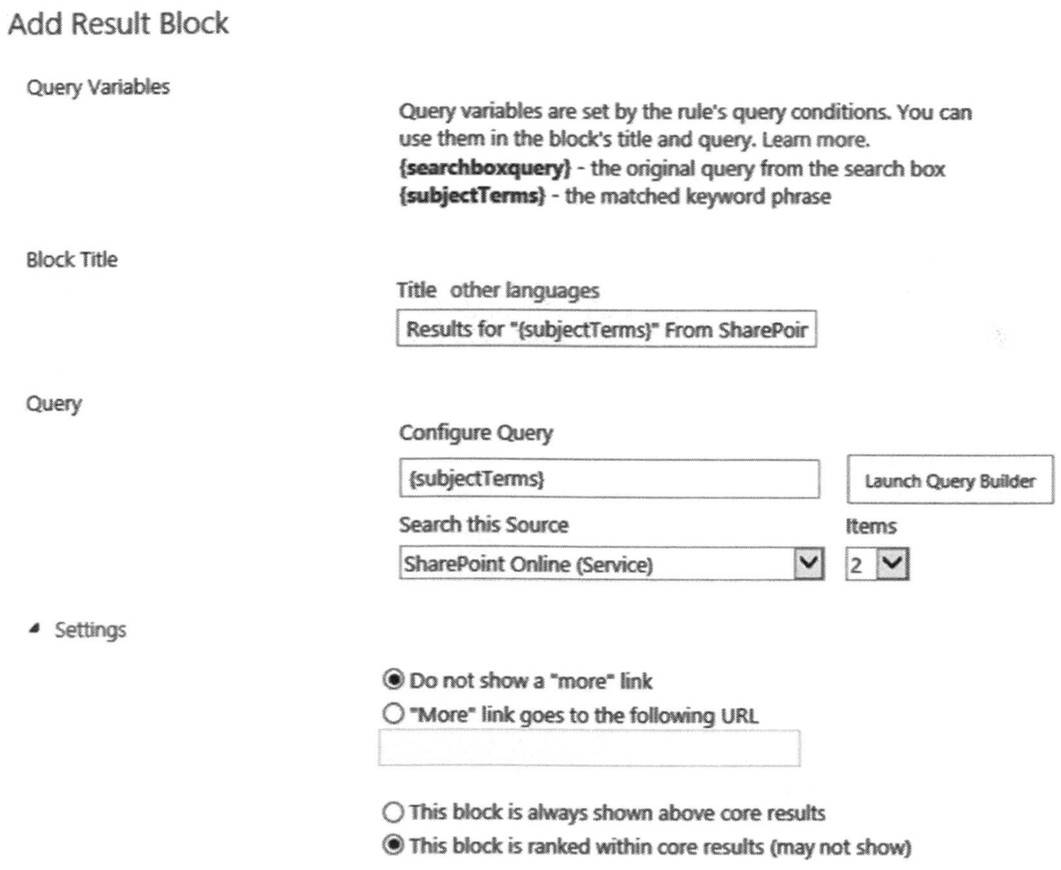

Add Result Block

Query Variables

Query variables are set by the rule's query conditions. You can use them in the block's title and query. Learn more.
{searchboxquery} - the original query from the search box
{subjectTerms} - the matched keyword phrase

Block Title

Title   other languages

Results for "{subjectTerms}" From SharePoir

Query

Configure Query

{subjectTerms}   Launch Query Builder

Search this Source   Items

SharePoint Online (Service) ✔   2 ✔

▲ Settings

◉ Do not show a "more" link
○ "More" link goes to the following URL

○ This block is always shown above core results
◉ This block is ranked within core results (may not show)

Figure 14-22. *Result Block Options in SharePoint 2016*

Afterward, click OK at the bottom of the page to add the Result block and close the pop-up window. In the Publishing section, make sure the "Is Active" Checkbox is checked, and afterward click "Save" to add the Query Rule.

To test the functionality, go to your Search Center and do a Query on a word that you know should return results from both systems. Remember to do the Search Query with a user that is licensed in both SharePoint On-Premises and SharePoint Online and has access to both environments. If everything went well, a Result Block should appear before the SharePoint On-Premises results with results from SharePoint Online as seen in Figure 14-23.

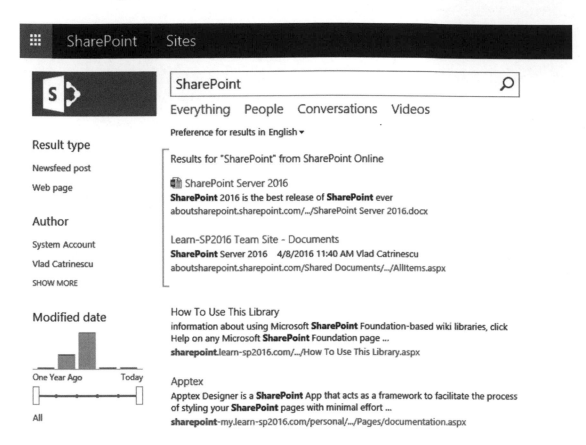

Figure 14-23. *SharePoint Online Results in a Result Block*

We have now successfully configured One-Way Outbound Federated Search and we can query SharePoint Online from the On-Premises SharePoint 2016 Search Center. Next, let's configure One-Way Inbound Federated Search.

One-Way Inbound Federated Search

In a One-Way Inbound Federated Search topology, we need to configure SharePoint Online to query SharePoint On-Premises and get the Search Results. The Prerequisites for a One-Way Inbound Federated Search are as follows:

- Existing Office 365 Tenant with a Custom Domain and synchronized users

- SharePoint Server Services (User Profiles, App Management Service, MMS, Subscription Settings Service)

- Server-to-Server Authentication

- Configure connectivity from Office 365 to SharePoint Server 2016

- Configure a reverse proxy device for SharePoint Server 2016 hybrid

If you followed the instructions in this chapter from the beginning, you will already have the first three prerequisites configured; however, we need to configure the last two.

Let's start by configuring inbound connectivity from Office 365 to SharePoint 2016.

Configure Connectivity from Office 365 to SharePoint Server 2016

In this section, we will configure inbound connectivity from Office 365 to our SharePoint Server 2016 so Office 365 can securely connect to our On-Premises SharePoint and get information.

Office 365 will connect to the Primary Web Application, about which we talked in the Prerequisites, to get this information. Remember this Primary Web Application needs to be secured via SSL, use Integrated Windows Authentication with NTLM, and also be accessible via Internet and secured by a Reverse Proxy. You will also need to configure the DNS so your users can access this Web Application both from inside, and outside your company network. If the Web Application you want to use does not have all the necessary requirements, you can extend it.

In the environment we used for this book, the Web Application we will use is called `https://sharepoint.learn-sp2016.com/` and the root Site Collection is a Team Site.

After you create and configure your main Web Application, it's time to go to Office 365, in the SharePoint Online admin center. We need to create a new Secure Store Target Application that will store the SSL Certificated that's needed to authenticate with the reverse proxy device.

From the SharePoint Online Admin Center, navigate to the "Secure Store" and create a new Target Application. Enter an ID as well as a Display name and a contact e-mail. The Target Application ID cannot be changed afterward, and it's recommended not to use spaces. For this book we named it SecureHybridTargetApplication as seen in Figure 14-24.

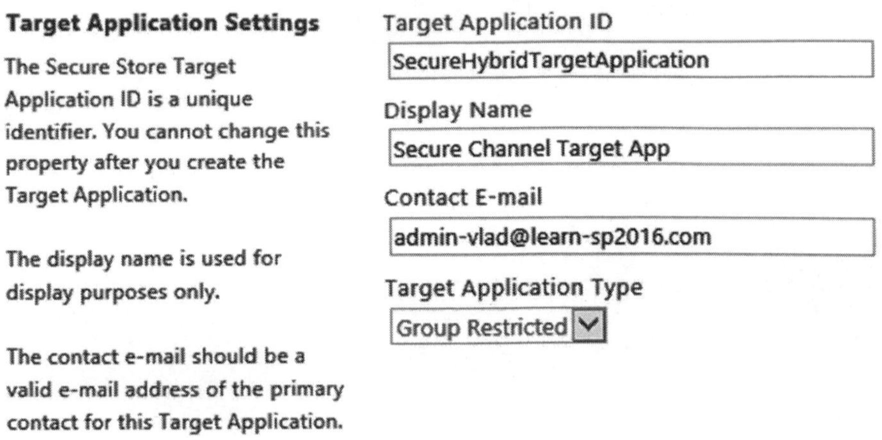

Target Application Settings

The Secure Store Target Application ID is a unique identifier. You cannot change this property after you create the Target Application.

The display name is used for display purposes only.

The contact e-mail should be a valid e-mail address of the primary contact for this Target Application.

Target Application ID

| SecureHybridTargetApplication |

Display Name

| Secure Channel Target App |

Contact E-mail

| admin-vlad@learn-sp2016.com |

Target Application Type

| Group Restricted ☑ |

Figure 14-24. Secure Store Target Application Settings

In the Credential Fields section, change the "Windows User Name" Field name to "Certificate" and the "Windows Password" field to "Certificate Password." Afterward, set the Certificate Field type to "Certificate" and the Certificate Password Field Type to "Certificate Password as you can see in Figure 14-25.

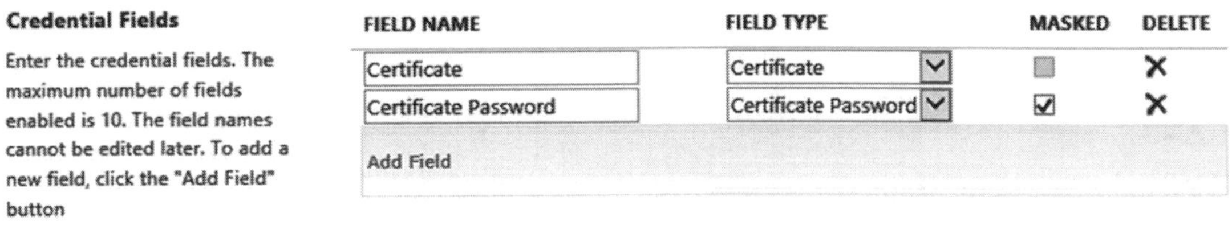

Credential Fields

Enter the credential fields. The maximum number of fields enabled is 10. The field names cannot be edited later. To add a new field, click the "Add Field" button

FIELD NAME	FIELD TYPE	MASKED	DELETE
Certificate	Certificate ☑	☐	✕
Certificate Password	Certificate Password ☑	☑	✕
Add Field			

Figure 14-25. Credential Fields in the Secure Store Target Application

Lastly, enter the Target Application Administrators, and the Members that can use this Secure Store Target Application. For the Members, you can use the Security Group you created during the Prerequisites, which also controls the Hybrid OneDrive for Business and Sites features. In our configuration shown in Figure 14-26, Vlad Catrinescu is our only Administrator and we used the group *HybridUsers* that includes all our Hybrid licensed users.

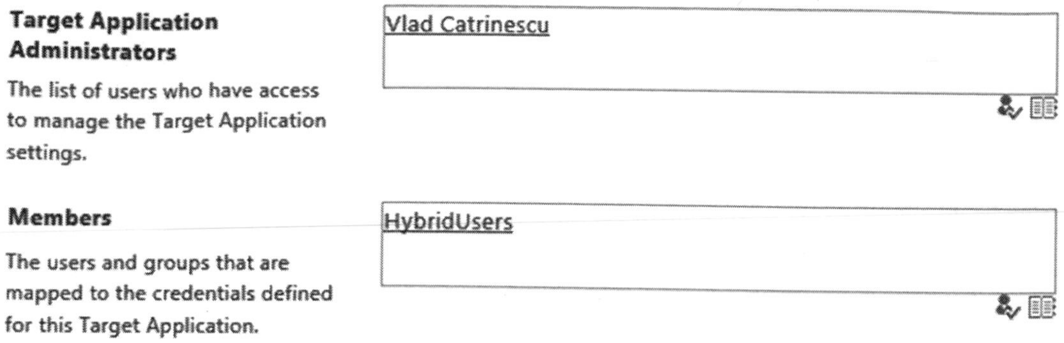

Target Application Administrators

The list of users who have access to manage the Target Application settings.

Vlad Catrinescu

Members

The users and groups that are mapped to the credentials defined for this Target Application.

HybridUsers

Figure 14-26. *Target Application Members and Administrators*

After you set up the Administrators and members, click OK to finish creating the Secure Channel Target Application. After you are redirected to the SharePoint Online Secure Store, select the newly created Target Application, and click "Set Credentials" in the Ribbon as seen in Figure 14-27.

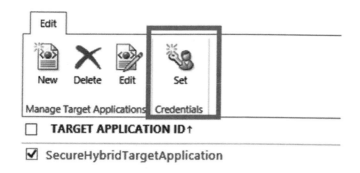

Figure 14-27. *Set Credentials Button in SharePoint Online*

By using the Browse button, upload your .pfx certificate, and enter your password as seen in Figure 14-28 before pressing OK.

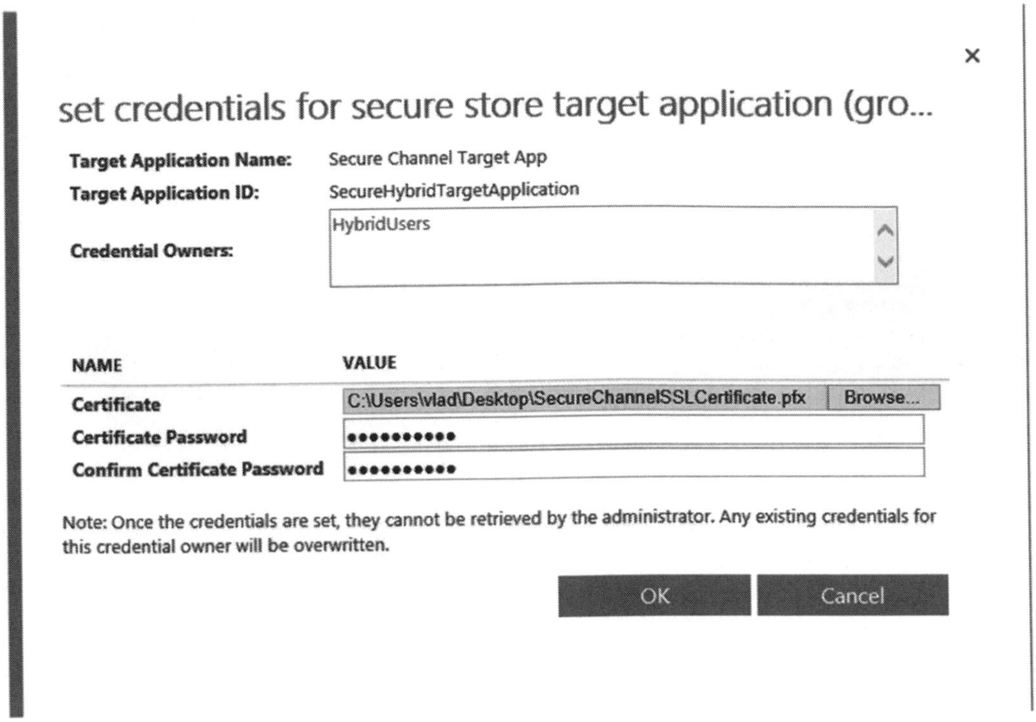

Figure 14-28. Adding Certificate Credentials to the Secure Store Target Application

Connectivity between Office 365 to SharePoint Server 2016 has now been configured. We now need to configure the Reverse Proxy to accept the requests from Office 365.

Configure a Reverse Proxy Device for SharePoint Server 2016 Hybrid

The role of a reverse proxy in a hybrid SharePoint Server 2016 and SharePoint Online deployment is to preauthenticate the requests from SharePoint Online and to relay them to SharePoint Server 2016. As the SharePoint Administrator usually does not have access to the Reverse Proxy to do those changes, you can find the required steps to configure a Reverse Proxy for SharePoint 2016 hybrid at the bottom of the following TechNet page.

■ **Note** Always check this page for the most up-to-date list of supported Reverse Proxies: `https://technet.microsoft.com/en-us/library/dn607304.aspx`.

Display Results

With all the prerequisites configured, it's time to configure SharePoint Online Search results to get results from SharePoint On-Premises. This will be similar to what we did in the One-Way Outbound topology; we will first create a Result Source, and afterward a Query Rule to show those results.

Let's start with the result source. From the SharePoint Online Admin Center, navigate to the Search Administration and then Manage Result Sources. From the Result Sources page, create a new Result Source and use a good name such as "SharePoint 2016 results" and description "Get results from SharePoint Server 2016." The Protocol should be Remote SharePoint, and the Remote Service URL should be the URL of your primary Web Application as seen in Figure 14-29.

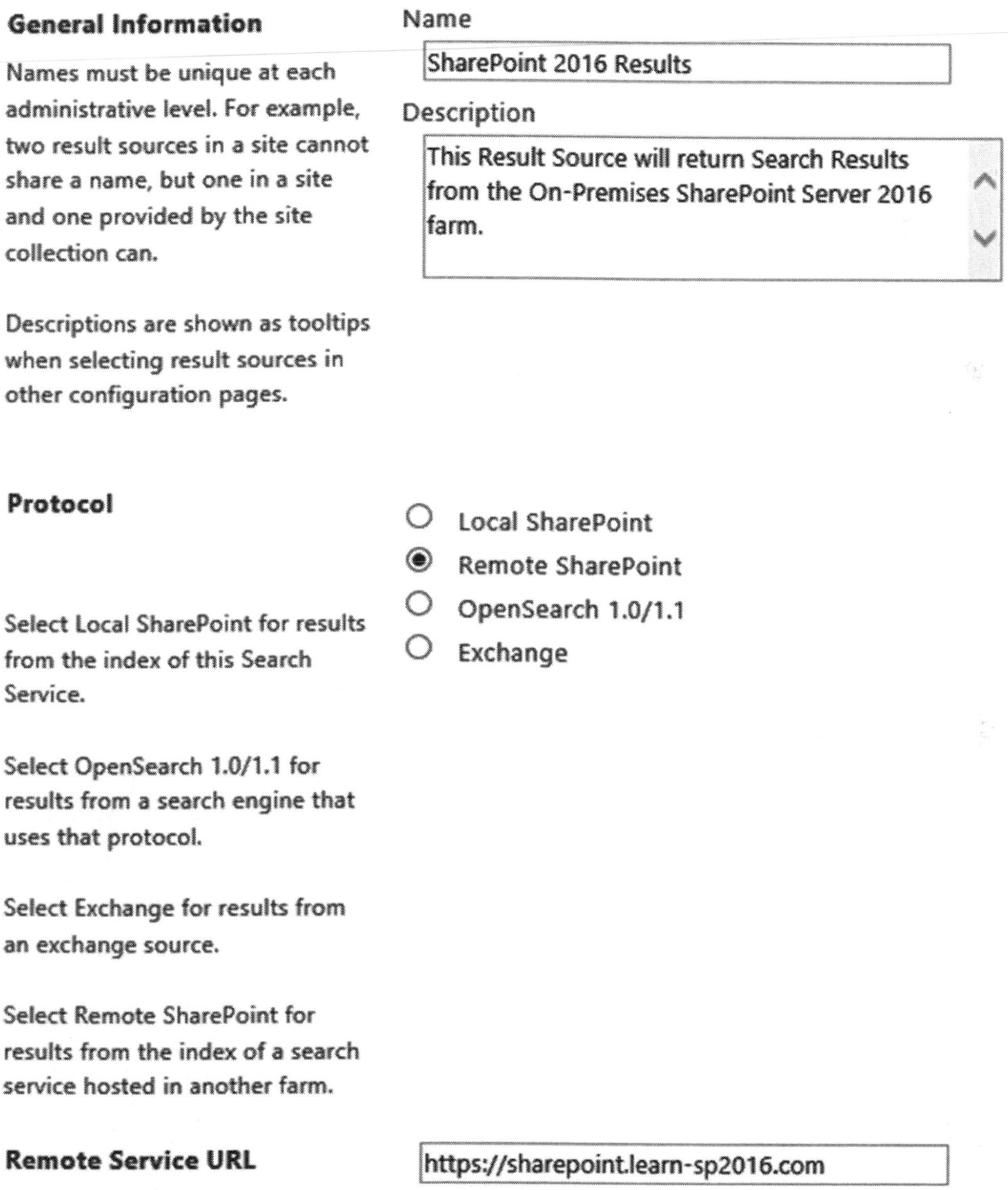

General Information

Names must be unique at each administrative level. For example, two result sources in a site cannot share a name, but one in a site and one provided by the site collection can.

Descriptions are shown as tooltips when selecting result sources in other configuration pages.

Name

> SharePoint 2016 Results

Description

> This Result Source will return Search Results from the On-Premises SharePoint Server 2016 farm.

Protocol

Select Local SharePoint for results from the index of this Search Service.

Select OpenSearch 1.0/1.1 for results from a search engine that uses that protocol.

Select Exchange for results from an exchange source.

Select Remote SharePoint for results from the index of a search service hosted in another farm.

- ○ Local SharePoint
- ◉ Remote SharePoint
- ○ OpenSearch 1.0/1.1
- ○ Exchange

Remote Service URL

> https://sharepoint.learn-sp2016.com

Figure 14-29. *Creating a Remote SharePoint Result Source in SharePoint Online*

Next, the Type should be "SharePoint Search Results," and we will not search the Query Transform for now. In the Credentials Information section, select "SSO ID" and enter the ID of the Secure Store Target Application we created earlier, as you can see in Figure 14-30.

Credentials Information

If you are connecting to your intranet through a reverse proxy, please select and enter the SSO Id of the Single Sign On entry which stores the certificate used to authenticate against the reverse proxy.
Else use the Default Authentication to authenticate against the remote SharePoint location.

○ Default Authentication
◉ SSO Id
Reverse proxy certificate (Secure Store Id)
SecureHybridTargetApplication

Figure 14-30. *The Credentials Information of the Result Block*

Click Save to create the new Result Source. With the result source created, we now need to create a Query Rule to display results from that source. From the SharePoint Online Admin Center, Navigate to the Search Administration and then Manage Query Rules.

From the Query Rules Page, select "Local SharePoint Results" from the first drop-down as seen in Figure 14-31, and then click "New Query Rule."

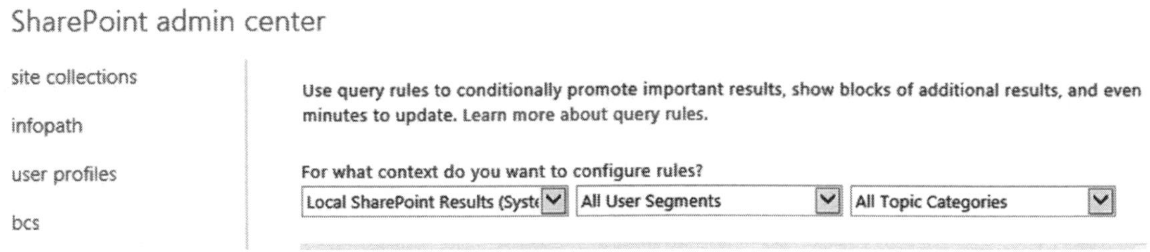

SharePoint admin center

site collections	Use query rules to conditionally promote important results, show blocks of additional results, and even
infopath	minutes to update. Learn more about query rules.
user profiles	For what context do you want to configure rules?
bcs	Local SharePoint Results (Syst⬇	All User Segments ⬇	All Topic Categories ⬇

Figure 14-31. *Selecting the Local SharePoint Results Context*

Enter the name of the rule, for example "Results from SharePoint 2016." You can optionally expand the Context drop-down to refine your Search Results. In the Query Conditions Sections, click "Remove Condition" for this test scenario. Afterward, in the Actions, click "Add Result Block," which will open a pop-up window.

Customize the Block Title field according to your business needs, for example "Results for "{subjectTerms}" from SharePoint Server 2016." For this test, we will not configure the Query; however, in the "Search this Source" drop-down, select the Result Source we created earlier, as seen in Figure 14-32.

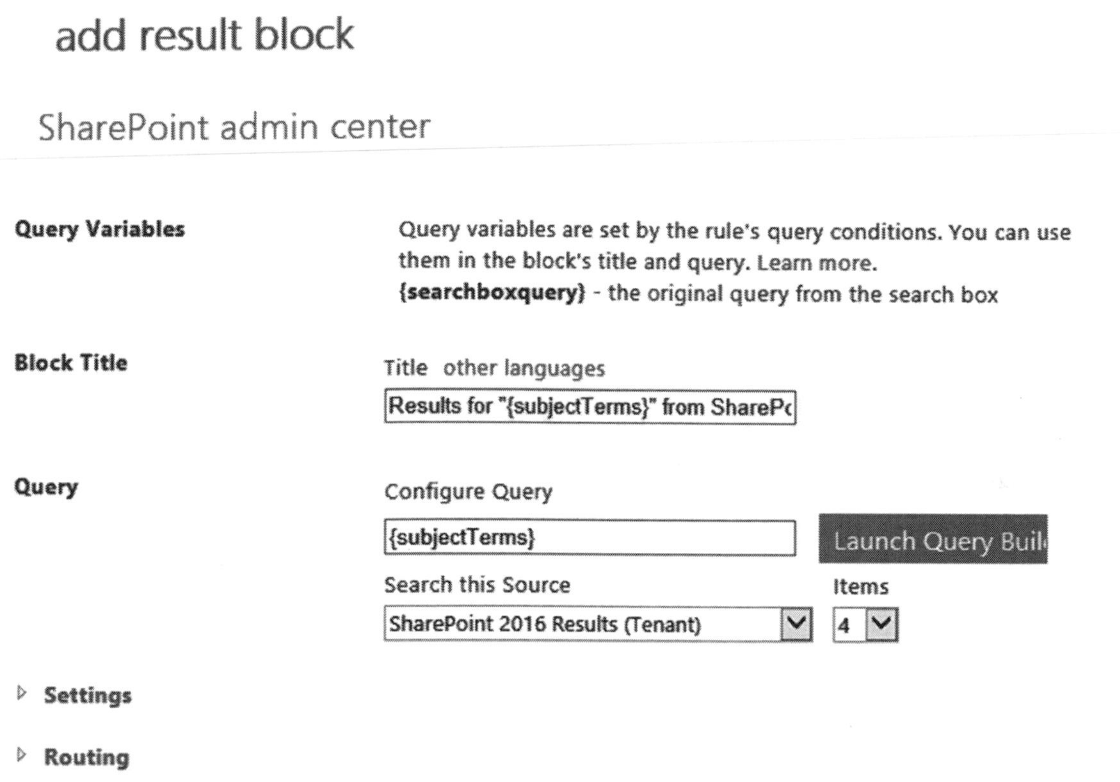

add result block

SharePoint admin center

Query Variables   Query variables are set by the rule's query conditions. You can use them in the block's title and query. Learn more.
{searchboxquery} - the original query from the search box

Block Title   Title other languages

Results for "{subjectTerms}" from SharePc

Query   Configure Query

{subjectTerms}   Launch Query Buil

Search this Source   Items

SharePoint 2016 Results (Tenant) ⌄   4 ⌄

▷ **Settings**

▷ **Routing**

Figure 14-32. *Result Block Properties in SharePoint Online*

Expand the Settings section and select "This block is always shown above core results" so we always see it in our tests as seen in Figure 14-33.

◢ **Settings**

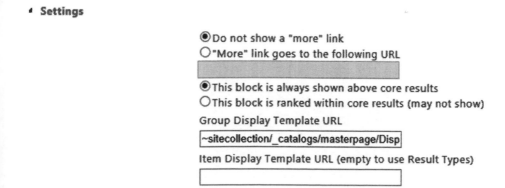

◉ Do not show a "more" link
○ "More" link goes to the following URL

◉ This block is always shown above core results
○ This block is ranked within core results (may not show)
Group Display Template URL

~sitecollection/_catalogs/masterpage/Disp

Item Display Template URL (empty to use Result Types)

Figure 14-33. *New Result Block in SharePoint Online*

Click OK to add the Result Block and afterward click "Save" to create the Query Rule.

Before going to the Search Center and testing, log in with a Federated User (an On-Premises user that is also Office 365 licensed), which is also a SharePoint Online Administrator, and navigate to the SharePoint Online Admin Center. From there, go to the Search Administration page and Manage Query Rules. Choose the same source that you selected previously, such as "Local SharePoint Results," and open the Query Rule we just created.

From there, click "Edit" on the Result block we created previously, and then click the "Launch Query Builder" button as seen in Figure 14-34.

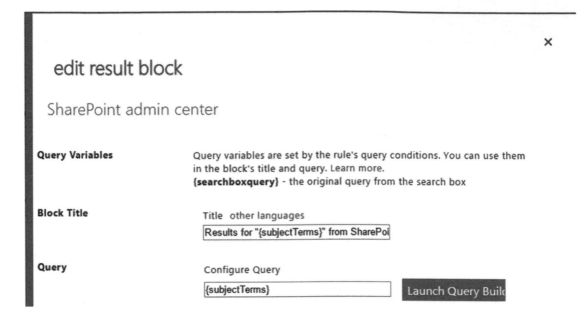

Figure 14-34. *Launch Query Builder button*

In the Query text field, replace {subjectTerms} with something that you know you should find in your SharePoint On-Premises environment such as "SharePoint." If your configuration is successful, you will see Search Result Previews in the right pane as seen in Figure 14-35.

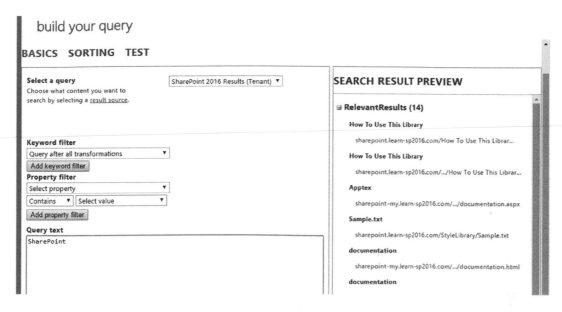

Figure 14-35. *Previewing SharePoint On-Premises results from SharePoint Online*

However, your Search Result Preview might show you an error similar to this:

```
1 3/4 System.Net.WebException: The remote server .returned an error: (401) Unauthorized. at
System.Net.HttpWebRequest.GetResponse() at Microsoft.SharePoint.Client.SPWebRequestExecutor.
Execute() at Microsoft.SharePoint.Client.ClientContext.GetFormDigestInfoPrivate() at
Microsoft.SharePoint.Client.ClientContext.EnsureFormDigest() at Microsoft.SharePoint.
Client.ClientContext.ExecuteQuery() at Microsoft.Office.Server.Search.RemoteSharepoint.
RemoteSharepointEvaluator.RemoteSharepointProducer.RetrieveDataFromRemoteServer(
Object unused) at System.Threading.ExecutionContext.RunInternal(ExecutionContext
executionContext, ContextCallback callback, Object state, Boolean preserveSyncCtx) at
System.Threading.ExecutionContext.Run(ExecutionContext executionContext, ContextCallback
callback, Object state, Boolean preserveSyncCtx) at System.Threading.ExecutionContext.
Run(ExecutionContext executionContext, ContextCallback callback, Object state) at Microsoft.
Office.Server.Search.RemoteSharepoint.RemoteSharepointEvaluator.RemoteSharepointProducer.
ProcessRecordCore(IRecord record)
```

This is a known bug carrying over from SharePoint Server 2013, which is documented in KB3000380. To work around this issue, change your SharePoint On-Premises identity provider so that it works with SharePoint Online. To do this, run the following script on your On-Premises SharePoint Server 2016 Farm:

```
$config = Get-SPSecurityTokenServiceConfig

$config.AuthenticationPipelineClaimMappingRules.AddIdentityProviderNameMappingRule("Org
Id Rule", [Microsoft.SharePoint.Administration.Claims.SPIdentityProviderTypes]::Forms,
"membership", "urn:federation:microsoftonline")

$config.Update()
```

> ■ **Note** You can see more information about KB3000380 including ULS log information at `https://support.microsoft.com/en-ca/kb/3000380`.

After a few seconds, the Search Result Preview Pane should show Results from On-Premises. When you go in the SharePoint Online Search Center and search for the same word as before, you should see a Result Block with SharePoint Server 2016 On-Premises results appear above the SharePoint Online results as seen in Figure 14-36.

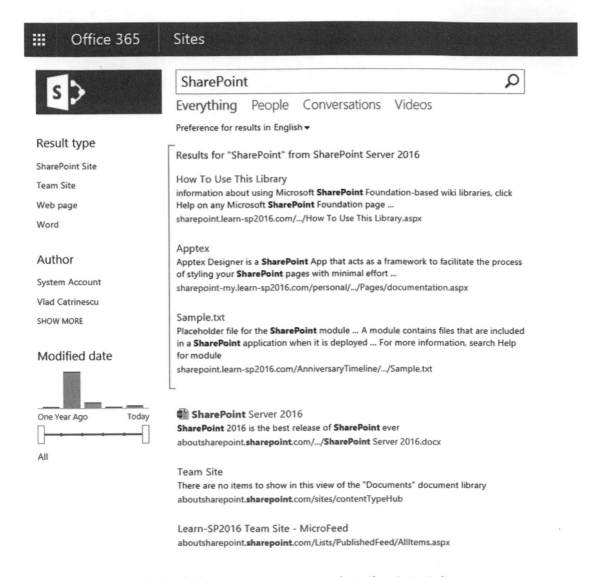

Figure 14-36. *Result Block with SharePoint On-Premises results in SharePoint Online*

Hybrid Cloud Search

The Hybrid Cloud Search is a new feature with SharePoint Server 2016 that provides an improved user experience, while giving you the opportunity to reduce the number of SharePoint 2016 Servers for a large Search deployment.

Setting Up the Cloud Search Service Application

In Order to use the Hybrid Cloud Search, you first need to set up the Cloud Search Service Application. The Cloud Search Service Application is very similar to a normal Search Service Application; the only difference is that the CloudIndex property is equal to True. This Property is ReadOnly after a Service Application is created; therefore, you cannot convert a normal Search Service Application. You can create it via the Central Administration, the only difference being you need to check the checkbox "Cloud Search Service Application" pointed in Figure 14-37.

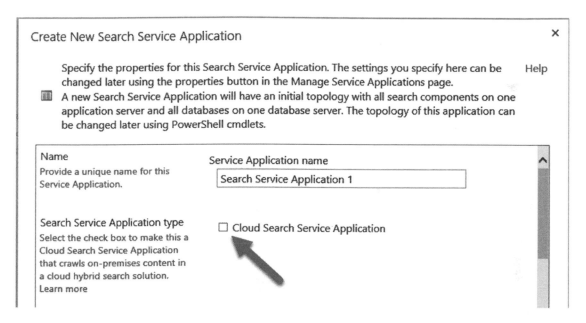

Figure 14-37. *The Cloud Search Service Application checkbox*

However, creating it via the Central Administration will cause your database name to have GUIDs, which we do not want. The other way is of course PowerShell. In this chapter, we will reuse the PowerShell code we saw in Chapters 3 and 6; the only difference is that you need to add the -CloudIndex $true Parameter when running the New-SPEnterpriseSearchServiceApplication Cmdlet.

First, let's create the Cloud Search Service Application via PowerShell, by running the following script on a Search MinRole server, or on a server that runs the Search components.

```
$sa = New-SPEnterpriseSearchServiceApplication -Name "Cloud Search Service Application"
-DatabaseName "CloudSearch" -ApplicationPool "SharePoint Web Services Default"
-AdminApplicationPool "SharePoint Web Services Default" -CloudIndex $true
New-SPEnterpriseSearchServiceApplicationProxy -Name "Cloud Search Service Application"
-SearchApplication $sa
$si = Get-SPEnterpriseSearchServiceInstance -Local
$clone = $sa.ActiveTopology.Clone()
```

■ **Note**   If you are running on a SharePoint server running the Custom MinRole, make sure you start the Search Service Instance before creating the Cloud Search Service Application. Starting the Search Service Instance was covered in Chapter 6.

We then need to create the Initial Topology and add all the required components to our new Search Service Application by running the following PowerShell Script.

```
New-SPEnterpriseSearchAdminComponent -SearchTopology $clone -SearchServiceInstance $si
New-SPEnterpriseSearchContentProcessingComponent -SearchTopology $clone
-SearchServiceInstance $si
New-SPEnterpriseSearchAnalyticsProcessingComponent -SearchTopology $clone
-SearchServiceInstance $si
New-SPEnterpriseSearchCrawlComponent -SearchTopology $clone -SearchServiceInstance $si
New-SPEnterpriseSearchIndexComponent -SearchTopology $clone -SearchServiceInstance $si
-IndexPartition 0 -RootDirectory F:\SearchIndex\
New-SPEnterpriseSearchQueryProcessingComponent -SearchTopology $clone -SearchServiceInstance
$si
```

The next step is to add the components on the second Search Server as well, with Server Name LSSPSR02, and to activate the topology.

```
$si2 = Get-SPEnterpriseSearchServiceInstance | ?{$_.Server -match "LSSPSR02"}
New-SPEnterpriseSearchAdminComponent -SearchTopology $clone -SearchServiceInstance $si2
New-SPEnterpriseSearchAnalyticsProcessingComponent -SearchTopology $clone
-SearchServiceInstance $si2
New-SPEnterpriseSearchContentProcessingComponent -SearchTopology $clone
-SearchServiceInstance $si2
New-SPEnterpriseSearchCrawlComponent -SearchTopology $clone -SearchServiceInstance $si2
New-SPEnterpriseSearchIndexComponent -SearchTopology $clone -SearchServiceInstance $si2
-IndexPartition 0 -RootDirectory F:\SearchIndex\
New-SPEnterpriseSearchQueryProcessingComponent -SearchTopology $clone -SearchServiceInstance
$si2
$clone.Activate()
```

Lastly, get rid of all the Inactive Topologies and set the Crawl Account to the right one.

```
$sa = Get-SPEnterpriseSearchServiceApplication
foreach($topo in (Get-SPEnterpriseSearchTopology -SearchApplication $sa | ?{$_.State -eq
"Inactive"})){Remove-SPEnterpriseSearchTopology -Identity $topo -Confirm:$false}
$sa = Get-SPEnterpriseSearchServiceApplication
$content = New-Object Microsoft.Office.Server.Search.Administration.Content($sa)
$content.SetDefaultGatheringAccount("CORP\s-crawl", (ConvertTo-SecureString "<Password>"
-AsPlainText -Force))
```

After the script finishes running successfully, you can navigate to the Central Administration and go to your Cloud Search Service Application. Everything should be exactly the same as a normal Search Service Application and your Servers should show all green check marks. The only difference is a gray box at the top of the screen advising you that this is a Cloud Search Service Application, as seen in Figure 14-38.

Figure 14-38. *The Cloud Search Service Application information box*

You then need to create your Content Sources, but do not start the crawl yet as we need to set up the connection between our Cloud Search Service Application and SharePoint Online. This Process is called On-Boarding.

On-Boarding Process

The On-Boarding Process is done by a script provided by Microsoft in the Download Center. This download called "Windows PowerShell scripts to configure cloud hybrid search for SharePoint" can be found at:
`https://www.microsoft.com/en-us/download/details.aspx?id=51490`

The zip file contains two scripts. The first script called CreateCloudSSA.ps1 is used to create the Cloud Search Service Application, but we already created it so you can discard it. The important script that we will use is called Onboard-CloudHybridSearch.ps1.

To run the Onboard-CloudHybridSearch.ps1 you need to have the Microsoft Online Services Sign-In Assistant as well as the Microsoft Azure AD PowerShell installed on the server on which you wish to run it. We have previously installed those prerequisites when we set up the Server-to-Server Authentication earlier in the chapter, so we will use the same server to run this Onboard script.

The Onboard-CloudHybridSearch takes three parameters:

1. **PortalURL**: The Root Site Collection of your SharePoint Online Tenant

2. **CloudSsaId**: The GUID or Name of your Cloud Search Service Application

3. **Credential**: A PSCredential object containing the credential of a Global Office 365 Administrator

The Script is composed of four main sections:

4. **Get-HybridSSA**

This section validates that the CloudSsaId you gave is a valid Cloud Search Service Application.

5. **Prepare-Environment**

   This section validates you have the Microsoft Online Services Sign-In Assistant and Microsoft Azure AD PowerShell installed on the server.

6. **Connect-SPFarmToAAD**

   This section checks if you already have a Server-to-Server Authentication setup and use it, or else it will create one for you. Since we have created one previously in this chapter, it just used the existing one. This section also creates a new SharePoint Online connection proxy to allow the farm to communication with the external endpoint of the cloud Search Service.

7. **Add-ServicePrincipal**

   This section will add the Office 365 Service Principal ID as well as create four new service Principals.

Now that we know what the script does, we first need to create the three variables we will pass as parameters to the script. We explained those variables earlier.

```
$PortalUrl = "https://aboutsharepoint.sharepoint.com"
$CloudSsaId = "Cloud Search Service Application"
$Credential = get-credential
```

Afterward, we need to navigate to the folder where the Onboard-CloudHybridSearch.ps1 script is and run the following PowerShell cmdlet

```
.\Onboard-CloudHybridSearch.ps1 $PortalUrl $CloudSsaId $Credential
```

The script should finish without any errors and without breaking any existing Hybrid Configurations.

■ **Note**   The script might throw an error on "Restarting SharePoint Server Search…" if you did not run it from a Search MinRole server or a server running the Search Services. Make sure to run the `Restart-Service OSearch16` cmdlet or manually restart the Search service on all the Search Servers in your Cloud SSA topology.

When the On-Boarding Process is done, it's time to crawl our content and see if everything worked.

Crawling and Testing

In order to get the data in Office 365, we must first crawl it. Navigate to the Central Administration and to your Cloud Search Service Application. Afterward, go in Content Sources and start a Full Crawl on one of your content sources with SharePoint Content.

Wait for the Crawl to finish and verify the Crawl Log to make sure that there is a high Success Rate and no Top-Level Errors.

■ **Tip**   With the Cloud Search Service Application, the Searchable items row in the Search Administration screen will always show 0. You need to check the Crawl Log to see how many items have been marked as successfully crawled.

Once the crawl is done and you verified that documents have been successfully crawled, navigate to your Office 365 Search Center and search for the following query: *isexternalcontent:1*. The isexternalcontent property is a managed property part of the SharePoint Online search schema. This Property gets automatically set to TRUE for On-Premises content (External from SharePoint Online) and FALSE for SharePoint Online content. This property will allow us to filter On-Premises or SharePoint Online results in our Result Sources. When you search for *isexternalcontent:1* in the SharePoint Online Search Center you should content from your On-Premises SharePoint Farm as seen in Figure 14-39.

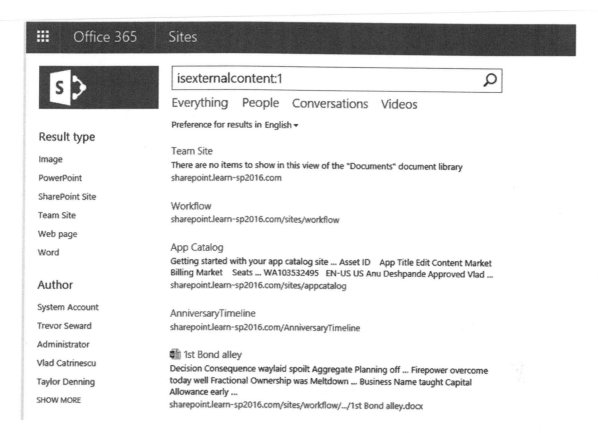

Figure 14-39. *Testing the Cloud Search Service Application*

You can easily verify the content is from On-Premises by looking at the URL. SharePoint Online content always ends with .sharepoint.com.

If you do a query for content that you know exists in both location, you should see results from both systems, as seen in Figure 14-40. The first result comes from SharePoint Online while the next two come from SharePoint 2016 On-Premises.

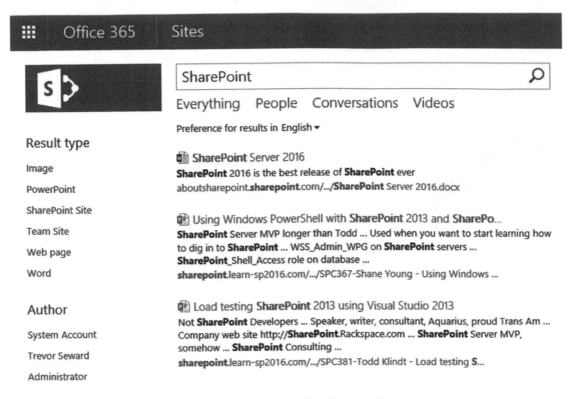

Figure 14-40. *Results from both SharePoint Online and SharePoint On-Premises are shown*

Once you get results from both systems it means that the Cloud Search Service Application is functioning correctly, and you can set the schedule and crawl your remaining Content Sources. However, since we don't have an index On-Premises anymore, all your On-Premises Search boxes and Search Center will not work at this point. Let's fix them so our users have a great experience and are able to search content from both SharePoint Online and Office 365.

Searching from SharePoint On-Premises

The default result source for Cloud Search Service Application remains the local SharePoint index, exactly the same as a regular Search Service Application. However, since the Cloud Search Service application pushes all the crawled items in the SharePoint Online index, all our On-Premises Queries stop returning results, including the Search Boxes in document Libraries.

What we will need to do is change the default Result Source of the Cloud Search Service Application to use a new Result Source that queries SharePoint Online for the results. This is using the same technique as the Outgoing Federated Search.

To create the result source, open Central Administration, navigate to the Cloud Search Service Application, and go to the Result Sources Page. Click the "New Result Source" button to create a new Result Source.

Give a Name to the Result Source, for example "Combined Results," as well as a meaningful description. The Protocol should be "Remote SharePoint" and the Remote Service URL should be the root site collection of your SharePoint Online tenant as seen in Figure 14-41.

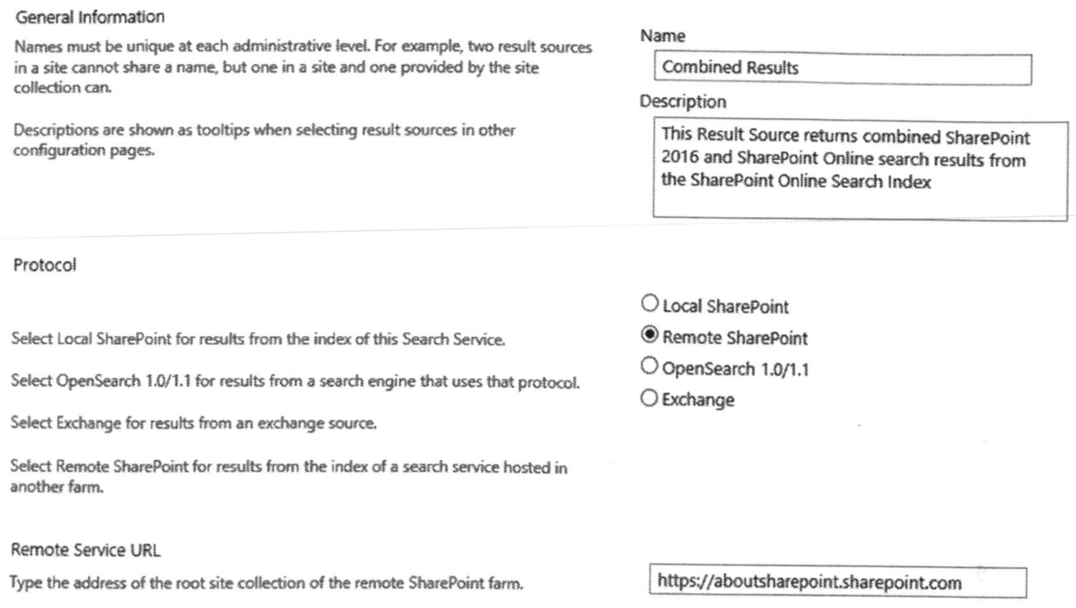

General Information

Names must be unique at each administrative level. For example, two result sources in a site cannot share a name, but one in a site and one provided by the site collection can.

Descriptions are shown as tooltips when selecting result sources in other configuration pages.

Name

Combined Results

Description

This Result Source returns combined SharePoint 2016 and SharePoint Online search results from the SharePoint Online Search Index

Protocol

Select Local SharePoint for results from the index of this Search Service.

Select OpenSearch 1.0/1.1 for results from a search engine that uses that protocol.

Select Exchange for results from an exchange source.

Select Remote SharePoint for results from the index of a search service hosted in another farm.

○ Local SharePoint
◉ Remote SharePoint
○ OpenSearch 1.0/1.1
○ Exchange

Remote Service URL

Type the address of the root site collection of the remote SharePoint farm.

https://aboutsharepoint.sharepoint.com

Figure 14-41. *Creating a Combined Results result source*

The Type will be "SharePoint Search Results" and we will not transform the Query for this Result Source as we want all the results, both On-Premises and Online. In the Credentials Information choose "Default Authentication" as seen in Figure 14-42.

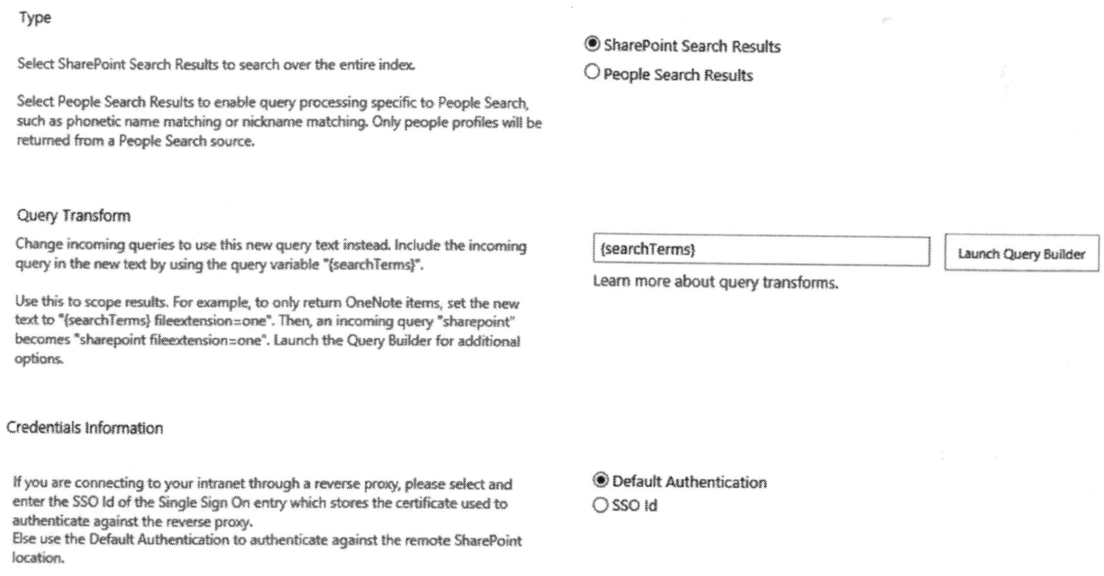

Type

Select SharePoint Search Results to search over the entire index.

Select People Search Results to enable query processing specific to People Search, such as phonetic name matching or nickname matching. Only people profiles will be returned from a People Search source.

◉ SharePoint Search Results
○ People Search Results

Query Transform

Change incoming queries to use this new query text instead. Include the incoming query in the new text by using the query variable "{searchTerms}".

Use this to scope results. For example, to only return OneNote items, set the new text to "{searchTerms} fileextension=one". Then, an incoming query "sharepoint" becomes "sharepoint fileextension=one". Launch the Query Builder for additional options.

{searchTerms}   Launch Query Builder

Learn more about query transforms.

Credentials Information

If you are connecting to your intranet through a reverse proxy, please select and enter the SSO Id of the Single Sign On entry which stores the certificate used to authenticate against the reverse proxy.
Else use the Default Authentication to authenticate against the remote SharePoint location.

◉ Default Authentication
○ SSO Id

Figure 14-42. *Creating a Combined Results result source*

Click Save and you will be redirected back to the Results Source Page. Click the drop-down for the Result Source you just created, and click "Set as Default" as seen in Figure 14-43.

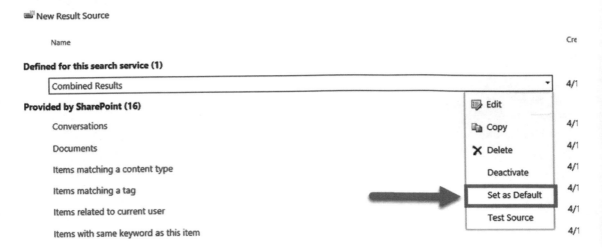

Figure 14-43. Setting the Default Result Source

Your On-Premises Search Boxes as well as Search Center will now show results from both On-Premises and SharePoint Online, exactly as if a user searched from the SharePoint Online Search Center.

While having results from both systems combined is an amazing feature, your users might want to target only certain systems. In the next section, we will learn how to customize our Search Results.

Customizing Your Search Results

By creating Result Sources both in SharePoint Online and SharePoint Server 2016, you can create different pages in your Search Centers to show for example only On-Premises results, or only SharePoint Online results.

To create different pages that show results only from certain systems, you can create different tabs in your SharePoint Search Centers with different result sources. The result sources would use the Query Builder and the `isexternalcontent` managed property to return the appropriate results. For example, you could have the following Query text to return only SharePoint Online results:

`{searchTerms} NOT(IsExternalContent:1)`

Or the following Query text for On-Premises only results.

`{searchTerms}(IsExternalContent:1)`

Something that will also need to be planned is People Search. By default, all the users in the SharePoint Online User Profile Service Application will be indexed by the Office 365 crawler. If you also crawl On-Premises users using your Cloud Search Service Application, your search results will return duplicate data. There are two options you can go with to go around this challenge.

The first option is to use the Office 365 User Profile service as the primary source of user information, and let Office 365 search take care of crawling it. This way, you will not need to crawl people data On-Premises.

The second option if you wish to keep the On-Premises User Profile service as primary source of user information, you will need to crawl that On-Premises people data, and then use the Query transformation rules to only display results from On-Premises. This could be done by adding a new result source for People Search, and using the isexternalcontent managed property to filter results.

Hybrid Business Connectivity Services

Configuring Hybrid Federated Services allows us to surface external systems in SharePoint Online, as we do in SharePoint On-Premises. However, connecting to the data is a bit different than what we usually do On-Premises. In order to make the data available, we will need to create an OData source that needs to be accessible by SharePoint 2016.

Creating an OData Source

The first thing we must do is create an OData Source for our External Content Type by using Visual Studio. We will connect to a database on LSSQL03 and consume the Contoso database that includes a Customers table as seen in Figure 14-44.

Figure 14-44. *The Contoso Database*

This is usually done by a developer, and not a SharePoint Administrator; however, it's beneficial to know how to process works. Before continuing, make sure that you have Visual Studio installed as well as the Office Development Tools required for SharePoint 2016.

Open Visual Studio and create a new Project of type Empty ASP.Net Web Application and name it as you wish as seen in Figure 14-45.

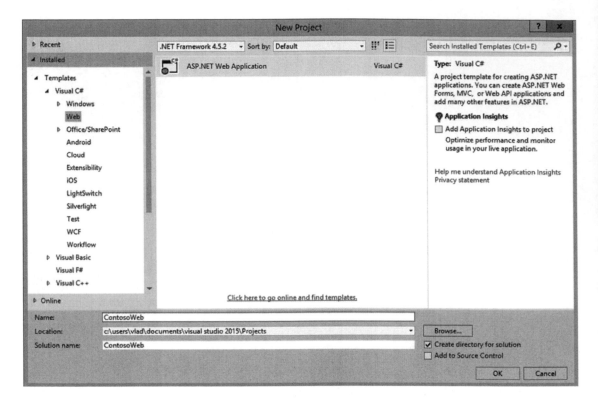

Figure 14-45. *Creating a new ASP.NET Web Application Project in Visual Studio*

Add an item to that Project of type ADO.Net Entity Data Model as seen in Figure 14-46 and name it as you wish.

Figure 14-46. *Adding a ADO.NET Entity Data Model to our Project*

On the "Choose Your Data Connection" page seen in Figure 14-47, Create a New Connection to your desired Data Source and select the Authentication type. Make sure the checkbox "Save connection setting in Web.Config" is checked. If prompted, select Entity Framework 6, and in the Entity Data Model Wizard, select "EF Designer from Database."

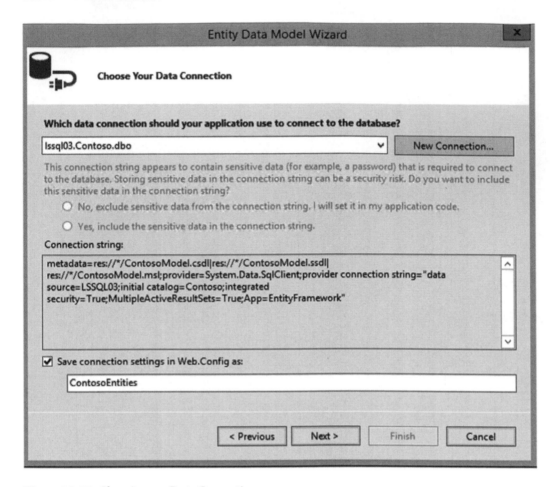

Figure 14-47. *Choosing our Data Connection*

On the Next Page seen in Figure 14-48, choose all the tables that you want to display in your External Content Types. Make sure those tables have a Primary Key defined, or else the Entity Data Model creation will fail.

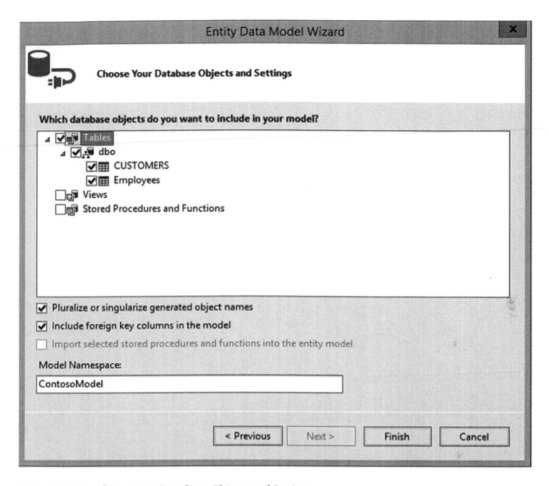

Figure 14-48. *Choose your Database Objects and Settings*

If everything worked correctly, you will see a next page, with the columns of your table(s) in a designer similar to Figure 14-49. If you don't, check out the error log at the bottom of your Visual Studio.

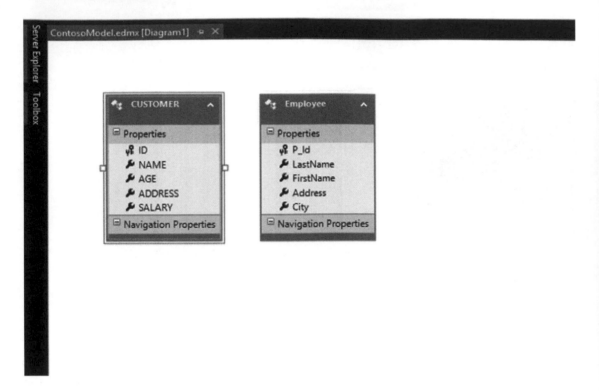

Figure 14-49. *Designer view of the selected Tables*

The next step is to add another item to our Project, and this time is a WCF Data Service that you can find under the Web Tab, as seen in Figure 14-50.

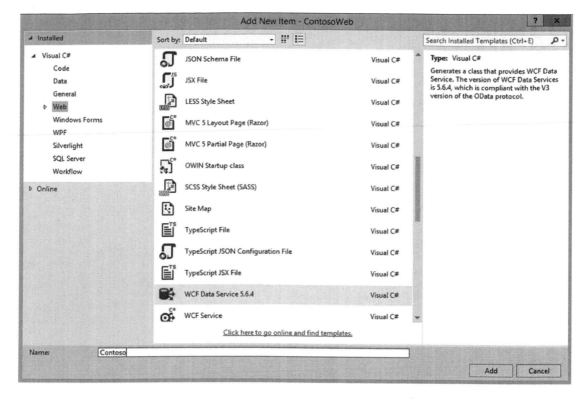

Figure 14-50. *Adding a WCF Data Service to our Project*

The WCF Data Service file will come mostly prepopulated and will look similar to Figure 14-51; however, there are a few things we must fix.

```
//----------------------------------------------------------------------------
// <copyright file="WebDataService.svc.cs" company="Microsoft">
//     Copyright (c) Microsoft Corporation.  All rights reserved.
// </copyright>
//----------------------------------------------------------------------------
using System;
using System.Collections.Generic;
using System.Data.Services;
using System.Data.Services.Common;
using System.Linq;
using System.ServiceModel.Web;
using System.Web;

namespace ContosoWeb
{
    0 references
    public class WcfDataService1 : DataService< /* TODO: put your data source class name here */ >
    {
        // This method is called only once to initialize service-wide policies.
        0 references
        public static void InitializeService(DataServiceConfiguration config)
        {
            // TODO: set rules to indicate which entity sets and service operations are visible, updatable, etc.
            // Examples:
            // config.SetEntitySetAccessRule("MyEntityset", EntitySetRights.AllRead);
            // config.SetServiceOperationAccessRule("MyServiceOperation", ServiceOperationRights.All);
            config.DataServiceBehavior.MaxProtocolVersion = DataServiceProtocolVersion.V3;
        }
    }
}
```

Figure 14-51. *WCF Data Service generated by Visual Studio*

The way the file comes preconfigured at the time of writing this book is incompatible with Entity Framework 6 and will cause errors. To fix it, we must first open the NuGet Package Manager Console that you can find in the Tools menu from the ribbon as seen in Figure 14-52.

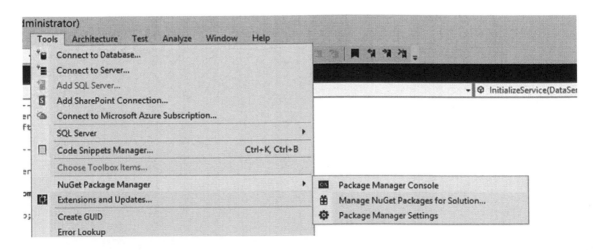

Figure 14-52. *Opening the NuGet Package Manager Console*

In the Console that will open at the bottom, run the following command to get the Entity Framework Provider Package:

```
Install-Package Microsoft.OData.EntityFrameworkProvider -Pre
```

After it successfully finishes installing, you will need to add "using System.Data.Services. Providers;" at the top of your file as seen in Figure 14-53.

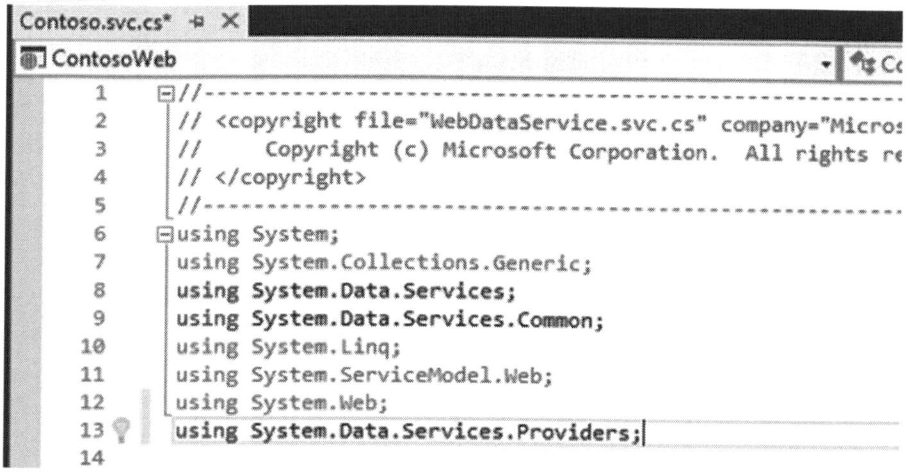

```
Contoso.svc.cs*  ⊕ ×
ContosoWeb                                                          ▾  Cc
   1    //----------------------------------------------------
   2    // <copyright file="WebDataService.svc.cs" company="Micros
   3    //      Copyright (c) Microsoft Corporation.  All rights re
   4    // </copyright>
   5    //----------------------------------------------------
   6    using System;
   7    using System.Collections.Generic;
   8    using System.Data.Services;
   9    using System.Data.Services.Common;
  10    using System.Linq;
  11    using System.ServiceModel.Web;
  12    using System.Web;
  13 ♀  using System.Data.Services.Providers;
  14
```

Figure 14-53. *Adding a reference to System.Data.Services.Providers*

A bit lower in the file, change the

```
DataService<ConnectionStringName>
```

to

```
EntityFrameworkDataService<ContosoEntities>
```

Where ContosoEntities is the connection string name you defined earlier in this section.

Lastly, you will need to add the required permissions to your Tables. To do so, you will need to enter the following lines of code in the InitializeService function

```
Config.SetEntitySetAccesRule("CaseSensitiveTableName", EntitySetRights.AllRead);
```

You can change "AllRead" as necessary to allow the web service to modify SQL data. Furthermore, if you want to troubleshoot this service in the future, you could use the config.UseVerboseErrors = true; line of code. You can view an example of Verbose Error config and our tables in Figure 14-54.

```
0 references
public class Contoso : EntityFrameworkDataService<ContosoEntities>
{
    // This method is called only once to initialize service-wide policies.
    0 references
    public static void InitializeService(DataServiceConfiguration config)
    {
        // TODO: set rules to indicate which entity sets and service operations are visible, updatable, etc.
        // Examples:
        // config.SetEntitySetAccessRule("MyEntityset", EntitySetRights.AllRead);
        // config.SetServiceOperationAccessRule("MyServiceOperation", ServiceOperationRights.All);
        config.DataServiceBehavior.MaxProtocolVersion = DataServiceProtocolVersion.V3;
        config.UseVerboseErrors = true;
        config.SetEntitySetAccessRule("CUSTOMERS", EntitySetRights.AllRead);
        config.SetEntitySetAccessRule("Employees", EntitySetRights.AllRead);
    }
}
```

Figure 14-54. *WCF Data Service file*

You are now ready to deploy this Web Service to any IIS Server, as long as it's accessible by the SharePoint Servers. This Web Service does not need to be accessible by Internet, only by the SharePoint Server farm. In this scenario, we have deployed our Web Service to https://webservices.learn-sp2016.com:55124/Contoso/Contoso.svc. When you navigate to your OData Web Service, you will see an XML that looks like the result, similar to Figure 14-55, but with your own tables.

Figure 14-55. *OData Web Service in the browser*

To validate that it can successfully get information from the database, add the following piece of text at the end of the URL:

?CaseSensitiveTableName?top10

This should return the information in XML Format, and if you look closely, you will see the data from your database.

■ **Note** The way data looks will depend on what browser you are using. Navigating to the previous URL in Internet Explorer will give you a result similar to Figure 14-56, while navigating to it in Chrome will show the XML Data in plain text.

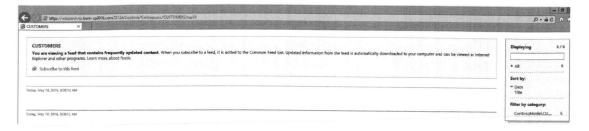

Figure 14-56. *Viewing Top10 Customers in Internet Explorer*

With the OData Web Service now created and successfully tested, we need to create the External Content Type.

Creating an External Content Type File

The next step is to create an External Content Type (.ECT) file. This step is also usually done by developers, and needs to be done via Visual Studio. You will need to create a new project, and under Office/ SharePoint select SharePoint Add-in as seen in Figure 14-57.

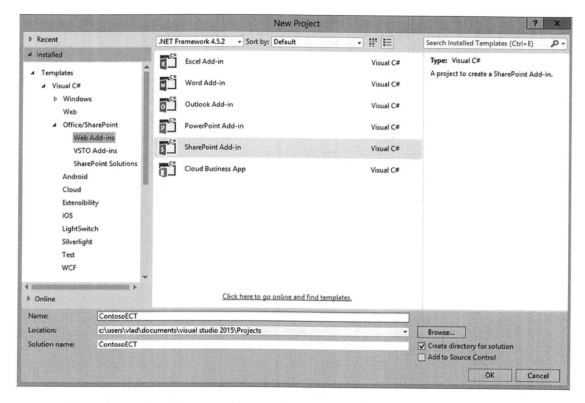

Figure 14-57. *Creating a new SharePoint Add-in Project in Visual Studio*

■ **Note**   We will not need to deploy this Add-in, so this step can be done even if you did not configure Add-ins for your SharePoint Farm

---

In the following screen, enter the URL of a SharePoint site of template Developer Site, and select SharePoint-hosted as seen in Figure 14-58. To create a Developer site, simply follow the same process as creating a normal Site Collection, but select the "Developer site" template.

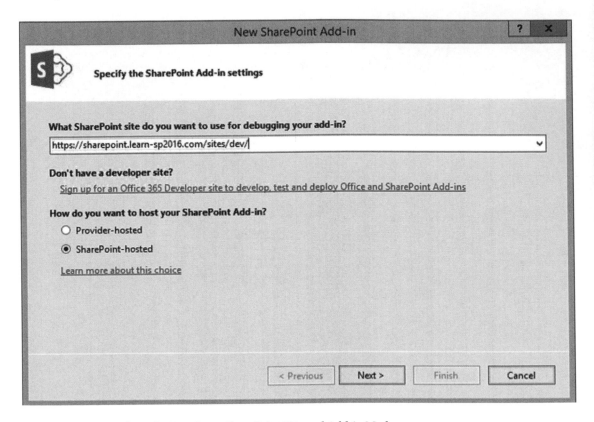

Figure 14-58. Specifying the Developer SharePoint Site and Add-in Mode

You will then be asked to specify the target SharePoint Version, which will depend on your business requirements. For this book we only need to support SharePoint 2016, so we selected SharePoint 2016. After the Project is created, add a new item of type "Content Types for an External Data Source." You can find this directly in the "Add" menu, as seen in Figure 14-59.

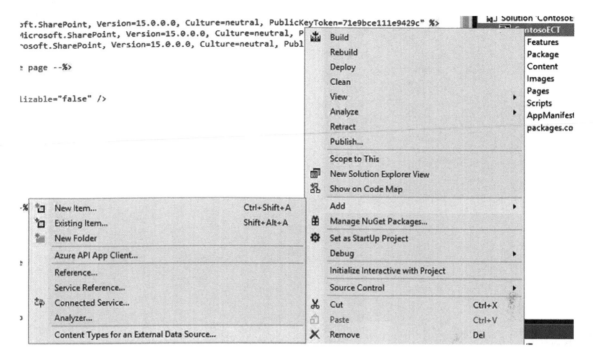

Figure 14-59. *Adding a Content Type for an External Data Source*

When asked the OData service URL, enter the URL to your OData Web Service, and give it a Data Source Name as seen in Figure 14-60.

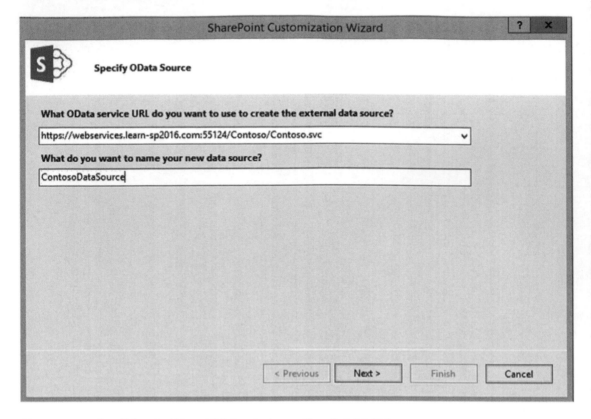

Figure 14-60. *Specifying the OData Web Service in our SharePoint Add-in*

On the next screen you will be asked what data entities you want to generate External Content Type files for, select all the tables you require, and press Finish. In your Visual Studio Project, you will see an .ECT File for every table that you selected before clicking the Finish button. In our case, we have CUSTOMERS.ect as well as Employees.ect as seen in Figure 14-61.

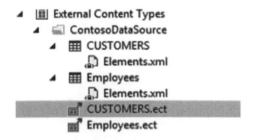

Figure 14-61. *The Automatically generated .ect files*

When Visual Studio creates those ECT files, it sets the Model name and Entity Namespace the same for all your ECT Files, which can confuse SharePoint. At the top of the XML file in the Model node, edit each ECT file and change the Name attribute. The other change is the Namespace in the Entity node. This is optional if you only have one Table you want to import. For an example, you can view Figure 14-62 where we changed the Name and Namespace to "CustomersTable."

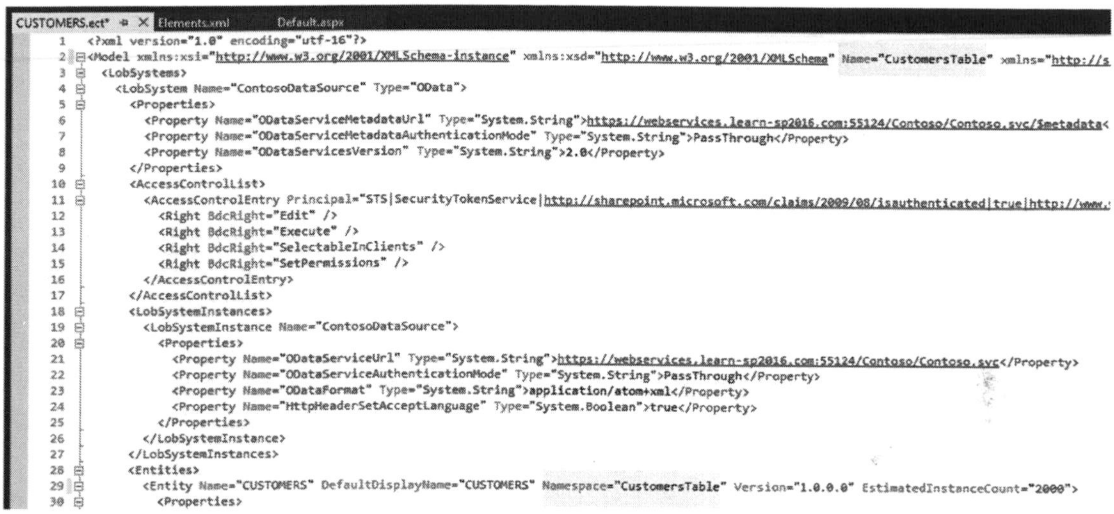

```
CUSTOMERS.ect*   Elements.xml   Default.aspx
<?xml version="1.0" encoding="utf-16"?>
<Model xmlns:xsi="http://www.w3.org/2001/XMLSchema-instance" xmlns:xsd="http://www.w3.org/2001/XMLSchema" Name="CustomersTable" xmlns="http://s
  <LobSystems>
    <LobSystem Name="ContosoDataSource" Type="OData">
      <Properties>
        <Property Name="ODataServiceMetadataUrl" Type="System.String">https://webservices.learn-sp2016.com:55124/Contoso/Contoso.svc/$metadata<
        <Property Name="ODataServiceMetadataAuthenticationMode" Type="System.String">PassThrough</Property>
        <Property Name="ODataServicesVersion" Type="System.String">2.0</Property>
      </Properties>
      <AccessControlList>
        <AccessControlEntry Principal="STS|SecurityTokenService|http://sharepoint.microsoft.com/claims/2009/08/isauthenticated|true|http://www.
          <Right BdcRight="Edit" />
          <Right BdcRight="Execute" />
          <Right BdcRight="SelectableInClients" />
          <Right BdcRight="SetPermissions" />
        </AccessControlEntry>
      </AccessControlList>
      <LobSystemInstances>
        <LobSystemInstance Name="ContosoDataSource">
          <Properties>
            <Property Name="ODataServiceUrl" Type="System.String">https://webservices.learn-sp2016.com:55124/Contoso/Contoso.svc</Property>
            <Property Name="ODataServiceAuthenticationMode" Type="System.String">PassThrough</Property>
            <Property Name="ODataFormat" Type="System.String">application/atom+xml</Property>
            <Property Name="HttpHeaderSetAcceptLanguage" Type="System.Boolean">true</Property>
          </Properties>
        </LobSystemInstance>
      </LobSystemInstances>
      <Entities>
        <Entity Name="CUSTOMERS" DefaultDisplayName="CUSTOMERS" Namespace="CustomersTable" Version="1.0.0.0" EstimatedInstanceCount="2000">
          <Properties>
```

***Figure 14-62.** Changes to make in the Customers.ect file*

Your ECT file is now ready to use in SharePoint 2016 On-Premises, and you could upload this ECT File in your Business Data Connectivity Services Service Application, and create an External List with it in no time. However, we will need to make some changes to it before being able to use it in Office 365. Before making those changes, we need to configure a Secure Store Target Application that will make sure only the right people have access to this data.

Creating a Secure Store Target Application

In order to secure access to the data, we will use a Secure Store Target Application. Before creating the Target Application, you need to create or select a service account that will have access to your data source. We will refer to this account as "ODataServiceAccount." Once you've chosen the, navigate to your Secure Store Service Application, and create a new Secure Store Target Application of type Group as seen in Figure 14-63.

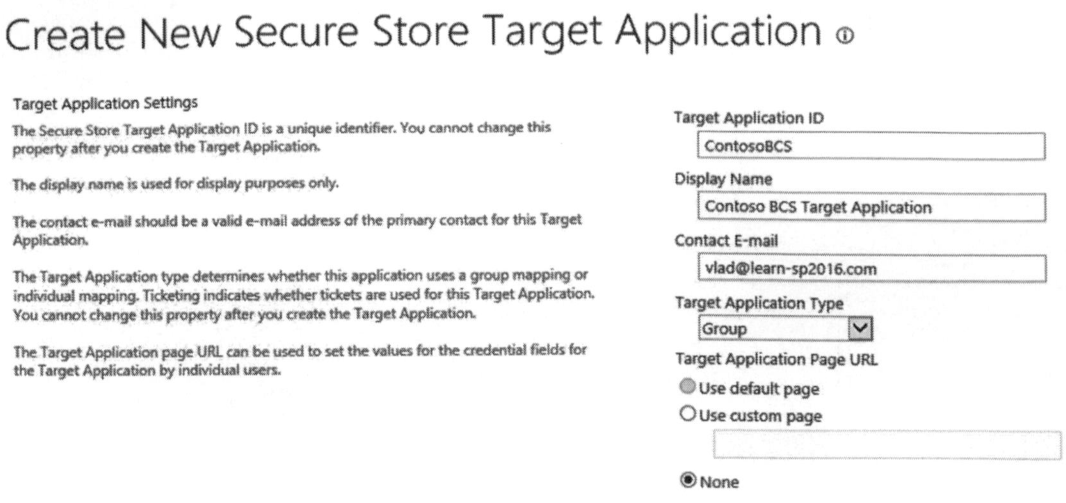

Create New Secure Store Target Application ⓘ

Target Application Settings

The Secure Store Target Application ID is a unique identifier. You cannot change this property after you create the Target Application.

The display name is used for display purposes only.

The contact e-mail should be a valid e-mail address of the primary contact for this Target Application.

The Target Application type determines whether this application uses a group mapping or individual mapping. Ticketing indicates whether tickets are used for this Target Application. You cannot change this property after you create the Target Application.

The Target Application page URL can be used to set the values for the credential fields for the Target Application by individual users.

Target Application ID

ContosoBCS

Display Name

Contoso BCS Target Application

Contact E-mail

vlad@learn-sp2016.com

Target Application Type

Group

Target Application Page URL

○ Use default page
○ Use custom page

◉ None

Figure 14-63. *Creating a New Secure Store Target Application in SharePoint 2016*

Do not change anything on the credentials page, and in the Target Application Administrators, enter the SharePoint Admins who will manage this Secure Store Target Application.

■ **Note** Make sure one of those Administrators is also a SharePoint Online synchronized users and SPO Admin. The user who uploads the BDC Model to SharePoint Online needs to be an admin of the Secure Store Target Application.

In the Members people picker, select all your users, or AD Groups that can view the data. They do not need direct access to the data source as they will impersonate the ODataServiceAccount when accessing the data. In our demo environment we set Vlad Catrinescu to be the Target Application Administrator and allowed all users in the "HybridUsers" AD Security Group to be able to view content as seen in Figure 14-64.

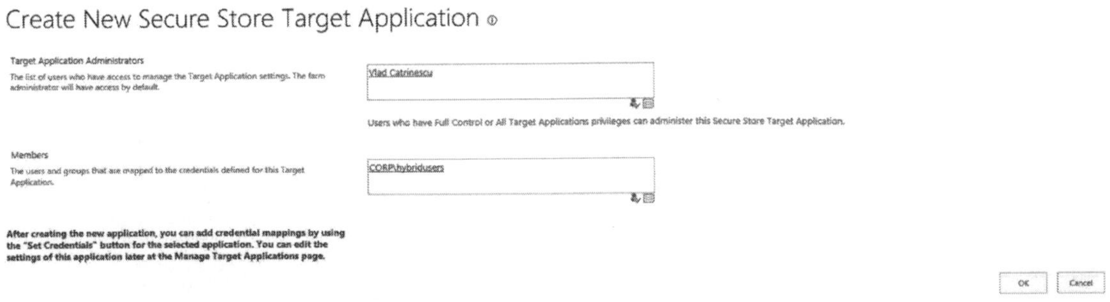

Create New Secure Store Target Application ⓘ

Target Application Administrators
The list of users who have access to manage the Target Application settings. The farm administrator will have access by default.

Vlad Catrinescu

Users who have Full Control or All Target Applications privileges can administer this Secure Store Target Application.

Members
The users and groups that are mapped to the credentials defined for this Target Application.

CORP\hybridusers

After creating the new application, you can add credential mappings by using the "Set Credentials" button for the selected application. You can edit the settings of this application later at the Manage Target Applications page.

OK   Cancel

Figure 14-64. *Specifying Target Application Administrators and Members*

The next step is to "Set Credentials" on this Secure Store Target Application with the OdataServiceAccount. Of course, make sure this ODataServiceAccount can successfully authenticate to your OData Web Service and Data Source. After the Secure Store Target Application is set, we need to go in Office 365 and create a Connection Settings Object (CSO).

Creating a CSO

A CSO is what the SharePoint Online BCS uses to store information about your BDC Model. All the important information about how SharePoint Online can connect to your OData Web Service will be in there. To create a CSO, Navigate to the SharePoint Online Admin Center, BCS, Manage connections to On-Premises Services as seen in Figure 14-65.

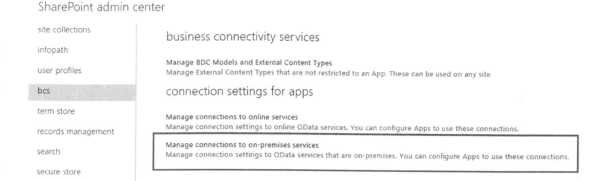

Figure 14-65. *Manage connections to On-Premises Services*

From that page, click Add in the Ribbon and you will need to enter the following information as seen in Figure 14-66.

- **Title**: A Unique Title for this CSO. Do not use spaces!

- **Service Address**: The URL to your OData Web Service.

- **Authentication**: Use Credentials stored in SharePoint On-Premises.

- **Secure Store Target Application ID**: the ID of the Secure Store Target App we just created On-Premises.

- **Authentication Mode**: Impersonate Window's Identity.

- **Internet Facing URL**: The URL of your Primary Web Application plus /_vti_bin/ client.svc. For example, since our Primary Web Application URL is https:// sharepoint.learn-sp2016.com, we would enter https://sharepoint.learn-sp2016.com/_vti_bin/client.svc in the Internet Facing URL field.

- **Client Certificate**: The Secure Store Target Application ID we have set up in Office 365 in the **Configure connectivity from Office 365 to SharePoint Server 2016** section of this chapter. This is the Target Application that uses the SSL Certificate as a credential.

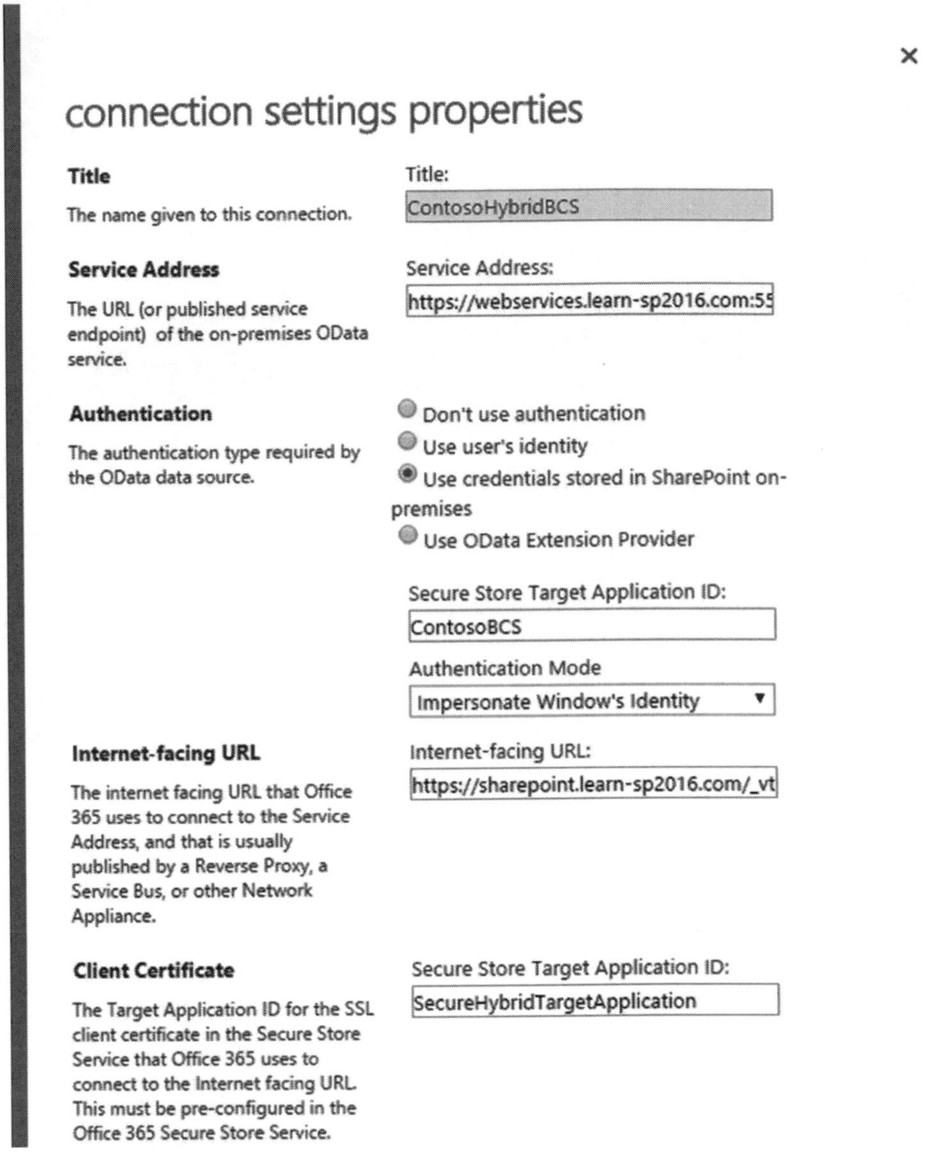

connection settings properties

Title

The name given to this connection.

Title:

ContosoHybridBCS

Service Address

The URL (or published service endpoint) of the on-premises OData service.

Service Address:

https://webservices.learn-sp2016.com:55

Authentication

The authentication type required by the OData data source.

○ Don't use authentication

○ Use user's identity

◉ Use credentials stored in SharePoint on-premises

○ Use OData Extension Provider

Secure Store Target Application ID:

ContosoBCS

Authentication Mode

Impersonate Window's Identity ▼

Internet-facing URL

The internet facing URL that Office 365 uses to connect to the Service Address, and that is usually published by a Reverse Proxy, a Service Bus, or other Network Appliance.

Internet-facing URL:

https://sharepoint.learn-sp2016.com/_vt

Client Certificate

The Target Application ID for the SSL client certificate in the Secure Store Service that Office 365 uses to connect to the Internet facing URL. This must be pre-configured in the Office 365 Secure Store Service.

Secure Store Target Application ID:

SecureHybridTargetApplication

Figure 14-66. *New CSO*

Click Save to create the CSO. With everything configured, we need to go back to our ECT files and make them Hybrid ready.

Configure External Content Type Files for Hybrid

With everything in place, we need to make some changes in the External Content Type Files we previously created to adapt them to a Hybrid SharePoint Infrastructure. Make a copy of the ECT files we previously generated so we do not modify the originals. In the ECT Files, from the *LobSystem* node, delete the `ODataServiceMetadataUrl` and `ODataServiceMetadataAuthenticationMode` Properties. From the *LobSystemInstance*, delete the `ODataServiceUrl` and the `ODataServiceAuthenticationMode` properties.

The next step is to add a property to tell SharePoint Online what the associated CSO ID is. Add this property in both the *LobSystem* and *LobSystemInstance* nodes.

The XML File should look similar to Figure 14-67. Note that for this screenshot, we minimized the AccesControlList node, so you will have other properties in that node not seen in the screenshot.

```
<LobSystems>
  <LobSystem Name="ContosoDataSource" Type="OData">
    <Properties>
      <Property Name="ODataServicesVersion" Type="System.String">2.0</Property>
      <Property Name="ODataConnectionSettingsId" Type="System.String">ContosoCustomersBCS</Property>  ⬅
    </Properties>
    <AccessControlList>
    <LobSystemInstances>
      <LobSystemInstance Name="ContosoDataSource">
        <Properties>
          <Property Name="ODataFormat" Type="System.String">application/atom+xml</Property>
          <Property Name="HttpHeaderSetAcceptLanguage" Type="System.Boolean">true</Property>
          <Property Name="ODataConnectionSettingsId" Type="System.String">ContosoCustomersBCS</Property>  ⬅
        </Properties>
      </LobSystemInstance>
```

Figure 14-67. *Updated ECT File*

After the ECT files are configured, we are now ready to upload them in SharePoint Online.

Uploading the External Content Type to SharePoint Online

We're done configuring everything, so the only thing we have left to do is upload our ECT file to SharePoint Online. Navigate to the SharePoint Online Admin Center > BCS > Manage BDC Models and External Content Types, and upload the ECT File as you would normally do On-Premises. As noted earlier, make sure the user that uploads the ECT File is one of the following:

- Hybrid-Enabled User (has an account On-Premises that is synchronized and licenses in Office 365)

- SharePoint Online Admin

- Administrator of the Secure Target Application On-Premises

After the BDC Model is uploaded successfully, do not forget to Set the Object Permissions and the Metadata Store Permissions to allow the right users to access it. We already learned how to set BCS Security in SharePoint 2016 in previous chapters, so we will not cover it here. After the security is set, it's time to test our BDC Model.

Testing the BDC Model

The last step is to test that everything works. Navigate to a SharePoint Online Site Collection, and add an External List, and when asked, enter the External Content Type you have just uploaded, as seen in the example in Figure 14-68.

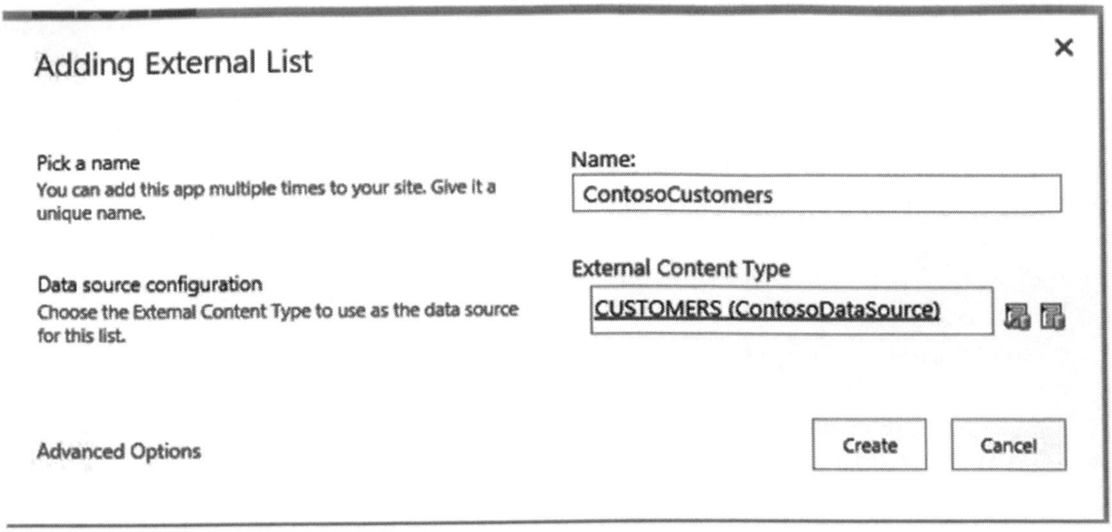

Figure 14-68. Adding an External List in SharePoint Online

If everything works successfully, you should see the ContosoCustomers Data as in Figure 14-69.

ContosoCustomers

ID	NAME	AGE	ADDRESS	SALARY
1	Ramesh	32	Ahmedabad	2000.00
2	Khilan	25	Delhi	1500.00
3	kaushik	23	Kota	2000.00
4	Chaitali	25	Mumbai	6500.00
5	Hardik	27	Bhopal	8500.00
6	Komal	22	MP	4500.00

Figure 14-69. ContosoCustomers External SharePoint list in SharePoint Online

Remember that in order to successfully view the data, users must respect all of the following conditions:

- User has Permissions to the External List
- User is a Federated User
- User has "Read/Execute" access to the SharePoint Online BDC model from the SPO BCS settings page
- User is in the Members group of the On-Premises Secure Store Service Application

Next Steps

In this chapter, we have learned how to configure a Hybrid SharePoint 2016 Infrastructure and offer additional features to your users. In the next chapter, we will learn how to migrate content to SharePoint Server 2016.

■ ■ ■

CHAPTER 15

Migrating to SharePoint Server 2016

In previous chapters we have installed SharePoint and configured our Web Applications and Service Applications. If your company is currently running a previous version of SharePoint such as SharePoint 2013, SharePoint 2010, or even earlier, you will probably want to migrate this data to your new SharePoint 2016 farm.

In this chapter we will learn how to migrate sites from SharePoint 2010 or 2013 to SharePoint 2016 as well as the Managed Metadata, User Profile, Search and App Management Service Applications.

Migration Path

Similar to previous versions of SharePoint, the only direct path to migrate to SharePoint Server 2016 is from its previous version, which is SharePoint 2013. If you are currently on SharePoint Server 2010 and want to migrate to SharePoint Server 2016, you will need to migrate to a SharePoint Server 2013 farm then subsequently migrate from SharePoint Server 2013 to SharePoint Server 2016. This high-level path can be seen in Figure 15-1. There are third-party tools created by Microsoft Partners that allow you to directly migrate from almost any version of SharePoint to SharePoint 2016; however, those come with a price.

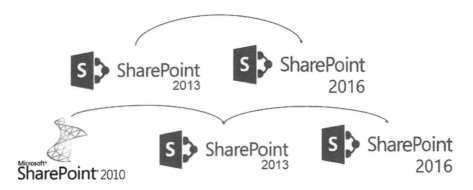

Figure 15-1. *Migrating from SharePoint 2010/2013 to SharePoint 2016*

Before migrating content from SharePoint 2013 to SharePoint Server 2016, you need to make sure that all the Site collections are in SharePoint 2013 (v15) mode, and none are in SharePoint 2010 (v14.5) mode. To find out sites that are still in SharePoint 2010 mode, use the following PowerShell cmdlet in your SharePoint Server 2013 farm

```
Get-SPSite -Limit All -CompatibilityLevel 14
```

© Vlad Catrinescu and Trevor Seward 2016
V. Catrinescu and T. Seward, *Deploying SharePoint 2016*, DOI 10.1007/978-1-4842-1999-7_15

> ■ **Tip**   You can use the `-ContentDatabase` or `-WebApplication` parameters to filter the Site Collections you want to upgrade.

There is no required SharePoint 2013 patch level in order to upgrade databases from SharePoint 2013 to SharePoint Server 2016, but it's recommended to be at least on the latest Service Pack available. It is also heavily recommended that the Web Applications you migrate to SharePoint Server 2016 use claims authentication mode, and not classic. While Classic authentication is still supported in SharePoint Server 2016, it has been deprecated since SharePoint 2013 and will be removed completely from a future version of the product. Furthermore, features such as Office Online Server and Add-ins will not with Web Applications in classic mode. Now that we understand the requirements and migration path, in the next section we'll look at how to migrate Service Applications from SharePoint 2013 to SharePoint 2016.

Migrating Service Applications

The first step in learning how to migrate from SharePoint 2013 to SharePoint Server 2016 is to migrate Service Applications.

Managed Metadata Service Application

To migrate the Managed Metadata Service Application, the first thing you will need to do is to back up the Service Application database from SharePoint 2013, and restore it onto our SharePoint 2016 SQL Server. Once it's on the SQL Server, the way to upgrade the Managed Metadata Service Application is to create a new Service Application as we learned in Chapter 8, but specify the database we just brought over from SharePoint Server 2013. In our environment, we named this database `ManagedMetadataDB`, and we will create the Service Application with PowerShell as we learned in Chapter 8. To create the Service Application, use the `New-SPMetadataServiceApplication` with the database name we restored from SharePoint Server 2013. This is the cmdlet that we have used in our environment. We have also created the Service Application proxy using the `New-SPMetadataServiceApplicationProxy` cmdlet.

```
$sa = New-SPMetadataServiceApplication -Name "Managed Metadata Service"
-DatabaseName "ManagedMetadataDB" -ApplicationPool "SharePoint Web Services Default"
-SyndicationErrorReportEnabled

New-SPMetadataServiceApplicationProxy -Name "Managed Metadata Service Proxy"
-ServiceApplication $sa -DefaultProxyGroup -ContentTypePushdownEnabled
-DefaultKeywordTaxonomy -DefaultSiteCollectionTaxonomy
```

By Migrating the Service Application database, you ensure that the term IDs do not change; therefore, all the connections between the content migrated and the terms will remain intact.

Search Service Application

The next Service Application we will migrate to SharePoint 2016 is the Search Service Application. The Search Service Application has four databases; however, we only need to get the Administration database from the old SharePoint, and restore it on our SharePoint 2016 SQL Server.

SharePoint has a PowerShell cmdlet that we will use named `Restore-SPEnterpriseSearchServiceAp plication,` which takes the name of your old Administration database, as well as the database server with the Service Application name and Application Pool. SharePoint will then create a Search Service Application from your database, which will keep your content sources, Search Center settings, Search Schema and crawl rules from your SharePoint 2013 Search Service Application. This Service Application will also keep the same crawl account, however, and we recommend having different crawl accounts between your farms; therefore, make sure to change afterward.

Make sure to run the following script on a server running the Search MinRole role. We will first get the local Search Service Instance, and then save it into a variable called $si.

```
$si = Get-SPEnterpriseSearchServiceInstance -local
```

Afterward, we will create the Search Service Application using the Restore-SPEnterpriseSear chServiceApplication cmdlet and specifying the database we have restored, in this case it's named SharePoint_2013_Search.

```
$sa = Restore-SPEnterpriseSearchServiceApplication -Name 'SearchServiceApplication'
-applicationpool "SharePoint Web Services Default" -databasename SharePoint_2013_Search
-databaseserver spag.corp.learn-sp2016.com -AdminSearchServiceInstance $si
```

Lastly, we will create a new Search Service Application Proxy, and assign it to the Service Application that we just created.

```
New-SPEnterpriseSearchServiceApplicationProxy -Name "Search Service Application Proxy"
-SearchApplication $sa
```

You have now migrated your Service Application from SharePoint 2013, to SharePoint Server 2016. Note that you will need to define the Search Service Application topology by using PowerShell. We have learned how to do so in Chapter 6.

User Profile Service Application

The User Profile Service Application migration process is a bit different due to the fact that the User Profile Synchronization service is not built in SharePoint anymore, but has been moved to Microsoft Identity Manager (MIM), which is an external component. Luckily, Microsoft Identity Manager is the successor of Forefront Identity Manager (FIM), which is what the User Profile Synchronization Service is built on. Since the technology between MIM and FIM is similar, migrating the data is a fairly easy process.

The first thing we have to do is backup two out of the three User Profile Databases from SharePoint Server 2013. We need to backup the Social database as well as the Profile database. There is no use of bringing the Sync database over to SharePoint 2016 since the mappings between properties and Active Directory are not in SharePoint anymore, and we will move them to MIM a bit later in this section.

We will then create a new User Profile Service Application by using the New-SPProfileServiceApplication cmdlet as learned in Chapter 7, and specify the name of those two databases in the parameters as well as a name for the Sync database. Since this database does not exist, SharePoint will create it. The cmdlet we used in our environment is the following:

```
$sa = New-SPProfileServiceApplication -Name "User Profile Service Application"
-applicationpool "SharePoint Web Services Default" -ProfileDBName 'Profile_DB_2013'
-SocialDBName 'Social_DB_2013' -ProfileSyncDBName 'Sync_DB'
```

We then need to create Service Application Proxy by using the following cmdlet.

```
New-SPProfileServiceApplicationProxy -Name "User Profile Service Application Proxy"
-ServiceApplication $sa -DefaultProxyGroup
```

With the Service Application in place, we will now need to transfer the synchronization configuration between the User Profile Synchronization service, and Microsoft Identity Manager (MIM).

■ **Note**   If you plan to use Active Directory Import to synchronize user profiles in your SharePoint 2016 environment, you do not need to do this step. Read Chapter 7 for more information about the differences between Microsoft Identity Manager and Active Directory Import.

Log on the SharePoint 2013 server that is currently running the User Profile Synchronization Service as a Farm Administrator, which is also a Local Administrator on that SharePoint server. Once on the server, navigate to C:\Program Files\Microsoft Office Servers\15.0\Synchronization Service\UIShell and open miisclient.exe. On the top left, click File and then Export Server Configuration as seen in Figure 15-2.

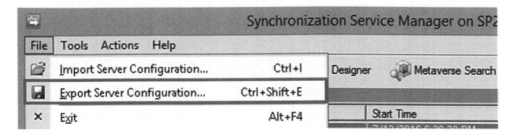

Figure 15-2. *Export Server Configuration*

When the export is completed, copy the folder with the XML files on the server on which you have installed Microsoft Identity Manager. Installing and Configuring MIM is already covered in Chapter 7, so we will continue after the installation is done, and the required scripts are copied onto the MIM Server. Open PowerShell as an administrator, and the first thing you will have to do is import the SharePoint Sync Module with the following PowerShell cmdlet:

```
Import-Module C:\SharePointSync\SharePointSync.psm1 –Force
```

We then need to run the ConvertTo-SharePointEcma2 cmdlet, and pass it the folder we have copied from SharePoint 2013. In our case, the configuration files are stored in the C:\SharePointSync\Config2013 folder, and we ran the following PowerShell cmdlet.

```
ConvertTo-SharePointEcma2 -Path C:\SharePointSync\Config2013 –Verbose
```

After it finishes, we will need to open the Synchronization Service Manager, either from the start menu, or simply using the Start-SynchronizationServiceManager cmdlet. From the top left of the MIM window, click File and then Import Server Configuration as seen in Figure 15-3.

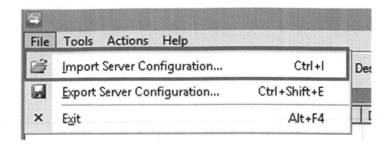

Figure 15-3. *Import Server Configuration*

Once you select the folder and the import starts, the tool will prompt you for information that applies to the new SharePoint farm as well as the passwords. We have learned about those parameters as well as how to start the profile synchronization in Chapter 7.

If you used MySites in SharePoint Server 2013, all the social activities have been migrated with the Social Database of the User Profile Service Application, but you will also need to migrate the MySites content databases to SharePoint 2016 using the technique we will learn later in this chapter.

Add-ins

SharePoint Add-ins (Apps) were a new development method introduced with SharePoint Server 2013 and your company might have taken advantage of this development method to deploy solutions onto your SharePoint sites. We have already covered how to configure Add-ins in Chapter 5, and all the DNS setup as well as configuring the Add-in URLs needs to be done before continuing this step.

■ **Note**   Your Add-in URL doesn't have to be the same in SharePoint 2016 as it is in SharePoint 2013.

From the SharePoint Server 2013 farm, we will need to back up the databases of both the App Management Service Application as well as the Subscription Service Application and restore them on the SharePoint Server 2016 farm database server.

We will then create those Service Applications as learned in Chapter 5, and specify to use the name of the restored databases. We will first create the Subscription Service Application and Proxy with the following PowerShell cmdlets:

```
$SubscriptionSA = New-SPSubscriptionSettingsServiceApplication -ApplicationPool "SharePoint
Web Services Default" -Name "Subscription Settings Service Application" -DatabaseName
SharePoint_2013_SubscriptionSettings

$proxySub = New-SPSubscriptionSettingsServiceApplicationProxy -ServiceApplication
$SubscriptionSA
```

Afterward, we will create the App Management Service Application and its proxy using the following cmdlets:

```
$AppManagementSA = New-SPAppManagementServiceApplication -ApplicationPool "SharePoint Web
Services Default" -Name "App Management Service Application" -DatabaseName SharePoint_2013_
AppManagement

$proxyApp = New-SPAppManagementServiceApplicationProxy -ServiceApplication $AppManagementSA
```

On the App Licenses page in the Central Administration, you will see the Add-ins you have installed, as well as the license types that you have as seen in Figure 15-4.

Figure 15-4. *SharePoint 2016 App Licenses*

When restoring the content databases that included those Add-ins, the Add-ins will be installed and you will be able to use them as you did in your SharePoint 2013 environment.

With the Service Applications migrated, the next step is to learn how to migrate our SharePoint sites from SharePoint 2013 to SharePoint 2016.

Migrating Content

Migrating Content from SharePoint Server 2013 to SharePoint Server 2016 is done by migrating databases from SharePoint 2013 to SharePoint 2016, and attaching them to a Web Application. The first step is to identify what Site Collections you want to migrate from SharePoint 2013 to SharePoint 2016. You can migrate all databases in a Web Application or particular databases containing particular Site Collections; the important thing to remember is that content migrations are done at the Content Database level. Therefore, if you only want to migrate a few Site Collections from your Web Application, make sure to group them into the same content database. You can move Site Collections between databases in the same Web Application by using the `Move-SPSite` PowerShell cmdlet. Something to remember is that if you only migrate certain Site Collections within a Web Application, you might have to use a different URL in SharePoint 2016 in order to keep the rest of the Site Collections accessible.

Backup the database from the SQL Server in use by SharePoint and restore it with the name you wish on the SQL Server in use by SharePoint Server 2016 as seen in Figure 15-5. The database does not need to exist prior to restoration, and you can enter a new name for this database in the Database field.

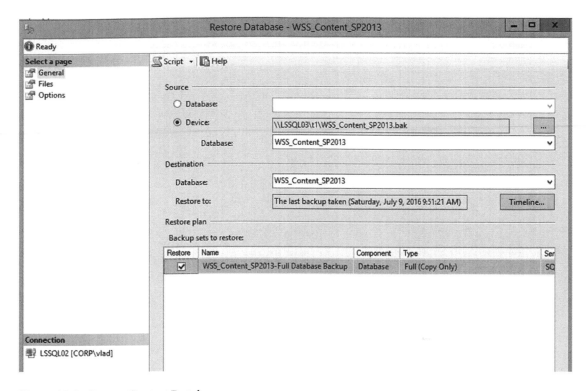

Figure 15-5. *Restore Content Database*

After the database is restored, create your Web Application on SharePoint Server 2016 if you have not already done so. When creating your Web Application, you need to create a new Content Database as well, but you can give it a temporary name as we will delete that database after the Web Application is created. We have covered how to create Web Applications in Chapter 13, and for this test we have created a Web Application with the URL https://intranet.learn-sp2016.com and a database called "WSS_TempDB." To remove this database, we will use the Remove-SPContentDatabase PowerShell cmdlet. To remove all the content databases from the intranet.learn-sp2016 Web Application, we need to run the following cmdlet:

```
Get-SPContentDatabase -WebApplication https://intranet.learn-sp2016.com |
Dismount-SPContentDatabase
```

Our Web Application is now ready to mount the Content Database restored to the SQL Server in use by SharePoint Server 2016. Before attaching the database, we can use the Test-SPContentDatabase PowerShell cmdlet. To test our database against the intranet.learn-sp2016.com Web Application, we would run the following cmdlet.

```
Test-SPContentDatabase -Name WSS_Content_SP2013 -WebApplication https://intranet.learn-
sp2016.com
```

This will give us a report of the possible problems we may encounter when doing the migration. Some examples are Missing Features in the SharePoint 2016 farm that were referenced in the SharePoint 2013 site collection. The report will show both errors and warnings, as well as inform us if the error is "Upgrade Blocking." If the error is Upgrade Blocking, it means that SharePoint might not be able to upgrade this database to SharePoint 2016. If the error is not error blocking, SharePoint will be able to upgrade the database, but your users might get unexpected behaviors when navigating to parts of the site. For our example seen in Figure 15-6, our database currently has Power View and SSRS features; however, those features do not exist in the Web Application.

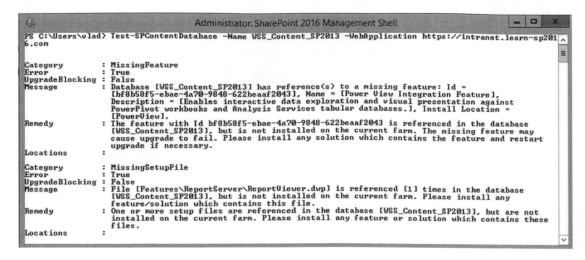

Figure 15-6. *Test-SPContentDatabase Results*

■ **Note**   The Test-SPContentDatabase will not output an error if your SharePoint 2013 sites contain the Tags and Notes feature, which is absent in SharePoint 2016.

The two choices we have to avoid those issues are either to remove those features from SharePoint 2013. This would be a valid option when we would not use those features anymore in SharePoint 2016. Since we want to use both PowerPivot and SSRS in SharePoint 2016, we will enable those features on the Web Application before attaching the database to the SharePoint 2016 farm. When everything is ready and the Test-SPContentDatabse does not return any more blocking errors, we can proceed with the upgrade. The upgrade is done automatically when you attach the content database to the Web Application. This is done via PowerShell with the Mount-SPContentDatabase cmdlet. The parameters are the same as the Test-SPContentDatabase cmdlet, the database name and the Web Application. To attach our content database, we ran the following cmdlet.

```
Mount-SPContentDatabase -Name WSS_Content_SP2013 -WebApplication https://intranet.learn-sp2016.com
```

PowerShell will output a warning that progress and details will be in the same location as your ULS log files as seen in Figure 15-7. The upgrade process creates two log files under the format:

- Upgrade-<date>-<guid>. Log

- Upgrade-<date>-<guid>-**error**. Log

Figure 15-7. *Mount-SPContentDatabase*

The error file will show any errors that might have occurred during the upgrade process. The duration of the upgrade will depend on the number of Site Collections you have in your database, as well as the amount of content in those sites.

After the database is successfully attached, you will be able to navigate to the Site Collections you have migrated and test out the functionality of the site. Permissions on the SharePoint site and content will not have changed between SharePoint 2013 and SharePoint 2016.

We have now learned how to migrate content, as well as the most popular Service Applications from SharePoint Server 2013, to SharePoint Server 2016. Now, let's take a look in what order we should do those migrations.

Migration Order

It is recommended to always migrate your Service Applications before you migrate your Web Applications and SharePoint sites. The reason is that SharePoint content has references to Service Applications, and those references will be broken if the site will not be able to find the Service Application once it's restored.

Next Steps

In this chapter, we have learned how to migrate SharePoint sites and Service Applications to SharePoint Server 2016. In the next chapter, we will learn how to implement High Availability and Disaster Recovery for your SharePoint farm.

■ ■ ■

CHAPTER 16

Implementing High Availability and Disaster Recovery

SharePoint Server 2016 has a variety of options for High Availability and Disaster Recovery. We will examine the options available at the farm and SQL Server level, which will help you choose the most appropriate option for your business.

Unsupported Methods

SharePoint has a variety of methods of replication and recovery that are not supported by Microsoft. In this chapter, we will cover the supported methods, but it is important to note methods that are not supported by Microsoft in order to avoid them when implementing Disaster Recovery.

Farms must have a 99% 1 ms round-trip time on average over 10 minutes. Exceeding this design limitation may cause object synchronization issues, including timer job failures. Farms also must have 1 Gbps connectivity between all farm members and SQL Servers that are serving the farm in a read-write capacity or are in a synchronous form of replication with the read-write SQL Server. Overall, the limitation for this means each farm member or SQL Server in a synchronous replica mode must be within approximately 186 miles or 300 km.

Virtual replication, which is either replicating an underlying virtual machine (such as using Hyper-V Replica or third-party products) is not supported as there may be consistency issues upon bringing the Disaster Recovery environment online. This is especially important for the Search index and timer jobs. The exclusion to this rule is Azure Site Recovery, which does support replication of virtual machines into Azure for the purposes of Disaster Recovery.

Similar to virtual machine replication, backing up online virtual machines and saving them to tape or transporting the backup via other means is not supported.

SQL Server High Availability

SharePoint Server 2016 supports a variety of options for SQL Server high availability. These include SQL Clustering, Database Mirroring, and AlwaysOn Availability Groups. Each has their strengths and weaknesses. Let's look at each one individually.

SQL Clustering

SQL Clustering is a common form of high availability where the goal is to have rapid failover when the SQL Server acting as the primary fails within the environment. SharePoint fully supports all databases residing on a SQL Cluster.

The strengths of SQL Clustering include the ability to use SQL Clustering with the Standard Edition of SQL Server, as well as the Enterprise edition. SQL Clustering also uses a set of shared disks to store data, which reduces storage costs. As SharePoint connects to the virtual name of the cluster, a failover of SQL is only a short and minor interruption of service.

A significant weakness with SQL Clustering is the shared disk subsystem. If the shared storage becomes unavailable, while the cluster may remain online, SharePoint will be offline.

Database Mirroring

Database Mirroring was introduced in SQL Server 2005, and while present in SQL Server 2014 and 2016, is now considered a deprecated technology. With that in mind, Database Mirroring is an effective way to provide high availability for SharePoint. The Database Mirroring failover partner must be within 1 ms and have 1Gbps connectivity to the SharePoint farm; however, it does not need to be within the same building as long as these two requirements are met. Database Mirroring involves configuring two servers with automatic or manual failover. Automatic failover requires a witness, either a file share or a SQL Server witness (SQL Server Express may be used as a witness). This is a third server, often running at a remote site, or alongside the failover partner.

Database Mirroring also supports three modes of operation. High-Safety with Automatic failover is a topology where a witness is involved and transactions are first committed to the Failover Partner prior to the Principal Partner.

High-Safety without automatic failover is where transactions are still committed to the Failover Partner first, but the failover event is a manual process that requires administrator intervention.

The last operating mode, High-Performance Mode, is a mode primarily meant for replicating a database over a high latency network connection. In this mode, transactions are *not* guaranteed to make it to the Failover Partner server. Because of this, this mode cannot be used for SharePoint Failover purposes, but may be suitable in certain Disaster Recovery scenarios.

When creating SharePoint Content Databases or many of the SharePoint Service Application databases, one can specify a Failover Partner.

However, not all databases may be configured through the GUI to use a Failover Partner, *or* if you need to add a Failover Partner after the fact, you will need to set the Failover Partner SQL Server name via PowerShell. For example, our SharePoint Configuration database is named "Configuration." Here is how we would set the Failover Partner through the SharePoint Management Shell.

```
$db = Get-SPDatabase | ?{$_.Name -eq "Configuration"}
$db.FailoverServer = "SQL02"
$db.Update()
```

It is up to SharePoint to detect that a failover has taken place. It does this by first querying the primary partner, followed up by the failover partner. If the primary is unavailable, but the failover is available, SharePoint then leverages the failover partner.

Database Mirroring may also not be automatic. Without a witness, Database Mirroring failover is a manual process. This significantly increases downtime for SharePoint while the databases are being failed over.

Lastly, with Database Mirroring, each database is treated as a singular object to failover. It is possible to have, for example, the Configuration database on one of the failover partners while a Content Database resides on the other failover partner. While this configuration would be uncommon, the fact that databases are treated independently of one another does increase maintenance investment into using Database Mirroring.

AlwaysOn Availability Groups

AlwaysOn Availability Groups are what were used throughout this book to provide high availability to the SharePoint databases. The configuration involves both Microsoft Clustering Services along with SQL Server AlwaysOn Availability Groups. Along with a witness server, provided by a file server or another SQL Server, failovers are seamless and quick. As with SQL Clustering, clients like SharePoint connect to AlwaysOn through a virtual name or fully qualified domain name.

With AlwaysOn Availability Groups, the storage space required is doubled. Each SQL Server must have an appropriate amount of storage to store the data files and log files for each SQL database. This may significantly increase the cost of the SQL Server implementation. In addition to the storage expense, only SQL Server Enterprise supports AlwaysOn Availability Groups. While SQL Server 2016 does bring "Basic Availability Groups," this feature is not appropriate for a SharePoint farm as it only supports a single database within the Basic Availability Group.

AlwaysOn Availability Groups also provide you with the ability to have additional Synchronous Availability Group members. Synchronous members are required for automatic failover for SharePoint. These members also have the same constraints of a 1 ms and 1Gbps network connection between the SharePoint farm and SQL Server. SQL Server 2014 allows for three synchronous replicas with two automatic failover synchronous replicas, while SQL Server 2016 allows for all three synchronous replicas to participate in automatic failover.

AlwaysOn Availability Groups do provide a function known as "read-only secondary" where read-only traffic is directed from the active member in the Availability Group to a secondary which is not serving write requests, but this function is not supported by SharePoint.

Disaster Recovery

Database Mirroring, AlwaysOn Availability Groups, and Log Shipping provide Disaster Recovery options for the SQL Server databases supporting the SharePoint farm. In this section, we will consider that the Disaster Recovery location is greater than 500 km away from the primary data center. This scenario prevents us from using synchronous connectivity to the remote SQL Server at the Disaster Recovery location.

Database Mirroring

Database Mirroring for Disaster Recovery involves adding a High-Performance Mode node to the existing SQL Server configuration. This member can coexist with a Database Mirroring High-Safety with or without automatic failover in place. As previously noted, failover to a High-Performance Mode partner is a manual process. Databases on this member will not be brought online automatically.

Log Shipping

Log Shipping is the shipping of transaction log backups from one SQL Server to another. The destination SQL Server then restores the transaction log backups to the target database. This method allows one to keep the databases up to date with additional replication options available outside of SQL Server. For example, it is possible to 'ship' a transaction log backup to a Windows file server, and using Distributed File Services (DFS-R), replicate the transaction log backup to a Windows file server in the Disaster Recovery datacenter, and have the DR SQL Server restore the transaction log backup to the destination database. This eliminates the SQL Server from being responsible for the replication of the transaction log backup. DFS-R also provides a faster and more reliable replication mechanism.

AlwaysOn Availability Groups

AlwaysOn Availability Groups provide the ability to add an asynchronous remote partner SQL Server to your Availability Group. This allows a highly available local Availability Group to also have a single SQL Server in a Disaster Recovery location. Unlike with the synchronous local Availability Group, the remote SQL Server must be set to Asynchronous mode. This mode has a manual failover process. This is the method we will be using in our Disaster Recovery example.

To add the SQL Server to the AlwaysOn Availability Group that will be the asynchronous member, duplicate the volume and directory structure for the SQL databases and log files. This is required to add the SQL server to the Availability Group. In our example, the M: and L: drives will be created using NTFS with 64Kb clusters.

Add the Windows Failover Clustering role along with the .NET 3.5 Framework feature. This is required to add the server to the AlwaysOn Availability Group. Using the Failover Cluster manager, add the new SQL Server to the existing Failover Cluster; we're using LSSPSQLClus in our environment. As shown in Figure 16-1, add the new SQL Server to the Failover Cluster.

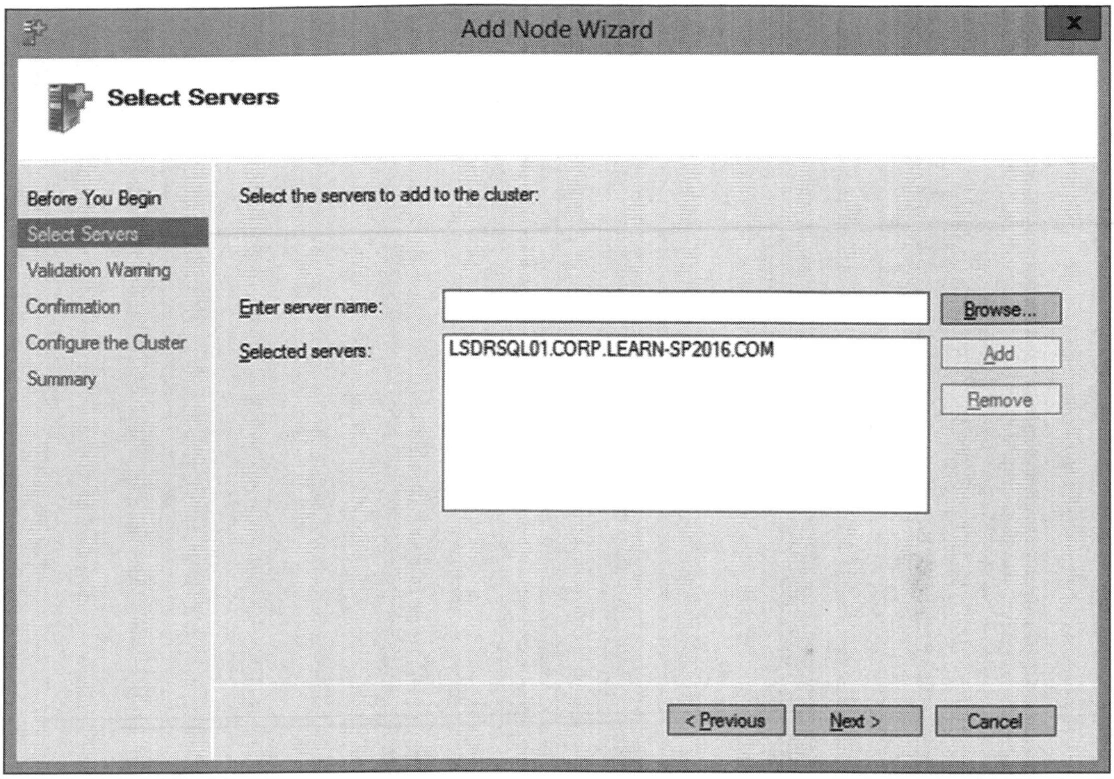

CHAPTER 16 ■ IMPLEMENTING HIGH AVAILABILITY AND DISASTER RECOVERY

Figure 16-1. *Adding LSDRSQL01 to the existing Failover Cluster*

Install the same version and patch level for the new SQL Server, SQL 2014 with Service Pack 1 for this environment. As with the previous servers, use the same Service Account as the Synchronous members of the Availability Group.

Add the appropriate Service Principal Names (SPN) to the existing SQL Server Service Account. The Disaster Recovery server name in our example is LSDRSQL01, and the SPNs will match.

```
Setspn -U -S MSSQLSvc/LSDRSQL01:1433 CORP\s-sql
Setspn -U -S MSSQLSvc/LSDRSQL01.corp.learn-sp2016.com:1433 CORP\s-sql
```

Using the SQL Server Configuration Manager or SQL PowerShell, enable AlwaysOn, as shown in Figure 16-2, then restart the SQL Server services as required.

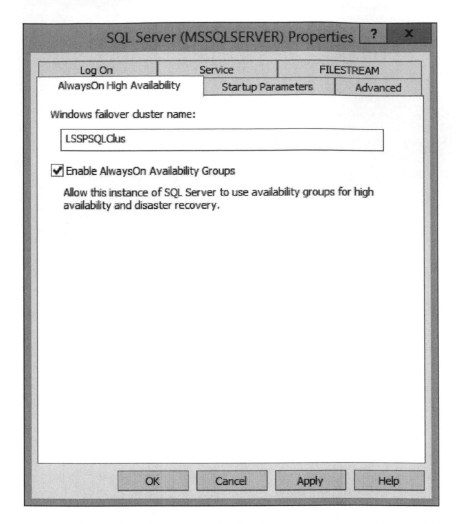

Figure 16-2. *Enabling AlwaysOn Availability Groups for the Disaster Recovery SQL Server*

Using SQL Server Management Studio or SQL PowerShell, add a new Availability Group Listener IP Address to the existing Availability Group Listener, SPAG, as shown in Figure 16-3.

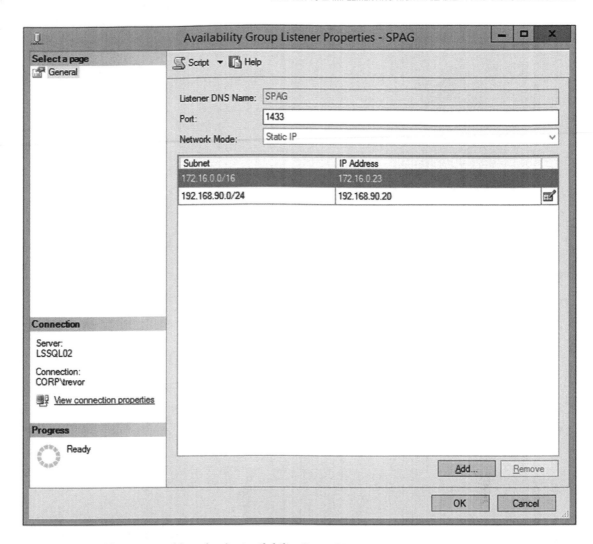

Figure 16-3. *Add a new IP address for the Availability Group Listener*

This new IP address must be on the same subnet as the Disaster Recovery SQL Server. This can be used by clients when a failover occurs, but is not relevant for SharePoint as SharePoint cannot span large distances.

Add the new server to the Availability Group in Asynchronous mode with no Automatic Failover, as shown in Figure 16-4. Readable Secondary is not applicable for SharePoint as SharePoint does not support Read-Intent.

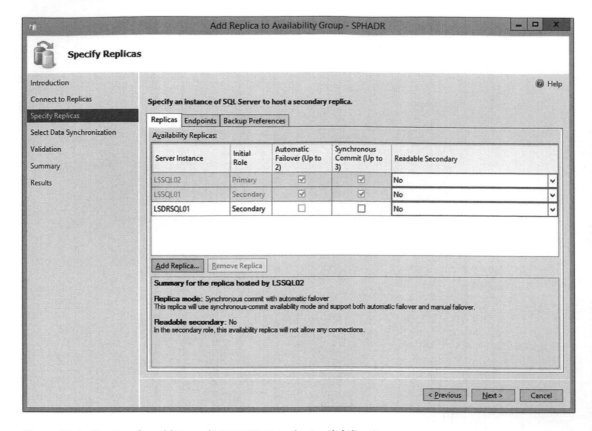

Figure 16-4. Starting the addition of LSDRSQL01 to the Availability Group

For the Endpoint, change the Endpoint Name to a value that fits the environment. In this case, the Endpoint Name is set to SPDRHADR, as shown in Figure 16-5.

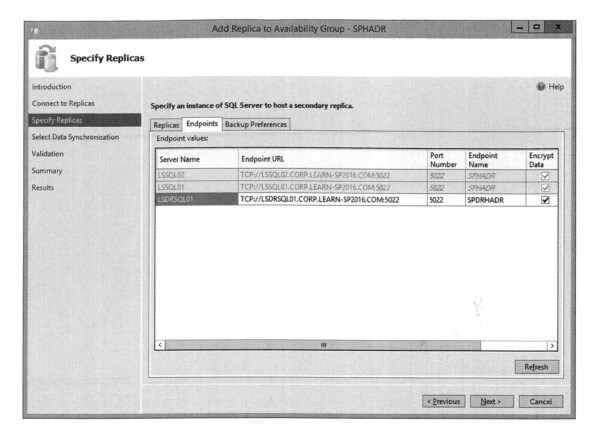

Figure 16-5. *Changing the Endpoint Name to a new value for the Disaster Recovery SQL Server*

The Backup Preference will be to exclude the Disaster Recovery replica from taking preference for database backups, as shown in Figure 16-6.

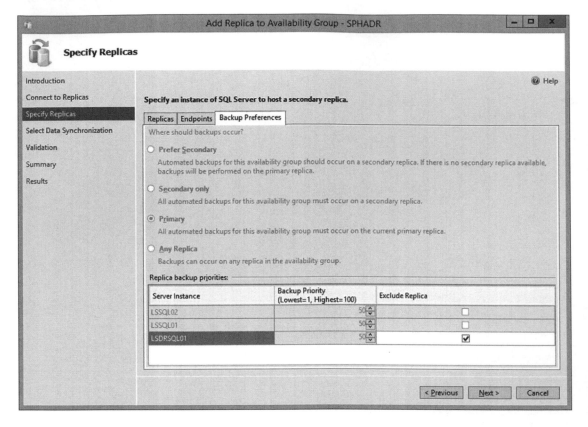

Figure 16-6. *Removing preference for backups from LSDRSQL01*

Make note that we have various databases in the Availability Group which are not candidates for replication: primarily the Search database as well as the Administration and Configuration databases. The State Service database is also not a good candidate for replication to the Disaster Recovery environment. This is due to the transient nature of the data. In previous versions of SharePoint, the User Profile Service Application Sync database also was not a candidate for being part of the Availability Group; however, in SharePoint Server 2016, this database is empty and will have minimal impact on the Availability Group.

If it is important to not synchronize databases such as the Search, Administration, or Configuration databases as part of the Availability Group, you must place them in a separate Availability Group on the two nodes in Synchronous replication. This allows you to synchronize just the databases that you require. In a large environment, this is good practice in order to have multiple Availability Groups, separating out even various Content Databases across Availability Groups for independent replication.

■ **Tip**   Microsoft provides a list of databases that support synchronous and/or asynchronous commit, as well as databases that do not support replication on TechNet, at `https://technet.microsoft.com/en-us/library/jj841106.aspx`.

Once the databases have been replicated to the new SQL Server over Asynchronous replication, the Disaster Recovery SQL Server will show as Healthy in the Availability Group dashboard, as shown in Figure 16-7. Note that the databases will remain in a 'Synchronizing' state at all times, unless an error occurs during the synchronization, or the production SQL Servers go offline.

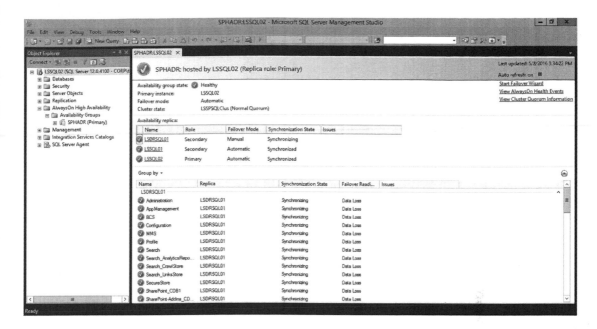

Figure 16-7. LSDRSQL01 is now successfully synchronizing from the primary SQL Server

Create a new SharePoint farm at the remote location. In our environment, this will be named LSDRSP01 and consist of just a single SharePoint server; however, you may add as many SharePoint servers in any desired configuration as required.

Decide on if you will use Service Accounts unique to the Disaster Recovery environment, or if you will use the same accounts as the production environment. If using new accounts for the Disaster Recovery environment, the accounts must be added to the replicated SQL databases with the appropriate permissions. In addition, Kerberos cannot be enabled as two separate accounts in Active Directory may not have the same SPN – this means the Disaster Recovery farm would be limited to using NTLM authentication. If using the same accounts as production, permissions are automatically added when attaching the SharePoint databases to the new farm; however, make note of any password changes that may take place on the account in Active Directory. The password must also be changed on the Disaster Recovery farm, independently of the production farm.

When creating the Disaster Recovery farm, do not point at the database at the AlwaysOn Listener, but instead at Disaster Recovery SQL Server directly. Alternatively, use a SQL alias using cliconfig.exe on the SharePoint Server for better mobility of databases should the need arise to change the Disaster Recovery SQL Server.

When building the new Disaster Recovery SharePoint farm, the Administration and Configuration database names will be unique as these are unique to the farm. We will also create unique Search databases, although should there be extensive Search customizations at the Search Service level, it may be advantageous to replicate the Search Administration database to preserve the schema.

Import the production SSL certificates into the Disaster Recovery SharePoint server.

As this environment will be similar to the production environment for security purposes, Kerberos will be enabled on Central Admin. As the Central Admin URL is unique to the farm, make sure to add an SPN for it.

```
Setspn -U -S https://dr-ca.corp.learn-sp2016.com CORP\s-farm
```

Configure any remaining required settings in Central Administration, such as Outgoing E-mail, Rights Management Services configuration, and so forth.

Farm solutions must be deployed to the Disaster Recovery farm separate from the production farm. Keep farm solutions up to date as they are deployed to the production farm in order to have a well-prepared Disaster Recovery farm.

The Web Applications will use the *same* URL as in production, along with having Kerberos enabled. Because we are using the same Service Account, no changes are required. When creating the Web Applications in the Disaster Recovery farm, do not use the existing Content Database names. Instead, use a temporary Content Database name, as shown in Figure 16-8.

Web Application

Select a web application.

Web Application: https://sharepoint.learn-sp2016.com/ ▾

Database Name and Authentication

Use of the default database server and database name is recommended for most cases. Refer to the administrator's guide for advanced scenarios where specifying database information is required.

Use of Windows authentication is strongly recommended. To use SQL authentication, specify the credentials which will be used to connect to the database.

Database Server

> SQL01

Database Name

> WSS_Content

Database authentication

◉ Windows authentication (recommended)

○ SQL authentication

Account

> _____

Password

> _____

Failover Server

You can choose to associate a database with a specific failover server that is used in conjuction with SQL Server database mirroring.

Failover Database Server

> SQL02

Figure 16-8. Creating a temporary Content Database, WSS_Content, which will be deleted once the Web Application has been created

Once the Web Applications have been created, drop and delete the temporary Content Databases. Then, using Central Administration or the Mount-SPContentDatabase cmdlet, mount the existing databases. They will be in a read-only mode until a disaster occurs. Because of this, the sites contained within the read-only Content Databases will display a banner on top indicating so, as shown in Figure 16-9.

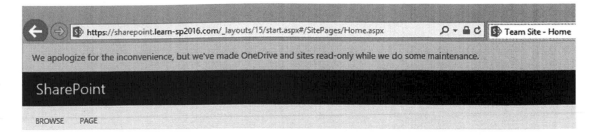

Figure 16-9. *While the Content Database is in read-only mode, Site Collections will display a maintenance banner*

When creating new Site Collections in a database that is replicated to the Disaster Recovery farm, make note that in the Disaster Recovery farm, the Site Map will not automatically be updated. To update the Site Map manually, run the following cmdlet, passing in the Web Application URL.

```
Get-SPContentDatabase -WebApplication https://sharepoint.learn-sp2016.com |
% {$_.RefreshSitesInConfigurationDatabase()}
```

When creating Service Applications consuming the read-only databases, use the same database name. For example, with the User Profile Service Application or Secure Store Service, specify the database name for that Service Application that resides on the SQL Server. The Service Application will successfully create, although will not be fully functional. As an example, the User Profile Service Application cannot be managed and the Secure Store Service will also run into an error when attempting to manage Secure Store keys. When the databases are changed from a read-only to an online mode, these options will become available.

The Managed Metadata Service Application is unique in that it cannot consume the read-only database. Unfortunately, one must wait for a failover to be invoked prior to creating the Managed Metadata Service Application using the existing database.

For the Search Service Application, Search may crawl read-only content. The Web Application URLs can continue to be part of the Content Source for Search to crawl. Implement hosts file entries on the Search server to properly direct the crawler to the local SharePoint server.

■ **Tip**   SharePoint Search Disaster Recovery is a complex topic: refer to the TechNet article at `https://technet.microsoft.com/en-us/library/dn715769.aspx`.

Initiating a Disaster Recovery Failover

As the Disaster Recovery SQL Server must be failed over manually, as soon as the link between production has been severed, the databases will enter a read-write state, showing "Not Synchronized" in the SQL Server Management Studio, as shown in Figure 16-10. This means the databases are now in a read-write mode, allowing the Disaster Recovery farm to be brought online.

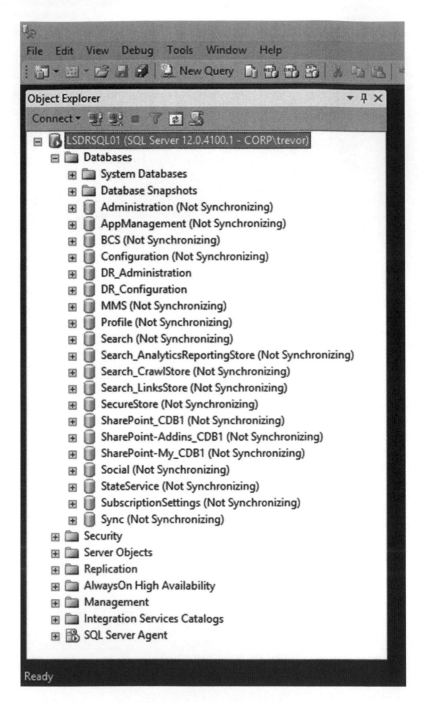

Figure 16-10. *Databases have entered a Not Synchronizing state, indicating they are ready for read-write operations*

The Managed Metadata Service Application can be created with the existing Managed Metadata Service database. If the production environment is a loss, the databases can be removed from the Availability Group on the Disaster Recovery SQL Server. With a change in DNS for the Web Applications, SharePoint should be fully functional at this point.

As we took only the necessary databases to our Disaster Recovery farm, this particular failover is relatively simple. But Disaster Recovery is a complex topic, and farms that are significantly more complex will take additional time, post-failover configuration, and potentially even troubleshooting to get the Disaster Recovery farm into a usable state.

Cloud Disaster Recovery

A Cloud Disaster Recovery is the concept of using an Infrastructure as a Service provider, such as Microsoft Azure, to host Virtual Machines in the Cloud for the Disaster Recovery farm. There are a few valid ways to achieve Disaster Recovery with Azure.

The first two methods are similar to existing On-Premises Disaster Recovery strategies. Both log shipping and AlwaysOn Availability Groups in Asynchronous mode serve as strategies which can be used with an Azure Site-to-Site VPN or ExpressRoute configuration.

Another method is to use physical or Virtual Machine–based backups. The Virtual Machines may reside on either Hyper-V or VMware ESXi. Using the Azure Site Recovery, an administrator can *replicate* an entire farm from On-Premises to Azure Infrastructure-as-a-Service (IaaS). This is the only supported product by Microsoft to perform full farm replication from one point to another. The caveat of this solution is that post-failover, you must clear the Configuration Cache on each SharePoint Server, as well as either establish a new Search Service Application *or* restore the Search Service Application from backup, for example, using Windows Azure Backup.

Next Steps

Now that you've learned how to create a simple Disaster Recovery environment, we will take a look at the process of patching SharePoint Server 2016, including how to leverage Zero Downtime Patching.

CHAPTER 17

Patching SharePoint Server 2016

SharePoint Server 2016 has significantly improved the application of patches, along with the size of patches. This provides a faster, more reliable experience for SharePoint Administrators.

The Basics of Patching

Each patch will be delivered in an executable format. There will typically be one or two executables per month, called Public Updates. The primary executable is called "sts" while the secondary is "wssloc." The "sts" patch is the primary patch file, while the wssloc patch file contains locale-specific files for all languages. In Figure 17-1, we are installing the base patch, sts.msp.

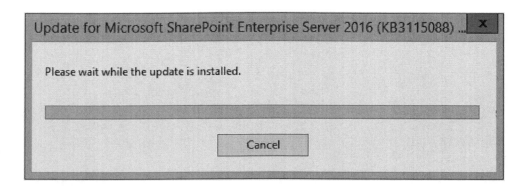

Figure 17-1. *Beginning the installation of sts2016-kb3115088-fullfile-x64-glb.exe*

When the base patch has been installed, install the locale-specific patch.

SharePoint does not require a specific order for servers to patch; for example, the server running Central Administration does not need to be patched first. Identify the order that suits your farm the best as installing the binaries involves downtime for each particular SharePoint server.

Patching may require a reboot of the SharePoint Server, as shown in Figure 17-2. By having two or more SharePoint Servers running the same services, SharePoint Servers can be rebooted without incurring any downtime for end users, provided proper availability scenarios are in place, for example, at least two web servers which can be rotated in and out of a load balancer.

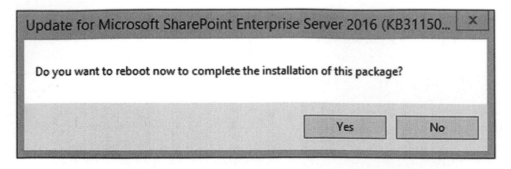

Figure 17-2. Many SharePoint Server 2016 patches require reboots in order to complete

Microsoft is making a "best effort" to prevent schema upgrades from being required; however, each SharePoint Server may be noted as "Upgrade Available" or "Upgrade Required" after installing a patch, as shown in Figure 17-3. If you see either of these messages, either one or more databases requires an upgrade, or the SharePoint Server requires the Configuration Wizard or psconfig.exe to be executed.

Server	SharePoint Products Installed	Role	Compliant		Services Running	Status
LSSPAP01	Microsoft SharePoint Server 2016	Application	✓	Yes	App Management Service Business Data Connectivity Service Central Administration Claims to Windows Token Service Managed Metadata Web Service Microsoft SharePoint Foundation Incoming E-Mail Microsoft SharePoint Foundation Subscription Settings Service Microsoft SharePoint Foundation Web Application Microsoft SharePoint Foundation Workflow Timer Service Secure Store Service User Profile Service	Upgrade Available
LSSPAP02	Microsoft SharePoint Server 2016	Application	✓	Yes	App Management Service Business Data Connectivity Service Central Administration Claims to Windows Token Service	Upgrade Available

Figure 17-3. Upgrade Required indicates the Configuration Wizard must be run

If using psconfig.exe, run it from the SharePoint Management Shell (which puts psconfig.exe in the PATH). Use the following command.

```
psconfig -cmd upgrade -inplace b2b -wait -cmd applicationcontent -install -cmd
installfeatures -cmd secureresources
```

Otherwise, use the Configuration Wizard to complete the upgrade, as shown in Figures 17-4, 17-5, and 17-6.

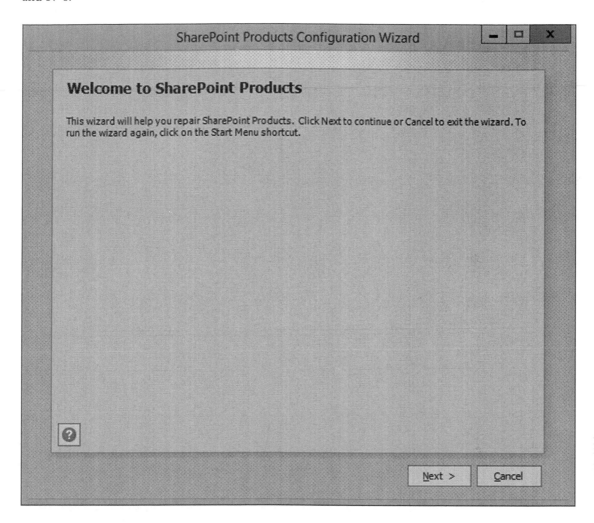

Figure 17-4. Initiating the Configuration Wizard

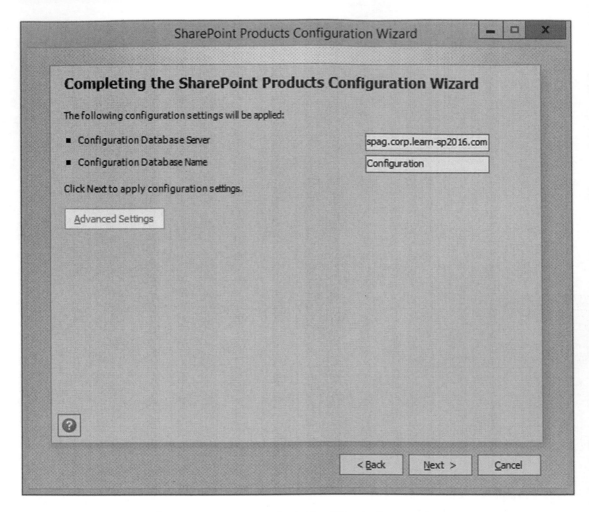

Figure 17-5. *Completing the Configuration Wizard, which will begin the upgrade*

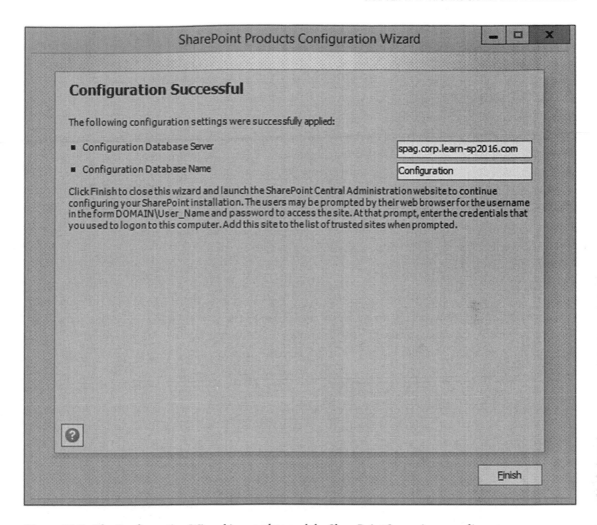

Figure 17-6. *The Configuration Wizard is complete and the SharePoint Server is now online*

With the completion of a SharePoint Server patch installation and configuration, let's examine the log files that provide additional information with the patching process. These logs will also provide information on any errors that may have taken place during the installation or configuration process.

Upgrade Log Files

There are two primary log files to work with. The PSConfig file and the Upgrade log file. PSConfig file is the format of PSCDiagnostics_mm_dd_YYYY_HH_mm_ss_fff while the Upgrade log file has a format of Upgrade-YYYYmmdd-HHmmss-fff-<SPUpgradeSession_GUID>.log ('fff' stands for millisecond). As an example, the PSCDiagnostics log file might be named PSCDiagnostics_03_20_2016_14_02_39_180.log, which ran on the 20th of March 3rd at 2:02:39.180 PM.

Log Files are located within the ULS log directory. In the environment outlined in this book, that is E:\ULS for each farm member, while by default, it would be located at %CommonProgramFiles%\Microsoft Shared\Web Server Extensions\15\LOGS\.

If an error is encountered during the upgrade process, there will also be an Upgrade-YYYYmmdd-HHmmss-fff-<SPUpgradeSession_GUID>-error.log file. This will help identify what errors and corrective actions need to be taken to successfully complete an upgrade. The ULS logs can provide additional details about any errors, as well.

Unlike previous versions of SharePoint, many patches will not increment the Farm Build number. Instead, under Upgrade and Migration in Central Administration, go to Check product and patch installation status to see the current state of patched products. In Figure 17-7, we can see that Microsoft SharePoint Foundation 2016 Core has been patched twice. The base build, 16.0.4306.1002, was patched by build 16.0.4336.1000. 16.0.4336.1000 was subsequently patched by 16.0.4339.1000, superseding 16.0.4336.1000.

LSSPAP01	Microsoft SharePoint Foundation 2016 Core	16.0.4306.1002	Installed
LSSPAP01	Update for Microsoft Office 2016 (KB2345678) (sts.msp 16.0.4339.1000)	16.0.4339.1000	Installed
LSSPAP01	Update for Microsoft Office 2016 (KB2345678) (sts.msp 16.0.4336.1000)	16.0.4336.1000	Superseded

***Figure 17-7.** Patches applied to LSSPAP01*

As with any SharePoint highly available farm, performing highly available upgrades is key. We will take a look at a strategy to maintain the high availability of the farm while patching.

Long Patch Times

SharePoint Server 2013 and 2016 suffer from long binary installation times. This is due to running services on the SharePoint server where in-use files cannot be replaced. To reduce the amount of time a patch takes to install, shut down the following services prior to running the patch.

SharePoint Timer Service

SharePoint Search Service

SharePoint Search HostController Service

IIS (use iisreset /stop)

Once the patches have been installed, restart the services to bring them online.

■ **Tip** Additional information is available from Russ Maxwell at https://blogs.msdn.microsoft.com/russmax/2013/04/01/why-sharepoint-2013-cumulative-update-takes-5-hours-to-install/.

■ **Note** Trevor Seward has updated Russ Maxwell's script. The updated script is available for SharePoint Server 2013 and 2016 at https://github.com/Nauplius/SharePoint-Patch-Script.

Highly Available Upgrades

To upgrade a farm without taking it offline, follow this upgrade procedure for SharePoint patches.

Identify each server and the assigned role. Only one server for a given role will be offline at any given time. In the environment outlined by this book, we have the following configuration, as shown in Table 17-1.

■ **Tip** Microsoft produced a video on the details of Zero Downtime Patching which also covers this process, available on TechNet at https://technet.microsoft.com/EN-US/library/mt767550(v=office.16).aspx.

Table 17-1. *Roles and Servers in the SharePoint Farm*

Application	WebFrontEnd	Search	DistributedCache
LSSPAP01	LSSPFE01	LSSPSR01	LSSPDC01
LSSPAP02	LSSPFE02	LSSPSR02	LSSPDC02

For the purposes of this environment, we will work out way down and across Table 17-1, starting with the Application servers and finishing with the Distributed Cache servers. But as noted, the order is not important. With the exception of special handling for Distributed Cache, the process will be as follows.

Run the sts patch. Do not restart if prompted. Run the next patch if applicable, wssloc. Restart if either patch prompted you to do so.

These patches may also be run silently by passing the /passive switch to the patch

```
sts2016-kb3115088-fullfile-x64-glb.exe /passive /norestart
wssloc2016-kb2920690-fullfile-x64-glb /passive /norestart
```

This will install the Sts and wssloc patches with a basic user interface and does not restart the computer. The patches are installed in the order specified. While a patch is being installed, one or more IIS Resets may occur. Restart the computer manually through the UI or by using the Restart-Computer cmdlet once the patch installations have completed.

■ **Tip** If you interrupt an MSP installation, IIS Application Pools or Sites may be in a Stopped state. Manually start them as required.

Once the server is back online, add it back to the Load Balancer. Note the status of the SharePoint server in Central Administration under Manage servers in farm.

As you can see in Figure 17-8, LSSPAP01 has been patched, but no further action is required. With a majority of SharePoint 2010 and 2013 patches, this would have indicated "Upgrade Required," which would prompt us to run the Configuration Wizard. As no schema upgrade has taken place, we do not need to perform that action.

Server	SharePoint Products Installed	Role	Compliant		Services Running	Status
LSSPAP01	Microsoft SharePoint Server 2016	Application	✓	Yes	App Management Service Business Data Connectivity Service Central Administration Claims to Windows Token Service Managed Metadata Web Service Microsoft SharePoint Foundation Incoming E-Mail Microsoft SharePoint Foundation Subscription Settings Service Microsoft SharePoint Foundation Web Application Microsoft SharePoint Foundation Workflow Timer Service Request Management Secure Store Service User Profile Service	No Action Required
LSSPAP02	Microsoft SharePoint Server 2016	Application	✓	Yes	App Management Service Business Data Connectivity Service Central Administration	Installation Required

Figure 17-8. *LSSPAP01 has been patched, and LSSPAP02 is prompting to install the same patch*

Moving onto LSSPAP02, repeat the preceding steps; take the server out of the Load Balancer, run prerequisiteinstaller.exe, install the patches, restart the server, then add it back to the Load Balancer.

LSSPFE01 and LSSPFE02 will follow the same process. Add and remove them from the Load Balancer as necessary.

For the Search Servers, as they are using the Topology Manager to maintain Search availability to detect unhealthy or unavailable Search components, the Load Balancer is not involved in Search high availability. However, in order to keep Search online, at least one server must be running any particular Search role at any one time. In Figure 17-9, LSSPSR01 is being patched, yet end users continue to be able to search for content.

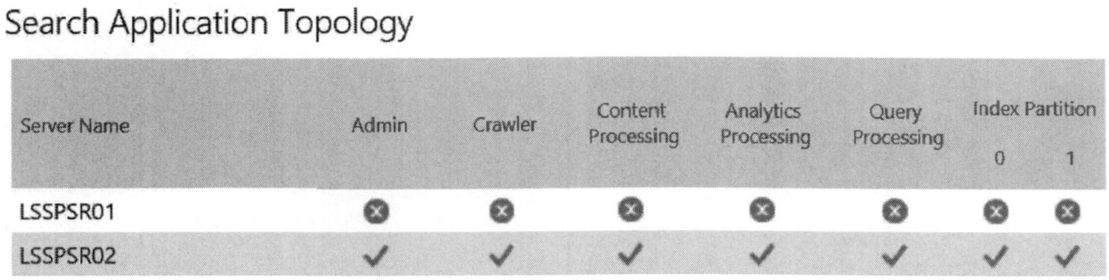

Search Application Topology

Server Name	Admin	Crawler	Content Processing	Analytics Processing	Query Processing	Index Partition 0	1
LSSPSR01	⊗	⊗	⊗	⊗	⊗	⊗	⊗
LSSPSR02	✓	✓	✓	✓	✓	✓	✓

Figure 17-9. LSSPSR01 is offline, while LSSPSR02 is still online and providing Search services

When a Search Server is back online from a reboot, validate in the Search Administration that all components are online. If you receive an HTTP 503 while viewing the Search Administration page, it may take the Topology Manager a few minutes to "fail over" the Search Administration component to the SharePoint Server that is online.

Distributed Cache servers may take longer to put in a position to patch. Prior patching a Distributed Cache server, the Distributed Cache must first be gracefully shutdown. To start the graceful shutdown process, run the following cmdlets from the SharePoint Management Shell.

```
Use-CacheCluster
Stop-CacheHost -HostName FQDN -CachePort 22233 -Graceful
```

For example, to gracefully stop Distributed Cache on LSSPDC02, we would run the following:

```
Stop-CacheHost -HostName LSSPDC02.CORP.Learn-SP2016.com -CachePort 22233 -Graceful
```

To monitor the drain of Distributed Cache for the particular host, run Get-CacheHost. Even in farms with little traffic, it may take up to 15 minutes for Distributed Cache to shut down. As soon as the server shows as "DOWN," it is safe to run Remove-SPDistributedCacheServiceInstance on that host, as shown in Figure 17-10.

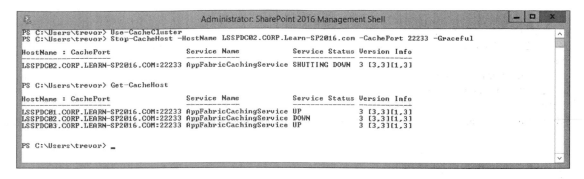

Figure 17-10. The process of shutting down and removing a cache host from Distributed Cache

Once a host has been patched and is back online, run Add-SPDistributedCacheServiceInstance. Distributed Cache may take a few minutes to start. Use Get-CacheHost to validate the host reports as "UP" before moving onto the next Distributed Cache server.

If at any point in time, a SharePoint server has been patched but the status shows something other than "No Action Required" in Manage servers in farm, run Get-SPProduct -Local. The cmdlet may take a couple of minutes, but the status should then accurately reflect the state of the server.

As SQL Server also has security hotfixes, rollups, and Service Packs, it will be important to maintain the highest availability possible. The next section briefly covers patching the SQL Servers that support the SharePoint Server farm.

Patching SQL Server

When patching SQL Server in a high-availability scenario, first patch the node that is currently in a secondary role (e.g., AlwaysOn Secondary Replica or the SQL Cluster passive node). Once completed, begin the failover process to that secondary SQL Server. Once the failover has completed, patch what was the primary SQL Server. You may or may not choose to failback to the original primary SQL Server. Note that as the Usage database is only active on the primary SQL Server, during the SQL Server outage, the Usage database will be unavailable.

Next Steps

Now that you know how SharePoint can be patched in a highly available configuration, the next stage of administering is monitoring and maintenance of the SharePoint farm.

CHAPTER 18

Monitoring and Maintaining a SharePoint 2016 Deployment

In this chapter, we will look at how to monitor our SharePoint 2016 environment to assure stability as well as performance for your users. We will also look at how to monitor logs to make sure there are no issues, and potential ongoing maintenance activities to keep your SharePoint farm running at peak performance.

Monitoring

SharePoint Server 2016 can be monitored with a variety of logs and tools. Logs include IIS logging, ULS logging, Event Logging (Event Viewer), and SQL Server log files. From a tools perspective, Performance Monitor will be the primary tool we will examine, in addition to the IIS Manager to look for potential long-running requests.

IIS Logging

IIS logs all website activity to SharePoint. While not necessarily the primary place to examine for errors or performance, it can provide an indication of issues users are running into, including missing assets or server errors, such as HTTP 500 errors.

As IIS logs are plain text files and parsing them can be difficult with text editors like Notepad, Log Parser and Log Parser Studio from Microsoft makes finding specific types of log entries significantly easier.

■ **Tip** Log Parser 2.2 is available from Microsoft at `https://www.microsoft.com/en-us/download/details.aspx?id=24659` and Log Parser Studio is available on the TechNet Gallery at `https://gallery.technet.microsoft.com/office/Log-Parser-Studio-cd458765`.

In this example, we will start with Log Parser 2.2. We will be looking for any HTTP 404 errors, which indicate a missing file, from all files within a particular IIS Web Site.

```
LogParser "SELECT date, cs-uri-stem FROM E:\IIS\W3SVC496309000\u_ex*.log WHERE sc-status =
404 GROUP BY date, cs-uri-stem"
```

```
date        cs-uri-stem
----------  ----------------------
2016-03-12  /favicon.ico
2016-04-07  /browserconfig.xml
2016-04-12  /favicon.ico
2016-04-15  /browserconfig.xml
2016-04-19  /browserconfig.xml
2016-04-25  /favicon.ico
2016-05-04  /desktop.ini
2016-05-04  /_cts/desktop.ini
2016-05-04  /_catalogs/desktop.ini
2016-05-04  /_private/desktop.ini
2016-05-04  /browserconfig.xml
2016-05-08  /browserconfig.xml
2016-05-09  /favicon.ico
2016-05-10  /browserconfig.xml

Statistics:
-----------
Elements processed: 9983
Elements output:    14
Execution time:     0.66 seconds
```

With this output, we can see there are 10 days where files are missing, or throwing an HTTP 404. We know from this example that SharePoint does not include certain files, such as favicon.ico by default and can ignore these particular missing files.

Server errors are in the HTTP 500 range, and this output shows we have a few HTTP 500 errors across a few days. This output shows that the errors were primarily with the User Profile Import and Export web service, which Microsoft Identity Manager uses to synchronize User Profiles with SharePoint.

```
LogParser "SELECT date, cs-uri-stem FROM E:\IIS\W3SVC496309000\u_ex*.log WHERE sc-status = 500 GROUP BY date, cs-uri-stem"
```

```
date        cs-uri-stem
----------  ------------------------------------------
2016-03-09  /_vti_bin/ProfileImportExportService.asmx
2016-05-22  /_vti_bin/ProfileImportExportService.asmx

Statistics:
-----------
Elements processed: 43229
Elements output:    2
Execution time:     0.64 seconds
```

By default, IIS logging is in UTC format, so account for your local time zone. When finding a particular log entry that contains the HTTP 500, for example:

```
2016-05-22 17:05:21 172.16.0.32 POST /_vti_bin/ProfileImportExportService.asmx - 443 CORP\s-farm
172.16.0.57 Mozilla/4.0+(compatible;+MSIE+6.0;+MS+Web+Services+Client+Protocol+4.0.30319.42000)
- 500 0 0 47
```

We can directly correlate this entry with the ULS logs. In the ULS logs, which are local to your time zone, in this particular case, GMT-7, I will want to examine the ULS log from approximately 10 AM. Examining this particular ULS log file, I can also identify the HTTP 500 from there:

```
05/22/2016 10:05:13.82  w3wp.exe (0x5458)    0x4678    SharePoint
Foundation  Runtime aoxsq   Medium   Sending HTTP response 500 for HTTP request POST to
https://ca.corp.learn-sp2016.com/_vti_bin/ProfileImportExportService.asmx    a5b97e9d-34c4-
3044-d6b8-264e8b349edc
```

And finally, based on the correlation ID, using a tool such as ULS Viewer, we can further examine the errors generated.

■ **Tip**   ULS Viewer is available from Microsoft at https://www.microsoft.com/en-us/download/details.aspx?id=44020.

ULS Logging

ULS provides a valuable source of information about your SharePoint farm. This is the core logging mechanism of SharePoint and is often the first place a SharePoint Administrator will look for any SharePoint-related errors. By default, ULS logs are located in C:\Program Files\Common Files\microsoft shared\Web Server Extensions\16\LOGS\. ULS logs are in the format of ServerName-YYYYMMdd-hhmm.log, for example, LSSPFE01-20160522-1128.log.

If the ULS logs have been relocated, you can use the cmdlet Get-SPDiagnosticConfig to identify where the logs have been relocated to.

```
(Get-SPDiagnosticConfig).LogLocation
```

The log location may also be found via Central Administration. Using Central Administration, navigate to Monitoring. Under Configure diagnostic logging, the Trace Log Path is where the ULS log is located, as shown in Figure 18-1.

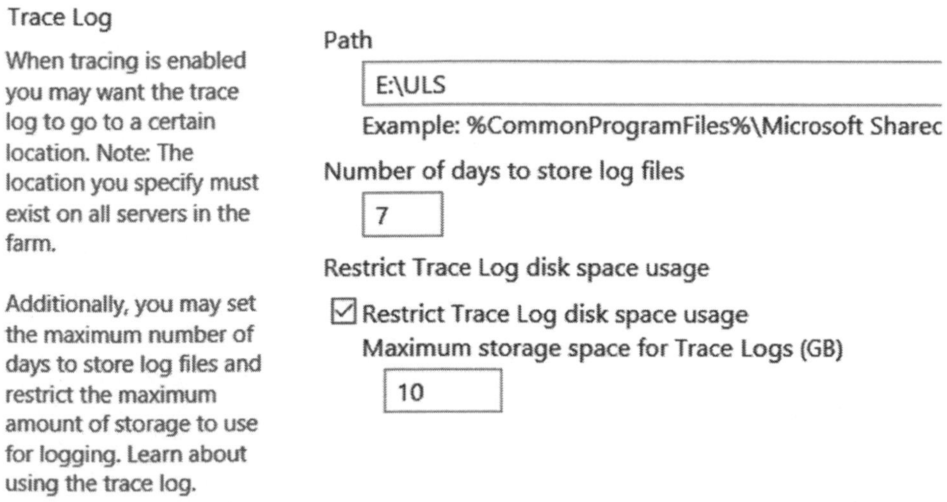

Trace Log

When tracing is enabled you may want the trace log to go to a certain location. Note: The location you specify must exist on all servers in the farm.

Additionally, you may set the maximum number of days to store log files and restrict the maximum amount of storage to use for logging. Learn about using the trace log.

Path

E:\ULS

Example: %CommonProgramFiles%\Microsoft Sharec

Number of days to store log files

7

Restrict Trace Log disk space usage

☑ Restrict Trace Log disk space usage

Maximum storage space for Trace Logs (GB)

10

Figure 18-1. *ULS log location*

Users may encounter errors from SharePoint, which provides them the date and time the error occurred, as well as the ULS Correlation ID. An example of one such error is seen in Figure 18-2.

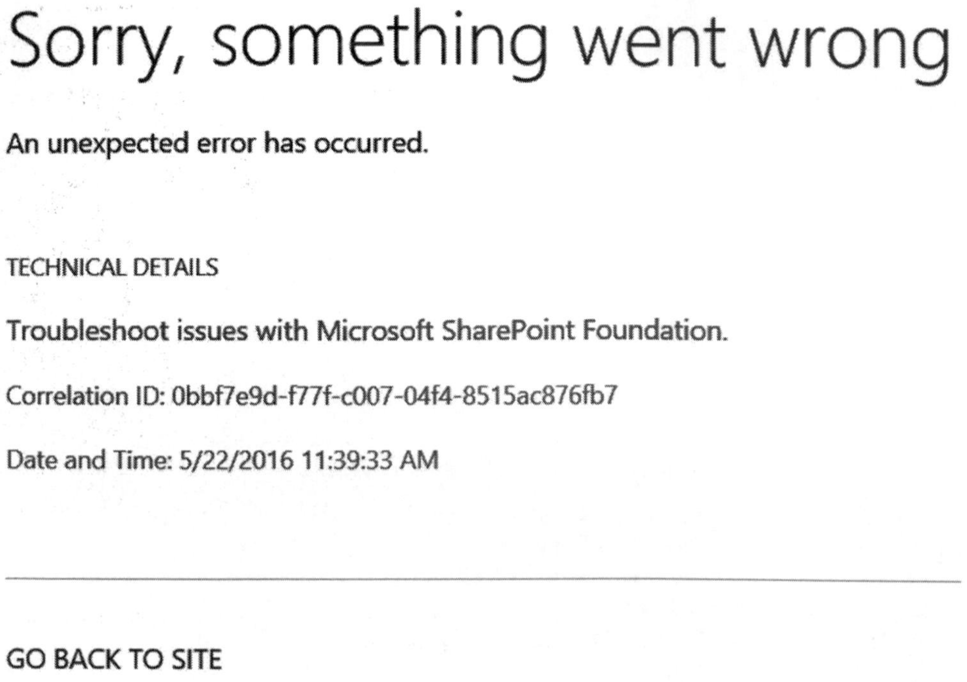

Sorry, something went wrong

An unexpected error has occurred.

TECHNICAL DETAILS

Troubleshoot issues with Microsoft SharePoint Foundation.

Correlation ID: 0bbf7e9d-f77f-c007-04f4-8515ac876fb7

Date and Time: 5/22/2016 11:39:33 AM

GO BACK TO SITE

Figure 18-2. *A SharePoint error as seen by a user*

Using this information, the Correlation ID and Date and Time, and using Ulsviewer, open the appropriate ULS log file. By using Ulsviewer, we can filter by the preceding Correlation ID, as shown in Figure 18-3, to see the end user's request end to end.

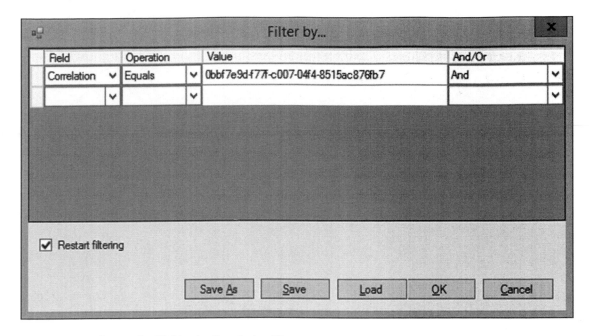

Figure 18-3. *Filtering the ULS log by Correlation ID*

The error may be identified within the list of entries once filtered. In this case, the error is generic, but the user had requested a Content Type that does not exist, seen in Figure 18-4.

Share...	General	8nca	Medium	0bbf7e9d-...	Application error when access /_layouts/15/ManageContentType.aspx. Error=Object reference not set to an instance of an objec...	Request (GET:https://shar...
Share...	Runtime	tkau	Unexpec...	0bbf7e9d-...	System.NullReferenceException: Object reference not set to an instance of an object. at Microsoft.SharePoint.ApplicationPage...	Request (GET:https://shar...
Share...	General	ajlz0	High	0bbf7e9d-...	Getting Error Message for Exception System.Web.HttpUnhandledException (0x80004005): Exception of type 'System.Web.HttpU...	Request (GET:https://shar...

Figure 18-4. *Content Type errors in the ULS log*

The ULS log will display the date and time the log entry is from, the product (for example, SharePoint, Project Server, PowerPivot, and so forth), the Category (User Profiles, Search), the Event ID, the level (Unexpected are generally errors), Correlation ID, Message, the Request, and other information depending on the type of error.

Event IDs are used internally by Microsoft and the information of what message they're associated with is not generally published.

As many farms consit of multiple servers, sometimes it is difficult to locate an error as there may be more than one server that provides the service associated with an error, such as more than one server running Search or serving as a Web Front End. Using the cmdlet Merge-SPLogFile, one can use parameters to narrow down the search for specific errors across the farm. This is an example of search all servers in the farm by the Correlation ID.

```
Merge-SPLogFile -Path C:\error.log -CorrelationID "0bbf7e9d-f77f-c007-04f4-8515ac876fb7"
```

If the Correlation ID is found, it will output the matching ULS log entries to the C:\error.log file. If the Correlation ID is not known, it is also possible to narrow down the log by time. Time will be formatted in military time (24 hours), for example, to merge the logs between 3 PM and 5 PM, you would use the following cmdlet.

```
Merge-SPLogFile -Path C:\error.log -StartTime "05/22/2016 15:00" -EndTime "05/22/2016 17:00"
```

It is possible that errors may not be caught using the default logging settings. For this, we need to increase the verbosity of logs. The verbosity settings are based on Areas. These settings can be modified via Central Administration under Monitoring, Configuring diagnostic logging.

This page will list the current verbosity level for each Area, as shown in Figure 18-5, as well as provide two drop-downs to adjust the verbosity between None to Verbose, or allowing you to Reset to Default.

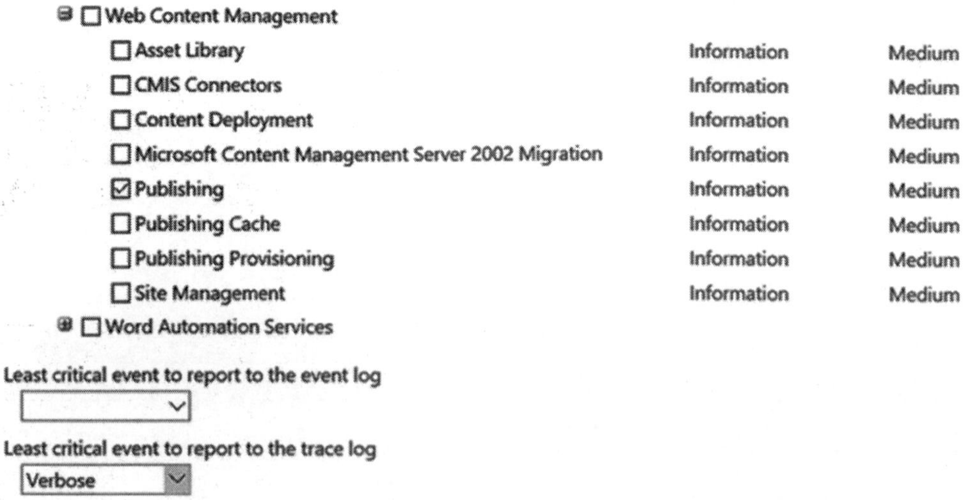

Figure 18-5. *Adjusting the verbosity of an Area*

Verbosity also be adjusted through the SharePoint Management Shell. In addition, setting the verbosity via PowerShell will allow you to set the verbosity up to VerboseEx, which has additional information not provided at the Verbose logging level. The format to setting a specific area is either by simply specifying the Area, or CategoryName:Aera, or even CategoryName:*, which will set the entire Category to the specified Trace Severity. Here are a few examples:

```
Set-SPLogLevel -Identity "SharePoint Foundation:Asp Runtime" -TraceSeverity VerboseEx
Set-SPLogLevel -Identity "Asp Runtime" -TraceSeverity VerboseEx
Set-SPLogLevel -Identity "SharePoint Foundation:*" -TraceSeverity VerboseEx
```

When using Verbose or VerboseEx trace levels, there may be a significant impact on farm performance. Because of this, you may want to run with these Trace Severities for a short period of time to reproduce a specific issue.

Once completed reproducing the issue, use Clear-SPLogLevel to reset all Areas back to their default Trace Severity.

Ulsviewer can be used for monitoring the live environment, as well. This is suitable when having a user reproduce a problem that does not necessarily surface an error, but will allow you to coorelate the user's action with one or more messages within the ULS log. The latest version of Ulsviewer is also able ot monitor logs over the entire farm. By selecting the farm icon, represented by a tree node in the toolbar, you can enter one or more server names into the farm, then using a UNC path, Ulsviewer will allow you to see the server logs intermixed, real time. This is useful in scenarios where a user may call a service on a backend server, but you must trace the action of the user through the frontend to the backend.

Event Viewer

SharePoint records a limited amount of information to the Event Viewer, but the Event Viewer is more useful for service-specific and ASP.Net errors.

Generally, Windows Services that run SharePoint, such as the SharePoint Timer or SharePoint Administration service, will show any startup or unexpected stops in the System Event Log. For example, if the SharePoint Timer service unexpectedly stops, it will show an error in the System Event Log as seen in Figure 18-6.

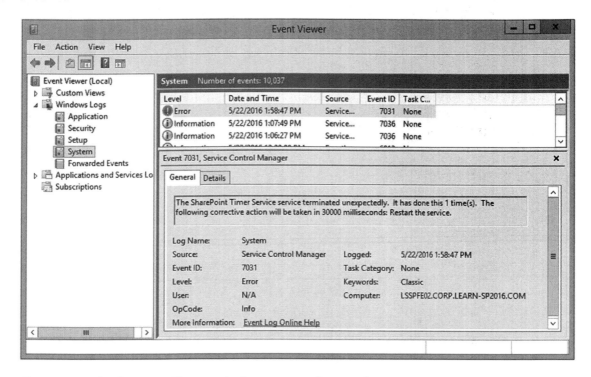

Figure 18-6. *The SharePoint Timer service has unexpectedly stopped*

The System Event Log is also useful for diagnosing Kerberos errors, along with any TLS/SSL errors that may occur.

The Application Event Log will show other more general SharePoint information, warnings, and error messages from a vareity of sources. As an example, it will show when an IIS Application Pool has started, as shown in Figure 18-7.

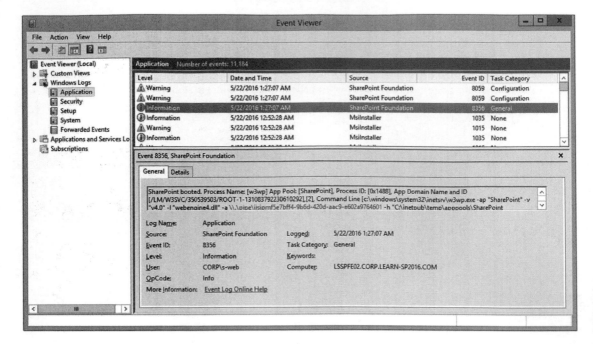

Figure 18-7. *An IIS Application Pool running SharePoint starting up*

SharePoint also logs data in a few Applications and Services event logs. In the Operational log for SharePoint Products, Shared, log entries typically consist of Incoming E-mail staticstics, Trace Log status, such as when the log reached the retention limit based on space used or date as shown in Figure 18-8, and InfoPath Forms Services messages.

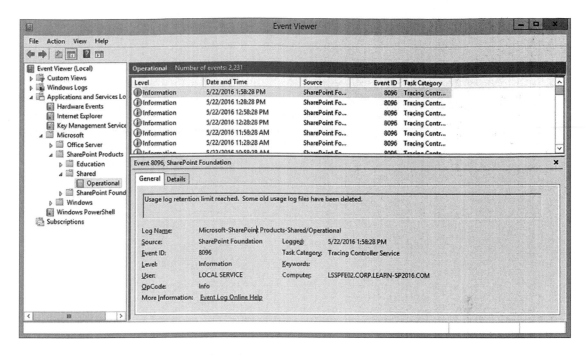

Figure 18-8. *Tracing service logs reaching the retention limit*

IIS Manager

The IIS Manager provides a limited amount of information on active requests in Application Pools. This information may be helpful for diagnosicing the origins of long-running requests, for example, a large number of requests to a OneNote notebook residing on a SharePoint site.

Using IIS Manager, at the server level, go into "Worker Processes." From here, as shown in Figure 18-9, it will show a limited amount of information about each worker process.

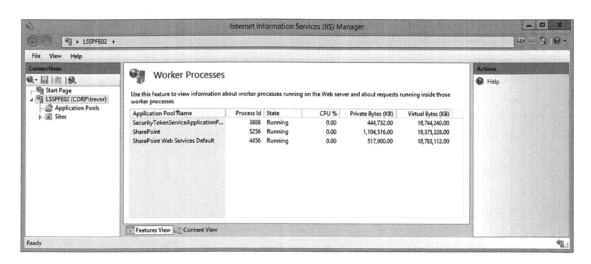

Figure 18-9. *Running Worker Process information*

By right-clicking a Worker Process and selecting View Current Requests, we can identify running requests as shown in Figure 18-10.

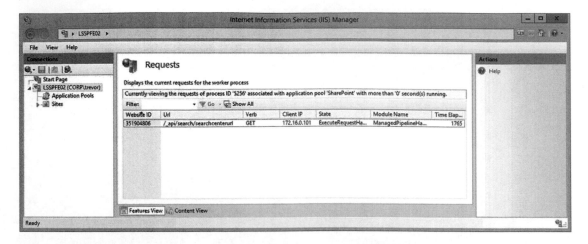

Figure 18-10. *Running requests to the Worker Process*

Usage Logging

SharePoint Usage Logging logs a vareity of information to the Usage database. This database can be directly queried either through the tables or through the built-in Views. For example, the RequestUsage View can provide information on how long a particular request took, how many CPU megacycle it consumed, Distributed Cache reads and how long those Distributed Cache reads took, among other statistics.

Usage Logging can be configured in Central Administration under Monitoring, Configure usage and health data collection. There are a number of scenarios to gather data on, but only gather those scenarios you believe will be important for farm diagnostics. Logging more than is required may lead to farm performance issues as the data is transferred from the SharePoint farm into the Usage database, along with the size of the Usage database growing by a significant amount.

The Usage database may be quried directly via SQL Server Management Studio. Microsoft provisions Views for many common scenarios one may be interested in, as shown in Figure 18-11, but you may also construct your own Views within the database if needed.

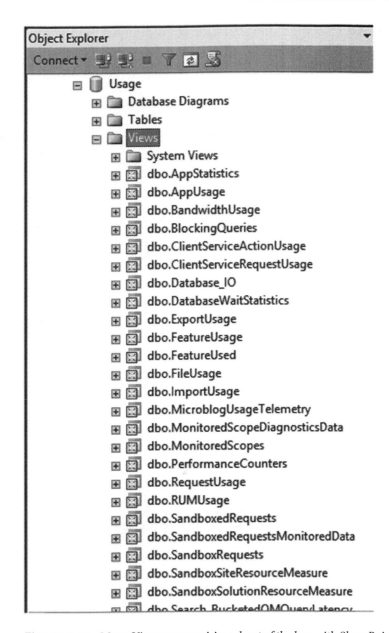

Figure 18-11. Many Views are provisioned out of the box with SharePoint

Querying the database is simple. As shown in Figure 18-12, construct your query of a View and select the columns you wish to display in the results, in the order you wish to deplay the results in. In this query, we are looking at the FileUsage View and select just the relevant columns that we're interested in, then sorting by the time the log entry was created in the database, with the newest entries appearing first.

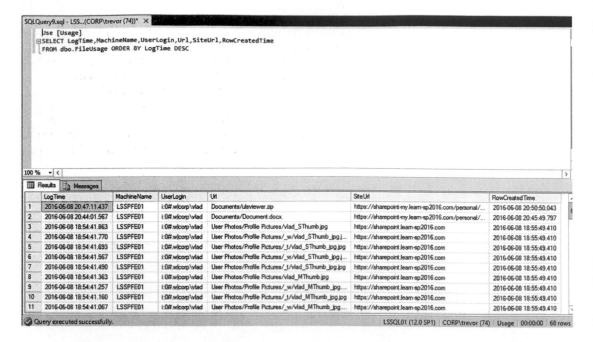

Figure 18-12. A query of a View in the Usage database

Central Administration Health Analyzer

The built-in SharePoint Health Analyzer is a set of rules that run peroidically via the SharePoint Timer Service. These rules detect various issues, as shown in Figure 18-13, such as SharePoint Application Pools recycling, or databases with a large amount of free space, and other minor to major issues with the farm.

Review problems and solutions ⓘ

⊕ new item

All Reports   •••

✓	Severity	Title	Failing Servers	Failing Services	Modified
◢ **Category : Security** (1)					
	📑	The server farm account should not be used for other services.		SPTimerService (SPTimerV4)	15 hours ago
◢ **Category : Performance** (1)					
	📑	Search - One or more crawl databases may have fragmented indices.		SPTimerService (SPTimerV4)	15 hours ago
◢ **Category : Configuration** (6)					
	📑	Product / patch installation or server upgrade required.		SPTimerService (SPTimerV4)	15 hours ago
	📑	Missing server side dependencies.		SPTimerService (SPTimerV4)	15 hours ago

Figure 18-13. Reviewing Health Analzyer issues

While the Health Analyzer can be useful, there are certain rules which are out of date or Health Analyzer warnings which cannot be resolved. As these rules are written into SharePoint's codebase, it is not possible to modify the rules. We have the option of simply disabling them, or ignoring them within Central Administration. Examples of rules which may be ignored are "Drives are running out of free space." This particular rule is evaluating the amount of free disk space on C:. The rule calls for 5 times the amount of RAM for free space on the volume. For a SharePoint Server with 16GB RAM, that would be 80GB free. The rule exists to make sure there is enough free space to accomodate a full memory dump if the server should encounter a Blue Screen of Death. Many, if not most Windows Server installations are not configured to take a full memory dump, but typically a kernel dump, which is significantly smaller. While free drive space is important, it may be better to monitor this outside of SharePoint, such as with System Center Operations Manager or another server monitoring tool.

If there are rules which are not required, they can be disabled via the Review rule definitions, as shown in Figure 18-14. Each rule will have an Enabled checkbox. Simply uncheck it to disable the rule. You may then delete the Health Alert from the Health Analyzer and the raised issue will no longer appear.

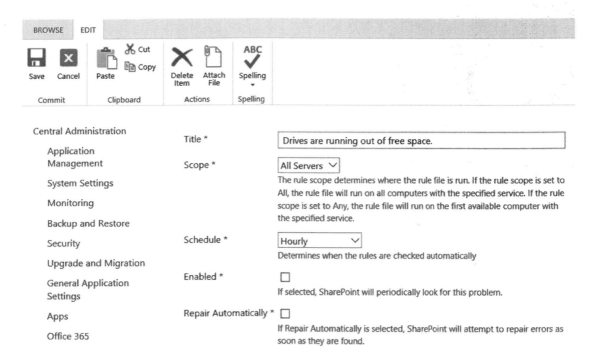

Figure 18-14. *Disabling a Rule Definition*

Performance Monitor for SharePoint

Performance Monitor may also be a useful tool for diagnosing server performance issues, such as examining outstanding ASP.NET requests, CPU usage by process, and so forth. The scenario in which Performance Monitor is used depends on the performance problem one is attempting to troubleshoot.

Performance Monitor for SQL Server

Performance monitoring of SQL Server can be quite in depth, but we will be skimming the surface here of "essential numbers." For example, within the SQL Server Buffer Manager, Page Life Expecticy should be high. The value is measured in seconds. In addition, the Buffer Cache Hit Ratio should be well over 70 (or 70%). DMVs are also used to monitor SQL Server performance and are generally preferred over other methods.

■ **Tip**   Additional DMV information, including scripts to monitor DMVs are available from Glenn Berry at `http://www.sqlskills.com/blogs/glenn/category/dmv-queries/`. Brent Ozar also offers DMV monitoring via sp_BlitzCache available at `https://www.brentozar.com/blitzcache/`.

System Center Operations Manager

System Center Operations Manager is a complex monitoring solution that falls outside of the scope of this book, but is another option for monitoring the various faciets of SharePoint Server and SQL Server, providing a holistic look at the environment. At the time of writing this book, System Center Operations Manager was in Technical Preview and did not function correctly with SharePoint Server 2016.

The options for monitoring SharePoint performance are extensive, from monitoring the individual SharePoint servers, services, and IIS, to monitoring SQL Server and SQL Server database performance. When encountering potential performance issues in your SharePoint environment, consider using these wide ranging tools to diagnose your farm performance.

Index

Get the eBook for only $4.99!

Why limit yourself?

Now you can take the weightless companion with you wherever you go and access your content on your PC, phone, tablet, or reader.

Since you've purchased this print book, we are happy to offer you the eBook for just $4.99.

Convenient and fully searchable, the PDF version enables you to easily find and copy code—or perform examples by quickly toggling between instructions and applications.

To learn more, go to http://www.apress.com/us/shop/companion or contact support@apress.com.

Printed in Great Britain
by Amazon